BATAAN
UNCENSORED

COL. E. B. MILLER

BATAAN UNCENSORED

First published by Ernest B. Miller, 1949; printed by
The Hart Publications, Inc., Long Prairie, Minnesota
Second edition published by the
Military Historical Society of Minnesota, 1991,

Printed in the United States of America
10 9 8 7 6 5 4 3 2 1

ISBN 0-9631642-0-1

**Library of Congress
Cataloging-in-Publication Data**

Miller, Ernest B., 1898-1959
    Bataan Uncensored
    1. United States—History—World War Two.
    2. Bataan, battle for 1941-42—Bataan Death March.
    3. Prisoner of war camps, Japanese. I. Title.

Library of Congress Catalog Card Number 91-67991

Epilogue as prologue

... an explanation as to why Bataan Uncensored is being reprinted.

Half a century ago, when the U.S. became a participant in World War II, it sent under-equipped military forces into desperate combat situations. The best the servicemen could hope for was to delay the enemy attack by offering their very bodies in sacrifice.

Their valiant efforts allowed the time necessary for a shocked America to awaken from apathy, to regroup and rearm and to ultimately defeat the warmakers who sought domination.

In the postwar period when arms were being dumped into the sea, an unusual patriot sought a means of convincing the public that liberty could not be taken for granted and that an adequate military defense was essential if democracy was to survive. The patriot was Colonel Ernest B. Miller, a National Guard officer whose unit, the 194th Tank Battalion, was stationed in the Philippines when the Japanese struck. The means he used was to tell the story of his battalion's experiences and the bloody fate of its members.

His book, Bataan Uncensored, takes the readers from peacetime to wartime and then back to peacetime. In the final chapters, he recommends changes that would bolster our military defense and better prepare our citizenry for the future.

Though he wrote the recommendations more than four decades ago, they are as meaningful now as they were then. That's why, rather than attempt to update those chapters, the material is offered as originally written. The very fact that what Col. Miller wrote so long ago still makes sense is testimony both to his insight and to the danger of recurring apathy on the part of Americans in times of peace.

Years ago, the original printing of Bataan Uncensored was sold, and there has been no way to satisfy continuing inquiries. Now, in this 50th anniversary year of America's entrance into World War II, a demand has been building for more and more copies.

We commend his message to all Americans.

ACKNOWLEDGEMENT

The Military Historical Society of Minnesota is profoundly grateful to the Stewart C. and Helen K. Mills Family of Brainerd, Minnesota, and to Colonel Miller's surviving children and their spouses, Marilynn (Miller) and Paul Bender, Tom and Jean Miller, Richard and Doris Miller and Patricia Miller Horner. This second edition was made possible by their encouragement and financial support. It is a testament to their continuing belief in the ideals for which Colonel Miller fought.

Introduction

AMONG THE REPORTS of World War II, this book has three distinctive qualities:

It is written by a citizen soldier, a non-professional military man—Colonel Ernest B. Miller of Brainerd, Minnesota—commander of the 194th Tank Battalion (National Guard).

Colonel Miller and his citizen soldiers were mobilized, and in the Philippines some time before Pearl Harbor. They covered the withdrawals into Bataan and became an integral part in that heroic siege against the overpowering Japanese hordes. They gasped for strength on the Death March, they elbowed death away in the confines of the hell ships, their sense of defeat fought with their American pride through the starvation and abuse of Jap prison camps.

This book tells that story—but the story is built on more than seared memory. For Colonel Miller, at risk of death himself, kept notes of what happened. Humiliated by defeat, he obtained affidavits from men who were there, smuggled his history-in-the-making past Jap sentries, hid the notes in Jap prison camps, remembered and recovered them when victory came.

Thus this book is unique. Colonel Miller writes as a patriot, rather than a professional. He survived the war's darkest hours. He relies on records as well as graven memory.

Some will dispute what Colonel Miller has to say, but none can match his right to say what he does. He did not put pen to paper until he was no longer in the Army. He is free of restraint. So he writes with candor. But his candor is the frankness of a man trying to preserve and protect a nation and a way of life—it is not the bickering and bitter frankness of a man striving to belittle or destroy individuals or institutions.

He has a vital interest in the United States of America. Not only did he undergo physical suffering for it, himself, but the day that he landed in Manila, freed from Japanese prisons, he was met with the tragic news that one of his sons had been killed on the Anzio Beachhead in Italy.

From this cauldron of experience has boiled this book. It deserves respectful reading.

The Minneapolis Tribune carried "Bataan Uncensored" in a series of articles which were in abridged form. Colonel Miller was assisted in this first draft by Bill Smollett, Tribune reporter. At the time, Miller was the State Commander of the American Legion—a whirling dervish existence of meetings, conferences, and speeches in every part of the state. Smollett rode with Miller, lived with him. He wrote this impression:

"I have met a man who actually knows the true value of a single slice of bread. He unconsciously lends drama to the routine procedure of every bite.

"But he is not acting. When he bites into a piece of bread, he is silently thanking Providence for it. You see—there was a time when his very soul cried out for a single crumb. That was through the bitter, starving days of Bataan. And through three agonizing phases of the infamous Death March. And through 19 days and 19 nights on a Japanese hell ship. And then through no less than five hell holes that the Japs called prison camps.

"Out of those endless days and nights of starvation, Colonel Ernie Miller found a new philosophy concerning food. It is a philosophy that he believes America could well afford to turn toward as something to grasp during a period of world-wide unrest.

"His philosophy: Be thankful for what you have.

"There is no pose in his attitude. His manner is not ingratiating. He speaks from personal knowledge and bitter experience. He has eaten practically everything that man could eat when man is imbued with the idea of saving his life. He shared the half-rations at Bataan, and the quarter-rations, and finally the rations that included horses and mules whose usefulness as food was more demanding than anything else.

"He partook of the meager portions of rice, handed out grudgingly, brushed the worms off, and later swallowed them, not being too particular. He slumped down, like the others, to face a tin can containing nothing but a sickly cucumber soup, and to stare at the rice that was composed mostly of sweepings.

"He recalls Rokuroshi where snakes were caught and roasted, where larvae from wasp's nests were roasted, where any root that could be chewed was used for food. He can remember the soup that contained nothing but pieces of common weed, jerked from the ground by work parties consisting of men who had only one aim—to live.

"Colonel Miller knows the terror of starvation. He knows how it feels to go to bed at night—hungry. To wake up each morning—hungry. To carry on throughout a long day with a ravenous, clutching feeling of never having enough to eat. He knows the nightmarish dreams that were a part of each black night during his prison life. Dreams that consisted only of food and more food. He remembers the everyday conversations in the prison camps, conversations that always turned to food.

"Yes, this man knows the value of food. He says: 'The bitter dregs of adversity have taught us to truly appreciate the simple things of life such as a crust of bread, a pinch of salt, a chair to sit upon, or a pipe of unadulterated tobacco.'

"And in his Americanism talks throughout Minnesota, he emphasizes that it is high time for Americans to appreciate what they have.

"Even a single slice of bread."

WILLIAM P. STEVEN
Managing Editor
Minneapolis Tribune

Preface

BATAAN UNCENSORED is just what the name implies. It is the true story of the Philippine Campaign and its tragic aftermath. Naturally, in presenting that story, individual contacts, together with the individuals themselves, had to be made a part of the narrative in order that it be told at all.

The 194th Tank Battalion was a National Guard outfit, composed entirely of citizen soldiers. They came from practically every walk of life.

It so happened that this battalion was decreed by fate to take part in the most crucial phases of the Philippine Campaign. It might have been some other outfit except that events determined otherwise.

Therefore, it has not been with any intention of slighting other units if they do not appear in the story. The 194th was actually engaged in these most important events, and except as otherwise stated, no other units participated.

It is also a fact that the true story of the withdrawals into Bataan, and some of the events that occurred on that blood-soaked soil, could not be told without the complete and detailed testimony of the 194th Tank Battalion, because of the crucial part it played, and the absence of other personnel and the higher commands.

As commanding officer, the writer actually saw and participated in these events, not only from a command post, but also in active and personal contact with all phases from the top echelons down through the lower elements.

The attempt has been made to portray the campaign just as it occurred, insofar as the 194th was concerned.

While it is true that the military must take their share of the blame for not making use of those things they did have at their disposal, and for adopting and fostering a Rip Van Winkle attitude, it is also true that if the American people had been actively interested in their own security during prewar years, the military would have been alert, and the inefficient system would not have been allowed to exist—and this story would not have been told.

The writer, having had more than 31 years service in the National Guard, involving active service in the Mexican Border Campaign, World Wars I and II, can testify to the extreme indifference of American citizens and Congress during the 23 years between those wars. Therefore, it only follows that the military was the victim of a system which never should have been allowed to exist in the first place.

There is no doubt in the writer's mind, that if Americans as a whole, had been more interested in their national security than they were in their own individual affairs, there would have been no World War II—or, at least, it would have been ended shortly.

About 75 percent of the Philippine defenders did not come back!

If the reader will bear in mind the foregoing, as the story unfolds, he will find no malice or thought of casting reflections in any direction. The only object is to focus attention on the results of apathy, in which thousands of Americans were sacrificed and the fate of the American Way of Life hung in the balance.

THE AUTHOR

Contents

TO THOSE
WHO DID NOT COME BACK

CHAPTER 1

Why?

I STOOD in the searing Philippine sunshine, wiped away the sweat with a grimy hand, and prepared to look at something which was to foreshadow the bleak months and years ahead.

We were the 194th Tank Battalion guarding the vital, strategic Calumpit Bridge and it was December 31, 1941. Tomorrow was to start another year—a year of defeat, of disgrace, of despair, for us and the American people.

Elements of the South Luzon Force had been withdrawing over the bridge on their way to Bataan. It trembled with the movement of vehicles choking the long stretch of highway which was the main road leading to San Fernando.

The one road to Bataan led out of San Fernando.

The famous Orange Plan (WPO-3) was in effect. The last Quartermaster units from Manila and the Port Area were moving into the areas destined to become the Philippine defender's last stand.

A young Tanker, his face expressing bewilderment, was speaking words never to be forgotten. They still ring in my ears and they constitute one of the reasons for the story I am telling.

"Hell—they're empty!"

I looked—and saw what I had seen before. The Tanker was calling attention to rumbling trucks moving through. Trucks that were *empty!*

There they were—trucks rolling toward Bataan that should have been crammed with life-sustaining food and pertinent equipment procurable only in Manila. My men counted between 100 and 150 *empty* supply trucks. They rattled like the bare skeletons which most of those watching Tankers were destined to become.

Food and equipment would have given us a fighting chance against overwhelming Japanese war power. But we were helpless—because someone had failed.

This was not the final shock—nor the first withering dismay we had felt since the campaign started. Each day and night had been filled with blundering, lack of planning, inefficiency. We had experienced it as a National Guard Tank Battalion ever since we were mobilized in February, 1941. It was our destiny to become the first Armored Force unit ever to leave the continental limits of the United States; we were destined to sit out the bombing of our grounded planes at Clark Field—to cover the withdrawals of our forces into Bataan.

Bataan! We didn't know it then, but Bataan's memories were to haunt us for years to come:

Good Friday—April 3, 1942—when the Japs launched their second invasion force in the all-out attack. Holy Saturday with its deluge of Jap bombs and shells and bullets. . . . Positions of the pitiful, starved and diseased defenders literally blown out of the ground. . . . Hell itself. . . . But even then a hope that would not die. . . . *Help must come!*

Easter Sunday. . . . The skies black with bombers and strafers—not ours—we didn't have any. . . . Services held by chaplains of all faiths amid the inferno of a one-sided war. . . . Services constantly interrupted by the merciless and unceasing pounding of the overwhelming, vicious Jap hordes.

Monday. . . . Tuesday. . . . Wednesday. . . . Days of agony and torment. . . . On the receiving end. . . . Nothing to throw back.

Black Thursday—April 9, 1942—the day the siege of Bataan became a flaming page in history.

The ragged, starved, disease-ridden *expendables* shuffling and stumbling into the March of Death—many to die on that march—many to die later in Japanese prison camps or on the hell ships—and the rest, a pitiful minority, destined to a living death of starvation, disease and abuse for three and one-half years in the hands of a nation which knew no code of ethics . . . human footballs that also wanted to live . . . the sickening realization always clawing at the mind that *help* had failed to arrive.

That knowledge was burned indelibly in our memories and also the knowledge of a faltering, staggering America subjected to terms of *surrender* not only through the all-out attack of a powerful enemy but also through the blundering stupidity of its own leaders—aided and abetted by a politically-minded

Congress and an apathetic majority of the American people during the prewar years of a smug and oily peace when the stake was *human life.*

Why? *Why?*

Why is it—with Congress always holding investigations attempting to place the blame on someone else—there has never been any investigation of Congressional *non-action* on preparedness during those prewar years? Why is it that more of the American people have not come forward—willing to share some of that blame?

Time dulls the memory. In some ways that is good. For the lessons we should remember—it is bad.

There are some things I cannot forget and still be a good American. Some of them still flash through my mind like a horrible nightmare filled with scenes that are impossible to comprehend:

Stupid delays in training—obtaining equipment and supplies. . . . The poison of apathy in our people, reflecting its Rip Van Winkleism seven thousand miles away. . . . Foolish snarls of red tape to trap citizen soldiers who had left school, professions, shops and stores—who wavered, appeared to collapse—then struggled to stand again because of their belief in the nation of their fathers. . . . The impossibility of even loading our tanks properly for shipment overseas. . . . No preparation. . . . Refusal to allow test-firing of our guns which had never been fired. . . . The fact that I, as commanding officer of a tank battalion, had no chance to fire a tank gun until the Japanese were actually in sight. . . . No high explosive shells for those guns in all the Philippines. . . . No gasoline for the tanks when gasoline *was* plentiful . . . the intense obsession of Major General "God Almighty" Kenyon Joyce at Fort Lewis, Washington, demanding all-out attention to details of the uniform over and above anything else and *to hell* with training and organization—his sarcastic reference to "latter day" soldiers which feeling was also displayed in the Philippines. . . . Badly needed parts for tanks and other vehicles which *did* arrive at Manila—which we could not get turned over to us or even find out where they were stored—and which the Japanese took over . . . scenes such as these—and many more.

Those were scenes that took place *before* war. What followed was a succession of nightmares; but they were nightmares as real as the lives of the men they affected.

There is no doubt that other men—both in the Philippines and elsewhere—went through the same agony as I did. But, perhaps because I was a commanding officer, had seen a great deal of service before, and knew a little more than the average of the early stages of preparation—or non-preparation—involving human life—the picture made a lasting impression which will be a part of me as long as I shall have life.

Notes, which I made in Bataan, were thorough and complete, omitting no details. These notes were destroyed by myself just prior to the end. However, they were vivid in my memory and as soon as we were in the first prison camp, I started the notes all over again, taking the testimony of pertinent individuals who had special knowledge and secreting those notes from the Japanese by various ways and means which will be described later on. Those notes were made religiously and accumulated throughout the three and one-half years as a prisoner of the Japanese. They were made on such scraps of paper as I was able to find. Not a single note was lost—not even one day when I felt the breath of a Jap guard on the back of my neck as I bent over my writings. Those notes were smuggled through Japanese sentries—in the Philippines, on the hell ship that took us to Japan, and into the prison camps on Honshu and Shikoku Islands.

The determination to tell this story was made in Bataan. That determination was not born of any desire or intention to besmirch the name of any individual but simply to call attention to why there *was* a Bataan and to fervently hope that it might help to awaken America.

The blame should not be placed upon any particular individual nor upon the military establishment other than those things which they could have corrected with the means at their disposal. The American people are basically to blame for allowing any such system to exist. The American people, through Congress, by their idealistic and apathetic attitude, allowed our military establishment to decay during the times of peace and did nothing about it, although grim warnings which went unheeded, were issued in plenty—by regular and citizen soldier alike—from the postwar days of World War I to the prewar days of World War II.

Brave men died needlessly. We felt the red tape and indecision that choked and strangled an American plan of strategy which did not even make use of those things that were available.

Perhaps no one could understand our innermost thoughts without having had the experience—that is understandable—but, surely, every American must understand what happened to us in part.

I promised God Almighty three things if I returned alive: First, to preach and teach Americanism with my whole being. Second, to tell the true story of our fiasco in the Philippines in all its nakedness—pulling no punches—with the hope that it might build a better and stronger America. Third, to attempt to drive home the point that our freedom will surely be lost if we again develop the apathy toward our national defense which we allowed to occur between our two world wars.

If there are those who would say that I am exploiting an issue that should remain untold, I humbly ask that they read with an open mind. Let the facts speak for themselves—remembering that the motive is entirely without malice.

History always asks questions, some of which are never answered. May I ask and humbly answer a few of those questions—some of which were running through my mind even when the enemy first struck?

Major General George Grunert was commander of the Philippine Department before McArthur was recalled to active duty which was toward the end of July, 1941. Why was General Grunert sent home to the United States in October, 1941? It was because he differed sharply with MacArthur in the defense plans of the Philippines. This could not be tolerated from a subordinate. It was generally conceded by officers close to the situation that Grunert was realistically sure of what was needed. MacArthur was steeped in the theoretical—and—MacArthur was the high command.

For several nights prior to and including December 5-6, strange aircraft were picked up and traced by our Interceptor Command. These planes operated to within a few miles of Lingayen Gulf. What of those "dry runs"? Was that information evaluated to mean it was all for fun? MacArthur and his staff knew all about the pilgrimages.

Why did MacArthur believe there would be no war with

the Japanese until about April 1, 1942? I cannot answer this
and would not raise the question except that it played a de-
cisive role in the events to come. However, I do know this
was the line of thinking we encountered when we arrived in
the Far East. This is also verified by General Lewis H. Brereton, commander of the Far East Air Forces in the early stages
of the war, and by General Jonathan Wainwright. It is denied
by MacArthur who stated to the press, when confronted with
Brereton's statement in his recent book, that the date of April
1, 1942, referred to, was the earliest possible date for the
arrival of the necessary reinforcements which would make a
successful defense of the Philippines possible and was not
merely an anticipated date of enemy action! And yet there is
no doubt that the mobilization and training schedule of both
the Philippine Department and of the Philippine Army was
based on the assumption that the Japs would not strike before
that time!

    Why were American planes lined up on the ground at Clark
Field when the Japanese bombed and devastated the area?
This was some hours after Pearl Harbor and we were all on
the full alert. The fact is—*they were waiting for orders*—which
were destined never to be received until they were actually
feeling the impact of the bombs!

    Why did our Air Force in the Philippines fail to bomb
Formosa the first day of the war, December 8, 1941 (December
7 U.S. time)? Missions had been previously assigned for operations on Formosa and permission had been requested of the
high command at 5:00 o'clock that morning to carry out the
plan. About December 1, 1941, MacArthur received a message
from General George Marshall which alerted him to the true
situation—rapidly deteriorating relations with Japan—and that
the first overt act to be committed should be by Japan. However, Marshall also stressed the fact that the message should
not be construed as meaning that a course of action should
be adopted that might jeopardize a successful defense of the
Philippine Islands. The overt act had already been committed
by Japan when bombs were dropped on Pearl Harbor. B17's
were actually loaded with bombs anticipating, naturally, that
bombing orders would come. When those orders failed to
arrive, calls were put in to the high command. The result—
orders to remove the bombs from the B17's! The idea seemed

to be that no attack would be made until Japan had committed overt acts on the Philippines. MacArthur has also denied the foregoing to the press, stating that no request was made for offensive action by the Air Force against Formosa. However, late that morning orders were received from MacArthur for both reconnaissance and bombing missions with Formosa as the target. The orders came too late. Japanese bombers erased Clark Field!

Why was not the Orange Plan (WPO-3) put into effect until December 23, 1941? This was the plan for the defense of the Philippines and carried the details of not only the scheme for defense but also *supply*. Why the period of indecision—16 golden days? Perhaps it was because of the prewar thinking of MacArthur which leaned toward the belief that it would be too expensive in men, money and materials for Japan to invade. Surely it was not because he thought the miserable, inadequate force and equipment available could stop an invasion by such a powerful enemy, once it started. And even if he did believe in that theory, how could he continue in that belief when most of his air strength was wiped out the first day?

What happened to the plans to evacuate the Port Area in Manila of pertinent supplies? What happened to that part of the Orange Plan concerning canned meats and such in the wholesale warehouses in Manila? Why was no rice moved from the vast storages at Cabanatuan—also a part of the Orange Plan? Why was Bataan put on half-rations immediately after the troops withdrew into the peninsula? The simple answer is that *there was this period of indecision* when foodstuffs, equipment and other supplies should have been hauled into Bataan and were not. Hence the *empty trucks.*

Why was it that in the hell of one of the first prison camps the satirical remark was passed around, "The United States has struck a medal for veterans of the Pearl Harbor Campaign. It's a replica of an ostrich with its head in the sand!" Meaning to ignore the fact that brave men lost their lives at Pearl Harbor defending their country? Not at all! It was grim commentary on certain facts the prisoners knew. Facts that revealed, shockingly, how someone had fumbled.

The most crucial withdrawal made in the entire campaign was the next to the last one before the final withdrawal into

Bataan. It was *16 hours after* that withdrawal before Wainwright's headquarters knew it had taken place. *And we told them!*

The complete story has never been told before, nor has any great part of it, because it could not be told without the detailed testimony of the 194th Tank Battalion. There would never have been a Bataan if the 194th had not been in certain strategic positions covering the withdrawals. It could have been another unit except that fate decreed otherwise.

General Wainwright gives no recognition whatever to this part of the campaign in his book describing the actions taking place during the retrograde movements to Bataan. His omissions were due to several reasons.

The two tank battalions were separate units designated as GHQ. They came under the direct control of USAFFE (United States Army Forces of the Far East). USAFFE was the extreme high command—General MacArthur. Control of the tanks was therefore exercised through the Tank Group Commander—Brigadier General James R. N. Weaver. General Wainwright, commanding the North Luzon Force, had to make his requests for tanks through Weaver. This rankled him to no slight degree.

Wainwright was a cavalryman of the old school and thoroughly indoctrinated with that branch of the service. As was the case with too many of our high ranking officers in World War II, he was not familiar with, nor cognizant of, the capabilities and limitations of tanks. He would tolerate no viewpoint, if adverse to his, on the use of tanks.

In relating this serious lack of unity and understanding, it is not my intention to detract from the stature of General Wainwright. The story could not be told without the details. He was a thoroughly brave soldier and subjected himself on many occasions to exposure from enemy fire when many men in his position might have seen no necessity to do so, nor would there have been any censure from any quarter.

Much of our tank operations he had no knowledge of. Apparently, some of those operations with which he was familiar were allowed to be forgotten.

One thing was crystal clear. Extreme jealously, concerning control of the tanks, mounted and became an obsession with both Wainwright and Weaver. And the fault lay not only with Wainwright.

Antipathy of one high ranking officer toward another and the complete lack of knowledge of most of the tank operations made our role exceedingly difficult. But it was only a part of the general picture of groping uncertainty that made Bataan a synonym for utter hopelessness.

CHAPTER 2

Prewar Mobilization of Citizen Soldiers

UNDER THE National Defense Act of 1920, the National Guard became an integral part of the Army of the United States—not only in name but in fact. It was the first line of defense along with the Regular Army. In the tables of organization of the Army, one tank company was allotted to each infantry division (square division) and was a component part of that division. The 34th Tank Company (34th Division) was located at Brainerd, Minnesota. It was a National Guard unit.

After World War I, even with the apathy displayed by Congress and the people towards things military, certain advocates in the Army began to think and speak of mechanized forces. This did not meet with the approval of the "Old School" who were in power. Nevertheless, this did not wholly deter armored advocates, even when ridicule became the order of the day.

This state of affairs existed until 1940 when Hitler rolled through France. Obviously, his success at blitzkreig war was due to his highly organized air-ground team. Mechanization was specialized to the nth degree which resulted in his so-called "buzz-saw" tactics and startled our "Old School" into doing something. The German idea of mechanization was actually born in the United States when German army officers witnessed the attempts of our enthusiasts, in the early years, to make their armored dreams come true.

The Armored Force was created on July 10, 1940, with headquarters at Fort Knox, Kentucky. The 194th Tank Battalion, GHQ, was created on paper. Brainerd became Co. "A"; St. Joseph, Missouri, Co. "B"; Salinas, California, Co. "C". All were the old square division tank companies and all were National Guard. Like groups were also organized from the balance of the National Guard tank companies in the United States.

Under orders from the President of the United States, we mobilized at our home stations on February 10, 1941. The organization of the 194th Tank Battalion would take place at Fort Lewis, Washington.

As early as October, 1940, I had made inquiries relative to the physical formation of a headquarters for the unit. Due to the fact that, as senior officer, and upon my arrival at Fort Lewis, my duties as commanding officer of Co. "A" would cease and I would assume command of the battalion. It should be remembered that the unit was organized only on paper. It was only common sense to set up a headquarters and staff ten days or two weeks in advance of the actual arrival of troops. No satisfactory answer was ever received and no authority was granted to create the headquarters even though I made repeated inquiries before actual mobilization.

We arrived at Fort Lewis on February 22, 1941, where we were joined by the St. Joseph and Salinas tank companies. A wild scramble ensued. We worked night and day. Housing was not yet completed. A Headquarters and Headquarters Company had to be organized. The battalion staff had to be selected. Due to the authority granted to enlist men over and above normal strength, proper uniforms were not available nor could the Quartermaster furnish them. Daily arguments—by mail and wire—with United States Property and Disbursing Officers of the several States had to be settled. Finance Officers of the Army had to be appeased—by mail—due to the endless procession of red tape created during the mobilization period; each man, during that period, was allowed a certain amount per day for home station housing, ration, etc. The company commander received the money in a lump sum by check. He was not allowed to put these funds in a checking account and pay by check. He had to cash the check and pay all bills by cash. Multitudinous certificates had to be made out for each expenditure. Instructions had been received from the Finance Office on procedure, but as is usual with Army finance affairs, it was made as difficult and technical as possible. Also, the instructions were not entirely clear nor were they complete. Having had experience with the Finance Department before and knowing they would follow me to the ends of the earth to make their point, I enlisted the aid of the United States Property and Disbursing Officer for Minnesota in helping me make out the certificates. I sighed with much relief when the job was done and everything in the mail. However, after reaching Fort Lewis, I found, to my consternation but not surprise, that even the expert aid received was not enough to satisfy Finance entirely and it was necessary to submit more paper work! Many other company commanders were in a much worse muddle than I.

Naturally, we had a serious shortage of officers due to the overnight expansion. They had to be assigned to many and varied duties. During the organization period it was possible for an officer to go to sleep at night as a subordinate and wake up as the company commander. An enlisted man summed the situation up one day when, in the heat of a supply tangle, he turned and said to another, "There's two ways of doing things. One is the right way and the other is the way the Army does it!"

At Fort Lewis, as commanding officer, I had to report to the Commanding General as soon as possible after arrival. This is Army procedure and it was instituted so as to aid materially in helping to establish and orient new arrivals in the area.

Before leaving Minnesota, new Army regulations had been issued for the dark "OD" shirt, trousers, cap and such. All officers in the Seventh Corps Area—Regulars, National Guard, Reserve—had all purchased this new regulation uniform.

I was wearing it when ushered into the large office of Major General Kenyon Joyce, later nicknamed by the men of my battalion as "God All Mighty" Joyce.

He sat at his desk staring at me. Directly in front of the desk was a rug, on which, the aide had informed me, I was expected to stand when reporting. I stood on the rug, saluted and reported.

Arising from his desk, he returned the salute in a very un-military manner and walked toward me. As I stood there at attention, he walked around and around me, giving me critical inspection much like a farmer would inspect a horse he was about to purchase. I fully expected him to open my mouth and look at my teeth. He stopped in front of me, reached out a hand and felt my dark shirt with sharp fingers."

"I don't know where you got that shirt," he said bluntly, "but we don't wear it here." Then he plunged into a lecture on the subject of "latter day soldiers." There was no word of welcome or offer to help us get settled. My past service flashed through my mind as he lectured on "latter day soldiers." Finally, he shook hands. It felt like holding a dead fish. I saluted and left his office feeling low and dejected.

In the Plans and Training Office, located in the same building, I stopped to inquire about training areas. A captain was answering my questions. He was wearing the same dark shirt as myself. I related my experience.

"Leave the shirt off for three or four days," he advised. "Then try it again. The General doesn't like the new regulation shirt. He would like to see us all wear serge."

General Joyce always wore shirts, the color of which I have never seen before or since in the Army. General officers are privileged to choose their own colors. On visiting the Post Exchange that same day, I found the dark shirt on sale! Returning to our area, I had our officers discard their taboo shirts for a few days. After that we put them on again and nothing was ever said.

General Joyce made it a point to make impromptu visits into training areas. Our area was no exception. His visits were feared because of his heckling attitude and impossible demands. Training was secondary to shirts being buttoned and neckties worn. Even when the Quartermaster could not furnish necessary clothing, the General would give the commanding officers "hell" for what he termed "improperly dressed soldiers."

On several occasions, conferences for commanding officers would be held at Joyce's headquarters. One of the procedures always followed in the Army, is never to reprove or reprimand anyone in the presence of his juniors. General Joyce did not follow that procedure. At all the conferences I attended, someone was "put on the carpet" in the presence of juniors and at one of these, two general officers in Joyce's command were reprimanded severely by him. Everyone in the room attending that conference was junior. I was only a major.

"Ike" Eisenhower became Joyce's chief of staff. He was a full colonel. Every time the General "messed" things up, Ike would follow through and pour oil on the troubled waters. I watched Ike work and was thankful for him. It was rumored at that time that Ike was "going places."

Some time in late Spring, a communication came through

from the headquarters of General Joyce. It asked for certain data on myself so that an efficiency report might be rendered. This was done once each year, the superiors reporting on the juniors. I replied by indorsement and called attention to the fact that the 194th Tank Battalion was attached to that headquarters for purposes of administration only and that any efficiency report rendered on me should be made by the Armored Force. I then contacted Armored Force Headquarters immediately at Fort Knox and protested being rated by people who knew nothing whatever about me. The protest bore fruit. The situation was corrected through Fourth Army Headquarters at San Francisco. It simply reiterated the original orders under which we came to Fort Lewis. It should not have been necessary, but with General Joyce, it was. From that time on, his headquarters dumped everything in our laps—even the correspondence which was already being channeled through them. In almost every matter, we were told to deal with the Armored Force. It was like a small boy showing his childish spite. Fortunately, the majority in his headquarters did not share his viewpoint and in spite of his policy, we did business with them.

Early in April, 1941, we received draftees to fill the battalion to war strength. They came to us all the way from the Middle West to the Pacific Coast. It was not long before they became an integral part of the battalion in everything from loyalty to vital cogs in the machine. We were the only Armored Force unit at Fort Lewis and it developed a very high esprit de corps which seldom slumped in spite of adverse circumstances.

We were 14 officers short in the 194th. Many of our non-commissioned officers were qualified except that regulations demanded completion of the 10 Series (qualification courses for second lieutenants) which these non-coms had not had. I requested this material so that schools might be held. It was flatly turned down with the information that any such schools would not be recognized and furthermore, the material was not available.

We knew that, unless we found some way to qualify 14 enlisted men in the unit, we would have assigned to us 14 outside officers and deserving men would lose out. Therefore a bold course was decided upon. A set of the 10 Series was actually purloined out of the Reserve office at Seattle. It meant concentrated effort. Everyone in the battalion cooperated. Twenty-five of our best non-commissioned officers were selected to take the Series with the understanding that the 14 highest would be chosen to go before the Board. I personally typed the stencils as we had to have enough copies of everything to give each candidate and instructor. Men in Headquarters, in addition to other duties, proofread the stencils and mimeographed copies. Officers acted as instructors. The 25 candidates had to be excused from some of their duties. Time was the essence. Other non-coms and privates took over these extra duties. Esprit de corps? *We had it!*

A communication was received from Fourth Army Headquarters in San Francisco calling my attention to the fact that we were 14 officers short and wanted verification. I replied that we were short at the present time but that the vacancies would be filled soon from qualified sources. About two weeks later a second communication was received from the same headquarters. It ignored my statement that the vacancies would be filled and stated that we would receive 14 reserve officers in July and August. I immediately replied and stated that a Board had been requested for qualified non-commissioned officers and would convene soon—that there was no necessity of assigning anyone as there would be no vacancies. I did not receive an answer.

The Board was formally requested. It was granted and the Board was convened. The President of the Board was a regular army colonel, practical in every respect and an individual who loved to cut red tape wherever possible. I carried in an armload of papers which represented the written work and examinations of the 14 candidates selected. The President exploded, "What in hell is that?" I then explained the whole situation and told him just what we had done. The Board then segregated the papers for each candidate and called them in, one by one. They finished their work by nightfall and the President sent for me. He stated that it was his extreme pleasure to inform me that all of the candidates had been recommended by the Board for commissions and congratulated the 194th on having enough initiative to circumvent red tape! The Board had concurred unanimously. In due time the 14 non-coms received commissions. *Nevertheless, in July and August we received 14 reserve officers.*

One grinning Tanker was heard to remark, "Everybody's gonna be an officer. A private is gonna be worth something around here!" We were never able to unload. It seemed that when the Army wheels started turning, only God could stop them. However, before long, the 14 reserve officers were duly accepted by the battalion and admitted into the "inner circles." They were assigned to various companies and put on the same basis as all the other officers.

There were no promotions for any of the original officers of the battalion until the last week in May, 1941, due to more red tape. I received my commission as a major on June 2nd although I had qualified for a lieutenant colonelcy before mobilization. The Board recommended my promotion from captain to lieutenant colonel which was concurred in by Fourth Army. The War Department had turned the recommendation down on the ground that it was a double jump even in view of the fact that the Board had submitted evidence of my qualifications together with previous service which included 17 years as a captain. One of my officers, Edward L. Burke, commanded Co. "A" as a second lieutenant from February into late November because of fumblings and failure to act by higher headquarters.

A week before Memorial Day, 1941, we received indirect information that "all hell might break lose" over the holiday week-end. We were told there might be a concerted effort to wreck airplane plants in various parts of the United States and that the Boeing plant in Seattle was on the list. The information was given us from Fort Lewis G-2 (Intelligence) sources. We were told of an important conference on a battleship with the FBI and Army Intelligence attending. This particular week-end was a long one with the usual lengthy holiday period. Many workers and others would be taking trips out of the areas involved. Some plants would be sabotaged by staging fake labor meetings at the front gates with enough violence to cause plant guards to rush to the scene. While the excitement was concentrated at this point, the plant would be sabotaged. We were then told that the Boeing plant might be either sabotaged or bombed. If bombed, it would be done by Russian planes! Fairy tale? Read the rest of the story and judge for yourself.

The day before Memorial Day we had as yet received no orders. The atmosphere around headquarters was tense. Most of the troops were in California on maneuvers. The Armored Force had decided against our taking part because of the training schedule which they did not believe should be interrupted. Only enough troops were at Fort Lewis to garrison the Post.

A great number of my officers and men wanted a pass over Memorial Day. I issued an order that passes would be held up until Memorial Day morning.

The night before, I sat in my quarters reading. It was a little after 9:00 P.M. when my adjutant, Capt. Muir, walked in.

"Heard the radio?" he asked. I told him I had not.

"A news flash just came over the air stating that all leaves had been cancelled at certain posts in the United States," he told me.

Just then the Orderly came running in. "You are to report immediately to post headquarters," he said. I hurried to conform with the order as fast as the jeep would carry me and found the C.O. seated at his desk. He shoved a radiogram at me which had come in code. The Signal Office had decoded it. I remember the exact wording.

"You may use troops as you see fit," it read. That was all but it was dynamite. To receive any such orders as that, in time of peace, is virtually a declaration of war.

By this time, the artillery and infantry commanders had reported. The C.O. asked us how long it would take to make the trip to the Boeing airplane plant. We made rapid calculations and he then outlined brief instructions of how he wished us to form a combat team. No information was given us as to the mission. He then gave me my orders:

"Service your tanks and other necessary vehicles for immediate movement. Mount your machine guns with *loaded belts.* Issue ball ammunition to the combat personnel. Tank crews will sleep alongside their tanks. You are on the full alert and will remain in that status until further orders."

I returned to our area and put the orders in effect. We only had eight outmoded tanks that needed constant work on them.

However, they would have done a great deal of damage in spite of being outdated. We remained on the full alert until Monday morning when orders were received the alert had been lifted.

Shortly after that, newspaper headlines screamed: *"Hitler moves into Russia!"*

CHAPTER 3

The Team Is Kicked Apart

IN EARLY July, 1941, two more tank battalions arrived from Fort Knox. They had just been activated, were untrained and had absolutely no equipment—not even a truck. Lt. Colonel S. MacLaughlin commanded one of the battalions and also was to act as the Group Commander of the three tank units at Fort Lewis. He was a regular army officer and one of the finest soldiers I have ever met. He was ever ready to help. Never did he attempt to use his rank except to represent the Tank Group in matters of supply, training areas and other pertinent phases directly affecting our welfare.

Soon after he arrived, I took my next phase of training to him for approval. We were sitting in his office smoking. He leaned back in his chair and said, "Now let's have an understanding early in the game. *You* are running your outfit and are responsible for certain results. You know what they need better than I. The Training Directive is laid down by the Armored Force of which you have a copy. From the way your outfit looks and functions, I don't think you need any help. From time to time, I will make inspections of all phases of training. If I see anything wrong, I'll tell you. Otherwise, *you* run your own show!" Here was the kind of soldier commanding officers dreamed about. His advice was always sound and his criticisms constructive to say the least. Above all—he fought for the Tankers whenever the need arose. He flatly refused the use of any of our trucks even though I offered to send two of them for the new battalions. His reply was, "Miller, you haven't even enough to take care of simple basic needs. Your outfit is the only one on the Pacific Coast that has any training. Get all of it you can with what little you have because I feel in my bones you will be called on damned soon and sudden!" Literally, I could have gone through hell for that man.

Sometime in July, orders from Fourth Army announced that the Pacific Maneuvers would be held in the Fort Lewis area to start on August 15th. The old bugaboo, relative to the use of tanks, which had been prevalent in the "Old School" ever since World War I, now raised its head again. The Directive stated that the tanks of the 194th would be split up so as to give both sides tank units. No other tank organization, either at Fort Lewis or Fort Ord, California, was in shape, as yet, to participate. I immediately replied with a carefully worded letter, pointing out that it was totally against Armored Force doctrines to split tank units; that they should function as a complete and composite battalion. My letter ended by calling attention to the necessity of allowing the 194th to participate as one team, for which they were created, and to gain the benefits of an enviable training phase which they had had no opportunity to participate in before. A copy of the letter was sent to Armored Force with the request for aid in solving our problem. Armored Force attempted to rectify the situation but was outweighed by the opposition. The morale of the Tankers was low.

In spite of equipment lacks, the battalion was beginning to function like a well trained football team. Up to the latter part of July, we had only eight tanks—the "Mae West" type (double turret)—1937 vintage, and just about worn out. Our maintenance crews worked like slaves to keep them running. However, we improvised and used our imagination. Two by four frames were constructed of approximately the same size as the crew compartment of the tank, inside of which men were placed to learn tank signals and coordination. We made frequent overnight bivouacs, assimilating war conditions, involving everything from tank establishments to river crossings and rapid convoy movements.

The latter part of July, we received a few more tanks. They were single turret jobs, also of 1937 vintage, but reconditioned. A few Jeeps and half-tracks were in the shipment. No one else at Fort Lewis had Jeeps. We were the envy of all. The morale of the Tankers went up!

About the 1st of August, late in the afternoon, Lt. Colonel MacLaughlin and myself were ordered to Headquarters. An order from Fourth Army was read which stated that a Task Force would be made up and sent to Alaska and that the 194th Tank Battalion would furnish one company for the Force. I asked them if they realized just what that order would do to my outfit; that it just did not make sense to train a team and then kick it apart! I was told coldly that it was an order from the War Department which could not be changed and was asked what company I would designate. My reply was that I would give an answer later that night so as to have time to think things over. The answer to my reply was to the effect that I would designate the company immediately. MacLaughlin jumped to his feet and almost shouted:

"Can't you give him a little time to feel his way?"

If the situation had not been so tense, I would have laughed. Mac had caught *rank* off balance. Facial expressions were something to behold. After a few moments of silence the decision came, "You may have until eleven o'clock tonight. That is all!"

Outside Headquarters, I turned to Mac and said, "If it were a matter of furnishing a cadre to train and help organize another battalion, there could be no argument. We expect that. But to just blindly walk in and take one whole company—."

Mac grabbed my arm, squeezed hard, "This is just one of those things. Don't let it get you down!" The look in his eyes and the words he spoke were more than a sermon.

Returning to our area, I called the company commanders together and explained matters. They had already heard the rumor! This was invariably the case with all confidential or secret orders coming through. Commanding officers and other pertinent personnel walked around with sealed lips with the knowledge that the secret had leaked out—and sometimes before the legal recipients knew about it themselves! The reaction of the company commanders was justified indignation:

Why was the battalion being used piecemeal when it was organized and trained to do just the opposite?

Why could not one of the other tank battalions furnish a company which would have made little or no difference to them in view of their state of training?

Of what use would the Armored Force be if it was to be used and torn apart at the whim of "swivel chair strategists" who knew little or nothing about mechanized forces?

I told them, frankly, that I was on the spot and it was absolutely necessary for them to aid me in naming the company. Therefore, more or less, I left it up to the staff and company commanders to decide who would go. They finally came out

with Co. "B", the St. Joseph, Missouri, company. When the conference broke up, we walked through the enlisted men's area.
They were congregated in groups outside the barracks. Conversation ceased as we walked through. Their faces were question
marks. They knew why we were in conference. Keep secrets
from the men? Hardly. They can almost literally smell a secret
with their eyes closed! What they didn't know was—what company? The news was soon announced. The morale of the
194th Tank Battalion sank to a hitherto unknown *low!* Co.
"B" started preparations the next morning. No information
was available as to the date of departure. We turned over to
them those tanks which were in the best condition.

It was with, perhaps, a selfish degree of satisfaction that I
officially notified Maneuver Headquarters of the latest events,
including the assignment of most of our tanks to Co. "B". We
were somehow just a little bit thrilled to know their carefully
laid plans for the use of tanks had been frustrated by the hand
of fate. However, like a cork on water which has been sub-
merged by a wave, they soon came to the surface with another
idea. In that no date was definitely set for the departure of the
Task Force, why could not the tanks of Co. "B" take part in
the maneuvers until they were needed for shipment to Alaska?
It might well be they would not leave the staging area of the
Task Force until after the maneuvers. Before their idea could
bear fruit, it leaked out and Task Force Headquarters issued
an order that Co. "B", together with all equipment, would
report immediately to the staging area. This definitely stopped further speculation. Maneuver Headquarters solved the
problem in the same manner that all problems were solved
at that time which involved lack of arms and equipment. Each
tank we had left would represent one platoon of tanks. If
additional tanks were needed, trucks would be labeled as such.
The battalion, less Co. "B", would participate as hitherto
directed.

About ten days before the maneuvers were to start, a group
of second lieutenants visited our area. In maneuvers, officers
are assigned to act as umpires. The lieutenants were to act as
tank umpires. The purpose of their visit, Headquarters announced to me over the telephone, was to talk over the use of
tanks, limitations, capabilities, view them, and to take a ride
if possible; they had never seen a tank and had been commis-

sioned a short time before out of school; it would be appreciated if we would spend as much time with them as possible
that afternoon. Train tank umpires in less than four hours!

Memories of a certain maneuver in the past flashed through
my mind when a tank umpire ruled one of two tanks (it also
represented a full platoon) out of action because it had been
theoretically fired upon by a .30 caliber machine gun! In essence, it would be like David trying to slay Goliath with a
spitball!

The lieutenants reported. They were a fine group of young-
sters who readily admitted their ignorance but were eager to
learn. We did all we could in four hours which was really
only a start but we tried to impress upon them an outline of
Armored Force Doctrines and also gave them a ride which
roughed them up but resulted in the thrill of their lives. It
cost the maintenance section of the battalion a good night's
sleep to put the tanks back into condition but they chuckled
as they worked.

On August 14th, the day before the Pacific Maneuvers were
to start, I received a long distance call from Fort Knox, Kentucky. It was about 11:00 A.M. and the Chief of Staff of the
Armored Force, Colonel Sereno Brett, was calling. His voice
was terse and he came right to the point. "Something big is
in the air. You are to report here immediately. Fly down!" I
told him the Pacific Maneuvers were to start the next morning; would I notify Headquarters and follow the normal procedure?

"Turn everything over to your executive officer and get
going!" he replied.

"What the hell now?" I asked myself.

Muir was standing nearby and had heard the conversation.
He anticipated my next move.

"Shall I call the Staff together now?" he asked. I nodded
and soon they were in my office and in possession of the latest
developments.

"Maybe we're going to be transferred to the Balloon Corps,"
suggested Capt. Johnson, Plans and Training Officer for the
battalion. Everyone laughed and it broke the tension.

Because of the maneuvers coming up, I had taken the
opportunity to send my dress uniforms to the dry cleaners.
Luckily, I had retained a dress coat. I told Capt. Muir to

make arrangements for my transportation and to call the cleaners to ascertain the status of my pants. He snickered and walked out. In a short time he reported back to say that the cleaners would have them ready to pick up on our way to the airport.

Not knowing what was in store for us, I gathered pertinent data together relative to the battalion, issued necessary instructions for the executive officer, and hastily packed. Running footsteps sounded in the hall outside my quarters. It was one of the sergeants from my headquarters. He saluted and held out his left hand containing my pipe and tobacco. "Thought you might need these, Major," he said. Death met him in the Philippines.

Captains Muir and Johnson were to accompany me to the airport so we might talk over last minute details. They soon drove up with the car. A Jeep roared up behind them. It was one of the officers from Co. "B", the unit designated for Alaska.

"What are you doing over here—Foreigner?" I greeted him.

His reply was hurried and jerky. "Just heard the news, Major. Don't forget we're still here. Pull for us when you're down there and maybe we can come back to the outfit."

Words were unnecessary. We shook hands and I climbed in the car. He stood alongside his Jeep and watched us out of sight.

Arriving at the cleaners, we were told that my trousers had been sent out to one of three places because of the rush of work and they had been unable to locate them as yet. Time was pressing and I had noticed that Johnson was wearing dress trousers. We were in the back seat of the car speeding for the airport. Evidently both Johnson and myself were thinking of the same thing.

"Give," I said.

"Certainly," replied Johnson as he started to take off his pants. "I wouldn't want our commanding officer to appear in public with anything but the best."

We succeeded in making the exchange but on arrival at the port, I found them to be much too long. I pulled them up as far as they would go and pulled the belt tight. Enroute, I was able to purchase a pair of suspenders. Without the coat, it looked as if I were wearing overalls. With the coat on, I felt truly girdled—but secure!

At 12:00 noon the next day, August 15th, I reported into Headquarters at Fort Knox and almost immediately was ushered into the presence of the Commanding General, Armored Force—Jacob Devers—and his staff.

CHAPTER 4

Secret Orders

THE GENERAL spoke briefly stating that the 194th **Tank Bat**talion had been ordered overseas for tropical service and that the movement was strictly in the secret category. At this conference and at a later one that afternoon, everyone except the General, his staff and myself, were banished from the vicinity.

General Devers asked me many pertinent questions about the battalion and then briefed his staff, after which certain phases of the movement were clarified. During the conversation, one of the staff officers blurted out:

"Now, when Miller gets to the Philippines—" he stopped abruptly biting his lips.

I had been well aware, during the conference, that I was not to be informed of our destination. When the break was made, I assumed the best poker face of which I was capable.

Then General Devers spoke with a sigh of admission:

"Well, the cat is out of the bag." He turned to me and sternly warned, "This must be kept absolutely secret!"

He shook hands with me, wishing us the best of luck and impressing upon me the important, historic significance of being responsible for the movement of the first armored unit ever to leave the continental limits of the United States. We then proceeded into the staff conference room down the hall to work out the details.

A loading chart was produced which had just been completed. It was for tactical loading (combat). We would load on the President Coolidge, which had been taken over by the War Department to be used for transport purposes. I was told to use every bit of effort in the name of the Armored Force to tactical-load that boat with our tanks and other equipment.

"You may have to come off the boat fighting," I was told. That statement was made with cold calculation.

Tanks were scarce. Evidently, the light tanks the United

States was turning out, were being shipped overseas to Britain on lend-lease, at least the great majority. The Armored Force was receiving only a few. In order to equip the 194th Tank Battalion with its full quota (54), one whole armored division had to be stripped of tanks! These would be shipped direct to San Francisco where we would load them on the boat.

Brisk argument got underway as to whether there was authority to send National Guard and draftees to the Philippines. One staff officer said he had heard of no law which made it possible, believing the bill called only for Alaska and the Hawaiian Islands. The Chief of Staff ended the discussion when he said there was no cause for worry relative to that detail. The order had come directly from General George Marshall, Chief of Staff of the Army. Colonel Brett produced the order and passed it around. (Congress did pass a bill, with a rider, authorizing the National Guard, Reserve, and draftees to be sent to the Philippines.)

During the conference, I brought up the question of Co. "B" which had been ordered to Alaska and requested it be restored to duty with the battalion. Somehow or other, which I cannot explain, I sensed an undercurrent. Sympathy was there, without a doubt, but other than that—nothing else. I was told that the decision had been made to give us another tank company which we would receive on arrival in the Philippines. It is my own personal opinion that the movement was already underway to break up National Guard units as much as possible but that the emergency in the Philippines put a brake on it for the 194th. The Armored Force had nothing to do with it except to be the instrument to carry out orders. They knew what was happening but were powerless to prevent it. This movement came from high quarters in the War Department and was part of a well planned and organized effort to discredit and disrupt the National Guard of the United States—an effort, which even General George Marshall, who did everything in his power to prevent it, could not stop! This movement was not new to the Guard. It started in World War I. Explanation of this movement appears in a later chapter. At all events, we had lost Co. "B".

It was nearly five o'clock in the afternoon and the end of the conference was in sight. There was one thing I wished to settle definitely before leaving and that was publicity.

"What will I be allowed to tell the press?" I asked.

"You can't tell them a damn thing," one spoke up.

"He'll have to tell them something," another officer said.

"My outfit is composed of citizen soldiers," I said. "Their families and friends are very much concerned as to where they are going and when it will happen. We are not in a state of war, as yet. If I do not have an authorized statement to hand the press, we'll have all of Congress on our necks!"

The Chief of Staff finally came up with a decision.

"You may publicly state," he said, "that the 194th Tank Battalion will sail on or about September 5th for tropical service. *Period!*" He then dismissed the staff and gave me some final instructions.

On my return to Fort Lewis, I was to go to San Francisco and work out the details of the movement with the Army Transport Service; I was to call my battalion at once alerting them for movement—official orders would follow; reports of our procedure in minutest detail from now until we actually landed in the Philippines, would be made by me to General Devers by *secret* letter and that the report would cover mistakes as well as success so that it might be used for future overseas movement of Armored Forces. He reminded me that we were making history.

"Colonel," I asked, "have I the authority to order my battalion out of the maneuver area into Fort Lewis tonight?" He must have been reading my mind for he gave me a broad grin.

"Major," he replied, "you have your orders and you are responsible that they are carried out. If I were in your shoes and with a mission such as you have, I would want to get started *right now*. Yes, you have the authority."

Lt. Colonel MacLaughlin's name was mentioned and I asked if it would be possible, officially, to allow Mac to work with me on some of the details. He replied that it was not only possible but he would include him in the orders which would allow Mac to accompany me to San Francisco. We shook hands and Colonel Brett left. As his footsteps faded away, I felt very much alone.

War seemed suddenly closer.

As I sat there, thinking things over in the big, empty room, my eyes came to rest on the telephone. The thought that I had a very pleasant duty to perform, warmed me immensely.

It did not take very long to put through the call to Fort Lewis. Luckily, Capt. Clinton D. Quinlan, S-4 for the battalion (Supply), had just come into the area on business for the maneuvers. My orders to him were to have the executive officer notify Maneuver Headquarters that the 194th Tank Battalion was relieved immediately from further participation and would proceed to Fort Lewis and prepare for an overseas movement. Clint was so surprised I could almost hear him swallow. I waited for his reply. Finally it came:

"Yes, sir." He repeated the instructions and then said: "Major, they have split up the outfit all over the area. I don't even know where the executive officer is. It will take some time to locate him."

"Then," I said, "you notify Maneuver Headquarters yourself and request them to make the contacts, after which, you—personally—find as many as you can and get them started. If I know this gang right, the news will spread and it won't take long!"

Clint died later on one of the hell ships.

The outfit was truly spread all over the landscape, as I soon learned. In most instances, tank commanders had been asked for their recommendations and they were accepted *if* they did not differ too much with the ideas of those to whom they were attached. Otherwise dispositions were made regardless of the advice of Tankers. There is no intention on my part to leave the impression that everyone was against us. We were simply the victims of thinking which had not been properly educated in mechanized warfare. Many of the people we came in contact with freely admitted they did not know a great deal about it and they were not obnoxious in giving their orders. However, they did have the rank and they did issue the orders and some of the dispositions made of tank installations and establishments would have meant utter annihilation in combat.

Quinlen lost no time. It was a duty that he relished immensely. If a bomb had actually dropped on Maneuver Headquarters, it could not possibly have created more of a furore. Quinlen's information was only that which I have related here. An air of mystery pervaded the scene. The Pacific Maneuvers were left without a single tank or tanker. What had been done to the battalion by higher authority, fate decreed should boomerang. It struck back at them at a most inopportune moment and it struck forcibly. They had to work fast and hard, turning some of their own trucks and Jeeps into tanks, pulling them from other outfits. They were getting a taste of their own medicine! Was our feeling one of revenge? I do not believe any of us felt that way, but we were only human and did have a feeling of smug satisfaction in the knowledge that even Fourth Army must bow to fate!

That night, I went by plane to Minneapolis and from there to Brainerd by car to have a short visit with my family. It was to be the last time I would see my son, Jim. He died on the Anzio Beachhead.

Later in the day, the editor of the Brainerd Daily Dispatch visited me and I gave him the exact statement authorized by the Armored Force Chief of Staff together with news items of the battalion. I saw an issue of the paper, at a later date, and he had stated nothing beyond what I had told him. But, naturally, he built a human interest story out of it and it *was news*. This was the home of Co. "A".

The next night I arrived, by plane, in Seattle. Muir and Johnson met me. From them I learned that coded orders had arrived at Fort Lewis from Armored Force Headquarters and that already a leak had developed.

"The men in our outfit," Muir stated, "are in possession of information that we are going to the Philippines!"

"Where did they get it?" I asked.

"Down at the Post somewhere. No one seems to know where it started."

Our destination—Philippines—was secret, together with certain details of the movement. It would not be strange for the men to be repeating what was already public knowledge—that we were sailing for tropical service on or about September 5th. That was the authorized public statement. But to be quoting "Philippines" as our destination was something else which might mean trouble for me and sure enough, it did! The next noon, storm clouds appeared in the shape of a telephone call from G-2 (Intelligence) at Headquarters, Fort Lewis. Knowing I would need help, especially in the first moments of G-2 hysteria, MacLaughlin jumped into the affair and helped to keep the storm from breaking before I had a chance to find out all the details. He succeeded in stopping it from becoming official for several days which was enough for me to gather ammunition. Had I been guilty, Mac would have been in the mess right along with me. He heard my story and that was enough. Can you blame me for thinking of the man as I do?

The Brainerd Dispatch, as I have stated, printed a story on what I had given them together with other pertinent details relative to Co. "A". It was sent in to the Associated Press per the regular newspaper channels and, of course, the radio head-lined it. *It was news!* Every officer and enlisted man in 194th was a citizen soldier; draftees, reserves, and the bulk—National Guard. *It was peacetime!* And it should be recalled that our politically-minded Congress had only just passed the measure, to retain the services of the citizen soldiers in the field, by the great majority of *one vote! Why shouldn't it have been news that a National Guard Battalion was sailing to a secret destination in the tropics?* Did the imagination of the newspapers and the radio need anything more?

It developed that the Pacific Coast newspapers, particularly from Tacoma and Seattle, had called Headquarters at Fort Lewis chiding them on the fact that other newspapers and radio broadcasts had known about this movement before they did—and here the 194th Tank Battalion was sitting in their own back yard! I know that the main reason for complaint was the fact that the source of the information came from a midwest town—Brainerd, Minnesota. Headquarters knew nothing of what I had been authorized to say. In fact, they did not know I had been authorized to say anything. None of this bothered me, but the one word—Philippines—did!

Up to the time we actually landed in the Philippines, I had never mentioned the "word," not even to my own wife when in Brainerd. Each night that I went to sleep, I uttered a silent prayer that the "word" would not pass my lips. The day after my return to Fort Lewis, I stopped in the officer's club. A regular army lieutenant colonel, whom I knew quite well, engaged me in conversation and said:

"Well, Miller, you're going to leave us pretty soon and where you're going—I wouldn't want to be!"

"Where are we going?" I asked.

"I'm not going to embarrass you," he replied, "but if you're interested, I have an album full of pictures which I think might help you in getting oriented. Come over to my quarters any time you say. You know, I had a tour of duty over there which ended just last year." I knew he had served in the Philippines! And so anxious was I to disassociate myself from the "word," I did not visit him.

In the meantime, some of my own agencies went to work for me. It was ascertained, and I was able to prove, that the first information of our movement had started not less than six hours after I had shaken hands with the Chief of Staff, Armored Force at Fort Knox, Kentucky! It was in the form of a letter from Knox, sent airmail, to one of the men in my battalion who had attended school at Knox and who was friendly with this individual, stating he had just learned that the 194th would be going to the Philippines soon! Also, I had in my possession, proof that within 30 minutes after the coded orders had been received at Lewis from Fort Knox, my men were in possession of the information, not only as to movement, but also our destination!

In due course of time, I received, not only an official communication from Headquarters, Fort Lewis, but also one from the War Department itself. Both demanded an explanation of how *secret* orders became the public property of the newspapers, the radio and the troops. The communications also reminded me that the press and radio had attributed the source of their statements to me! I answered these communications officially as I wanted them to be made a matter of record and reiterated what I had been allowed to say (neither Fort Lewis nor the War Department had had enough foresight to check into that phase). Then, I charged that the leak of pertinent information, relative to destination, must have been released from the Signal Office at Fort Lewis, and related other circumstances relative to previous secret orders. No mention of the leak at Fort Knox was made. I was sure this breach of confidence was a matter not related to maliciousness and could be settled by a word of warning for the future. Leaks had happened at Fort Lewis too often to be anything but malicious and it needed a thorough house cleaning.

Mac took my official answer down to Headquarters in person. I requested him to do so because I reasoned that certain verbal conversation must accompany it and he was in possession of enough information to advise them to clean their house. Logically, I could not do this. He returned, walked into my office, saluted and very formally said, "Sir, the mission has been accomplished!" We had a drink! I never heard anything more, officially or unofficially, from Fort Lewis or the War Department relative to the matter.

The next morning, at daybreak, Mac and I were on our way to San Francisco—one thousand miles away. Our transportation was my command car, a Ford, which I had received as a part of the Tables of Organization. Mac had been issued a Plymouth. All the way to San Francisco, he extolled the virtues of the Plymouth. We hit 90 miles an hour but this did not satisfy him. Knowing that we would be compelled to return to Fort Lewis before the battalion moved out, that my command car would then be loaded with other organic equipment of the battalion and that we must precede the outfit into San Francisco, we made a bet as to whether or not his Plymouth could make the Oakland Bay Bridge in less time than my Ford. Believe it or not, the second trip with his Plymouth was only about 30 seconds behind the Ford! It was so close that we both shook hands and declared all bets off.

We drove directly to Fort Mason, San Francisco, which was Headquarters of the Army Transport Service. We immediately visited the huge office. As we walked through the sea of desks, we were constantly amazed by the number of letters laying face up on desks with the large word *"secret"* stamped across the top. Many of the desks were unattended! Had we so desired, we could have read several of the letters without interference. We were both in uniform but never were we asked for any identification whatever!

CHAPTER 5

Operation "Movement"

WE FOUND the pertinent Army Transport Officers, introduced ourselves and stated our business. I pulled the tactical loading chart out of my pocket and laid it on the desk.

"What is that?" I was asked.

"That," I replied, "is a tactical loading chart which I am required to follow."

They first looked at it with a great deal of interest. It soon changed to amusement. An officer reached into a drawer of his desk and brought out a roll of blueprints.

"Take a look," he suggested. "This is the President Coolidge."

It was apparent that it would be impossible to make a tactical loading.

The President Coolidge was a luxury liner, taken over from the Dollar Line and reconverted for Army transport use. It had but recently returned from the Orient where it had been picking up our nationals. It was then in drydock undergoing repairs.

We were next shown the official orders which had been received direct from the War Department. The orders stated that the personnel and *all* tanks of the 194th Tank Battalion would be shipped on the President Coolidge. Nothing else was mentioned!

"It has been impressed upon me very forcibly," I told the group, "that we may have to come off the boat fighting. I think the people at Fort Knox knew what they were talking about. If we ship the tanks alone, we will have no combat efficiency whatever. We must have service vehicles and other necessary equipment right along with us."

"But look, Brother," I was told, "you're not the only outfit going on this boat!"

There would be two battalions of anti-aircraft (200th CA—National Guard), the 17th Ordnance Company—which was to service our tanks in fourth echelon maintenance, quite a number of casuals—both officers and enlisted men, part of the organic equipment for the foregoing, and in addition, a large shipment of airplanes and other paraphernalia. The War Department order had specified only the troops and their bare combat equipment. No provision whatever was made for servicing, tools, gasoline—not even ammunition for our weapons. The "swivel chair" strategists evidently expected us to come off the boat fighting—with our fists!

We were given permission to visit the drydock and take measurements of the cargo hold for the storage of the tanks. The type of tank we were receiving was the M-3 (light tank), a product and brain child of the Ordnance Department. It was not designed by the people who had to fight in them and the Ordnance Department resented any recommendations or ideas from that source. This was true, not only with tanks, but with other equipment and weapons as well. The past history of that branch of our Armed Forces will bear this out.

After arriving at the dry dock, we found that very little change was being made for the carrying of military equipment. It was still an ocean liner primarily for transport of troops. Mac and I measured the space allotted for tanks and found we could load them all *if* the turrets of 19 were taken off. This would render them unfit for combat for many hours after arrival at our destination.

Contact was immediately made with the staff of the Armored Force at Fort Knox to whom we gave all the details and requested a change in orders—either to allow us to load more equipment on the Coolidge or to put us on another ship. The answer was received that the Commanding General, Armored Force did not desire to interfere with the plans of the Army Transport Service. That was that! It was nearly 6:00 P.M. when the message was delivered. It had been a hard day, with nothing but disappointments all along the trail, and I must have reflected the discord of feelings within myself. Mac started to laugh.

"The end of a perfect day," he quoted sarcastically.

"Situation normal—*snafu!*" I replied.

Then we both started to laugh. We were standing in the lobby of the Hostess House at Fort Mason where we had gone to await the message. A one star general walked by eyeing us suspiciously. From the way he looked at both Mac and myself, I am quite sure he fully expected to see a bottle between us.

"Thought for a minute the old buzzard was going to stop and introduce himself," offered Mac. "Anyway, you can't say that all of our luck is bad!"

"Well," I said, "if you're going to look like that, when you become a general, I want to disassociate myself from you right now!"

"I'll be a Chinaman's grandpappy if I ever look like that—Say! Why don't we forget all this business for awhile and go down and visit Chinatown?"

The idea was good and it helped considerably. While partaking of Chinese food (invented in America) the thought came to us that the Commanding General's message in no way prohibited us from trying to get the 194th routed on another ship. The more we talked about it, the more feasible the plan became and it was decided to make this the first order of business in the morning.

Bright and early, we made our appearance and submitted the plan in detail. The officer who was handling our movement shook his head. "I know exactly what you are up against," he said, "and if there was anything I could do about it, you may rest assured it would be done. I want to call your attention again to the fact that this is a War Department order from which we cannot deviate. It would have to be changed in Washington and it would take real rank to change it. And, if it were changed, we would then be compelled to deal with the unions. The staff of the other boat would have to be enlarged and reorganized to meet the union demands. That is the picture."

"Isn't there some way possible to load part of our service equipment with the tanks and half-tracks?" I asked.

"If you don't include too much," was the reply.

A list was submitted and we departed.

G-4 (Supply) of Ninth Corps Area, with headquarters at San Francisco, had been designated to correlate details, relative to our supply in the Philippines. We visited him and talked over these matters, and particularly on gasoline and ammunition. Our tanks were equipped with the radial type airplane motor and used aviation gasoline. We were concerned with whether or not this gasoline would be available. If not.

arrangements would have to be made for special shipments from the United States. I dictated our requirements as to all pertinent items and G-4 sent a radio to Manila making the necessary inquiry. Several days later, he called me long distance to advise that Manila had replied, stating all the items were on hand and would be available to us on our arrival. I was struck with the G-4 quoting the word "Manila" over the telephone and in the clear. Secret orders!

In the meantime, preparations had steadily gone ahead at Fort Lewis. Multitudinous details had to be consummated, dealing all the way from Post clearances of issued items to transfer and replacement of enlisted personnel. Congress had written into the law various ramifications dealing with marital status, age and what-have-you. It was very confusing to say the least. Congress, as usual, was straddling the fence—unwilling to face an obvious national emergency—interested, primarily, in the vote back home. And, evidently, the great majority of the American people were not interested—at least, we did not hear any protest. Men, who were to be transferred because of prohibitory clauses of the law for overseas duty, had to be replaced by other men from other outfits who were eligible. Luckily, we did not have a great number in that status. Otherwise, we might still be at Fort Lewis! Our old equipment was turned over to the other two tank battalions. They were very happy to get it. As the last vehicle, of the whisker-age vintage, limped out from our area, I observed one of the men of our outfit thumbing his nose at it and then, very nonchalantly, blew a kiss in its direction.

Several days before the battalion was due in San Francisco, Mac and I took off on our second trip. Arrangements had to be made with both Fort Mason and Fort McDowell (across the bay) for housing, feeding, medical shots, additional clothing, visitors, acceptance of tank shipments and other equipment, records and many other details too numerous to mention. Every step we had taken, at Fort Lewis and San Francisco, I had very carefully written up in the secret reports and submitted to Fort Knox as ordered. These reports were voluminous and were used, later, in movements of other armored units in overseas movements. It was a real headache at the time because of other responsibilities, but (and I hope this thought will be pardoned) I took a great deal of justifiable pride in these reports, after we had landed in the Philippines and the job was done.

During the course of checking off the unending list of things that had to be done, Mac and I came to a complete halt when he exploded with: "Holy smokes! We haven't called on the Commanding General yet!"

"So what?" I asked. "You're a regular army officer. I'm just a "latter day" citizen soldier. That's the reason you're along— to remember military etiquette!"

"Hear! Hear!" said Mac. "Well, let's go see what he looks like."

"If he looks like the one we saw the other day, I don't want this trip spoiled," I replied.

We walked down to headquarters and just outside the door, Mac said:

"We'll have to make friends with the sergeant in charge of the outer office. He is the one who can really help us."

"Certainly," I said. "I used to be an enlisted man. That's where I got my start."

Mac turned around and looked at me.

"What a start you got!" he returned. And as I laughed, he said, "Wipe the hilarity off your face and let's go!"

We stepped into the office. A master sergeant was in charge. He was very courteous and had the usual answers. He knew the game from A to Z and could, if called upon, have ushered us to the category of thumbing a ride on the open highway. However, without being egotistical, Mac and I knew the ropes. He was quick to recognize it. Before we had exhausted our conversation, we had his confidence and cooperation, and we also had a desk in his office together with stenographic help. He proved to be a real aid to us and he knew we appreciated it. He disappeared into the Commanding General's sanctum sanctorum.

Mac said, "Polish your belt buckle. We're on our way!"

"Did you clean your teeth this morning?" I asked.

Before he had a chance to reply, the sergeant opened the door and gave us a big smile. "The General would like to see you."

We passed through the door and almost immediately felt at home. The sergeant had most certainly paved the way. Don't ever pass up a sergeant! Brigadier General Lee was in complete charge of the Port of Embarkation. He rose from his desk and shook hands with us in a most cordial manner, pushed a box of cigars over and invited us to help ourselves. Then he said: "Sit down and tell me what I can do for you."

He was entirely familiar with the movement of the 194th Tank Battalion and also with our problems. He expressed his regrets that he could not help us in loading tactically and reiterated what Army Transport officers had already told us. I know that he realized our predicament, because, when we rose to take our leave, he shook hands with me and said:

"Major, I wish you the best of luck in where you are going. It will be a hot spot. I want you to know that if it were within my province to change those orders, I certainly would do so. If there is anything other than that, let me know."

Mac and I left his office a great deal more sober minded than when we first entered.

We now learned that the President Coolidge would be laid up in dry dock longer than had been anticipated and that the sailing date was delayed to September 8th. This was good news rather than the opposite. Much still remained to be done. The 17th Ordnance Company had just arrived and we went into a huddle with the company commander. They were familiar with the M-3 tank and we wanted them to know the details of loading. It was agreed that they would furnish the detail to strip the nineteen turrets and also, to help load the tanks. This was a relief to me. Our people had never seen the M-3 and I had been wondering how we could accomplish the almost impossible.

The night before the scheduled arrival of the battalion from Fort Lewis, Mac and I had worked until the small hours of the morning. The schedule stated the time of arrival as 6:30 A.M. September 5th. At 6:00 o'clock, we were waiting, alongside the tracks below Fort Mason as we wanted to board the train, before arrival, and acquaint the officers with the detraining procedure. We found that the train would be late and we decided to have breakfast in a restaurant adjacent to the tracks. I will never forget that breakfast. We had hot cakes and sausage—plenty! Our appetite was really enormous. While waiting for the first installment of breakfast, I placed a nickel in the jute box and pushed the button. It came up with Concerto in B Flat Minor. I had heard it before, but at this particular time and for no apparent reason, I was so enthralled with the deep chords that I played it again and again. Mac liked it too but after about three encores, he protested along with the management. The chords struck something in me, that morning, that was really responsive. I was nearly kicked out. It was to be a part of a coincidence I will never forget.

The special train, bearing the battalion, arrived at about 7:30 that morning. Mac and I boarded it as it passed slowly by the restaurant. I know that both of us were thrilled as the gang recognized us. We gave out the necessary instructions and prepared for the stop at Fort Mason. The troops had to be transported, by ferry, to Fort McDowell (across the bay). The route passes by Alcatraz and also makes a stop there. The purpose of taking the battalion to Fort McDowell was to give them the start of necessary medical shots for tropical service, check on records, and to issue pertinent clothing. The outfit loaded on the ferry and were soon "bedded down" at McDowell.

Crews from the 17th Ordnance Company, accompanied by details from the maintenance section of the 194th, were dismounting turrets from the tanks and loading them on the Coolidge. They had quite an argument with the port authorities. All of the tanks had some aviation gasoline in the gas tanks. One of the regulations stated that all gasoline must be removed from vehicles. Aviation gasoline is high test and very dangerous. This was a particular point. The details were told that there was no time to remove the gasoline and to load the tanks on the ship as they were. They did.

Many relatives and friends of the 194th made the pilgrimage to San Francisco to see us off. It was the last time the great majority would see each other again.

The troops were brought over from Fort McDowell at about 3:00 P.M., September 8th. They were unloaded and checked up the gang plank. They filed on slowly, answering their names, and as I think back over that scene and the unaccountable feeling that came over me, it was but an omen of the things yet to come.

After the troops had been checked and quartered, I made a last inspection to see if my list of vehicles had been included on the Coolidge. *They were not.* Frantically, I tried to get action. The total result was that *one truck* was loaded. With a feeling of total frustration, I entered the item in my secret report, sealed it, and turned it over to the military police for mailing.

About ten minutes before the gang plank was removed, an orderly paged me and I accompanied him to the dock. There stood Mac. He had been ordered earlier in the day to Fort Ord, 100 miles away. He had driven back just to see us off. Many of the uninitiated, perhaps, think there is no sentiment in a military organization—just a hard boiled makeup of *duty*—armorplated over and beyond sentiment. I think I may safely state that this is the myth of all time. Sentiment runs deep in the Armed Forces—perhaps because of the close mutual affiliations and the sharing of a common life with the dangers involved. Whatever it is, Mac displayed it that night. No words were wasted. For once in his life he could not wisecrack. He thrust out his big hand, swallowed hard, and said, "Good luck, Ernie."

I grasped hard and squeezed. He turned rapidly away and strode for the nearest shadows of the big buildings on Pier 45. That was the last I saw of him.

We sailed at 9:00 P.M. that night, September 8, 1941, to the accompaniment of last good-byes, fluttering handkerchiefs and unashamed tears in the eyes of many. I stood along the rail watching the lights of San Francisco fading away and suddenly awakened to the fact that we were directly under the Golden Gate bridge. One young Tanker, standing nearby, put his farewell into poetry:

> "So long to you, oh Golden Gate,
> I'll soon be back and we'll have a date."

Strange thoughts we have at moments like these.
He never came back!

CHAPTER 6

The Battle of Supply

ONE OF THE requirements, demanded by the Armored Force, was that the radial motors, with which our tanks were equipped, be turned over daily by hand so that the cylinders would not "freeze." The first day out, our crews went down into the hold. In a short time the maintenance officer and sergeant reported back.

"Major," they said, "we turned a couple of the motors over. The fumes nearly knocked out some of the men. There's no way for those fumes to escape and there's danger of an explosion!"

I ordered the men out of the hold. The tanks should never have been loaded on the ship with any gasoline in them, without making provisions for ventilation. And we were dealing with aviation gasoline! Needless to say, there were no more motors turned over during the entire voyage. Numerous inspections were made but that was all.

We arrived in Honolulu Saturday morning, September 13th, at about 7:00 A.M. Our share of the ship's guard was relayed so that everyone would have the opportunity of going ashore. At about 5:00 P.M. that day we set sail again. Everyone reported in good shape.

From now, until we reached the Philippines, our course was south of the Great Circle—off the beaten track—and we traveled by blackout. Our convoy was the USS Astoria, a sleek cruiser. Several times, smoke was observed on the horizon and, each time, the cruiser made for the spot at full speed to investigate. Nothing out of the ordinary happened.

As we entered Manila Bay on September 26th, I called a staff meeting. When they were all seated, I announced:

"The destination of the 194th Tank Battalion is the Philippines!"

They all laughed heartily and so did I, more heartily than any of the others. So securely had I kept the "word" locked inside me, I now found myself feeling almost guilty that I had spoken.

A party from shore came on board while we were still out in the bay and a conference of commanding officers and adjutants was held. The 200th CA, 17th Ordnance Company, and 194th Tank Battalion would be taken to Fort Stotsenburg (about 60 miles north of Manila) by bus. I made the necessary arrangements to leave the maintenance section detail at Manila for the unloading and guarding of our tanks and half-tracks although it took strenuous argument before the Port Area Quartermaster would agree. We debarked at about 3:00 P.M. and were soon on our way. I was taken by command car in advance of the movement. The route lay on Highway 3, the main road, north of Manila, leading to Lingayen Gulf and the Baguio area. This was the route on which war would come to us.

Travel was comparatively slow. The highway was paved with concrete, but highways in the Philippines are used as sidewalks, by not only the Filipinos themselves, but also by dogs, chickens, pigs and everything else. Little children were the worst hazard of all. The Filipino is curious by nature and constantly strives to increase his knowledge. Adults and children, loitering on the highways, causing accidents and near accidents, was not done for any other reason except to satisfy the insatiable desire of the Filipino to see what was going on at close range! My first impression was that they were a discourteous and rude people with their staring and crowding. I was soon to learn that they were just the opposite.

Our car arrived at Stotsenburg after dark. Darkness comes quickly in the tropics after the sun goes down. A guide met me and together we went into the area in which we would bivouac. I was groping my way over the unfamiliar ground— my mind a jumble of thoughts. Suddenly, I heard a voice.

"Major Miller!" someone called from the darkness. I answered.

"Come over here, will you please?" said the voice.

Still groping, I moved toward the sound. It was the Commanding General of Fort Stotsenburg, Brigadier General Edward King, and his aide. He immediately introduced himself in the darkness and shook hands, welcoming me to the Post. He apologized for not being able to assign us better

quarters, stating no notification of our coming had been released in time to provide housing. However, he had had tents
put up which were equipped with cots, and he had made arrangements for supper that night and breakfast the next
morning, which would allow us ample opportunity to set up
our own kitchens. He was extremely solicitous regarding the
welfare of the enlisted men, and impressed upon me that this
was the first thing to be taken care of; to forget everything
else, including formalities, until this was done. He did not
leave the area that night until the men had arrived and were
taken care of. His attitude then, and in the future, was to discard red tape to meet the practicality of a situation. Here was
the man who would be given command of Bataan, in the
final days of that bloody holocaust, and who would refuse to
allow anyone but himself to accept responsibility for the surrender order issued on that historic day—April 9, 1942!

By 10:00 A.M., the next morning, all tanks had been unloaded from the President Coolidge. The Port Area Quartermaster was contacted and the request for aviation gasoline was
submitted so as to get the tanks to Stotsenburg. The reply was
that it would have to be ordered from Cavite—Naval Supply
Base—and would take about one and one-half hours. I had
assigned Capt. Spoor (Battalion S-2, Intelligence) to handle
the convoy from Manila to our area. Shortly after 1:00 P.M.,
he again reported to the Quartermaster office to see if the
gasoline had arrived. After searching for someone in authority, he found Major T. Smythe, who was later to become the
executive officer of the Tank Group under Brigadier General
James R. N. Weaver. Smythe had been with the 7th Infantry
at Fort Lewis but had recently been sent to the Philippines
and assigned to the Quartermaster of the Port Area. His
branch was Infantry. He advised Spoor to become acquainted
with the custom of taking a siesta at that time of the day and
to come back later!

Spoor took things in his own hands and put through a call
for Cavite. Finally, after making connections with the proper
parties, he found that no request for gasoline had been made.
He therefore ordered it in the name of the Port Area Quartermaster, and the Navy promised to send it in. At 7:00 P.M., it
finally arrived and the tanks were serviced. It was not until

9:00 P.M. that they were able to secure a police escort to the north boundary of Manila.

That trip would take another book to relate the details. It was precarious to the nth degree. Travel was on the left hand side of the road in the Philippines. We were not used to that as yet. Tanks are hard enough to handle in the daytime without adding darkness, and unfamiliar driving regulations, to the ordeal. Filipinos had never seen a tank before. Particularly, at night, the highways are used as sidewalks. Groups are continually going back and forth on foot, visiting with each other and taking advantage of the cool of the evening. Visualize, if you can, tank drivers straining, twisting, dodging, sounding their sirens—60 miles of it—amid the screechings of children darting suddenly in the path of the oncoming tanks, curious Filipinos blocking the way, dogs yapping, oncoming traffic including both automobile and carabao carts—constantly having to remember to drive on the "wrong" side of the road—visualize, and you will have some idea of that trip. Several stops were made and the vehicles were instantly surrounded by man and beast. Adults and children both, looked and touched and marvelled. It was an event!

The tanks arrived at Stotsenburg about 4:00 A.M. the next day. To the credit of the Tankers, only two minor incidents had occurred—knocking a piece of concrete from a small bridge and causing a carabao to make for the jungle, dragging the cart behind. Nothing serious resulted.

We had arrived in the Philippines during the rainy season—and it rained! Native type barracks were completed for us about the 15th of November. During this period, there was no storage space whatever for equipment and other supplies except out in the open. We also had the equipment, including 17 tanks, of a company which did not exist as yet. Clothing and other pertinent paraphernalia had arrived on another boat. In between tropical rains, we had to spread things out to dry. It was a continuous battle taking care of Ordnance. This was in addition to the training schedule.

As soon as we arrived, it was apparent that we would fight the Battle of the Bugaboo of Supply.

Aviation gasoline was requisitioned for the tanks immediately. The M-3 tank was new to us. Outside of driving them from Manila, no one in the battalion had had any experience

with that type. We needed training and we needed it badly.
We were told that an administrative difficulty existed. The
gasoline would have to be transferred from the Air Corps.
Clark Field, with huge storages of gasoline, was a part of
Fort Stotsenburg until shortly before war when it became a
separate entity. It was not until about November 1st, more
than 30 days after we had arrived, that we were able to procure gasoline to run the tanks!

In the meantime, I had been called upon to submit an estimate of our needs relative to gasoline, oil and grease. The
estimate was made up carefully and based on absolute training needs for one month. I was met with an attitude which
made me almost believe, for a time, that perhaps I might be
insane in the matter of our requests. I was told to remake the
estimate on an intelligent basis—that they did not use that
much gasoline and oil on the Post in a whole year and we
had submitted requests for only one month! There seemed to
be no understanding whatever of the modernization of the
Army. After considerable argument and explanation, the
Quartermaster agreed to put the request through but shook
his head unbelievingly as he did so.

Our tanks were equipped with 37mm guns which had never
been fired. We requested recuperating oil and ammunition so
as to test fire these guns and also train the men. No one had
fired the 37mm gun although we were conducting schools on
nomenclature and functioning. The request was flatly turned
down! The first firing of our 37mm guns was done when the
Japanese were actually in sight!

In early October, I received a copy of the manifest, listing
tank parts being shipped us on the steamship Yaka. It docked
about the middle of October. From that time until war actually broke out, I used every means at my disposal, striving to
locate those parts. Never was I able to get any information
whatever and Port Area did not seem to care! We did not get
the parts. The Japanese eventually possessed them! The shipment was the equivalent of from 12 to 14 carloads of parts!

Quartermaster property also arrived which actually was delivered to us at Fort Stotsenburg. It was billed to us and included needed parts for trucks, reconnaissance cars and Jeeps.
These parts were taken from us and put in the Quartermaster
Pool and under their control completely. It almost became

necessary to have an act of Congress to release even a cotter pin. For instance, the muffler on my command car had deteriorated to the extent of where it rotted off. We requisitioned for a replacement about the middle of October. After repeated follow-ups, and a direct request to the Commanding General himself, the muffler was issued just a few days before war broke out in December!

The short wave radios we had for our tanks were not designed for the M-3 tank. The Armored Force instructed me to install this radio, after we reached the Philippines, as a stopgap measure. As soon as possible, they would send the radios which had been designed for this type of tank. This we did, soon after arriving at Fort Stotsenburg. In order to install the radios, it was necessary that we eliminate one .30 caliber machine gun in each tank. This was located on the right side, in the sponson, and was controlled by the driver. This left a good sized hole, which exposed the crew to bullets, shell, and bomb splinters. Realizing that it would be a long time before we received the proper radios, I made a formal request to the Ordnance Department in the Philippines, to weld a piece of metal over the holes, as a temporary measure. This was flatly refused on the grounds that they could "make no modifications on the M-3 tank without proper authority of the Ordnance Department." This meant that a request would have to be made, through channels, and that it would have to go back to the United States, through multitudinous channels, before we would receive an answer. I thought it over very carefully, and came to the conclusion that before we would receive an answer through those mediums, either we would have a war or we wouldn't!

Soon after, we were bombed, and the war was on. On the same day that hostilities commenced, and after we had been bombed on Clark Field, I ordered the 17th Ordnance Company, to cover the holes, by welding on pieces of steel from old tractor plates. This, they did without delay. The 17th Ordnance Company had wanted to do it before, but lacked the authority.

The situation became so difficult that, one day in the Ordnance Office at Stotsenburg, my temper got the best of me.

"We don't even get a damned answer to our communications!" I ranted.

The Ordnance sergeant in charge that afternoon, looked up at me and laughed aloud.

"Major," he grinned, "after you've been here awhile, you will realize that if you get an answer to your communications within 30 days, it will be considered as immediate action!"

I laughed with him. There wasn't anything else to do.

General King was one individual who seemed to recognize that a serious emergency existed and that we were facing war. He did everything in his power to set the house in order but he was working against odds. I know that he did not share the belief of MacArthur and others, that the Japanese would wait until about the 1st of April to strike. King was like General Grunert—not interested, so much, in the state of readiness we would be in on M Day, but how ready we would be if the blow fell *before M Day!* General King had other duties which took him away from Stotsenburg much of the time. He was responsible for, and had to visit, Philippine Army installations in various parts of North Luzon. His trips were tough ones.

Soon after our arrival, we had our official conference with him. He explained the Orange Plan (WPO-3) for the defense of the Philippines. It was a three phase affair.

Phase One: Beach action. If that failed—

Phase Two: Retrograde movements involving delaying actions, holding up the enemy's advance as much as possible, and finally—

Phase Three: Withdrawal into Bataan where it was contemplated we could hold out for about six months which would allow the Navy to clear a way for reinforcements.

The General, after orienting us, asked what recommendations we wished to make in the way of primary missions. We explained to him the absolute necessity for detailed reconnaissance studies of the terrain so that we might determine where tanks could and could not be used. He immediately agreed and assigned the surrounding area adjacent to Stotsenburg and Clark Field. We were to ever widen out so as to enlarge these reconnaissance studies and to report each area to him when it was finished. This was to be done by submitting overlay maps of the areas.

The plan was immediately put into operation under Johnson and Spoor (Battalions S-3 and S-2, respectively).

During the early part of November, orders were received that maneuvers would be held at Camp O'Donnell, about 20 miles to the north of Stotsenburg. Again, the same line of thinking entered into the plans for the use of tanks as we had encountered in the Pacific Maneuvers.

Orders were issued by Major General Jonathan Wainwright, who was at that time commanding general of the Philippine Division (Scouts), that the 194th Tank Battalion would be split up between the two forces. I protested, as before, but in addition called attention to the fact that we had strange equipment (much more than we had ever had before), had never been allowed to stretch out the battalion for road space in convoy, and in no way had been given opportunity to be trained as a composite unit. Finally, that maneuvers would do this for us and if denied, would circumvent what we had been sent to the Philippines for. In reply, I received a letter entirely ignoring the technical points involved. It blindly ordered us to abide by the original decision.

It was then that I made a trip to Fort McKinley, just outside Manila, where General Wainwright's headquarters were located. I found Colonel Harrison Browne, Wainwright's chief of staff, who took me in to see the General. Colonel Browne was an old friend of mine having served as Regular Army Instructor of my old National Guard regiment in Minnesota. We had been on many fishing and hunting trips together and were more than ordinary friends. He said:

"Well, Ernie, I wish you all the luck in the world, but I don't think you're going to get very far, and if the General says 'no'—don't press the point!"

General Wainwright, tall and slim, received me very courteously. There was no stiffness about the visit and I felt at ease. It did not take long to come to the point. In essence, he told me it was absolutely necessary that the tanks be split for the maneuvers and that he would like me to go along with him without any further protests. He said that he would soon be taking command at Stotsenburg and that he would see to it, personally, that we received the type of training we so desired. In spite of my disappointment, as I left his office, I could not help but like "Skinny." He had let me say the things I had wanted to say and in my own words. He was not dictative in any way—merely firm in his decision. I had argued and lost.

The maneuvers were suddenly cancelled later on. Transportation difficulty was the reason given. After about a week, orders were again issued that maneuvers would be held. Later they were cancelled the second time. The same reason was given.

General King now assigned me another mission. I was to work out an Alert Plan for the use of tanks in the protection of Clark Field. This was to be done in conjunction with the commanding officers of Clark Field and the 200th CA. Lt. Col. Lester Maitland commanded the field. The plan was worked out with the tanks taking station on and around Clark Field, primarily to repel any airbourne troops with which we might be faced. It was submitted to King who approved it in its entirety.

On the day that we finished the Alert Plan, Col. Maitland and I sat in his office. We were alone. He was the type of officer that wanted to see things done but had run up against the same kind of stone wall which we had encountered. He felt frustrated and very much discouraged. It was he, who had made the first non-stop flight from San Francisco to Honolulu, quite a number of years before. There was no doubt in his mind that war was imminent. It was here that Maitland confirmed a rumor regarding an alert held at Stotsenburg, a short time before we had received our orders to leave for the Philippines. I had tried to confirm this rumor after we arrived but could only get denials. Maitland told me the whole story. There is no doubt in my mind that this was the reason why we were sent over in such a hurry and why I was told we might have to come off the boat fighting. Everything fitted into the picture.

Maitland sent a patrol daily to fly north from Clark Field over Lingayen Gulf, then southward over the China Sea, along the west coast of Luzon, to the southern end and then back to Clark Field. This route covered the vulnerable parts of Luzon, where a hostile landing force might normally invade.

On one of these patrols, one plane was flying at a lower altitude than the rest and the pilot noticed something on the water in Lingayen Gulf. He investigated and found it to be a buoy with a flag on it. Then he found other buoys with flags at approximately 1,000 yards apart extending out into the China Sea for about 30 miles. By the time the pilot reached Clark Field, to make his report, it was nearly dark and too late to do anything about it that night. Maitland traced the course of the buoys to the northwest and found that the line intersected a Japanese controlled island on which a powerful radio station was known to exist!

The next morning at dawn, a special patrol was sent up to investigate. The buoys had been taken up at night. A fishing craft, in the vicinity of the line of buoys, was making rapidly for shore. The hold of the craft was covered by tarpaulin in which, according to Maitland's viewpoint, the buoys had been placed. There was no means available whereby the plane could communicate with friendly agencies on shore and by the time the report was submitted, it was too late to make any check. The alert went on which, evidently, spurred the War Department, belatedly, into trying to do something about it. This was the area in which the Japanese put their main landing force!

CHAPTER 7

There will be No War with Japan

MORALE HAD ITS difficulties even concerning the Armored Force shoulder patch. At Fort Knox I had been informed that the triangular patch had been approved by the War Department and I immediately placed an order to take care of the entire battalion. At San Francisco notification was received that it had been disapproved!

This was an outgrowth of the fight which had been waged between proponents of a separate mechanized force and the anti's who wished to retain this force within their own branches. The Armored Force evidently scored the first victory, with the result that a premature announcement was made. However, their opponents finally outweighed them in the end.

Every man is proud of his branch of the service, no matter what it is. Personnel in the 194th was no exception. The decision lowered the morale of the outfit. Every other branch of service had their own distinctive insignia. The decision left the officers of the 194th wearing tank insignia on their shirt collars and lapels of the coats. There was nothing denoting tanks on the uniform of the men.

We had an idea which was put into effect upon arrival in the Philippines. Chinese tailors at Fort Stotsenburg were contacted. They had Filipino women, experts on embroidery, in their employ. We made a deal with the tailors to embroider yellow silk tanks on the overseas caps of all the enlisted men in the battalion. It was the same type of embroidery that was regulation for officer's insignia on the cotton uniform. Morale went up!

Several times I was asked by higher authority if this was the practice in the States to which I replied in the affirmative.

Stress was placed, at Fort Stotsenburg, on the personal appearance of both officers and enlisted men. This was necessary and entirely justified up to a certain point, but at times, it seemed to transcend all attempts to prepare for war. Many times, during the *working day*, our officers and enlisted men would have occasion to go out of our area on official business. Tanks are very hard on clothing because of grease, oil and metal. Therefore, in a tank unit, both officers and men wear coveralls and, in the Philippines, we had a hat known as the "Sloppy Joe." It had a soft brim which not only protected individuals from the rays of the sun but also, to a great extent, kept the neck and ears free from greasy dirt.

Our people were constantly being stopped and sent back to the area because they were not in "proper uniform." I tried to explain our predicament to headquarters but was met with a blank refusal to allow any leeway. It bacame mandatory for anyone to change clothes, if he left the area. If personnel had not been on official business, dealing with everything under the sun to keep tanks and other vehicles running, there would have been justification for such an order.

One particular Saturday morning, a group of my men had been promised a pass, from noon to Monday morning at reveille. They had been working like beavers all week long—and working through the heat of the day when many of the "regulation enforcers" were taking their siestas. We had to send some of these men out of the area that morning on missions of business, relative to the servicing of vehicles and weapons. There was no time for them to change uniforms. It had to be done and they were ordered to go as they were.

About 11:00 A.M., the men reported back. They said that they had fulfilled the mission, but in doing so, had run afoul of the military police. Shortly, headquarters called by telephone, stating that the men would be confined to the area over the week-end as punishment.

Immediately, I jumped into a Jeep and went to headquarters and explained the incident and stated that I had ordered them on that mission. It did no good—they were sorry but orders were orders. Just as I came out of the door, General King walked in. He shook hands with me and wanted to know if there was anything he could do for me. I told him there certainly was something he could do, and then explained my predicament. He heard me through, and after chuckling to himself, told me to disregard headquarter's decision and let the men have their pass. Then he said: "Don't put me on the spot too often. You know, I'm scared to death the military

police may find me, some day, with one of my buttons un-
buttoned!" General King was a very human individual, but
he could also be a mighty strict disciplinarian—if the occasion
warranted.

For some time, we had been hearing persistent rumors that
another tank battalion was on its way to the Philippines, and
that it would be the 192nd—another National Guard unit.
The rumor was confirmed, officially, several days before the
ship was to arrive. General King ordered me to proceed to
Manila on November 20th and attach myself to the boarding
party which would visit the transport in Manila Bay before
it docked. This was the regular procedure so that instructions
could be given the commanding officers for debarking from
the ship. The General's orders were to help the new arrivals
over administrative rough spots so there would be the least
amount of delay in bringing them to Stotsenburg.

November 20, 1941, was Thanksgiving Day. Capt. Muir accompanied me. We arrived at Pier 7 and immediately reported to the officer in charge of the landing party. He was already
on the small boat which would take us out to the transport—
the President Scott—a much smaller liner than the Coolidge.
General King's orders were explained but I was met with instant refusal to allow me to accompany the party. My name
was not on the mimeographed list with which the officer was
armed! While we argued, the boat shoved off. This automatically made me a member of the party, under formal
protest—of which I never heard any repercussions.

After boarding the President Scott, I met a colonel and a
major—both Tankers. The colonel was James R. N. Weaver,
regular army, and would be the Tank Group Commander.
The major was T. Wickord, National Guard, commanding
officer of the 192nd Tank Battalion. The 192nd and 194th
would form what was to be known as the 1st Provisional
Tank Group. The troops debarked in good order and were
piloted over to the area where they would board busses for
Fort Stotsenburg. Much to my surprise, military police told
me, the troops would go by train instead of bus. I asked them
if this was a recent change in orders, to which they replied,
it was not; that the schedule for movement by train had been
in their hands for at least a week! This made a great deal of
difference in taking care of the incoming troops. All arrange-

ments had been made by General King for the buses to unload the 192nd directly in their own area. Coming in by train,
the men and their baggage would be deposited about two
miles from that area—hungry—and no transportation!

Taking the commanding officer of the 192nd, we drove to
Stotsenburg as fast as possible. There was a delay in long distance calls and we could not wait for a clear circuit as the
train had already moved out. I had a good idea as to where
I would find General King on our arrival—and sure enough—
he was there, waiting alongside the road which led into Fort
Stotsenburg, to greet the 192nd in person when they arrived
by bus! I told him what had happened. He had not been informed of any change in the original schedule sent him some
time before.

Then came an unpleasant duty, that might just as well have
been unnecessary if the Port Area Quartermaster had been a
little more concerned with planning than he was with siestas!

My outfit had just sat down to their Thanksgiving dinner—
the first away from home. They had planned for it and the
holiday spirit was in the air. We had to rouse them out of it
and put them to work, transporting the 192nd, with their baggage, to the new area. They had to leave their dinner setting
on the tables to get cold. Our plans, to feed the 192nd, were
based on a bus movement which would have prevented the
confusion which now followed. General King stayed with us
until everyone had been taken care of before he had his dinner.

Colonel Weaver arrived a day or two later from Manila and
took command of the Tank Group. We were not long in find-
ing it out! Tank Groups were composed of two or more separate tank battalions, such as the 192nd and 194th. These battalions were organized so as to administer themselves. Armored
Force regulations stated definitely that Tank Group Headquarters would not be administrative but only tactical, and
the Tables of Organization for Tank Group (strength and
types of personnel), precluded the possibility of it ever becoming administrative. This was only intelligent, as the only
reason, why the Armored Force ever created the tank group,
was to coordinate the separate tank battalions for tactical purposes. That battalion might be working with one outfit today
and another tomorrow.

Colonel Weaver immediately issued an order that the Tank Group would be administrative as well as tactical and that everything would be sent through his headquarters. When I remonstrated, no answer was made. With the amount of administrative detail that we were compelled to put through Tank Group, it meant a bottleneck. It was just another bottleneck, when smooth, unified preparation was sorely needed.

A "Rip Van Winkle" world was the Philippines! Lack of basic knowledge of the Army of the United States was prevalent. For instance—my headquarters received a communication from the Adjutant of the Philippine Department at Manila. He requested a copy of National Guard Regulations so that they might know how those regulations could be correlated for more unification! I stared at the letter unbelieving, scarcely able to comprehend that the adjutant, in his important post, could be so uneducated concerning Army Regulations. I wondered just how far this lack of knowledge reached in the high command.

When a national emergency has been declared to exist (we had been in that state for more than a year), under call of the President of the United States, the National Guard is mobilized and becomes a part of the Army of the United States and functions under Army Regulations as does every other component and individual. Knowledge of Army Regulations is part of the peacetime training of the Guard. It functions in its home station under National Guard Regulations for the obvious reason that it is not in the active service, and therefore, federal regulations could not apply. However, it trains under, and is inspected by, the Regular Army.

My adjutant, Captain Muir, was sent to Manila in person to determine, if he could, what the Department Adjutant had in mind. Muir came back the same day and reported to me. We were right. We had read the letter correctly. The adjutant was unfamiliar with the regulations and had even suggested that it had been thought the governors, of the several states from which we had come, might have some authority relative to our use in the Philippines! The thinking expressed, indicated that we might be a relic of the 13 colonies!

The letter was answered officially referring the Philippine Department to the National Defense Act of 1920!

We continually fought to keep our organic equipment intact. At one time, an order came through, from the Quarter-master at Fort Stotsenburg, instructing us to turn our 10-ton wrecker over to Post QM immediately. It was the only piece of equipment, of its type, that we had. Without it, we would have been at a loss to properly operate in the maintenance section. We used a little politics.

The Ordnance Department was presented with the order and shown that we could not service and maintain the tanks without the wrecker. The tank was the Ordnance brain child. This aligned them with us. The Quartermaster dropped the issue.

About nine days before the outbreak of war, an order was received from General MacArthur's headquarters that some of our Jeeps, reconnaissance cars, and trucks would be sent immediately to Manila and turned over to the Port Quarter-master. My protests were in vain—MacArthur had issued the order. It was Saturday morning.

Early that afternoon Lt. Swearingen was sent in with the vehicles. He could find no receiving officer to sign for them. Everyone had gone home for the afternoon. My orders were the same as any commanding officer would give—not to leave the equipment until a responsible officer had signed for it. Swearingen called the Port Quartermaster, Lt. Col. Quinn, on the telephone and found him at home. He was informed the vehicles were on hand ready to be turned over.

"Just leave the equipment," the QM replied.

Swearingen reiterated my orders.

"Well, I'll be damned if I'm coming down," the QM said. "After you've been in the Philippines long enough, you won't be so anxious to disturb people on Saturday afternoons. Leave the equipment there and go back to Stotsenburg."

Swearingen again repeated my orders and reminded the QM that the order for delivery that afternoon had come from General MacArthur. He requested the QM to send some responsible officer down to sign.

The Port Quartermaster replied in conversation not quite printable, but refused, point blank.

Swearingen was also stubborn. He locked all the vehicles, retaining the keys, and notified me of his action. It was too late to do anything about it that day.

The next morning (Sunday), I sent Captain Riley, com-

manding officer of Headquarters Company, and Lt. Swearingen into Manila. It finally developed that they actually had
to locate the residence of the Port Quartermaster, so as to get
the proper signature for delivery of the vehicles!

About one week before we were bombed, another tank company was assigned to us. It was a National Guard tank company from Harrodsburg, Kentucky, and had arrived with the
192nd Tank Battalion on November 20th. The unit became
Co. "D". There was no chance whatever to train this company as a part of our outfit. It was like a football team—getting ready to call signals at the start of the game only to find
that a strange, new face had appeared in the backfield. The
stake in this game, however, was human life.

With Colonel Weaver in command of the Tank Group, I
showed him the Alert Plan together with the approval endorsement of General King. He kept the plan to look it over.
The next day, during a conference with him, he said that he
was not satisfied with the plan. When I asked him what was
wrong, he replied only in general terms, not pinning down
any one point. Then he said that he would think it over.
Several days before the Japs bombed, we talked again about
the plan. He accepted it in full without further comment!

Our military policy, in respect to the Philippine Islands,
had undergone a radical change. The original policy of not
defending the Islands was tossed out of the window, evidently
during the early summer of 1941. Sometime, during that
period, the policy was reversed and it became the intention
of the War Department to garrison the Philippines with an
adequate force. However, probably due to MacArthur's thinking that the Japs would not strike before April, 1942, planning for reinforcements was too late. Perhaps other factors entered the situation also, but the fact still remains that the
mobilization and training schedule of both the Philippine
Department and of the Philippine Army was based on the
April assumption. The schedule for reinforcements was also
based on that program. That schedule, on file with the Port
Quartermaster at Manila, planned for the docking of some 70
odd ships, between October, 1941, and February, 1942, with
men, equipment and supplies. Had that schedule been consummated, there would have been no Bataan. It, no doubt,
was forgotten, that the Japs also knew about that schedule!

Major General George Grunert went back to the United States in October, 1941. He had been the Commanding General of the Philippine Department before MacArthur took over the latter part of July. I stood on Pier 7 that morning, having had to come to Manila on business—the business of trying, personally, to locate the tank parts that had been shipped to us, and which had arrived. As stated before, I was unsuccessful. I was one of the spectators who watched both General Grunert and General MacArthur as the propaganda show was staged. The band played and all things, on the surface, were displays of mutual admiration, amity, and regrets. This was for public consumption. General Grunert's face, at times, belied the "friendly" leave-taking and pictured, more plainly than words, his innermost feelings. He was leaving because he had the courage to be a realist and to stand up and say so. He disagreed with MacArthur and because he did—he went home!

On about December 1, 1941, I made arrangements with the Stotsenburg G-2 (Intelligence) for a conference with Captain Spoor (Battalion S-2). The purpose was to coordinate the information we had accumulated on our terrain reconnaissance with G-2 secret maps, documents and other pertinent records. The conference was also meant to bring closer coordination between the 194th and the higher command. Spoor reported back to me late in the afternoon. He stated that he had been in conference with the G-2 since about 1:00 P.M. He was told that, in the opinion of the G-2 (Lt. Col. Linebach), the 194th had done a great deal of unnecessary work because of the fact that it would be absolutely impossible for the Japanese to attack the Philippine Islands successfully! Also, that the Japanese had everything to lose by going to war and nothing to gain; that there would be a great deal of drum beating but no war! Linebach showed Spoor secret maps and documents pertaining to the "Triangular Defense Plan." This plan was built around Hongkong, Singapore, and the Philippine Islands—hence "Triangular Plan." The G-2 said that it would be mostly naval operations. Our naval forces were supposed to be strong enough, that by working with British naval forces and British bases, we could block any invasion of the Philippines from either the China Sea or the Pacifiic long before the enemy had cleared the waters of Formosa! Spoor questioned

Linebach about subversive activities in the Philippines, particularly a society in Pampamga Province (Fort Stotsenburg was located in this province) known as the Soktalosta. Linebach replied that the Filipinos were very loyal and we had nothing to fear. It is interesting to note that the 5th Column, after the war started, emanated from Pampamga Province! This is not surprising. Pampamga has always been the revolutionary center of the Philippines. I then ordered Capt. Spoor to check with the 26th Cavalry (Philippine Scouts) and artillery units at Fort Stotsenburg as to what their dispositions would be in the event of attack. We were both astonished at the answer. It would be the plan of higher headquarters!

About the middle of October, I requested that the 194th Tank Battalion be granted permission to make a road march to Lingayen Gulf. The purpose was to stretch ourselves out in convoy with all equipment under assumed war conditions. I explained, carefully, that we had never had the opportunity to do this and it meant much in the way of training. The request was immediately turned down. After waiting a few days, I again made the request directly to MacArthur's headquarters—through channels. I was called to headquarters by Fort Stotsenburg G-1 (Adjutant), Lt. Colonel Merrill, and asked if I realized how much gasoline this would take. I answered to the effect that the amount did not interest me, that the request was made in the interests of pertinent training which was a part of our schedule. He then stated that we would wear out the equipment with such long movements! I tried to explain to him that tanks were supposed to make long jumps, in this age, but needed the practice to actually do it. He remonstrated at further length until I said:

"Well, Colonel, my request is directed to the high command. Put it through and let's see what happens." He did so, under protest.

Sometime in the early part of November, the high command answered. It gave us permission to make the trip! There were a number of unnecessary restrictions but it was permission and we rejoiced. I found out in a prison camp that permission was granted simply to make a show of strength and not because we needed the training! We made the trip with two incidents. The first was made by the 17th Ordnance Company which I had requested should accompany us. One of their pick-up trucks struck a small Filipino girl. She had darted out in front of the truck as the column passed. They stopped, but Filipinos came out with knives, and remembering previous instructions, the crew and truck moved out. These instructions, given to us soon after arrival, were that, if we had an accident involving the running-down of a Filipino, to stop and give aid *if* other Filipinos were not in the vicinty. If they were, move on! The reason for this was the danger of becoming involved in a fight which meant life and death. The Filipinos were not hostile to Americans. They were hysterical in nature, which is one of the inherent characteristics of the Oriental, and would do things in the heat of excitement which might create a serious incident. The instructions also were to stop at the next Philippine Constabulary Office and report the incident. This was done. The second episode was when a sharp curve was reached. The tank was on its own side of the road. On rounding the curve, it crashed through the entire right side of a bus. The bus was parked on the highway *over the center line*. This was not surprising. We had found vehicles parked on the highway before. It was common practice in the Philippines for buses to stop at various and sundry places, along the route, to allow the passengers to relieve themselves. Sometimes, the driver would park on the shoulder of the road—if convenient. This time, evidently, it was not convenient and he had parked on the road and across the center line. Luckily, no one was in the bus when it was hit. We stopped the entire column and brought a member of the Philippine Constabulary on the scene. He saw the whole picture and assured me that he would report in our favor. The driver of the bus also admitted that he was in the wrong. Two days before we were bombed, I received an immediate action communication from MacArthur's headquarters asking for details of the accident. Accompanying it, was a letter from the Bus Company claiming damages to the amount of 2,000 Pesos ($1,000). There was also a letter and an affidavit from the Philippine Constabulary stating that we were in the wrong and had taken pictures, in reverse, to prove it! Such is the working of the Oriental mind. The Constabulary worked on the Oriental principle that the United States could afford to pay the bill, regardless of the fact, that we were not to blame! Luckily for me, in this instance, *war came!*

CHAPTER 8

War Comes

DURING THE NIGHT of December 5-6, 1941 (December 4-5 U.S. time), unidentified aircraft, approached the west coast of Luzon from the China Sea, in the vicinity of Iba, an American airfield. Iba is to the west of Fort Stotsenburg and Clark Field. This had occurred for several nights prior to that date. We were informed that it was thought the Japanese had made a "dry run."

The 194th had been ordered on the half alert, since December 1st. The half alert was, all tanks actually in position as per the Alert Plan and manned by half the crew—with no ammunition.

That past week, the press and radio had carried statements by General MacArthur refuting all rumors that there was any kind of an alert in the Philippines. The Manila newspapers had also carried a headline story quoting President Quezon. It was a story depicting the extreme bitterness of Quezon toward the United States, and in particular President Roosevelt, for failure to provide adequate defense of the Philippines. It also indicated that he might "play" with the other side. The tirade—and it was a tirade—was one of extreme, bitter vindictiveness. The thought had often been expressed, among both civilians (Americans) and pertinent members of the Armed Forces, that it would not take very much to cause Quezon to "throw in" with the Japanese. His statements in the press certainly sounded as if he were ready to do so—soon! On Bataan and in the prison camps, it was the firm conviction of many who knew the true situation, that Quezon was not a voluntary guest of the United States but was a political prisoner. At any rate, we were all glad that he had not had the chance to collaborate with the Japanese.

Saturday morning, December 6th (5th U.S. time), orders were received to pick up and distribute ammunition of various types. It was then that an ugly rumor was confirmed. *The only ammunition available for our 37mm tank guns, was*

62

armor piercing shells. No high explosive shells were to be had! This, of course, had been included in the radio message sent Manila, prior to our sailing, and to which they had replied in the affirmative. Armor piercing shells are merely large bullets, of the caliber indicated, capable of piercing certain thicknesses of armor plate. This is of little or no use against personnel. High explosive shells burst on contact, exploding shell fragments over a wide area. This type of shell *was nonexistent in the Philippines.* We would be compelled to depend entirely on our machine guns against enemy personnel. Our light tanks were extremely vulnerable and depended on speed, maneuverability, and fire power for their own protection. High explosive shells were most important for use against anti-tank guns and encroaching infantry. The success of our operations, either offensive or defensive, depended a great deal on availability of high explosive ammunition. In the latter days of Bataan, the Ordnance Department manufactured a few rounds of homemade high explosive shells for us, but for the critical campaign ahead—*none!*

After receiving the allotment of ammunition, I inquired about recuperating oil for the 37mm guns. They could not be fired without that oil. I reminded the issuing agency that we had requested the oil a long time before. The usual reply was made—it would be taken care of. It was *not!* It was eight hours *after* the bombing had taken place before our guns were serviced with recuperating oil! *Our 17th Ordnance Company actually had to go to Manila and get it, after the Japs had dropped their eggs!*

All leaves and passes were cancelled, by higher authority, that Saturday morning. All men were ordered held in the barracks area with the exception of those required to man the Half Alert. Apparently, the high command was ready to admit that the Japs might strike much sooner than had been anticipated. Much could still have been done that was not done. That was our weakness—the things left undone. This policy had been followed so long, that, even with the black clouds of war directly overhead, it was well nigh impossible to quicken the tempo of a military force afflicted with the theoretical and siesta-itis. However, one thing was absolutely sure. We were warned in ample time and we were on the alert! There could be no excuse for not making use of those things that *were* available.

Sunday, December 7th (6th U.S. time) was very peaceful. We discussed the situation at our noon meal. Our alert positions were visited and the half-crews inspected. Things were too quiet. That night, I sat outside my quarters, listening to radio music and conversing with some of my officers. I decided to go to bed about 10:00 P.M. The final number on that particular radio program was Concerto in B Flat Minor. It was the same piece of music that had enthralled me in San Francisco, and on this last night of peace and quiet, it made a deep and lasting impression on me which has never abated. It was the last American music I was to hear until after the war. At times, in the prison camp, I would awaken at night and hear it plainly.

The next morning, Monday, December 8th (7th U.S. time), I walked into the mess hall for breakfast, at about the usual time, 6:30. As I entered the hall, I sensed an unusual buzz of conversation. The words "Pearl Harbor" and "bombing" struck my ears. I noted an unusual lack of bantering among those present. Taking a seat at the long table, I pulled a cup of coffee toward me.

"What's the news?" I asked.

Several officers joined in the answer. They had heard a very short radio broadcast from Manila, they said. Pearl Harbor had been bombed by the Japanese!

When you have planned on war, the announcement is something like an anti-climax. I thought of the many times articles had been written by experts; the studies made in the War College; all of them a grim warning on the capabilities of the Japanese and the vulnerability of the Hawaiian Islands, with the advent of the airplane. I thought of those who had "pooh poohed" the idea and labeled those prophecies as "pure jingoism."

We listened to the next newscast at 7:00 A.M. There was little additional information other than—Pearl Harbor had been bombed.

Arriving at our headquarters, I made a pretense of looking over correspondence—waiting for developments. The wait was not long. The telephone rang. The Tank Group Commander ordered me to report. He was calm, and coldly stated what we already knew. He had no further information but had received orders to go on the full alert and to be prepared for any contingency.

As part of the Alert Plan, my rear echelon (administrative, supply, and maintenance sections) under the command of the executive officer, was to retire out of the barracks area to selected positions, far enough away from the combat area so they might continually function in the supply and maintenance of the forward echelons. This was standing operating procedure. Positions had been selected when making up the Plan.

Company commanders were immediately called into conference and I issued orders that the Alert Plan would be put into effect with no delay. The value of a Plan is that no time is wasted. Everyone concerned is familiar with all the details. I had given them the order to move out when the telephone rang. It was the Group Commander again, Col. Weaver. In a voice devoid of any emotion, he announced that Japanese planes had been sighted over Northern Luzon and were headed south.

"Get going!" was his terse order.

The balance of our battalion, not already on the half alert, were all loaded and ready for orders. It was merely a case of company commanders taking control and moving personnel into positions on and around Clark Field. My command post was located adjacent to Co. "A", on the north edge of the field.

At about 9:00 A.M., we received information that the Japanese planes, sighted, had been over Lingayen Gulf and that our air patrols, which had been up since early morning, had evidently discouraged them from coming further south. The enemy had swung to the east and bombed Camp John Hay at Baguio. This camp was not important. It was maintained as a rest camp for both officers and enlisted men and was located in the mountains, directly east of Lingayen Gulf. A short time before, some English women and children had arrived from Hongkong and Singapore, it being thought they would be in a comparatively safe place, if hostilities started!

The rest of the morning was comparatively quiet with little or no new developments. Our planes had been active all morning. They had been ordered on the combat alert beginning at daylight. At about noon, the planes landed at Clark Field for refueling and further orders. At just about that time, I received a message from the Tank Group Commander. It read as follows:

"Skies over Luzon are clear. You may go back on the half alert."

Does suspicion make a man stubborn? Or does knowledge of red tape and incessant blundering, make him suspicious? At any rate, I found it impossible to agree with the message. We knew hostile action had taken place—not only at Pearl Harbor but also on Luzon. To be sure that there would be no misunderstanding or rumors, I immediately had my radio operator call all company commanders to the command post. At the same time my S-2, Capt. Spoor, was sent in to the CP of Col. Weaver to check on the message.

In a short time, my company commanders were assembled, together with the staff. I read them the message and then re-iterated that hostile action had taken place.

"Inasmuch as the message is not an order," I told them, "we will maintain our present positions on the full alert until further orders have been received." When they were dismissed, the time was about 12:25 P.M.

About ten minutes later—or 12:35 P.M.—we heard the roar of motors, coming from the northwest. The roar was like the deep growl of many powerful beasts—snarling as one. It was unmistakable.

The command post was located under the trees, at the edge of the field. We did not have clear visibility in the direction of the roar. Suddenly, we saw the planes—directly overhead. They were flying at an altitude of what must have been more than 20,000 feet. They were distinguishable only as navy planes.

What can you expect of an American soldier who has learned to believe in the promises of his country? One of the men at the command post called out: "Who said the American Navy didn't have planes over here?"   ;

We kept our eyes glued to the skies. The planes, we soon could plainly determine, were in two groups of 27 each and were navy bombers. They came over us in perfect formation. The best of Nippon's pilots must have been in those planes!

Then they dropped their load of *bombs—bombs* that glistened in the sunlight—*bombs* that fell with determined aim to land on field installations and our grounded airplanes, lined up like ducks on a pond! *Bombs! Hundreds of them!*

The bombing was diabolically accurate. The scenes of ruination and horror that followed were unbelievable—even though they took place right before our very eyes. No matter how much one had visualized the price of unpreparedness—it couldn't be—it was impossible that the sovereignty of the United States of America could be challenged with impunity!

But there it was!

Violent explosions that pierced the eardrums—unending explosions that shook the entire world; flash fires and dense smoke that seemed to spread a pall of mourning over the area; clouds of dust that choked and clogged all vision; trees and the long Cogan grass around the field, on fire, roaring and crackling like an evil beast—swooping down upon the tanks. *The whole world was on fire—the inferno of hell itself!*

As the bombers cleared Clark Field, Jap fighter planes moved in at low altitudes. They appeared to come from the south and flew in circles, from south to north. We were unable to determine how many of these planes were involved because of the smoke and dust. They continually circled the field, strafing with machine guns, and, with what was later determined to be, 20 mm guns.

We had been given orders, as part of the Alert Plan, not to fire on any hostile plane unless it was preparing to land. Our mission was to repel any airborne infantry which might be landed on or adjacent to the field. It was generally thought that if any attempt was made to bomb Clark Field, it would be followed immediately by landing of airborne troops.

One of the members of Co. "D" could not contain himself. Forgetting that he might be exposing our ground positions in the case of airborne landings, he manned the .30 caliber machine gun, mounted on the turret of his tank. He brought down a fighter plane. The 192nd Tank Battalion, which was in reserve position at Fort Stotsenburg, also had an over-enthusiastic Tanker who did the same thing with the same result. These were the only Japanese planes brought down that day to my knowledge, although it has been stated differently.

The 200th Coast Artillery (AA), was also in position on the full alert with us. This regiment had left their calibrating equipment (or most of it) in the hands of the Ordnance Department at Manila, when they had landed, with us, in September. Up to the time of the bombing, it had not been returned to them! This equipment had been left with Ordnance for adjustment.

Therefore, about all they could do, was to fire blindly in the air! They were also equipped with antiquated fuses which, for the most part, was all they had for the rest of the campaign. For each six shells fired by the 200th Coast Artillery at hostile planes, only about one exploded! That was the average. In spite of that tremendous handicap, after receiving the calibrating equipment, they made an enviable record. We always felt very good to have that outfit around us!

The raid, in its entirety, was over at about 1:00 P.M., or shortly thereafter. Why the Japanese did not bring in paratroops and airborne infantry will always remain a mystery. Explosions and fires continued nearly all afternoon. The tanks of Co. "A" were within 40 feet of an intense grass fire. It was not laughable then, but we did laugh afterwards in recalling the "running play by play" account, of the fire, from Lt. Costigan's tank. His platoon was closest to the actual fire and, naturally, he was intensely interested in its progress. When the fire stopped, it was about 150 feet from my command post. At his location it was only about 40 feet! The fire was hot where we were. It must have been *very* hot where he was. I was determined not to move any of our tanks until it was absolutely necessary because of our mission and also because any move on our part would expose those positions to the enemy, making us a target before we could launch an attack—presupposing the Japs would land. Costigan was equally determined to keep me informed as to the progress of the fire in his area and also—the heat. He was a fluent commentator over the radio that afternoon and we knew just how each inch of the fire front, in his area, was progressing, together with up-to-the-minute information on how well cooked they were. Finally, the heat became so intense that he shouted over the speaker, "Shall we move now?" I told him to hold it until he received orders. There was no reply but we could hear him mumbling to the crew of his tank something to the effect that, "the Major thinks we've got asbestos suits on!" A trail paralleled our positions a short distance to the front. The fire stopped there and Costigan's insistent demands were quelled.

An immediate survey was made of our tank installations. The Japs had not found our positions. We had one dead in Co. "D" and several others in the battalion wounded. Otherwise, we had escaped. However, Clark Field was a shambles. Airplanes were burning and exploding. Gasoline dumps were on fire. All buildings that would burn were going up in flames. Dead and wounded were strewn about. A number of Filipino workmen, engaged in construction work on the field, were dead and wounded, together with Air Corps personnel.

The station hospital at Fort Stotsenburg was not adequate to take care of the large number of cases, but doctors and nurses improvised and worked like demons, unmindful of their own safety or comfort.

I learned from my executive officer, Captain Charles Canby, that the Tank Group Commander, Col. Weaver, had violated the Alert Plan. Canby had actually moved the rear echelon into their positions as per that plan. Weaver had, a little later, contacted Canby and asked where the rear echelon was. Canby told him and reiterated that it was a part of the Plan. Without any explanation, and without notifying me, Weaver ordered Canby to bring them back into the barracks area! Luckily, the order came to late to do anything about it until after the bombing. At about 2:00 P.M., I contacted the Group Commander to ascertain why the Alert Plan had not been followed. I also requested permission to send the echelon to their alert position. I was given no information or reason as to his orders but was told they would stay in the barracks area until further orders and also, that we would retain our present positions, for the time being!

It will be remembered that I had sent Capt. Spoor, my S-2, back to Weaver's headquarters to ascertain the authenticity of the message I had received at noon. Here is Capt. Spoor's deposition:

"Major Miller ordered me to proceed to the headquarters of the Tank Group Commander and check on the message, received at noon, to the effect that we might go back on the half alert. I found Col. Weaver, not at his headquarters, but at the headquarters of the Air Corps on Clark Field. I asked him about the message. He told me that it was correct and that it had come from higher authority and for me to return to Major Miller and so state. While I was there, at Air Corps headquarters, I overheard an order, which came from the supreme commander in the Philippines, that no planes were to leave Clark Field. All planes, including bombers, fighters, and observation, were lined up on Clark Field, ready for combat, many with their motors running, and some, with the pilots in the cockpits. As I left the headquarters, my driver pointed out a large formation of planes approaching from a northwesterly direction, and said they looked like Navy planes. The first bomb struck the Clark Field PX (Post Exchange), as we cleared the field gate, at approximately 12:35 P.M. In the bombing and strafing which followed, most of the planes on the field were destroyed, about 300 personnel killed and wounded, and hangers and installations, such as fuel and ammunition dumps, hit and set afire. After the bombing, which both my driver and I watched from a ditch, I returned to the command post of Major Miller."

In a prison camp, when men were faced with death—and talked—I was told by Air Corps officers, that at the actual time of the bombing, orders, which they were waiting for, *were received!*

A radio broadcast, from the Manila radio, *shortly before the bombing,* stated that Clark Field had been bombed. *It has never been explained.*

Censorship had not, even yet, been clamped down. I took advantage of it to send a cable to my wife that all was OK with the outfit. It went through!

We learned, later in the afternoon, that Iba, on the west coast of Luzon, had also been hit. This, as stated before, was an American airfield. The planes, bombing both Clark Field and Iba, had come from Japanese carriers in the China Sea. This explained the "unidentified" aircraft making their "dry runs" before war.

One American plane, about to land at Iba when the Japs struck, managed to get away and came to Clark Field, intending to land there. Before he had a chance to land, however, he was knocked down by the Japs raiding Clark Field. He landed near the rear echelon of the 194th Tank Battalion.

It is difficult to analyze the feelings one has, during and after such a bombing. The first reaction is one of almost complete disbelief, disbelief that we could be caught in such a deplorable and helpless condition. In the morning, we had watched with pride, our air patrols, searching the skies, eager to find the Jap who challenged the sovereignty of the United States of America, hoping he would appear! A few hours later—Clark Field—the Gibraltor of the Far East—the colossal Giant (as depicted in the news reels) writhing in its death struggles—the American Eagle—*struck down!*

My mind went back to the many defense talks I had given in the prewar years—when it was unpopular to do so—when students in our colleges were carrying banners denouncing war—when idealistic citizens were helping to weaken national defense—when Congress was beseiged with letters urging them to vote against national defense appropriations (which they did). I thought of the time I had been invited to address a luncheon club on Arimstice Day, in which I had given a national defense talk, at which I had stated that the War College in Washington, had evaluated the Philippines; that Japan could take the Islands any time they desired to do so because we had nothing to defend them with. And, after I had made the talk, as is the custom with luncheon clubs, members come forward to shake hands with the speaker, congratulating him on his talk, in which there had been no exception in my case; and how one—smug—conceited—self-satisfied individual stopped, shook hands, and said:

"Miller, that was a mighty fine talk you gave but, of course, you belong to the National Guard, and are, therefore, enthusiastic about our national defense—probably over enthusiastic." Then, he clapped me on the shoulder and said, "I wouldn't worry too much about the Philippines. Uncle Sam has an ace up his sleeve there!"

I thought of these things—then—and perhaps, the resolve to tell the whole story, was born—amid the shambles—and ashes—of America's sovereignty—at Clark Field.

Strange thoughts to have, when the veritable holocaust was being enacted before our very eyes!

The next reaction was a natural one. It is one with which human minds are blessed; one which played so important a part in our future, even with the magnitude of that violence we had witnessed.

That reaction was *hope. Hope* that things were not as bad

as they seemed. *Hope,* that now we were baptized with fire and blood, the veil would be lifted—and vision would be clear and in the right direction!

We had a piping hot meal that night. It was not only good—it was a veritable life saver. What a wonderful morale builder—*food! Hope* started all over again; for *"hope* springs eternal in the human breast!"

Conversation revealed that *hope,* as nothing else could, among both the officers and the men. We all ate together in the field. It was conversation full of optimism and even cheer. The events of the day had welded us together, as nothing else could. You could hear and feel that optimism and cheer, as we tackled the good, warm food and allowed the warmth to revive our spirits.

"Nobody will do that to Uncle Sam and get away with it," volunteered one Tanker to another.

"Wait 'til the Navy moves in and clears the path," said another.

And a third expressed the thoughts of all of us:

"We'll show those yellow bastards—and it won't be long either!"

The thought, of becoming prisoners of the Japanese, was not a part of our thinking. We did not know that *hope* would carry—*some of us*—through nearly four years of starvation, disease, and abuse, before Uncle Sam found the "ace up his sleeve," so carefully hidden by that smug, self-satisfied individual of the luncheon club, who, religiously—each week—contributed to his country's welfare, by pledging allegiance to the Flag of the United States, sitting down to a good meal, singing a few songs, with much gusto—belching, also with much gusto—and again, contributing to our country's welfare (the war effort) by buying war bonds—with interest accruing—of course!

CHAPTER 9

The Rice Storage at Cabanatuan

HAD THE GERMANS been against us, in the Philippines, instead of the Japanese, it is extremely doubtful if we would have reached Bataan. Targets of opportunity would present themselves to the Jap air force—targets that just about stood up and shouted—but, seldom would the Jap divert himself, from his original mission, to take advantage of these things. Only one road led into Bataan. This was from San Fernando. While the Japs did bomb portions of this road, there was never any serious threat to that vital artery.

Of absolute, essential importance, was that part of WPO-3 (Orange Plan) devoted to *supply*. Later, on Bataan, where we were reduced to starvation rations, that importance loomed like an ugly specter.

Part of the Supply Section of WPO-3, was the establishment of a rice depot at Cabanatuan. It consisted of setting aside about 50,000,000 bushels of unthreshed rice. This amount was to be kept on hand at all times. The depot was also used by the civil government for the feeding of the Filipinos. Before the war, the island of Luzon did not raise sufficient rice to meet all of their needs. Much had to be brought in.

A high quartermaster officer, assigned to Supply, and who worked on this part of the Plan, assured me that the entire amount was on hand at the start of hostilities. It had been checked. The requirements of that part of the Plan were met.

Details were built around the troops as follows:

(A) Americans—10,000—180 days (6 months)—eight ounces of rice per day or 900,000 pounds for the entire presupposed six-month period.

(B) Philippine Scouts—6,000—180 days—sixteen ounces of rice per day or 1,080,000 pounds for the above period.

(C) Philippine Army—50,000—180 days—sixteen ounces of rice per day or 9,000,000 pounds for the period.

The total rice requirement, therefore, for the entire period, was 10,980,000 pounds.

73

Americans were half-ration (rice) so it could be balanced with other food.

The NARC (National Agriculture and Rice Corporation) storages at Cabanatuan were chosen years before and incorporated into the war plan, for the following reasons:

1. Amount available in the storage area, at all times, was nearly twenty times the computed requirements.

2. Capacity for milling of the rice.

3. The only one place where this large quantity was always on hand.

4. Total capacity was plenty, while nowhere else, was this true.

A sack of rice is normally one cavan (114.4 pounds). To make more leeway and for simpler figuring, use 100 pounds of rice to one cavan—or—one sack. Our requirements of 10,980,-000 pounds, or 109,800 sacks, could easily be met at any time, since the amount available, as stated above, *was nearly 20 times our computed requirements.*

We had on hand about 750,000 pounds of rice in our own depot and that of Corregidor. It was never allowed to fall below that figure. Movement of 10,000,000 pounds of rice (100,000 bags) to Bataan could be handled this way:

One carload (box car) would equal 40,000 pounds (400 bags). Divide 100,000 bags by 400 and you have 250 carloads required. Using a conservative estimate, had the effort been made, 25 coarloads per day could have been moved, out of Cabanatuan, with very little difficulty. This would have meant about 10 days of hauling. The Japs gave us from December 8th to at least December 27—23 *days*—to do the job. *It was not done.*

The railroad from Cabanatuan, to a point south of Lubao (where it ended), was open at all times during this period. The rice could have then been hauled by truck into Bataan. Twenty-five carloads per day will make 200 average truck loads. As much as 40 carloads per day could have been hauled from Lubao by truck. The quartermaster officer, referred to above, states that box cars, in more than sufficient numbers, *were available!*

The argument might be advanced, that not enough **trucks** were on hand to haul rice and other foodstuffs to **Bataan**. *This is not true.* A vast number of commercial trucks **were** available, as were many military trucks, not only in the Quartermaster Pool, but those on hand with troops, *and not being used.* Many of our trucks, and also those of the 192nd Tank Battalion, were assigned to the rear echelons. They carried baggage, supplies and equipment which would not be used, ordinarily, unless the unit was set down at one place. From December 8th until we actually retired to Bataan, these trucks accomplished absolutely nothing except to hold the paraphernalia with which they were loaded! If necessary, these excess trucks could have been unloaded at dumps, had there been proper planning. Both trucks and certain personnel of the rear echelons, could have been used to haul food and other supplies to Bataan—if found necessary. However, there was this period of indecision—December 8th to 23rd—before it was finally determined that the Orange Plan was in effect. It was *secret* and I was not even allowed to divulge that information to my staff!

Not one grain of the rice at Cabanatuan was touched! Although a vital part of the war plan, none of it reached Bataan!

The warehouses at Cabanatuan were bombed, and most of the rice was burned by the Japs—*but not until the very last of December!*

During this period of indecision, Japanese bombers paid little or no attention to roads or railroads. They had specific missions from which they seldom diverted their efforts.

Imagine, then, my feelings, at the strategic Calumpit Bridge, when the young Tanker exclaimed about the *empty trucks,* winding their way to Bataan! Since the early morning hours of December 29th, the 194th Tank Battalion had been in position, on and around that bridge. We were in absolute command of the area. We saw everything that passed and everything that went on. *Those empty trucks were no myth!*

Perhaps it was fortunate, that, as we bivouacked amid the smoking ruins of Clark Field on that first day of war, we could not see these things that were yet to come—food and materiel of war, sabotaged by that same mismanagement and indecision, which had destroyed our air power. Our faith was—now that war had come—we would wipe the slate clean, starting out with singleness of purpose—and unity—to make full use of those things we had left. And so—we prepared for the second day of war.

At about 2:30 A.M., the air alarm sounded, and we prepared for another bombing. The planes were soon within hearing, but they were to the east of us and proceeded south. At about 3:00 A.M., we heard the dull roar of bombing, which later, proved to be Nichols Field at Manila. We heard the planes return along the same path of travel. Other targets were also bombed that night but we were not disturbed. At dawn, an undamaged plane at Clark Field attempted to take off. It struck a bomb crater, exploded and burned before our eyes.

Later, that morning, I visited the command post of Tank Group and recommended the advisability of moving the 194th to new locations, but still in the vicinity of our old ones. I pointed out that the element of surprise was now over and our positions probably known, and that a huge store of bombs and gasoline were cached in the woods to the rear of Co. "A". I also strongly advised completing the Alert Plan and moving the rear echelon to its prepared positions out of the barracks area which might be bombed. I received no answer to my requests except, that we would maintain our positions until further orders. There were no unpleasantries accompanying the orders. Col. Weaver was very courteous. He was just unwilling, probably, to admit that he had made a mistake in ordering the rear echelon back into the barracks area. Perhaps, if I had separated my requests, he might have given permission, then, to at least, move the battalion.

Reaching my command post, we decided to reorganize a part of our positions, so as not to be exactly in the same spot and still not violate Weaver's orders. We had hardly started on the plan, when the commanding officer of the 192nd Tank Battalion visited the CP and stated he had just received orders from Colonel Weaver to take over part of my area with his battalion, and that I was to proceed with new installations near Mabalacat, a short distance from Clark Field. This was what I had recommended a short time before! I visited Group Headquarters immediately and Weaver confirmed the orders. No explanation was given. We moved into our new area after the 192nd arrived.

Meanwhile many telephone calls came into the various headquarters. Most of them originated from 5th Columnists. They purported to be giving "hot" information—all the way from Jap landings by sea, to paratroop invasions. At first, these calls caused a great deal of inconvenience. The Japs had not, as yet, displayed their intentions. There was no pattern or precedent. Every precaution had to be taken. In one instance, a call came in that Jap paratroops had landed in an area nearby—"many," came the hysterical voice. On investigation, it was found to be true—except "many." A Jap plane had either been hit or was otherwise out of commission and the crew jumped. The Filipino often exaggerates, not because he wishes to do so wilfully, but simply because it is one of his characteristics.

The forces on Luzon, had been divided into what was known as the North Luzon Force and the South Luzon Force. Major General Parker commanded the latter force, with headquarters in the Batangas area, south of Manila. Major General Jonathan Wainwright commanded the North Luzon Force, with headquarters at Fort Stotsenburg.

It should be explained, at this point, that the Luzon Forces were not affiliated, in any way, with the forces on Corregidor Island and vice versa. They were separate and distinct. We could expect no reinforcements from Corregidor, because of the important mission which they would have to perform, in denying Manila Bay to the Japs, or in other words—Harbor Defense.

There were about 10,000 American soldiers in the forces on Luzon, of which the great majority were not equipped or trained as combat elements. For the most part, they were Engineers, Signal Corps, Quartermaster, Military Police, and Air Corps—without planes.

The Philippine Scouts (part of our regular army) had numbered about 6,000, as a maximum. An increase to 12,000 was attempted, before war. This effort was not wholly successful, due to the high standard set by the individual Scout himself. No finer soldier was ever found. It was the highest ambition of the Filipino to become a Scout. And the Scout made sure that the so-called "intrusion" would not lower that most enviable standard. A great proportion of the Philippine Scout strength was on duty with the Corregidor Harbor Defense.

The Philippine Army was composed of Filipinos from all provinces. Different dialects were spoken. Some could not understand the others and vice versa. They were hardly in the

kindergarten stage, as far as training was concerned. Some
had been drafted as late as December. Weapons were completely strange to them—what few weapons there were to give
them. The great majority knew not what the war was all
about. They never had a chance to weld themselves into an
army. They were a motley force at best—due not to any fault
of theirs. They probably numbered, at the start of hostilities, about 50,000. It was much less than that after the first
shot was fired.

This was the miserable force, lacking the essentials, even of
bare equipment, that was to face the well trained, fully equipped, vastly numerically superior Japanese hordes.

Several days after the war had come upon us, my headquarters received a pamphlet which was labeled "Confidential." It was the G-2 (Intelligence) War Department's estimate
on Japan.

The pamphlet had been prepared by the G-2 Section of the
War Department—charged with the responsibility of enemy
intelligence. It was supposed to give an accurate picture and
evaluation, so far as possible, of the enemy situation regarding manpower, state of training, morale, physical capabilities
of the individual, equipment, and organization of the Japanese Army.

There is no reason why this pamphlet should not have been
issued long before. It made little difference, however, as it was
only a pitiful attempt at the most—an almost worthless analysis. As I studied it, my thoughts wandered and went back to
Fort Stotsenburg, shortly after Colonel Weaver arrived, when
he scheduled a meeting for all officers. His aide read to us
confidential reports that had accompanied the Group Commander from the United States, reports that were from one
to two years old—*on the German army.* The 194th had procured those same reports, held schools on them at Fort Lewis,
before we knew we would be assigned to the Philippines! As
one of my lieutenants said afterwards, on the way back to
our area: "Now, ain't that something."

There were many blank pages on the G-2 pamphlet. For instance—the heading over a page would be "Heavy Tanks" and
then pertinent data was supposed to follow. The page would
be blank. This would be true of many other items. And with
the war already begun, there was no chance for my staff or

myself to read and evaluate what little information there was in the pamphlet.

Friday morning, December 12th, Capt. Spoor and myself went into our barrack area, to check on conditions, leaving Capt. Johnson (S-3) in charge of the combat elements. Canby, my executive officer, urged me to make one more attempt, to secure permission from the Tank Group Commander, to move the rear echelon out of the barracks area.

"It must be done," he asserted. "I've been holding my breath for fear the Japs will be moving in to bomb this place."

I told him it would be done even at the risk of a reprimand. Capt. Spoor and I then stopped at our quarters where we decided to allow ourselves the luxury of a quick shower bath. In the middle of the bath, we received word that Jap bombers were over northern Luzon and headed south. Spoor was a little faster than I, and had succeeded in putting on most of his clothes. I had just finished drying myself when the bombers came swarming over. They came in from the northeast, and they were flying low. The sky was overcast. The formation moved directly over our barracks area, dropping bombs as they came in. Perhaps it was due to the fact that the low altitude bombing caused many of the bombs to fall as duds. That was on our side of the ledger. However, several buildings were blown up. Through the grace of God, there were no casualties in the 194th.

The Japs had filled their bombs with rivets, spikes, and what-have-you. A red hot rivet blew through one end of the building and landed at my feet. Before I could get my clothes on, the bombers returned again—over the same path. This time they dropped no bombs.

And then we showed how human we are. Every man grabbed whatever weapon he could reach and began taking pot shots at the planes. It eased our feelings. Foolish as it sounds, I picked up my caliber .45 pistol and stood on the back steps of our quarters, shooting at the planes until the gun was empty. I might just as well have been hurling rocks. And then I heard laughter. It came from Capt. Quinlen (S-4) and some of the men who were in shallow fox holes, nearby—and then I realized that the commanding officer was standing nude, firing at planes with a .45 pistol!

The adjacent area, occupied by the 200th Coast Artillery,

was hit badly and some casualties resulted. In our own area, one of the latrines and bath houses had received a direct hit and were blown out, almost completely. One of our men was in the latrine at the time but escaped any injury. The sight he made, with pants down, hurriedly making his exit, was one to remember.

Some of the bombs were dropped on Fort Stotsenburg proper. One of our Jeeps and motorcycles were on their way to the warehouse area, when the bombing started. They stopped and jumped for cover as quickly as possible. One of the bombs dropped very close, entirely destroying the Jeep and a paint storage shed nearby. When the smoke had cleared, all four men were unharmed, but they were entirely covered, from head to foot, with bright yellow paint!

Throwing my clothes on, I visited Tank Group Headquarters without delay, and made the request, once more, that we be allowed to consummate the full alert plan and send the rear echelon out of the barracks area. Permission was granted immediately!

At 3:00 P.M. that day, I received a message at my C.P. to report at Group Headquarters to act as Group Commander during the absence of Colonel Weaver who had been called to USAFFE Headquarters at Manila.

At about 6:00 P.M., North Luzon Force Headquarters alerted me with a warning order, that the 194th Tank Battalion would proceed to the Calumpit Bridge area that night. At about 7:00 P.M., the confirming order came from Colonel Weaver at Manila, by telephone, and in addition, to report at Fort McKinley with two half-tracks and reconnaissance personnel, by 7:00 A.M. the next morning. It was to be a movement that tried the very souls of both officers and men—a night movement that was totally unnecessary—had a little common sense and planning been used.

I visited my desk, at our headquarters in the barracks area, before leaving Fort Stotsenburg on the night movement. Everything was just as I had left it on the first day of war, except for dust and dirt that had accumulated. Staring up at me was the correspondence from MacArthur's Headquarters, relative to the 2,000 Peso damage claim, in connection with the tank and bus collision. It seemed to leer evilly at me—and I leered back. This time, it was my turn to score. Taking the correspondence, I slowly and methodically tore it into bits, throwing it all over the office. Muir, standing over his desk, looked up in bewilderment:

"What's the matter?" he asked. "Going nuts?"

"No!" was my reply. "I am!"

CHAPTER 10

Invasion

THAT NIGHT OF December 12-13, it rained—one of those slow, misty, drizzly rains that chilled us to the very marrow of our bones. We had 162 vehicles in the 194th Tank Battalion. Fifty-four were light tanks and 19 were half-tracks. The rest were trucks, Jeeps, reconnaissance cars and a few motorcycles. We had to move without lights, down the one main highway towards Manila. Other traffic—also without lights—was on the road. Most of this traffic consisted of buses and trucks with Filipino drivers.

The strain on drivers and vehicles, particularly tanks, is severe enough in daylight driving. To drive at night, without lights, in a continuous rain, and against other traffic is enough to give anyone a severe case of extreme jitters. It should be remembered that the tanks and half-tracks had no windshields. To drive a segregated vehicle in this manner is not too bad, but we were moving a mechanized unit, by platoons. We had to maintain road spaces and time elements as much as was humanly possible.

No prior reconnaissance had been made of the area we had been ordered into. We did not know where we could bivouac. All that we knew was—it must afford adequate cover from hostile air observation and, at the same time, fulfill the mission of being in close proximity of Calumpit Bridge. I immediately dispatched reconnaissance detachments, under Lt. Spaulding, to precede the column and accomplish the "impossible."

Then. began the nightmare. A number of tanks and other vehicles went off the road—into ditches and over fills—some to regain the roadway under their own power—others needing help. One tank went over the shoulder and turned bottom side up. The crew, miraculously, escaped serious injuries, except for severe bruises and cuts which they carried with them for a long time after.

It seemed to be an evil omen that night, as we went through

San Fernando, that at one of the turns, several tanks missed that turn and went down the road to the southwest. *That was the road leading to Bataan!* It was along this road that later events caused us to withdraw into Bataan. *And still later, we traveled that road in the march of death!* I was riding in a Jeep that night, and luckily, checked the column. A guide had been posted by the reconnaissance detachments, but for some unexplainable reason, some of the tanks missed him. He reported the incident to me and we started in pursuit. After some distance we overtook them and guided the vehicles back into column.

We finally reached the bivouac area, the last elements arriving about 6:00 A.M. The drivers and their reliefs were worn out mentally and physically and were almost nervous wrecks. Everyone was wet to the skin. To be in that condition, in the early morning hours, in the tropics, is a great deal more discomforting than under similar conditions in the temperate zone.

The reconnaissance detachments had done an excellent job. However, they had been compelled to bivouac us in three separate areas, in order to obtain adequate cover. The Calumpit Bridge is located in an extremely open country with numerous rice paddies.

Waiting, while the two half-tracks were being serviced, I sat on the front steps of a country school and soon stretched out on my back. I had a half-smoked cigar clenched between my teeth. It pointed straight up in the air, and without intending to do so, I fell asleep. About ten minutes later, Capt. Johnson awakened me to state that the half-tracks were ready. I can remember him saying, "Major, that's the first time I ever saw anyone, who could chew tobacco and snore, at the same time!"

Not knowing yet what the mission was, I left the executive officer in command of the battalion and proceeded to Fort McKinley with Capt. Spoor, the reconnaissance detachments and the two half-tracks. We arrived and I reported to Colonel Weaver. It was then that I learned just how absurd and unnecessary the night movement had been.

USAFFE, it was disclosed, had determined to place the 194th Tank Battalion with the South Luzon Force, for the time being. It was not known just where the enemy would strike. Orders had been given that the battalion would be moved to the South Luzon area. The reconnaissance detachments and half-tracks had been ordered to Fort McKinley for the purpose of making a reconnaissance for the bivouac area of the battalion. The outfit would not move into that position until the next day! Our night movement had merely been an initial start—and what a start! The whole movement could have been consummated during daylight hours, by platoons and small groups, with no fear whatever of hostile air action. That night trip took as much, if not more, of the physical and mental stability out of the outfit, as any later events of the war. At the very least, reconnaissance detachments should have been allowed to perform their mission, in advance of the battalion, during daylight hours. It would have saved untold hardships on both personnel and equipment.

Colonel Weaver accompanied us, in search of a suitable place, from which we might operate efficiently with the South Luzon Force. It was found, just north of Muntinlupa, and had excellent cover from large mango trees. We also visited the Batangas and Nasugbu beaches. These two areas, together with Lingayen Gulf to the north, constituted the three most probable danger spots, at which, the Japs might land.

Feeling that Col. Weaver would, in all probabilities, issue another night movement order, I recounted the hazards and hardships of the night before, and outlined a plan, to move the battalion by sections and platoons during daylight hours, without fear of air attack. He finally agreed to this and issued the order. The next day, Sunday, we made the movement without one, single incident. All elements were in the bivouac by 7:00 P.M.

It was very evident, from the beginning of the war, that the 5th Column was well organized. Any time the 194th had made any kind of movement, whether by day or night, rockets would be observed, somewhere in the vicinity, signalling the event.

In our new position, south of Manila, we had issued orders, through the Constabulary in Muntinlupa, that no lights would be allowed during the hours of darkness. This was our only means to eliminate signalling, at night, in our immediate vicinity. The Filipinos were very cooperative. Our first night in the new area disclosed quite a number of lights that could have been signals. Several nights, after the order had been issued, a flashlight was observed in the distance, blinking from one of the houses in town. My guards immediately fired and we had no more trouble from that quarter.

Also, at about this time, the men in our maintenance section, brought a young woman to my command post. She was very good looking and seemed to be well educated. We were all agreed that she was not a full-blooded Filipino. She had been frequenting our maintenance installations. This was not unusual, because the Filipino is very curious by nature. We were constantly chasing them away from our tank establishments.

In her case, however, the men had become suspicious for two reasons. First, she was very persistent, and second, she asked questions that were too intelligent to be casual. I sent my S-2 (Intelligence) to Manila with the girl in custody. He was to report to the G-2 section of USAFFE. He also had another mission. Lt. Fleming, communications officer for the battalion, had reported unauthorized radio activity somewhere in the area. He had recommended that we ask the Signal Corps for aid with a radio detector, to locate this particular one.

Captain Spoor, the S-2, made the trip and reported back with the information, that the Signal Corps would take care of the matter immediately, and would send a detail with the equipment. It was interesting, but not surprising, to find that nothing was ever done.

As to the girl, Spoor had acquainted the G-2 section with her activities, and requested that she be held under surveillance, so that we would not be bothered with her in the area. He was promised everything possible would be done. but it was also added, that they were not quite sure anything could be done unless positive and actual proof be submitted that the girl was engaged in subversive activities. Spoor then asked if it would not be possible to, at least, keep her in Manila, under suspicion, so there would be no chance of endangering our installations. He was told, in effect, this would be done.

A very short time after he had reported to me, the girl strolled down the highway, with bright smiles for everyone in sight, and wholly unperturbed! She had been released, because

USAFFE claimed they had no authority to hold her! This, with a war going on! We were compelled to set up heavier guards. That same night, the guards brought in a Filipino whom they had found prowling around our establishments. This time, we did not go to USAFFE. We lodged the man in the local Philippine Constabulary jail, preferring charges against him as a spy. We knew this would keep him locked up, without any further action, until we had evacuated the area.

Intensive reconnaissance was pushed, from the time we occupied our new position, to December 24th. We had never been in this section of Luzon and were totally unfamiliar with the terrain. South Luzon Force was kept informed of our accomplishments.

Progress was somewhat slow, due to the absence of maps. Very few military maps were available. Complete topographical surveys had been completed years before and maps had been printed. With the few troops we had in the Philippines, there was no excuse whatever for the limited supply. It meant only printing them during the time of peace.

I was able to procure exactly *one* of these maps. My staff, company officers, and non-commissioned officers had to pick up ordinary oil station maps which showed only main roads and towns. Luzon is filled with rivers and mountains. These, and other topographical features, were not shown on the oil station maps. Captains Johnson and Spoor, mysteriously acquired two military maps like my own. They did not volunteer any information, as to where they came from, but I noticed that the stamp of higher headquarters appeared thereon.

During the ensuing operations, our troops were never furnished with any guides whatever. That, certainly, should have been an integral part of the war plan. In many instances, guides would have been of inestimable value to us, in the way of river crossings, trails and such. There is no doubt the Japs were equipped with adequate and experienced guides. That was obvious, by the rapidity in which they made river crossings and short cuts, after bridges had been blown.

New Bilibid Prison was located a short distance out of Muntinlupa. Adjacent, thereto, was a concentration camp, which had been established after war started. Japs and Germans had been rounded up in Manila and brought to this camp. Americans were in charge. About 400 had been interned. The only telephone available for our use, and on which we could depend, was located here. It had a direct line to USAFFE. The internees had every privilege allowed them by international law—even visitors. They were very arrogant and continually demanded additional rights. Major Sherry, a reserve officer, was in charge. No better individual could have been chosen. His method was not one which involved toughness, although he could be tough, and on a few occasions, he had to display that quality. He would hear their story out with extreme calmness and courtesy. Then, he would render the decision and tell them the reason why. If they objected, it would be in vain. He never became angry, but simply dismissed the objectors, with courtesy and good humor. Neither the German or the Jap could quite cope with this sort of thing and were somewhat dumbfounded. However, they did realize he was fair. At our first prison camp at O'Donnell, the Japs presented Major Sherry with two small roasted chickens and a few cigarettes. Also, a little later, when the generals and full colonels were segregated from the rest of us, Sherry was detailed to accompany them. This group never received any better treatment than we did. The "presento" to Sherry, and his segregation from the "common herd," was the Jap way of acknowledging the fair treatment he had given the internees. The debt was paid. They could now kill him—and be "sorry"— but that would be all right! Such is the inscrutable way of the Jap!

Sometime, about the 20th of December, the Manila newspapers headlined a Japanese assault and attempted landing on the beaches of Lingayen Gulf. In official releases, purported to come from General MacArthur's Headquarters, the landing was described. The story said that the Japanese had been repulsed with heavy losses; that the Philippine Army had come into its own; that it was eager to close with the hated Japanese. The story even pictured a wounded Filipino, who described the terrific battle.

Later, in the prison camp, the truth of this story was told me. The narrator, was a regular army major, who was actually on the scene and in command of a battalion of the Philippine Army.

On this particular night, some of them thought they saw

lights out in the gulf. From then on, they thought they saw many things pointing to an enemy landing. They fired out into the gulf with everything at hand. The major said it reminded him of the Fourth of July back home. He stated there was no Japanese landing whatever, and no Japanese were in sight! The wounded soldier, whose picture appeared in the newspaper, must have received his wounds from his own people.

On December 22nd, I was called to Manila by Tank Group Headquarters. The headquarters had been transferred from Fort Stotsenburg, so that it could, immediately, make itself available to either force—north or south. It was now with USAFFE, inside the old walled city, at Fort Santiago. This was also MacArthur's headquarters before the war. Capt. Johnson accompanied me and we arrived at about 6:00 P.M.

Sometime earlier, the Tank Group Commander, Colonel Weaver, had been promoted to Brigadier General. We met with him and his staff. The General stated that the Japanese had landed in force at Santo Tomas in Lingayen Gulf; that undoubtedly, it was the main effort; that withdrawals might have to start and, therefore, I would prepare my battalion for possible movement to the north. The 194th Tank Battalion, he said, was to be the rearmost element in any withdrawals. This meant that, as the units withdrew, all would clear through us, after which, we would put ourselves between them and the Japanese. I pointed out to the General, that we would be in a very precarious situation. It would be dark, during these operations, and we would be compelled to run without any lights. The movement would be slow, in many instances, and it would be entirely possible for the enemy to by-pass us, on foot. They could easily place mines ahead of the tanks, or hurl explosives as we passed by. I requested that the Infantry be made a part of our operations so that we might have some protection. General Weaver agreed with me and said it would be done. Where the fault lay, I was never able to find out. Although I made numerous reports and inquiries—*we never had a single infantryman accompany us on any of the withdrawals!*

The Japs had landed comparatively small forces at Aparri and Vigan early in the war—the night of December 9-10. Both these locations are in northern Luzon. On December 13th, they landed at Legaspi—in southern Luzon. No resistance was offered, because of extreme distances involved, lack of personnel and equipment to send against them, and the fact that the Japs could not launch an effective offensive against us from those points. Our forces waited for the main effort.

General Weaver asked for my recommendation, as to whether or not we should:

1. Take offensive action, as the rear guard, with the tanks or—

2. Adopt checkerboard tactics (take up successive positions) in withdrawals.

His attention was called to the fact, that the operation would be made during the hours of darkness, precluding any offensive by tanks, and that tanks were canalized to roads (impossible to operate off the roads) with innumerable bridges, which would act as perfect tank traps. Therefore, the lesser of the two evils would be, the checkerboard proposition.

Much to my surprise, he agreed, and also, to another daylight movement, conducted in the same manner as on December 14th. One exception was, that we leave one company with the South Luzon Force. The General then ordered me to be ready to move north, at a moment's notice.

The next day, December 24th, I received orders, at about 11:00 A.M., to proceed to the vicinity of Carmen, on the Agno River, where he would receive further orders.

Co. "C", together with necessary servicing details, was left with the South Luzon Force. We moved up the main highway by platoon and section until we reached Manila. Co. "A" was routed through the Cabanatuan area, and the balance of the outfit, up Highway 3. This was done, in order to detract attention of the movement from the Japanese. As usual, rockets were observed all along the route.

We reached our objective about 7:00 P.M., and dispositions were made along the south bank of the Agno River in lieu of further orders.

As the section, I was traveling with, neared Clark Field, we could see Jap planes circling. Clouds of dust and some smoke hung heavy in the air. We prepared for an attack but the planes were evidently too busy to pay any attention to us. Co. "A" had been bombed heavily in the San Jose area—with no casualties or damage.

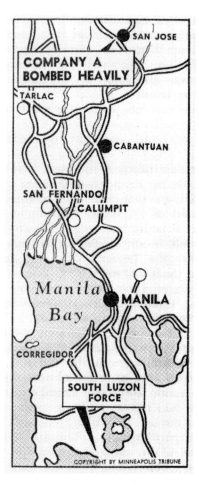

As we made our dispositions that night, and wondering if we would have an opportunity of giving our tanks a badly needed servicing, we did not know, that on the morrow, we would be holding 25 miles of line with only 30 tanks and 5 half-tracks!

CHAPTER 11

The Agno River Rat Trap

AT ABOUT 4:00 o'clock the next morning, December 25, 1941—Christmas—Capt. Spoor and I went to the rear, to check on our supply and maintenance echelon at Gerona. At 6:00 A.M., we had completed the inspection and started north to the Agno River. The dawn was just breaking. Across the street from the bivouac, was an old Catholic church, built in the days when the Spaniards held possession of the Philippines. The congregation was already assembled. There were no lights in the church except candles. Spoor stopped the Jeep and we looked within. Nearly everyone was kneeling. Mass had not yet started. We looked at Christ upon the Cross. It seemed that He moved. We sat—almost paralyzed. A rythmical sound beat itself upon our senses. We turned in its direction. A very old Filipino lady was approaching, hobbling on a cane. We watched her, fascinated. She seemed to eminate something indescribable; her every movement was determination. She arrived between us and the open doors of the church, stopped and turned towards us. She smiled—the most beautiful smile I have ever seen—and said, "Merry Christmas! Gold bless you." She disappeared, within the church.

All of my previous Christmases flashed through my mind. I suppose Spoor had the same thoughts. He broke the spell when he said, "That ought to carry us through Christmas!"

It was a day of brilliant Philippine sunshine. I think we both started the day with life anew. Anyway, the drive back, was with an eagerness of something unexplainable.

After setting up the command post at San Manuel, Capt. Johnson and I proceeded to the Agno River to contact General Weaver. We met him in the early afternoon at Carmen, located on the south bank of the Agno, through which, Highway 3 runs north and south. He gave me the orders.

We would organize the south bank of the Agno River, beginning on the west of Carmen, thence westerly to Highway 13, a distance of 25 miles.

Because of the long run we had made with the tanks, and
with no opportunity for proper servicing, only 30 tanks and
five half-tracks were available for the job. It should be remembered that one company was with the South Luzon
Force. This was called to the attention of General Weaver,
and to another fact, most pertinent.

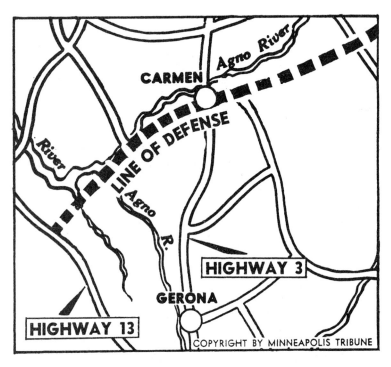

A dirt road roughly paralleled the Agno River, on the
south side, *but* did not go all the way through to Highway 13.
At some distance west of Carmen, this road crossed the river
to the north side, and then went west to connect with Highway 13. The terrain between this highway, and the point
where the road crossed the river, was impassable for tanks,
being all jungle. This meant the outfit would have to be split,
with no chance for contact between, because the bridge would
be blown. And, if this was the line to be held, all of the tank
units east of the jungle area, would of necessity, be compelled

to withdraw into Carmen or—in other words—the same way in which they had entered the area.

It was an extremely bad situation. One of the basic principles in the use of Armored Force units, is to provide a back door or another outlet.

The General made no reply to this, but merely reiterated the order, and that it would be carried out.

The line west from Carmen to the point where the road crossed the river, was allotted to Co. "A" and Co. "D" (minus one platoon), with Co. "A" on the right. The line west of the jungle to Highway 13, was allotted to one tank platoon from Co. "D", and the five half-tracks. There was no contact with this western element except by radio.

Remembering that 25 miles were involved, it was necessary that these units work in platoons. It is evident that a vast amount of line was left between the platoons, over which, it was humanly impossible for the tanks to have any control. Elements of the Philippine Army were put into position, both in the tank areas and in the vacant spaces between tank platoons.

There was much Japanese air activity Christmas Day; however, nothing unusual occurred.

Before daylight of December 26th, an orderly reported from the south, to my command post with an urgent message ordering me to report to General Wainwright, whose headquarters was now at Bambam. Capt. Spoor accompanied me.

General Wainwright was eating breakfast, and invited us to partake. He then outlined his proposals. I was in a quandary, due to the fact that our orders were supposed to come directly from USAFFE (MacArthur) through General Weaver, and not from Wainwright. However, I could not very well remind the General of this, so remained silent.

He showed me the plan for the withdrawals, on the several phase lines, and stated that the Bambam River line would be held at all costs. He then said that he had not been satisfied with the use of tanks up to the present time.

I knew what he had in mind, because I had already heard the story. On December 22nd, the Japanese had landed in force. The 192nd Tank Battalion, which was in the Lingayen area, was called upon, by General Wainwright, for action against the Japs.

Not much information was available on the strength of the Japanese at that time, nor was a great deal known of the dispositions, except that they were supposed to be heading south on the road. General Weaver had received the request (or order—I was never able to determine which) and he sent one platoon north on this road to meet the enemy. There was no opportunity for reconnaissance. The road was very narrow, making it impossible to turn around. *The inevitable happened.* The platoon ran into a perfect tank trap, and was shot to pieces. The lead tank had received a direct hit. The other four tanks, in column, could neither return the fire nor turn around. The 47mm guns of the Japs ripped through our tanks like a knife through butter.

This is what General Wainwright had in mind when he stated he was not satisfied with the use of tanks up to the present time. In his book, he tells of this instance. It is his only reference to the tanks. He blames the tank group commander, General Weaver, for not sending more tanks on this mission. In all fairness to Weaver, the only blame is, that he sent any tanks at all! If General Wainwright had had his way, he would have used all the tanks and none of them would have survived.

Even the layman can understand that the value of light tanks lies in speed and maneuverability. It was very foolish, in the first place, to send tanks up a narrow road with no reconnaissance. In the second place, had there been hundreds of tanks on the road, the whole column would have had only the frontal fire power of *one* tank. The only thing necessary to trap the column would be to knock the lead tank out of action. The tanks in the rear could not get off the road due to the topography; nor could they turn around on the narrow road.

General Wainwright then went on to state that he wanted me to make a thorough reconnaissance of the area immediately south of the Bambam River. He told me to present a plan, for the use of tanks in this area, incorporating a smashing action.

I called his attention to the fact that the area was composed of jungle and rice paddies, that we had already conducted a reconnaissance of that section before the war, and that it had been eliminated, as far as we were concerned for the use of tanks.

He became very impatient and reiterated, that he was not satisfied with the use of tanks, up to that time. I ventured to say, that in order to operate, light tanks needed terrain, which would lend itself to a successful smashing action, rather than making the tanks fit into any particular phase line. To this, there was no answer except that the area would be organized for the use of tanks, and for me to go into session with G-3 (Operations) and be prepared to submit my recommendations.

After I was dismissed, with my mind truly in a quandary, I walked into the next room. There I found General Weaver, tank group commander, pacing the floor. While he did not tell me directly, that he was displeased at my being called into conference with General Wainwright, I could see that he was very much perturbed. I told him what had occurred and what the General had ordered me to do, and also, the objections lodged.

He told me to go ahead and have the conference with G-3, and to go through with the reconnaissance. My sympathies were with General Weaver. Literally, he was "between the devil and the deep blue sea." USAFFE held him responsible for taking orders only from them. At the same time, he was confronted, continually, with higher commanders in the field, who had the idea, apparently, that tanks could do anything—after everything else had failed.

Conferring with G-3, and making necessary arrangements for the reconnaissance, Capt. Spoor and I returned to my C.P. On arrival there, we could hear heavy artillery fire on the Agno River. Capt. Johnson and I left immediately for the area. We were forced to park our Jeep some distance from the river, because of heavy artillery and mortar fire.

The fire was being delivered by the Japs. We had no artillery or mortars, except a few half-tracks, which mounted a 75mm gun, which would dash in between the tanks, and deliver a few shells at the Japs, and then seek a new location. The result was, that the "spot" would receive undivided attention from Jap artillery and mortars. Literally, it was one hell of a mess! One of our ammunition trucks was on fire and exploding profusely. Stopping beside a large tree, we tried to survey the situation. An exploding shell from the truck, deposited part of the tree at our feet. "When I signed up for this war," Johnson quipped, "I didn't agree to be a target for our own artillery!"

We found that our tank units had been heavily engaged since early morning. They had a field day, the first few hours. The Japs had attempted to cross the river at several places, and tried to set up gun positions, in plain sight, on the north bank of the river. It took a long time for them to learn.

It was in this action, just west of Carmen, that the absence of high explosive shells, for our 37mm guns, was felt. While our armor piercing ammunition did help materially in knocking out observed gun positions of the enemy, it was of little good for use against enemy personnel. Despite this drawback, at least 500 Japanese had been disposed of. This was a conservative estimate, and was based upon actual count, after deductions had been made for conjecture.

By now, the tanks had been forced to change positions frequently, due to hostile aircraft and direct observation from the north bank of the Agno River, also due to our friends, the half-track artillery (both of them). Tanks are most vulnerable when not in motion, especially light ones. It was evident the Japs were bringing up more concentrations of artillery and mortars.

At about 2:45 P.M., I walked toward one of the tanks of Company "A". When about 10 feet away from the vehicle, a mortar shell came over and landed in the top of a tree directly above the tank. It had been moved just a short time before. The explosion severed one of the tree limbs, which hit me on the helmet and knocked me down. For a few moments, I was dazed. Then I heard cries from within the tank.

The driver helped me open the front doors. The tank commander, Sgt. Herbert Strobel, fell out past the driver into my arms. He had not had the chance to close his turret, after moving, and he had received the direct blast from the mortar shell. He was badly mangled. The tank driver had received a piece of the shell through his foot. The other two members of the crew were unharmed, but badly stunned.

Two of us carried Strobel out to the road while the other assisted the tank driver. A truck, coming down the road, was stopped and it was found that several other wounded were passengers and were being taken to an aid station nearby. We loaded Strobel and the tank driver into the truck. I knew that Strobel was mortally wounded. At about 3:00 P.M.—he died— the first whom I had known intimately. He was from Brainerd, Minnesota, my home town. He had a milk route before the war, and the thought kept repeating itself in my mind, "Herb won't deliver milk any more."

Japanese artillery and mortar fire became increasingly heavy. The Philippine Army had evacuated long before. The only thing left was the battalion tanks.

The 31st U.S. Infantry and most of the Philippine Scouts, the only front line units we had, were in Bataan or vicinity. This was necessary, in case the Japanese tried to land on that important and strategic peninsula. Therefore, we had no support whatever.

Not having received any orders, at about 5:00 P.M., Capt. Johnson and myself started for the command post. We found our Jeep missing and an almost complete wreck in its place. We found out who appropriated it, later, and took remedial action. Our arrival at the C.P. was delayed until about 6:30 P.M.

General Weaver and his aide awaited us. I was covered with blood; this was the topic of conversation for some time. After relating the front line situation, I told him that it was apparent the Japs would attempt a river crossing that night, and that we had nothing but the tanks to stop it. I asked him what our orders would be.

He did not reply directly but talked only in general terms. His attention was again called to the fact, that most of our units on the Agno River, were in a rat trap, and that no Filipino infantry whatever, was on the line. There was no reply. I again took the initiative and said, that it would be necessary for two men from each tank, to physically occupy the river bank to watch for enemy crossings; that there would be nothing for local security; that the vacant spaces between platoons would be totally without observation—*that the entire 25 miles of line,* as far as I could determine, *was being held by the 194th Tank Battalion with 30 tanks and 5 half-tracks.*

This sort of conversation went on until a little past 7:00 P.M. I finally asked the General the question which was uppermost in my mind:

"When do we withdraw?"

He did not reply for a long time. Finally he replied:

"You will stay in position until 5:00 A.M. tomorrow morning; then you will withdraw."

We had heard an unconfirmed rumor, that a withdrawal was scheduled for that evening, shortly after dusk. I asked General Weaver if there was such an order. He did not reply. As a final question, I asked if the 192nd Tank Battalion, which held positions to the east of us, had received the same order. This was a very important question that any commander would ask. The most vulnerable part of any force is its flanks. We were particularly concerned with all elements on our right. The left flank was anchored into the mountains. The right was wide open. In reply to my question, the tank group commander replied that the 192nd had not, as yet, received the orders but they would.

After the mess was all over, I found that the 192nd Tank Battalion had never received these orders, but had taken direct orders from General Stevens, who was in command of the elements to our right. The orders issued by him, were that all troops would withdraw at 7:00 P.M. Whether or not the 192nd should have taken their orders from General Stevens, or waited for General Weaver, which they were under orders to do, is beside the point. We were left alone on the entire front—and didn't know it!

Due to the fact that the Philippine Army had evacuated—voluntarily—earlier in the day, the elements of the 192nd Tank Battalion (directly to the east of us) had actually moved out about 6:40 P.M. They had not notified us, presuming we were doing the same. The time is confirmed by an American major, regular army, who was in command of a composite Filipino battalion, astride the Carmen road, and taken prisoner at dusk that night trying to find his battalion (they had "evacuated"). Naturally, we did not know this story until quite some time after the events occurred.

At about 7:30 P.M., Captain Johnson and I prepared to go back to the front line, with the orders given by Weaver. Suddenly, we heard a tank coming down the road at high speed. It was dusk but the concrete pavement could still be plainly seen. In the darkness, the tank missed the command post, and continued on down the road. The roar of another

tank was heard. We manged to make ourselves seen and stopped it. The tank was commanded by Sergeant McComas of
Co. "A." One cylinder of the motor was completely blown
out. McComas told me what had happened.

His platoon, under command of Lt. Costigan, was in position just to the west of Carmen. Captain Burke, of Co. "A",
had been out inspecting his platoons at dusk, and had parked
his Jeep in the vicinity of Carmen. He had started on foot, in
the darkness, when he was suddenly fired upon. He was reported dead. We learned later, in the prison camp, that he
had been badly wounded and crawled into a ditch, where he
was found the next morning by the Japanese and taken prisoner. The firing had come from a strong party of Japanese.
Lt. Costigan, who was outside of his tank in the area, immediately ordered the tanks to open fire with their machine guns.
This was done. Then realizing that something had happened,
of which he was not aware, Costigan contacted the tanks of
his platoon and ordered them to follow him out, before they
could be trapped.

The tanks started up the road—toward Carmen—firing all
their guns. As they reached the outer edge of Carmen, they
found a road block had been set up by the Japanese. Probably, because of the determination of the Tankers, and by the
grace of God, they broke down the block and proceeded on
into the town.

The American major, referred to as having been taken
prisoner earlier, had been tied up by the Japanese, and was
held on the opposite side of the intersection of Highway 3 and
the road on which the tanks were coming out.

He stated, afterwards, that Carmen was full of Japanese
and that they had set up heavy guns and mortars. The tanks
were in column and firing steadily. They had to make a right
turn, firing almost in the face of the tied up major. Why he
escaped injury from that fire will always be a mystery. He
said he was unable to physically verify the fact for some time
after! We met both him and Capt. Burke later at Cabanatuan
Prison Camp.

As the tanks turned the corner, they were fired on by heavy
guns. Mortar fire pursued them until out of range. Somewhere, in the darkness, the Japs had placed a thermite bomb
on one of the tanks, just above one of the ammunition trays,

on the perfectly flat, top deck, armor plate, so kindly designed by the Ordnance Department (in the days of peace, when the testimony of combat soldiers was promptly discarded—or treated as heresy). It burned its way through the armor plate and dropped into the ammunition tray—in the crew compartment! The crew immediately evacuated the tank with no casualties, and were picked up by the tank in the rear. By this time, the ammunition inside the tank, was exploding and the aviation gasoline had caught fire. It was an inferno in less time than it takes to tell it.

CHAPTER 12

Confusion

SGT. McCOMAS WAS sent to the rear as his tank motor was still functioning, even with one cylinder blown out. Two tanks at my C.P. were immediately placed in position for a road block. Another tank from Costigan's platoon, together with a half-track from the C.P., completed the block. All other vehicles and personnel were sent to report back at our rear echelon.

Our radio operators were immediately ordered to get in touch with the other elements on the Agno River. We knew that the other platoons, to the west, were not heavily engaged as yet, because of the distance at which they were located. The radio operators reported a great deal of static in the air. They were unable to make contact. We never knew whether that static was man-made or otherwise. However, we tried unsuccessfully all night to get contact.

Realizing we would have trouble with the radio, I sent Capt. Spoor to the rear on a dual mission. First, he was to notify Tank Group Headquarters of what had occurred. Secondly, he was either to proceed himself or send someone else south to Tarlac and then proceed north on Highway 13 to contact the extreme western elements of the 194th and try the radio from there. If that failed, he was to immediately contact, cross-country, our units east of the jungle area and instruct them to attempt a negotiation of carabao cart trails in a westerly direction, so as to come out on the railroad grade to the west. If they could guide themselves that far, they could follow the grade to the southeast and intersect Highway 3 north of Moncada, which would be to our rear. The moon would be up soon and it would be easy to see. Everything depended on contact and time was the essence. Spoor left on the mission.

A short time later, a half-track, mounting a 75mm gun, came down the road. It was commanded by a lieutenant. He had been a short distance from the area where the trapped tanks had been located. Luckily a cane field had been found through which he had detoured. This brought him out on Highway 3, just to the north of our road block. We requisitioned him and put the gun into position.

At about 11:00 P.M., General Brougher came up from the south. He was in command of the Philippine Army west of Carmen. He was on his way to check on previous orders given his command that afternoon. I related what had happened and he told me that the withdrawal order for *all* the troops had been issued early that day *to start at 7:00 P.M.;* that he had given orders for his troops to proceed west to the railroad and not try to come through Carmen, because of anticipated Jap control of that area; that two special trains would be coming up to evacuate those troops to the next phase line south, and that my tanks were supposed to protect the railroad crossing on Highway 3 (this was quite a distance to the south of our block). I told him that we had received no withdrawal orders for 7:00 o'clock. General Brougher was a very outspoken soldier and voiced his opinion in no uncertain terms. After the explosion, he commended the formation of the block, and impressed upon me the absolute necessity of being at the railroad crossing no later than 4:00 A.M. and at the phase line at daylight. He was informed that we would do this but would remain in position until the last moment, to which he agreed. He left soon after.

At about 2:50 A.M., we were still in position at the road block. All stragglers had been cleared and sent to the rear including a Philippine Army patrol. Nothing but thin air was between us and the Japs. We had no knowledge of the turmoil which was going on in the rear echelon and Tank Group Headquarters, nor of the failure of Capt. Spoor's mission. We were not to learn about it until hours later.

Suddenly we heard a motorized movement from the north. It later proved to be the advance guard of a Jap armored column. We never determined its size. The lead vehicle came down the road with dimmed lights. We had laid our guns in fixed positions, so that the entire highway, including ditches, was completely covered at several angles. The signal for firing had been pre-determined. I was to fire the first shot with my 37mm gun.

When the lead vehicle of the Japs was about 150 feet away, a shot was fired. Capt. Johnson and his tank crew must have had a premonition that I was about to fire. It has always been an argument as to which of us fired the first shot. To my knowledge, only one shot was fired back at us. Our 75mm gun opened up and at that close range, it practically swept the road. All the tanks and the half-track fired steadily for about 15 minutes.

It had been agreed upon, that when ready to move, my tank would bump Johnson's tank to start the block to the rear. We were acutely aware that if we stayed in position too long, once we had been committed to action, we might jeopardize the entire road block by leaving it in an extremely vulnerable position for hostile action by enemy ground troops. We had no local security whatever. I touched the driver's head and he bumped Johnson's tank. The block moved out at full speed and then reorganized as we had planned, about one kilometer down the road. We proceeded slowly and reached the railroad crossing about 10 minutes before the two train-loads of Philippine Army came through. There was no enemy action.

Up to this time, a great part of the efforts of the Japanese was directed through the Carmen area down Highway 3. Whether or not the road block determined the future action of the Japs, the fact remains that their main effort was now directed to the east, in the Cabanatuan area. This was the long way around and left Highway 3 entirely clear for the withdrawals of our forces. Had the Japs pressed on down that highway, it is extremely doubtful that we would have reached Bataan. Eye witnesses at Carmen (prisoners) stated, that after the road block affair, the Japs organized Carmen for defense, thinking that a counter attack was, or would be, in progress. Most certainly, had the Japs pushed us, they could have split the North Luzon Force, which would have resulted in a debacle of utter confusion.

The night before, I had requested General Brougher to see to it that orders were specifically issued to allow no bridges to be blown until we had given the clearance. To my personal knowledge, the General did this. He also took all other steps possible to insure the order was obeyed.

As stated before, there are innumerable streams in the Philippines. Nearly all have high banks. In the scheme of retrograde movements, or withdrawals, the mission was to blow all bridges after our troops had crossed. On this night, we learned that if we wished to hold a bridge intact, we would be compelled to place our own armed guards on that bridge with orders to shoot anyone who attempted to blow it without our authority. It must be remembered that all other troops would withdraw, leaving us alone. It might be hours before we traced their line of march. Filipino Engineers would be left at bridge sites to blow them. Always the orders were, *not* to blow until the tanks had given orders. The hysterical characteristic of the half-trained Filipino Engineer, would cause him to blow a bridge prematurely at the slightest provocation. The breeze in the trees—the rustling of leaves or bushes—the darkness—*the unknown*—would cause him to go into immediate action. How we wished for the Philippine Scouts to be with us on those missions!

As we proceeded south, we found a bridge blown. Luckily, it was a small one. But it was impossible to make the crossing without the bridge. By dint of back-breaking work, torn and lacerated hands, ingenuity and what-have-you, we rigged a crossing. If that opening had been one foot longer, we never could have done it. It was past daylight when we crossed the long bridge out of Moncada. I stopped and talked with the Engineers and told them that other tanks of our outfit would be following soon. An American officer was in charge of the Filipino Engineers. I felt we had nothing to fear. We reached Gerona, the new phase line, at about 8:30 A.M. December 28th. The line was just forming and we helped organize it.

Shortly thereafter, messages began to come in from Tank Group Headquarters. They were rather incoherent and the gist of these messages was such as to throw me into a complete tailspin. One of the messages said something about "Come out of your position fighting." We began to think the high command knew more of the situation than we did. I fully expected a Japanese to leer evilly from around the tree against which I was leaning. Another commander in the same area was getting the same type of messages from another source.

It must have been realized by the high command, at this time, that the Philippine Army could not be depended upon. This should have occasioned little surprise. MacArthur had been told that before. These people had no chance for proper

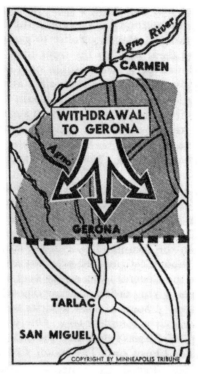

training and had not handled firearms before. The Filipino is no coward. He was untrained—a part of a mob. Americans have had ample experience to clearly show the folly of placing untrained personnel against a well-trained and well-equipped army. Our history is full of it—if we will just take time to read. Our national capitol was ransacked and burned, by a numerically inferior force of the British, with a casualty list on our side of only 14 killed and wounded! Our Declaration of Independence was saved by Dolly Madison, wife of the President, in that fiasco, who had presence of mind to tuck it under her arm when the evacuation was on and many were running—to save their own skin! Why should anyone have thought that the Filipino was any different? In addition, he was by no means as enlightened as the American, nor did he know anything about modern warfare. The Philippine Scout is a shining example of the bravery of the Filipino.

Almost at the first shot fired, a great portion of the Philippine Army would voluntarily evacuate to the rear. This necessitated the forming of Military Police to gather up the stragglers and bring them back to the front line. They were lost sheep and followed back into position only to do it all over again. Invariably, they had lost their rifles and were "looking for my companion." We could always count on them having two things—their gas masks and a stick of sugar cane.

It was here that I received a message, as did other commanders, that any soldier seen to evacuate without orders would be summarily shot. The order came from General Wainwright.

Capt. Spoor rejoined me at about noon and told me about the events of the night before. He said that when he had arrived at San Miguel (Tank Group Headquarters) on his mission, the General had already heard from Lt. Costigan, who had missed the command post in the dark. Weaver had threatened to shoot Costigan and everyone else in the outfit. Spoor said that the General was a raging man, running around in his underwear, giving orders, sending one vehicle at a time, north on Highway 3. Some of these vehicles were overmanned. Others were without a complete crew. One was broken down completely. Sgt. McComas's tank was one ordered north. This had one cylinder blown out. The motor had functioned all the way back but after being turned off, naturally "froze." We had this experience several times. The radial motor would keep on running until stopped. It was then stopped for good. Each vehicle had no definite mission except to go north and join me. General Weaver ordered all and sundry, including himself, to get out in the road and stop all vehicles—turn them around—and head them north—vehicles which belonged to other outfits—busses, trucks—anything that moved. It seemed that he had suddenly taken command of the entire North Luzon Force!

Spoor tried to explain his mission to the General. He was told that the Tank Group would handle it immediately. Weaver was in a state of semi-hysteria. This state of affairs was confirmed by the others in the rear echelon. He ordered Spoor to take a half-track and join me.

Spoor started out and reached Gerona where he met a half-track which had been sent up to the road block by Weaver.

The crew in this vehicle had been sent up earlier by Weaver and did not know the state of affairs in the rear. I had given them orders to return as far as Gerona and stop any more from joining me. We had our block formed and did not wish any superfluous personnel or equipment in the area. They would have been of no use whatever and might have placed the block in jeopardy. Spoor was unable to state definitely that Tank Group had completed the mission. His opinion was that they had' not. He had gone back to Headquarters that morning but had been unable to learn anything about it.

Shortly after this, I was visited by the new executive officer of Tank Group, Major T. Smythe, who told me just where General Weaver could be located. I found him south of us, near Tarlac, at his field C.P. On reporting, I found him extremely courteous—and doing all the talking. He almost immediately told me that the mission had been taken care of. He then stated that my orders were to remain in position at Gerona; that there would be another withdrawal that night to the Tarlac line and that we would cover that withdrawal.

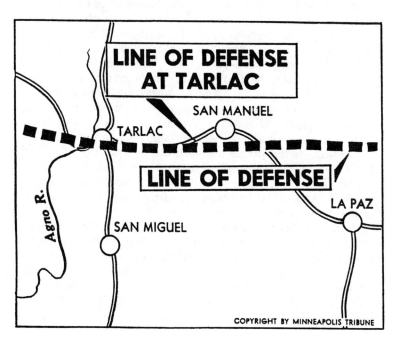

LINE OF DEFENSE AT TARLAC

SAN MANUEL

TARLAC

LINE OF DEFENSE

Agno R.

LA PAZ

SAN MIGUEL

We were to be in readiness for any eventuality because of heavy pressure developing to the east, in the Cabanatuan sector. I found the high command had no information on our sector other than that which had happened the night before.

The Tarlac line was reconnoitered for positions, guides posted and orders relayed. There was no action with the Japs that day. However, the pressure on our right flank, to the east, was steadily growing. The withdrawal from Gerona was without event except the usual 5th Column activity of rockets and some grenades thrown from the darkness which did no damage.

That night, the entire story of the Agno River affair came to light. *The mission had not been completed nor was it ever started.* Units, trapped by the Carmen affair to the west, had not been engaged very heavily with the Japs. On receiving no orders that night, Capt. Jack Altman took a half-track and crew early the next morning down the road towards Carmen. They arrived in the area which had seen the fighting of the night before and were immediately fired upon by the Japanese who were well organized and in full possession. They returned the fire and turned the half-track around, succeeded in traveling several kilometers west, when the motor died. On examination, they found the radiator riddled. Destroying the vehicle, they continued on foot.

The day before, the Tankers had conducted a reconnaissance for themselves. This is standing operating procedure with armored forces. They had been briefed previously on the main topographical features, between themselves and Highway 13 to the west. They therefore knew that the railroad lay to the west of the jungle area. An old carabao cart trail had been found and they reasoned that it might lead to something better. If it would run generally south, it would intersect the railroad. At least, they would be farther away from the rat trap and the position could be no worse.

It was out of this "back door" that Altman now took the tanks. It was slow process and almost impossible without guides. They had to guess when other trails appeared. They encountered some Filipinos but were unable to get any information. One tank became separated from the rest during this trek and never did rejoin us. This tank was commanded by Lt. Hart. While in Bataan, Philippine Scouts who were operating between the Guerillas and ourselves, informed me that the tank and crew were operating near Fort Stotsenburg. They had talked with the crew and brought me their names to prove it! Three of them died later. The fourth is still in doubt.

Altman and his Tankers kept going and eventually found the railroad. They took the grade southeasterly until it brought them to Highway 3. There was much rejoicing and they proceeded south to Moncada. *The bridge was blown completely!* This was the same day we had received assurance that it would not be blown. No Japs were even anywhere near the area! The river at this point is very wide and deep. Altman's men carried a number of wounded with them.

Using his initiative, Altman ordered the tank guns and pieces of tank mechanism removed and hidden, deep in the jungle. It was his plan to cross the river, find our forces and attempt to get guides for a river crossing. They negotiated the river, with their wounded, by means of girders and by swimming. They did not join us, however, until 1:00 A.M. at the Tarlac positions. Pressure on the right flank now made it impossible to even consider any return for the tanks. That flank was in danger of being turned. The South Luzon Force was being steadily pushed back (north) by Japanese who had landed on the southeast coast of Luzon. It was mandatory that all withdrawals be carried out on a uniform line.

Later, at a conference of the high command and which was attended by General Weaver, the whole blame for the loss of the tanks was placed on the Engineers. The American officer in charge had gone to sleep while waiting for the tanks to appear and the bridge—going up—awakened him! At least, that is the story.

To this date, to my knowledge, no blame was ever placed on General Weaver for failing to take proper and necessary precautions in the establishment of tank positions on the south bank of the Agno River; for failure to order the withdrawal at the proper time; for failure to get the withdrawal orders to the 192nd Tank Battalion, and for failure to allow Capt. Spoor to complete his mission, or in lieu thereof, to complete it by Tank Group.

Perhaps General Weaver had to blindly obey orders in the matter of tank dispositions on the Agno. This, I do not know.

However, I do know that he was directly responsible for the rest. Had we received the withdrawal orders on time, and had Tank Group functioned and coordinated the movements of the 192nd and 194th, the Japanese would have made no river crossing as soon as they did. All units would have come out safely. That river crossing was made without opposition of any kind and it was made about 1,000 yards to the east of Carmen. *No one was there to oppose them!*

The failure of Tank Group Headquarters resulted in leaving the right flank of the 194th Tank Battalion entirely exposed!

CHAPTER 13

Empty Trucks — and Death

DURING THE DAY of December 28th, the Tarlac line was strengthened as much as possible. Some units of the 192nd Tank Battalion were given me for the purpose. Capt. Spoor and our reconnaissance detachments worked all day, combing the area for "back doors," favorable spots for road blocks, and other combat plans. Elements of the rear echelon were moved forward and literally poured grease and oil in the starved tanks. Minor adjustments were made. We didn't dare remove any armor plate for other servicing because of the proximity of combat. Pressure on the right flank was building up more and more. We sent out patrols to our front but no contact with the Japanese was made. It became apparent that the situation to our right would demand a withdrawal that night to the next phase line—the Bambam River. Capt. Johnson and I had made a last minute check on our combat units and returned to the command post at about 7:30 P.M. to see if any orders had been received. We found General Weaver and his aide waiting for us.

He verified the fact that another withdrawal would take place and then told me that I would take the 194th Tank Battalion, minus a small portion of the combat elements, and proceed again to the Calumpit Bridge area—the movement to be immediate. I decided to leave the 192nd units plus one platoon of the 194th to cover the withdrawal and proceed south with the rest. The Tank Group Commander ordered me to hold the Calumpit Bridge at any cost and to shoot anyone who attempted to blow it.

The bridge was a strategic point. The South Luzon Force had to cross this bridge in order to reach San Fernando out of which the road led to Bataan. Elements of the North Luzon Force, in the Cabanatuan area, also had to withdraw across this bridge *after* the South Luzon Force had made its crossing. The plan for withdrawal into Bataan was that the South Force would withdraw first across this bridge. Coming from the south, their movement would be covered by the North Force, after which, it would withdraw across the bridge. The importance of this strategic point is apparent. If not held, it meant that the South Luzon Force, together with part of the North Force, would be bottled up by the Japanese and unable to reach Bataan.

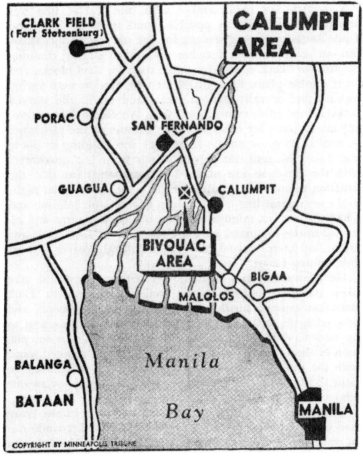

We were nearing the vital part of Phase 2 of the Orange Plan. The success of all our retrograde movements depended upon the maneuver soon to be conducted in the San Fernando-

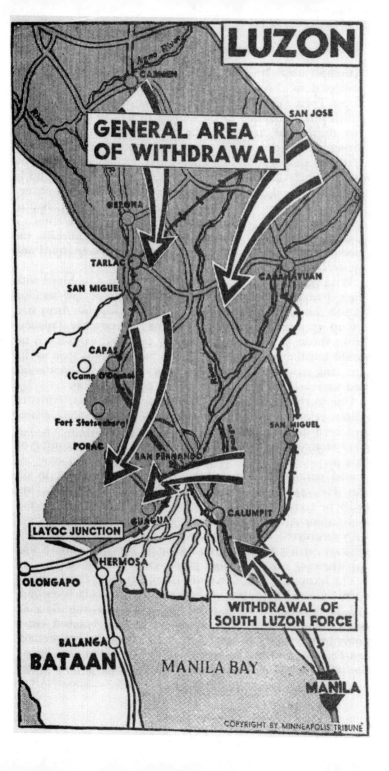

LUZON

GENERAL AREA OF WITHDRAWAL

LAYOC JUNCTION

WITHDRAWAL OF SOUTH LUZON FORCE

CARMEN

SAN JOSE

GERONA

TARLAC

CABANATUAN

SAN MIGUEL

CAPAS

(Camp O'Donnell)

Fort Stotsenberg

SAN MIGUEL

PORAC

SAN FERNANDO

GUAGUA

CALUMPIT

HERMOSA

OLONGAPO

BALANGA

BATAAN

MANILA BAY

MANILA

COPYRIGHT BY MINNEAPOLIS TRIBUNE

Calumpit area. In order that our forces from the south be
protected in their movement through this area, the North
Luzon Force must make a wide swinging retrograde operation,
which can be likened to the closing of a huge door—through
180 degrees of arc—with the enemy attempting to come
through the opening, or smashing through the door itself.
With the enemy pounding unceasingly, retrograde movements
are extremely difficult operations when merely backing up in
one direction. The outer edge of our "door" had to change
directions from south to west to north. Obviously, Bataan
depended upon the success of this "impossible" operation.

Our orders meant another night movement. Luckily, the
moon was out. Visibility was excellent. Orders were issued and
we were soon on the way.

Wild rumors were rife among the Filipinos. Combined with
their hysterical nature, it meant the necessity of sending
patrols down the road ahead of us. The Philippine Army had
set up 37 mm guns covering the road in case the Japanese
broke through. Had our patrols not preceded us, there is no
doubt but that we would have been fired upon as soon as the
first tank moved into sight. The trip was made without event
and we reached Calumpit Bridge by early morning.

Due to the initiative, and that alone of the Quartermaster
officer, referred to earlier in this story, tank gasoline drums
had been dropped at various points for our convenience. We
were eternally grateful. Had it not been for the planning of
this particular officer, our gasoline problems would have assumed paramount proportions. He was not ordered to do
this. He forsaw the need and he acted without orders. One
order he received from G-4 (Supply) of USAFFE was for the
establishment of certain supply dumps in Bataan. It carefully instructed him to place them in defilade. This is the
military term used for protection against artillery fire. Nothing whatever was said about protection from the air!

The reconnaissance element of the 194th immediately prosecuted an intensive patrol of the area, and particularly around
San Fernando, the focal point for retirement into Bataan.
Ammunition and gasoline dumps were being bombed accurately by the Japs—too accurately to be casual. Dumps around
San Fernando seemed to be receiving the most minute attention. This location was in Pampanga Province—a hotbed for

subversive activities. We were at a loss to understand how these dumps were located so soon after being established. One of our reconnaissance half-tracks solved the riddle.

The crew found, in one particular case, five Filipinos standing at pertinent points around the dump. Ostensibly, they were watching Japanese reconnaissance planes. Each Filipino had a mirror in his hand. When the plane approached the area, the mirrors would be flashed into the sun. The plane picked up the flashes, locating the dump as being somewhere within the mirrored circle. Needless to say, the 5th Columnists evacuated the area soon after. The Jap plane would make contact with bombers and the dump would be disposed of. My men killed three of the five Filipinos and wounded the fourth. The fifth man escaped. This information was passed out to our forces and also to the Filipinos in the vicinity. I know that at least on two occasions, after this, the Filipinos themselves took care of two groups of 5th Columnists equipped with mirrors. It is interesting to note that no more dumps were bombed in that vicinity.

A detachment from the 200th CA (AA) was put into position close to the bridge. They were very welcome! Soon after their arrival, a flight of Jap bombers made their appearance flying fairly low. The 200th let loose a barrage that seemed to lift the Japs up into the sky. At least three of the planes were hit badly. Smoke poured out and the Japs did not drop a single bomb! It was comical to see the way they came in— and went out. Everyone had a good laugh.

It now became apparent that Bataan was to become a land of want. Persistent rumors had it that we would be on half rations after withdrawing to the peninsula. Our rear echelon was put to work salvaging anything worthwhile from the wreckage at dumps and along the roads. We found commercial trucks ditched and abandoned when Jap air activity stepped up its tempo. Some of the trucks were repaired with little trouble. The men went to work with a will. Between now and about January 4th, the rear echelon of the 194th Tank Battalion salvaged and moved to Bataan, about 12,000 gallons of aviation gasoline and about six truck loads of canned food. This was done entirely on our own initiative. Everything was dumped at a location in Bataan just south of Orion.

We put guards on it who functioned admirably. "Foreigners" didn't even get close to that dump.

Several more attempts were made to bomb the bridge which met with complete failure. The anti-aircraft detachment was most certainly on the job.

Early in the afternoon of December 31st, a report was received at my command post from the combat element guarding Calumpit Bridge. It stated that an atempt to blow the bridge might occur. I sent Capt. Spoor to investigate and to make doubly sure that our personnel understood that their orders were to shoot anyone—no matter who—if they tried to blow the bridge.

Spoor reported back in about an hour. He said there had been quite a session with a colonel of Engineers, who had intimated that the bridge might have to be blown, at any moment, regardless of what orders we had. Spoor reiterated the orders I had given and also told the colonel from whom these orders emanated (USAFFE). No answer was forthcoming. There was no need to recheck the Tankers guarding the bridge. They would have blasted MacArthur himself if no countermanding orders had been received!

Much of the South Luzon Force moved over the bridge that day on their way to Bataan. The movement also included elements from the Port Area at Manila. We had watched traffic carefully since taking control of the bridge. We knew exactly what was going on. It was no myth when that young Tanker exclaimed, "Hell! They're empty!" *They were—empty trucks!* Trucks that could and should have been used to haul needed supplies into Bataan. It developed that there had been no detailed plan for the evacuation of food and supplies from the Port Area and from the wholesale warehouses in Manila. The pertinent question had been asked by our friend, the realistic Quartermaster officer, as to just what plans were laid and he was told, with a wave of the hand, that the whole job could be done in two days. This was shortly after war had started. No estimates had been made for the number of trucks needed, nor did anyone have an idea as to labor or where they would come from. As a matter of fact, instead of two days, the job would have taken nearly two weeks! The Japs gave them *three weeks* and still practically nothing was moved! That part of the War Plan relative to taking inventory of the Wholesale Warehouses for food, was actually carried out. *That was all!*

At about dusk, the rear echelon of Co. "C" rolled across the bridge. It will be remembered that this company had been left with the South Luzon Force on December 24th when the rest of the 194th was ordered north to the Agno River. The combat elements of Co. "C" had been ordered into the Baliuag area, on the other side of the bridge and to the northeast, to give assistance to those units of the North Luzon Force, which were engaged against the Japs south of Cabanatuan. The rear echelon of this company was ordered into the battalion rear echelon area.

The mission of holding Calumpit Bridge was nearly complete. The South Luzon Force, with the exception of a few elements at Baliuag, had crossed and were either in or on their way to Bataan. All that remained of the balance of our forces would cross tonight. Later on, in the evening, the combat elements of Co. "C" rejoined the battalion. They had an ugly story to tell of their part in the fighting to the south.

The Japanese had landed on the east coast of Luzon in the vicinity of Lucban. The South Luzon Force attempted to meet this attack. The region was mountainous and difficult for combat. They were practically without any equipment for such a fight. Fighting was heavy in the north and no help could be expected from that direction.

A platoon of Co. "C" tanks were ordered to go up a narrow trail, travel like "hell," and shoot the guns. The platoon leader told the major, who was giving the orders, that a reconnaissance should be made first to determine the terrain and to check what might be out in front. The major told him the mission was primarily to impress the Philippine Army and to raise its morale.

The platoon leader suggested it was known the Japs had landed and evidently were progressing eastward. The major said he had specific information the Japs had nothing more than small arms or .50 caliber machine guns at the most, and that they were on the other side of the mountains. The platoon leader again urged the need for reconnaissance. He was met with a blank refusal and was told to get going.

The five tanks started out. Following armored force doctrine, they moved in column, each at such distance from the other, to allow visible contact. Upon rounding a sharp curve, the second tank could not see the first tank. The driver of the second tank, as a natural reaction, stepped on the accelerator to try to close the gap. This saved the tank from getting a direct hit.

An anti-tank gun of the Japanese had fired directly at this tank, the shell landing just in the rear. The crew realized that what they had feared had happened. There was no place to turn around. The driver roared down the trail at full speed.

They now faced a road block of logs thrown across the trail. The Japs had built fires around the block and had thrown green wood on top of the dry so as to create smoke. Visibility was almost zero at the block. The tank hit the block and went through, zooming out of the smoke into the clear only to be confronted with a 77mm gun set up by the Japs in the middle of the trail. The driver did not hesitate but crashed into the gun and crew, overrunning it. They proceeded this way for nearly a quarter of a mile, continuing to overrun gun positions and firing their own weapons as they rolled along.

Finally, they found a spot where the tank could be turned around. The tank commander had made up his mind that the only way out was the way they came in. They started back, spotting more machine gun nests and other gun positions which they promptly overran. The Japs were thick in the area and many casualties resulted.

Just before they reached the spot where they had been first fired upon, they saw why they had lost sight of the first tank in the column. It had received a direct hit in the front which had knocked off both front doors. The tank had plunged off the trail into a rice paddy. It was later disclosed that Jap machine guns had poured their fire into the tank. The crew had all been killed. Lt. Bob Needham, platoon commander, had been in the first tank.

The crew of the successful second tank were patting themselves on the back, believing they might get out safely, when they received a direct hit which knocked off the idler sprocket and sheared off rivets, driving them all around inside the tank. This was one more item, the combat troops had argued about with the Ordnance Department, prior to the war and which was received with deaf ears. Later on, tanks were built by welding instead of rivets.

One of the rivets went through the neck of Eddie De Benediti, a member of the crew. The tank rolled over a bank and finally came to rest upright in a rice paddy. The tank driver shut off the motor. All exit doors were carefully examined to see if they were securely locked. The crew peered through the slits of the tank. They had run into an area the Japs were using as a springboard to launch the attack. The Jap infantry was now jumping off and the artillery was giving support. The other three tanks had been stopped dead in their tracks. A small part of the crews escaped but the majority of the platoon was dead.

The tank commander told the other three men to be perfectly quiet and play dead. Soon a party of Japanese tried to open the tank. The crew members held their breath. They were startled when a Jap said in English, "Americans all dead." The party of Japs departed.

The Jap attack was steadily rolling forward. Later in the day, another party tried to get into the tank. They stayed for more than half an hour and then left. That night, just before dark, more Japs came. They removed the cable from the outside of the tank and tried to open the doors. They jabbered back and forth until someone on the bank yelled at them and they, too, disappeared.

The tank crew was exceedingly thirsty. They had no water, and the tropical sun had been beating down all day. The armor plate became almost red hot and the inside of the tank became a living hell. The crew could make very little movement.

A Japanese kitchen was located only about 20 feet from the tank. Every little while someone would come down to examine the tank. That went on until about 3:00 A.M. the next day. It was at this time that the American-Filipino 75mm guns (very few in number) started to register on the Japs who apparently believed it was a counter attack. They did a great deal of yelling and jabbering, and placed trees and logs in the middle of the road as a block. Some shells landed very close to the tank. One shell wiped out three trucks and the kitchen. The firing lasted about two hours. The crew licked the sides of the tank for any moisture present.

At about 5:00 A.M. the Japs left the area and started up
the road. By 7:00 A.M. all movement had ceased. The crew
made a careful survery through the eye openings, took their
pistols and ammunition, and quietly slipped out. They started
to work their way into the jungle and almost bungled into a
party of Japanese loading machine gun belts at a shack nearby. At the same time, they heard other Japs approaching.
Their entrance into the jungle was made precipitately. Eddie's
wounds had been dressed as best as could be done under the
circumstances. Every time be breathed, it sounded like a death
rattle.

After walking about five hours, they heard tanks on the
road and found them to be Japanese. That area was left behind in a hurry. From that time on they traveled almost entirely through the jungle and over the mountains.

It was early the morning of December 26th when they had
left the tank. The next two days they spent in painful effort,
to put as much distance between themselves and the Japanese
as possible. They met some Chinese who said the Japs were
now in Majayjay; therefore they had to stay on the mountain route. They contacted Filipino guides. It was fortunate
they had some money. Some guides would take no money.
Others had to be paid.

The night of December 29th, they stayed in Lilio. Just before this, they had met two men from the other tank crews
who had escaped. Both were in bad shape with wounds and
other injuries. They had to be practically dragged over the
tortuous mountain trails. A Filipino doctor in Lilio gave the
wounded much needed medical attention. The morning of
December 30th, all felt much refreshed and rested. With
guides, they came to Nagcarten. Here, the Catholic priest gave
them something to eat and told them to take a certain trail.
Japs were moving up from Banoga. They left Nagcarten and
started for Calauan. The guides left soon after they had
started because the Japanese were coming in from all sides.
The Tankers took to the jungle and plodded through to a
point near Dayep. Filipinos told them that the Japs were in
front of them and also in back. They finally negotiated with a
guide to pilot them to Manila Bay, after which, the guide
procured a small boat for them. They left St. Benito that
night, crossing over to the town of Cordona, which was reach-

ed at midnight. The Filipinos gave them coffee, rice cakes and a good place to sleep.

The New Year dawned and they walked to Binangonan. There, they managed to get a boat which took them to Manila only to find that the American-Filipino Army had evacuated. They took the wounded to the Philippine General Hospital in Manila. Eddie was turned over to the doctors who operated immediately. The rest were told to contact the Red Cross (Filipino). It was lucky they did. The Red Cross took them to the Port Area where they were just in time to catch the last boat leaving for Corregidor. It was just before the Japs came into Manila. Reaching Corregidor about 2:00 A.M., January 2nd, they were put in the hospital for three days. They needed it! After this, they were taken to Bataan and left at Mariveles to find the 194th Tank Battalion. Everything was in a state of flux. No one knew where we were. They stayed at Mariveles—but not for long. Japanese bombers came over and nearly got all of them. Walking to the north, they shifted for themselves and finally came to something which looked familiar. Ragged, dirty, and unshaven, they just stood—and looked. It was our rear echelon bivouac! They found their voices and let out a yell. The Tankers responded. One of the cooks, noted for his hard-boiled manner (which was merely armor plate to cover up his emotions), strolled over and said, "Now that you're here, I suppose you'll be bellyachin' for somethin' to eat!" With that, he turned around and went to the kitchen. Everyone knew what would happen. He busied himself with preparations for the meal, continually grumbling to himself in which audible snatches of his one-way conversation could be heard such as, "What the hell they think this is? Short order restaurant?" In a comparatively short time he yelled, "Come and get it! Think I'm gonna waste all my time with you birds?" The meal, he had provided, was of the very best we had. Someone said, "Thanks." The cook said, "Nuts!" Then he sat down and listened with avid interest to the story told.

It was a joyful reunion, even for men who knew they were to be on Bataan until they were killed or captured.

CHAPTER 14

The Road to Bataan

IT WAS NOT until some time later that another story came to light concerning Co. "C" which had been left with the South Luzon Force. Evidently, they were going to let someone else do the telling. General Jones, who had commanded the area they were in, told it with recommendations for decorations to be awarded to the participants. He had wanted to make a personal reconnaissance and had taken a half-track and crew of Co. "C" as his protection. He was in his own vehicle. While riding down a certain road, the party was ambushed by a strong Japanese patrol. The half-track, which was preceding the General's conveyance, abruptly stopped and returned the fire with everything they had. The half-track was completely disabled from enemy fire. It was literally riddled. Whether all the Japs were killed, who participated in that ambush, will never be known. However, when the fire ceased, the crew made a thorough investigation. They found many bodies but none alive. They had no idea, whether or not, other forces of the Japanese were in the vicinity. They calmly and methodically dismounted the machine guns from the half-track, gathered up their equipment, and hiked back to friendly territory. They brought every weapon with them intact!

I know that everyone in the battalion felt the same as I did that night of December 31st. Co. "C" was back with us! We hadn't seen or heard of our "adventurers" as yet, but the *team* was, once again, complete.

About 10:00 P.M. that night, General Weaver and his aide, Major Pettit, visited my command post. They notified me officially that I had been promoted to Lieutenant Colonel effective December 19th. All other officers of the battalion, whom we had recommended, were promoted on the same order, including Burke, whom we thought had been killed at the Agno River. After being sworn in, General Weaver gave me orders to proceed with my battalion to the area east of San Fernando, which would be the next strategic point.

This point was part of the swinging movement of the North Luzon Force, east of the all-important road which led into Bataan. The Japs must have realized by this time, that we were withdrawing into Bataan. They were too late to seize the Calumpit Bridge. The South Luzon Force had crossed. Only the combat elements, involved in the retrograde movement in the Baliuag area, had to cross and this would be accomplished tonight. The completion of the swinging movement now depended on the successful withdrawals in the Mexico area, east of San Fernando. Japanese pressure here was very great.

We reached the new position about 4:00 A.M., January 1, 1942, and contacted the combat elements. This was the New Year. I believe we all were thinking the same thing—what was in store for us? We knew that our trials were, daily, to become more grim as time went on. What we didn't know was—*for how long?* Anyway, everyone gave vent to that age-old salutation, "Happy New Year!" The spirit was there even though our bodies were beaten. The hand clasps, that night, were truly in comradeship. We did not know whether we would live or die. One thing was sure—we had survived thus far. And when everything was over—the war ended—returning to our land of dreams—we remember those hand clasps—casual, nonchalant hand clasps—with *dead men*—and we *remember!*

Nothing eventful happened January 1st except a one-sided affair. A patrol of our tanks and half-tracks caught Japanese tanks east of Mexico. A hot fire, lasting for not over ten minutes, knocked out five Jap tanks. As per their usual blundering, they had stopped without a reconnaissance of their surroundings. Our patrol, luckily, was under cover and poured a murderous fire into the assemblage. There were no casualties on our side. Japanese air activity, on New Year's Day, was very lively but without a great deal of effect. Late in the day, we received orders that we would cover *all* withdrawals south and east of San Fernando. This was the last phase of the "swinging door" maneuver. The 194th Tank Battalion was to be the last unit through San Fernando—and would give the clearance order for blowing the bridge on the south side of the intersection.

The Philippine Army, in our area, had had a field day with the Japs. In spite of Jap superiority of men and equipment, the Filipinos had given battle, and chased the enemy out of their positions. Once they started after the fleeing Nipponese, it was just as hard to make them join the withdrawal movement, as it was in other operations, to bring them from the rear to take the offensive, after being pushed out by the Japs. It took quite a session of convincing before they could be turned towards San Fernando again. To have let them continue, would have meant that the Japs on both sides, would have closed in, and they would have been hopelessly surrounded, and a huge gap in our withdrawing lines would have resulted.

The Philippine Army troops started to withdraw after dark and cleared the 194th at about 1:00 A.M., January 2nd. We covered their movement with no unusual occurrence and arrived at San Fernando about 2:00 A.M. The last unit from the south, a contingent from the 192nd Tank Battalion, cleared the bridge shortly thereafter. As the last tank of the 194th passed the intersection, the signal was given and the bridge was blown.

San Fernando was truly a ghost town. As our tanks moved through, covering the withdrawal, no active contact with the Japs was made. However, hand grenades were hurled at us as we passed dark alleys. There was nothing to do but fire back. Our mission was to cover the withdrawal and no time could be wasted in ferreting out these 5th Column rat's nests.

The last elements of the North Luzon Force (to the north of us) were withdrawing southwesterly through Angeles. All units of the North Force were to reform on what would be known as the Guagua-Porac line. Guagua was on the main highway leading to Bataan. Porac was to the northwest. At Betis, several kilometers to the northeast of Guagua and on the main highway, an outpost was left, for which I furnished one platoon of tanks from Co. "C". The 194th was put into position on the right of the line, or just in the rear of Guagua. The consensus of opinion was that the Japs would push down the main highway and attempt penetration through Guagua. We reached this position at about 5:00 A.M., January 2nd. No enemy activity that day was observed.

The Tank Group Commander and his aide visited our position. We had to stay on the highway with the tanks due to the physical impossibility of operating them off the road. Aware

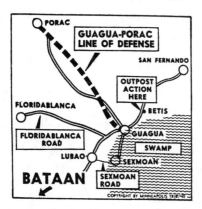

of our responsibility to provide our own local security, we had established two road blocks to the southeast of us. One was to watch the Sexmoan road to our right rear, and the other the Florida-LeBlanca road to our left rear. Thus we would be protected from either right or left in case of Japanese infiltration from those directions. The main body of the 194th was staggered in depth from front to rear. The road blocks consisted of tanks and half-tracks.

General Weaver had seen the two blocks on his way up to our position and asked what they were for. I explained they were for our local security. He immediately stated that the blocks were unnecessary as the Sexmoan route was impassable for the Japs and as long as we had friendly troops to our left, the Florida-Leblanca block was superfluous. He also went on to say that it was merely "frittering away" combat vehicles. Knowing by this time, that an argument would be useless, and would perhaps precipitate a direct order to remove them, I called his attention to something else and changed the subject.

On January 3rd, the enemy contacted the outpost at Betis. After considerable action, the outpost was driven in and the platoon from Co. "C" rejoined the battalion. Jap artillery fire started to register that day and by nightfall was fairly heavy. We had little or nothing to throw against them. Some Jap infiltrations were made through our lines but were disposed of very quickly. Nearly every Jap infantryman carried a one-man mortar. It was very effective. We did not even have the common trench mortar!

The morning of January 4th, hostile artillery fire became intense. By late afternoon, there was no doubt but what the main effort of the Japanese would be against our flank, the right. Strange to say, there was not much enemy air activity against us that day.

Early on the morning of January 5th, it was evident that something would happen. Our right flank was being pounded unmercifully. Mortar and other fire added to the pressure. Enemy air activity stepped up. By noon the position was almost untenable. At about 1:00 P.M., orders were issued for a complete withdrawal from the Guagua-Porac line. This was the first and only daylight withdrawal of the entire campaign. The order stated that the entire line would evacuate toward the left flank (Porac), thence south, via trail and cross country to a point to be designated, thence easterly and reestablish a new line to our rear, astride the main highway. This would be the last line established before retiring to Bataan. The orders went on to state that the 194th Tank Battalion would remain in position on the right flank, protecting the withdrawal, until a clearance order was given. We were then to move to the rear on the highway and establish a temporary line, orders for which would follow.

At about this time, indirect hostile small arms fire was coming through our position from the east—at right angles to us. We were in an extremely precarious situation. The Philippine Army on the right flank with us, was completely shot to pieces and hardly any of them were in position when the orders were received.

We were very much concerned about the two road blocks to our rear. We tried to gain radio contact with them. There was no answer. I sent my S-2 and S-3 in their tanks down the highway to Lubao to check on the blocks. A short time later, they reported by radio stating there were no blocks in place! The following testimony appears in Capt. Spoor's (S-2) affidavit: "When I arrived in Lubao, I found the road blocks had been removed entirely, and later learned, on orders from the Tank Group Commander, that they were to accompany our medical detachment back to Hermosa where Colonel Miller had ordered them that morning. I notified Colonel Miller and he ordered my tank to hold this position until additional combat vehicles could reach the point. Two tanks and two half-tracks, under command of Capt. Fred C. Moffitt reported and took over the position, and a short time later successfully engaged a large column of Japanese on the Sexmoan road."

General Weaver had never notified me in any way that the blocks had been removed. Why he had them accompany the medical detachment, in friendly territory, will always be a mystery to me. Had the block not been in place, the Japanese would have established themselves in our rear, set up a road block of their own, and destroyed us later in the afternoon. The column of Japs included artillery as well as infantry. They had been literally cut to pieces. There ware approximately 500 of them and were led, up the road, by Philippine Constabulary with white flags. Our block was unable to distinguish them from friendly troops until they were quite close. The guns of the block had been laid on ditches as well as the road. There was no escape from that withering fire. A favorite trick of the Japs was to force Filipinos to lead their columns in hopes that the ruse would aid them in their operations.

Immediately following this action, the Japanese air force, as if in vindication, came in and bombed Lubao very heavily. The town was virtually destroyed. It was an inferno.

The bridge, just south of Guagua, had been blown when the withdrawal of the troops to the east was started. This was done as a safety measure so that the Japs could not immediately put too much pressure on our right flank from the front.

At 2:30 P.M. we were still holding our position. Hostile fire became increasingly heavy. Chunks of concrete were blown out of the highway on which the tanks were waiting. Several of the tanks were struck but no serious damage resulted. About this time, Lieutenant Black, liaison officer between Tank Group and ourselves, reported with one of the usual incoherent orders from General Weaver. This never seemed to fail whenever we were in a hot spot. The orders stated that the 194th Tank Battalion would counter attack Guagua immediately!

It was apparent that the Tank Group Commander did not know the true situation. I asked Black (an old 194th officer) if the General knew that a withdrawal was in progress—a *daylight withdrawal*. He replied he was quite sure the situation was not known as he only found it out himself on arrival in our area.

The order for the 194th to counter attack was evidently inspired by the fact that the General had ordered Co. "A" of the 192nd Tank Battalion to launch an attack early that morning against the Japs up a trail which he had picked from his map. It was a trail which did not exist! The company commander, Lt. Bloomfield, had sent back a message stating that no trail existed in that area and that it was impossible to launch any kind of tank attack through the jungle.

Coupled with the order which Lt. Black had brought me, was an order for the 194th, that night, to establish a temporary line in the vicinity of Remedios and that Infantry would be there to meet us. Also, that we would receive further orders at that point. Apparently, the General thought the withdrawal would occur that evening. The Japs did not wait for the usual procedure!

Co. "A", 192nd Tank Battalion, had been in position just to the west of Guagua. It was to follow the troops to the west and then take the Florida-LeBlanca road easterly back to our main highway, in our rear, where it would revert to my command until further orders. At about 3:00 P.M., the company arrived at the prescribed point. They were very glad to see us and we were most happy to see them! I sent this company to the rear to occupy the Remedios position. It warmed our spirits to know that we had a reserve.

At about 3:30 P.M., Major Moses, clearance officer of the withdrawing forces, joined me. After loading quite a number of wounded on a truck, he gave me the clearance order. We proceeded toward Lubao. Hostile fire swept through us from east and north. We returned the fire blindly and finally ran out of it. On the way, we rescued a half-track mounting a 75mm gun. We placed it in our column. After arrival at Lubao, which was still an inferno, we picked up the road blocks together with Captains Johnson and Spoor. Then we moved south to the Remedios position, arriving there about 7:30 P.M.

No Infantry was on hand, nor did any show up. The only troops on the line that night was the 194th Tank Battalion and Co. "A" of the 192nd. No officers from higher headquarters appeared, nor did we get any further orders. Arrangements had been made that afternoon for the kitchen trucks to bring up a hot meal. Capt. Quinlen arrived with them at about the same time that we reached the line. As usual, the spirits of everyone soared most noticeably.

We fully expected someone to come up to our area that evening from Tank Group with orders. Positions were selected, which proved to be the best of any we had had previously. We were astride the highway along an old creek bed. Capt. Altman had reported with a few Bren gun carriers which we had picked up earlier in the campaign from a shipment that had been destined for Singapore. They had been routed to the Philippines from the U.S. War had come before delivery could be made. We had mounted .30 caliber machine guns on the Bren carriers. Half-tracks, tanks and carriers were disposed in line. The command post was about 100 feet in the rear. An outpost was placed at each flank and one down the highway to our immediate front. These outposts consisted of half-tracks and their crews. The moon came up quite late in the evening and gave us excellent visibility—the only locality we had seen where rice paddies or jungle did not exist. It was an old turnip field and we had a wonderful field of fire.

About midnight, becoming greatly concerned with the lack of contact between ourselves and the higher command, and also the withdrawing troops who were supposed to be forming the main line to our rear, I sent Captain Johnson (S-3) to the rear for the purpose of locating Tank Group for further orders and to find out where the main line of resistance was to be formed.

We all needed sleep very badly and it was with a grateful feeling that I fitted myself into the excavation, I had made in the ground, for my hip bones. It felt good. And then, Captain Spoor got restless.

Spoor was uncanny in the way he could almost literally smell trouble. He seemed to have a premonition every time we were about to get into a hot spot. I tried to sleep. Spoor was close by. He was restless from the very start, and finally, it became downright irksome.

"What in hell's the matter with you?" I asked, rolling over.

"I have a hunch we're going to get hit," he replied.

"We have made dispositions and have every bit of security

that is possible," I told him. "If we do get hit, we're in pretty good shape to take care of it."

"I hope so," said the dubious Spoor.

He stretched out, but he didn't go to sleep—and neither did I. My feelings were akin to resentment that he had thrown a wet blanket over our need for rest, and at the same time, I knew he was right.

At about 1:50 A.M., we heard a challenge from our outpost on the road to the north. We could hear voices, sounding like those of Filipinos, in reply. We immediately climbed into our tanks, not knowing what to expect. A group of men had been challenged by the outpost, as they came down the road. When challenged, the reply was made by Filipinos that they were a patrol sent out by our forces and that they were just returning. That was a common occurrence and we had to be careful. That is the reason why I had placed Master Sergeant William Boyd in command of the outpost. If ever there was a combat soldier, who possessed leadership and judgment, Bill Boyd was the man.

A shot was fired by the outpost. We heard the unmistakable guttural howls of Japanese in the patrol. One voice came through, very clearly, in the strange—almost animal-like—Japanese-English.

"We are the peepul who are not afraid to die by boolets," it howled. Japanese always work themselves into a frenzy before attacking. They are taught to howl and chant for their inspiration, much in the same manner as the Indians did in our pioneer days.

Almost immediately, the Japs attacked. They came across the open field in bright moonlight, and started to use what we thought at first was gas. However, it proved to be smoke. A slight breeze came up and blew the smoke back into the Jap lines.

On our left, the Japs attacked in fairly open order. But, east of the road, and particularly toward the right flank, they attacked in column. All of our guns were in operation and the slaughter was terrific.

One of the characteristics of attacking Japanese is infiltration through the opposing lines, by individuals or small groups. Several of these individuals succeeded in reaching our lines but were quickly disposed of. Our machine guns had a certain amount of tracer ammunition in the belts. Either some of these tracers set fire to the grass, some distance in front of the tanks, or it might have been set by Jap tracers. The fire centered in front of Lt. Petree's tank.

Realizing that if the fire gained headway, it might endanger the tanks and set fire to them, and also that the light of the flames would place our tanks in silhouette, Petree climbed out of his tank. Without regard to his own safety, and in the face of extremely heavy enemy fire, he ran toward the fire. He used his coat and put out the conflagration. Miraculously, he received no wounds from the attacking Japanese. *He was shot in the back from the rear of our lines!*

For some reason or other (probably to disguise themselves as Filipinos) many of the Japanese wore white shirts. It was the policy of the Japanese to compel Filipinois to accompany the combat forces so as to present a screen of "friendly" aspect.

At just about the time that Petree was shot, I noticed a movement in one of the trees to our left. With the help of one of my tank crew, we manned the anti-aircraft machine gun on top of the turret. We fired into the tree, using as our target a patch of white, which later proved to be a white shirt. A body dropped from the tree. It was one of the Japs who had infiltrated behind the lines. The men with Petree stated that the shot which struck Petree came from this direction. It was their belief that our "prize" was the one responsible for Petree's wound. He died about one week later. The DSC was awarded posthumously.

Several white flares went up at intervals along our line of tanks. This was always the indication given by Jap infiltrators when they had reached American lines. That signal, however, did not indicate that they would stay in that status very long. They were taken care of immediately.

There was no possible chance for the Japs to make any headway across the open field. I was particularly concerned about our flanks. We had no infantry. Had the Germans been attacking us, a feint would have been made on our front, while the main effort would have been made in an enveloping movement on one or the other flanks. Had the Japs done so, we had nothing to stop them. They did not adopt those tactics that night and we had very little trouble with our flanks.

At about 3:00 A.M., they withdrew, leaving masses of their dead and wounded behind. It was impossible to estimate the number of Japanese casualties. From what we could see, it was tremendous. Nothing was heard from the Japanese until two whole days later—January 7th.

And that was extremely fortunate!

CHAPTER 15

Behind the "Gates"

CAPTAIN JOHNSON had not yet reported back. Knowing that
our situation was precarious, to say the least—realizing that
our orders were to join the new line to our rear before daylight—having no knowledge whatever as to where that line
would be formed—I ordered all wounded to be picked up immediately and taken to the aid station at Hermosa. We later
learned our medical unit had been bombed heavily and much
of our medical equipment and supplies completely destroyed.
After our wounded had been evacuated, orders were issued
for the battalion to move out to the south. In getting the
column organized, one tank went over a steep embankment in
the darkness and overturned. Luckily, no one in the crew was
seriously injured. We tried to rescue the tank but the grade
was so steep that it was impossible. We removed the weapons,
twisted off the gasoline valves in the crew compartment, and
shot 37 mm armor piercing bullets through the motor, setting
the tank on fire. We were entirely unmolested.

Plans for movement to the rear were made on the spur of
the moment. We would make short jumps of perhaps two
kilometers and rapidly deploy, astride the highway. If nothing developed, we would do the same thing again. I was in
hopes that Johnson would soon arrive with information and
orders.

At our first stop, we came upon some 155mm guns (World
War I vintage) being set up. The battery commander told me
he had been ordered, late that afternoon, to place the guns in
this position as a reserve for the Guagua-Porac line! I asked
him if he had not heard of the withdrawal made that afternoon, and if he had not passed through our troops forming
a new line. He replied that he had not heard of the withdrawal, nor had he seen anyone on his trip north. I then inquired if he had not heard the firing a little earlier in the
vicinity of Remedios. To this, he replied in the negative. This
was due to the fact that his guns were tractor drawn.

I told him what had happened. He probably was the most grateful man I have ever met. Had he been allowed to go into position, the Japs would have captured all the guns. The top speed of these tractors was about six miles per hour! We didn't know it then, but those 155's were to be something that we almost worshipped in Bataan. The battery commander immediately turned around and took the guns to the rear. We covered his movement as best we could. There was no enemy contact.

About 5:00 A.M., we proceeded very slowly to the rear. Daylight, as I recall it, came at about 6:30 A.M. We hunted for cover and disposed the battalion into position along the railroad grade and astride the highway. It was a very poor position with little field of fire, but was the best we could find.

At about 7:15 A.M., having heard nothing further, I took a Jeep and proceeded to the rear. After traveling about one kilometer, I met Capt. Johnson on his way up. With him was Colonel Moran, one of the officers of the withdrawing forces. He said that the troops had had an extremely tough time of it making their way cross country. They were completely fatigued. He stated they would be put in line as soon as possible, along the railroad tracks, where we already had our tanks. It was about 5:00 P.M. that day before the troops were on the line. No Jap hostility, except a few scattered shells of shrapnel, was encountered. The 194th has always wondered what would have happened to Bataan, if they had not fought the action with the Japs, in the early morning hours of that day. The survivors of both the 192nd and 194th Tank Battalions are also wondering why General Wainwright completely ignored tank actions in his book.

Capt. Johnson accompanied me back to the command post of the 194th and told me the story of what had happened to the mission I had sent him on at midnight, the night before. After receiving his orders from me, he had picked up the battalion communications officer, Lieutenant Fleming, who was anxious to check communication installations with Sgt. Aaram at our rear echelon. He had been denied this opportunity the day before, the story of which appears later in this chapter.

Arriving at our rear echelon, Johnson immediately contacted Major Canby, 194th executive officer, and Capt. Muir, S-1. He learned that Tank Group Headquarters was located in the immediate area. Awakening the G-3, he was informed that the Tank Group Commander was asleep. Johnson made a report of our operations of the past 24 hours and then asked why we had not been informed as to where the new line would be established. The G-3 stated that Tank Group had no information whatever. Johnson then said that it was apparent he would have to find General Wainwright's headquarters (North Luzon Force) and get the information there. G-3 suggested that it was a good idea but only knew the general area in which the headquarters was located.

Johnson and Fleming traveled to the area and parked the Jeep about a half mile off the road. They floundered around in the darkness for quite a time, finally found the creek bottom, which had been one of the general directions, traversed this for a quarter of a mile—and located Headquarters North Luzon Force.

Colonel Merril, G-3, was awake and in conference with another officer whom Johnson did not recognize. It was about 5:30 A.M. Johnson reported and asked where the new line would be formed. The Colonel stated that there would be no change at this time.

Johnson asked him if he realized what had happened during the last 24 hours. The reply was that there had been very little change! It was evident that the headquarters had received no report, at least relative to the fighting around Guagua, Porac, Lubao and Sexmoan. Therefore, Johnson gave him the entire report in detail and ended up by saying that these positions were not only under control of the Japanese but were occupied by them. The G-3's answer was to the effect that this information must be wrong.

Then Johnson, realizing the immediate danger to our entire force and the future of Bataan, exploded with something that a junior officer does not usually say to a senior.

"God dammit, Colonel! I know I'm right! *I was there!*" And he again reiterated the details. Naturally he knew nothing of our latest engagement with the Japs after he had left on his mission.

The G-3, apparently realizing that the information was correct, thanked him for it. He knew Johnson personally, having had associations with him at Stotsenburg before the war pertaining to our S-3 matters. But he could offer no information whatever as to the new line, or any other pertinent information. There was nothing else for Johnson to do except to depart and come back up until he found the 194th.

Thus it was that 16½ hours, *after this crucial withdrawal had started,* headquarters of North Luzon Force, under the command of General Wainwright, knew nothing about it! Are we egotistical in stating, that had not the 194th Tank Battalion been located at the right places, and the right times, there would have been no Bataan?

Lt. Fleming then told me about the mission I had sent him on the day before, when the fighting was heavy in the Guagua area. We were much concerned with our radio communications between forward and rear installations. Fleming had been engaged that morning in Guagua, removing cans of food supplies from a box car which was on the tail end of a train that had been bombed and was burning. He and his men removed a good portion of the supplies and had loaded them on a truck which we had salvaged from the ditch. It was a Filipino commercial vehicle. Jap artillery fire splintered the box car and Fleming, with his men, drove the truck proudly into the tank area. I told him to send the truck to our dump in the rear, check communications, and to also give Capt. Quinlen some instructions on gasoline and other supply arrangements. This was about 1:00 P.M. He dispatched the truck and a little later started out in his Jeep.

Just prior to reaching the Supply Point, he met the Tank Group Commander, who stopped him and asked where his half-tracks were. Fleming told the General that he had no half-tracks, that he was the battalion communications officer. Weaver certainly should have known Fleming. He had "kidnapped" him the night of December 31st, *after* he had given me orders to move the 194th in the area east of San Fernando. I was without my battalion communications officer until we arrived at Guagua on January 2nd! Weaver had ordered Fleming and his crew to remain on the Calumpit Bridge, and never notified me of his order! Nor was Fleming ever used for whatever the General had in his mind.

Weaver now told this officer to take a half-track and go to Guagua. The General pointed out a half-track setting alongside the road. Fleming replied that he had just come from Guagua on a direct mission for me. He also pointed out that the vehicle, designated by the commander, had been sent to the rear because of mechanical failure which had not been repaired. In spite of this, Weaver insisted that Fleming go to Guagua. The only mission seemed to be that he would reinforce the 194th. After much difficulty with the clutch, the half-track was put in motion and moved toward Lubao and Guagua.

After limping to within one-half kilometer of Lubao, Fleming had to stop because of tanks and trucks moving against him down the road. These were the vehicles of Co. "A", 192nd Tank Battalion, which I had ordered to the Remedios area for the initial establishment of the temporary line we were to occupy that night. No other troops were allowed on this highway. It was reserved for the 194th and the attached Co. "A", which was holding the entire right flank for the withdrawing troops to the west. Fleming patiently waited for the column to pass.

Several minutes later, General Weaver advanced down the road in his Jeep. At some distance, he stopped and sent for Fleming. On reporting, the lieutenant was asked why he had stopped, to which he replied that the road was jammed and he had to stop. The General then asked for Fleming's map, and marked thereon the temporary position the 194th would occupy that night.

About this time, the company of tanks started to pass. The Tank Group Commander ordered Fleming to stop one of them, turn it around, and go back to Lubao and lead the 194th through the town. He stated that we were opposed by a strong enemy force and were in serious trouble.

The tank already had a full crew but Fleming piled in on top of them, despite their vociferous protests, and was able to get as far as the bridge in the southern part of Lubao before traffic again forced him to stop. Luckily, he encountered Captains Spoor and Johnson, whom, it will be remembered I had sent down to investigate our missing road blocks. He found that the situation had not changed and was told why they were in the area. Fleming did not dare to start out on his mission for me again, for fear of running ino the General. Therefore, at the advice of Johnson and Spoor, he attached himself to them and, at the same time, kept a wary eye out for the Commander.

And now, back to where we left off the morning of January 6th, establishing the new line along the railroad grade. General Weaver came up about noon and told me there would be a withdrawal that night, into Bataan, and that we would cover it. He also showed me, on the map, the position the 194th would occupy after covering the withdrawal. He stated that he and Major Smythe (executive officer of Tank Group) had selected this position with a view of giving the battalion's personnel badly needed rest, and a chance to have our maintenance platoon service the tanks. Our tanks were track-laying vehicles, and needed service continually, if they were to be kept in operation. We had been on the move almost constantly, from one end of Luzon to the other. There had been no chance for maintenance and service other than the proverbial "lick and a promise."

Both officers and men of the battalion were nearly out on their feet from lack of sleep. After riding in a tank, for even a short distance, the individual's equilibrium is impaired for some time to come. This is due to the terrific vibration, jolting, and noise of these mechanized vehicles.

Add to this the night marches we had conducted, the fighting we had been engaged in, the irregularity of meals, and the continual strain of being the rearmost elements in the withdrawing forces—one can readily realize the condition most of us were in. And we had no infantry whatever to cover any sneak attack at night on the tanks.

When General Weaver spoke the welcome words—where we could rest and have maintenance—morale shot up one hundred percent!

The withdrawal started after dark that night. It was entirely without event and we crossed the bridge, near the Layoc Junction, at about 2:00 A.M., January 7th. Phase 2 of the Orange Plan (WPO-3) had been successfully completed—as far as troops were concerned. The 194th Tank Battalion was the last unit to go into Bataan.

We had been given to understand that Bataan was impregnable and that fortifications and other strong points had been built up. We were also told that a strong line had been formed at the extreme north end of Bataan, known as the Layoc Junction line. Imagine our feelings and utter amazement to discover that hardly any preparations had been made,

other than a few minor excavations—fox holes—where individuals had made them! The line, in our vicinity was held by
the 31st U.S. Infantry.

Arrangements had been made with Major Canby to have a
hot meal ready for the battalion, as soon as we arrived at the
trail junction leading into our area. We arrived and pulled off
the road and up the trail. It was bright moonlight now. Major
Canby was there with the kitchen trucks. He called me aside
and said that he had disobeyed the Tank Group Commander's orders. I asked him what he meant. Canby replied that
the General had ordered him to take all of the rear installations into our new area that had been picked for rest and
maintenance. He had made a thorough reconnaissance of the
area and found it to be a veritable rat trap. Therefore, he had
not moved the rear echelon until he could talk to me. He also
stated that we would be much closer to the front line than
perhaps I had thought. I asked how far that was and he replied not more than 500 yards! I told him, if we were called
on by the General, to state that he had conferred with me and
I had decided not to move the echelon until conferring with
the General. Canby was a conservative individual and if he
thought the area was a rat trap—*it was!*

We had our meal and the world looked bright again. Then
we looked at the area in question. We found that Canby had
been downright modest in his description. It was not only a
rat trap—it was *the* rat trap, if there ever was one. The trail
into the place was loaded with hairpin curves over very
treacherous terrain. Under no circumstances could it be negotiated at night unless the moon was up. The area itself, was
high up on an elevation. It was flat and provided fair cover.
It was, as Canby said, about 500 yards behind the front lines.
This meant, that any combat at all with the Japanese, would
result in our position being immediately under fire! This
would also mean, due to the one-way entrance into the place,
that there would be no chance of getting out of it or of conducting any warfare of a mobile nature, if a break-through
were made. The area between the front line and ourselves
was jungle and precipitous. It precluded any possibility of
moving tanks in that direction. In view of what General
Weaver had told me, that this was the area for rest and maintenance of equipment, it led me to believe that he had no

knowledge of where the front line really had been established.

At about 8:00 A.M. that morning, January 7th, Japanese artillery began to register very heavily and accurately in our vicinity. Shortly before this, General Weaver and his aide visited our position. I told him our rear echelon had not been brought in, and worded the explanation in such a way as to lead him to believe the decision had been left to me. He accepted my remarks without further comment.

The 192nd Tank Battalion had preceded us into the area the night before and their Co. "A" had been turned back to them. Our maintenance platoon waded through the Japanese barrage and did what little servicing they could, between the whines of Jap shells. We sent them back about noon.

The General pointed out another area on the map, to the rear, which he had selected for rest and maintenance, entirely ignoring the previous day's orders. He said we were to enter this area at any time that night after darkness.

The Jap artillery had raised havoc with some of the few 75mm gun positions of our forces, and had scored direct hits. This was the first time I had witnessed their artillery as being very effective. Usually, they were not. They evidently had direct observation. Although shells landed in our area all day, there were no casualties.

At about 6:30 P.M. that day, part of our front line broke. They had been hammered unmercifully, all day long, in their unprepared positions by Jap artillery, mortar and small arms fire. They had little to throw back other than their own small arms fire. A break at this point had occurred earlier in the afternoon, but had been closed again within a short time.

When the second break was made, it came directly through our tank positions. As senior officer, I immediately ordered both battalions to prepare for movement and assemble in column on the main road to the east. This was our only chance. How those two battalions negotiated the trail can be credited only to the nerve and determination of the drivers. It was dusk but still light enough to distingush, faintly, the outline of the route.

Assembling on the main road, we threw out local security and prepared as best we could to take care of eventualities as they occurred. At about the same time, the executive officer of Tank Group appeared with an infantry commander. After conferring with them on the situation, I found that another withdrawal was scheduled and that the advance units had already started. The next line would be the Abucay-Hacienda line which was further south. The executive officer had been sent up to confirm the General's order for us to proceed to the area mentioned in his order.

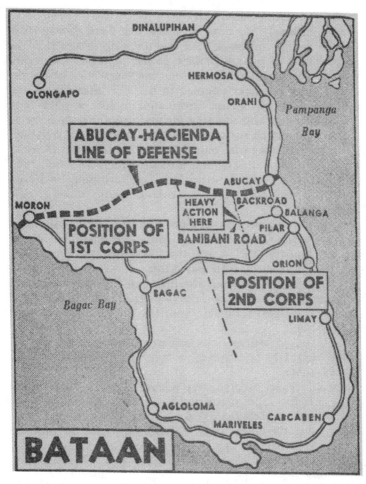

A messenger was immediately dispatched to our rear echelon, with orders for the kitchen trucks to meet us at our new bivouac position with a hot meal. We had eaten nothing but iron rations, early in the morning, due to the impossibility of bringing the trucks or kitchen personnel through the Jap artillery fire.

We arrived about 1:00 A.M. The moon was up and the trucks were on hand to greet us. I issued orders for everyone to eat before bivouacking.

Then we heard a loud roar.

Looking across the clearing, I saw the Tank Group Commander in his underwear. He was shouting orders that the tanks should be placed in their proper positions. No reconnaissance had been made and no one knew just where the proper positions were supposed to be. The area was on the northern slope of Mount Samat and heavily wooded. The Commander was also shouting for me in no uncertain terms.

The sight struck me so funny that I burst out laughing. Perhaps I was somewhat punch drunk. Probably we all were. Anyway, we were all laughing without being very loud about it. I quickly hid behind a truck. Lt. Ted Spaulding, who happened to be behind the truck, was also making noises of subdued mirth.

"If you ever want to do me a favor, do it know," I told him. "Report to the General and tell him I'm somewhere in the area but probably still out on the road. And tell him it was my orders to feed the battalion before we did anything else." If I had faced the General that night, in his underwear and under those circumstances, I know that I would have burst out laughing right in his face and that would not have been good—for me!

Ted mastered his emotions and struck out bravely. He repeated what I had told him to say. The conversation was clearly audible.

General Weaver ordered, very vehemently, that the vehicles be put in their proper places and under cover before the food was served. He said there was no need to make such a rumpus, anyway, when the tanks came in. Too much noise, he insisted. He then went back to bed. A temporary Tank Group Command Post had been set up right in our area. That was not very comforting.

Spaulding reported back. Orders were relayed to the Tankers. The vehicles were put away as best we could. In spite of the injustice of the whole affair, very little grumbling was heard! I always did suspicion, however, that some of the tank motors made more noise than was necessary! Every once in awhile, one man would look at another and start laughing.

Had it been daylight with danger of air observation and had we been liable to combat duty in this area, there would have been an excuse for the order. But we were at least 10 kilometers behind the Abucay-Hacienda line, which was already occupied by troops together with artillery installations.

As soon as daylight arrived, the tanks were properly placed and soon our maintenance crews, from the rear echelon, were at work. This was the first rest for the combat elements since December 24th.

Early that morning, the General sent for me, and I joined him together with the commander of the 192nd Tank Battalion. Nothing was said relative to the night before. A general discussion followed as to the situation and I was told that we would go into complete maintenance and servicing. He was most affable and courteous. There were times that I liked the General very much. I admired his choice of English and his courtesy. His bravery, I could never question. But there were other times when I almost hated him.

CHAPTER 16

The Abucay-Hacienda Line

AT ABOUT THE time of the withdrawal from the Layoc Junction line, the North Luzon Force under General Wainwright, became I Corps. The South Luzon Force under General Parker, became II Corps. Bataan was divided up between the two corps, with II Corps occupying the line from Manila Bay, west through Abucay to a point west of what was known as the Hacienda. The sector of I Corps started in the vicinity of Moron, on the west coast of Bataan, and thence easterly to meet II Corps. The point of contact was not physically occupied. This point of division was in thick jungles and in an extremely mountainous region. Because it was not actually occupied by troops, combat patrols were used to cover the breach. They made periodical visits. Without any reflections on the high command, this proved to be our weakest point in the organization of that line. We had not yet learned that the Japanese were strongest when participating in jungle warfare. When a piece of terrain was evaluated (in the white man's mind) as being impossible, we were interrupted by the Japs making use of it.

For the most part, from this time on, the 194th Tank Battalion's activities were with II Corps. It was now, that it was truly brought home to us, the sad lack of tank parts which were badly needed. How we could have used even a fraction of that shipment received at the Port Area in Manila, but which was left for the Japs! Our maintenance crews dug to the bottom of the bag, improvised, and created miracles. The meager amount of tank supplies that we carried in the maintenance section, was exhausted. No other parts were available except a small supply which was normally carried by the 17th Ordnance Company. This was the unit that serviced both tank battalions in what was known as Fourth Echelon Maintenance—major overhauls.

As for food—on entering Bataan on January 7th—orders greeted us that all troops would go on half rations. This was not too difficult at first. We served two meals a day, at 8:00 A.M. and from 4:00 to 5:00 P.M., dividing the half ration between the two. We also apportioned the food we had salvaged, into the two meals. Everyone in the battalion was made to go through the mess line, so as to eliminate any suspicion that someone else was getting more than his share. Our salvaged food helped a great deal but not for long. There was not enough of it.

For two or three days, our personnel received a good rest. By this time, the Abucay-Hacienda line had been organized in the II Corps sector. I Corps had also organized.

The Japanese started their main push against the right of the line, in the Abucay area. The 57th Infantry (Philippine Scouts), together with the rest of their combat team, was located here. What little artillery we had, was composed of 75mm and 155mm guns—all of World War I vintage. The actual number of guns was very few.

The Japs had modern equipment. They had the new 105mm gun which outranged our old 155mm rifle. In spite of this, our artillery was handled so much better than the Japanese, that there was no comparison in the damage done. The Jap did not seem to know how to use his artillery intelligently. Had our forces been equipped with modern weapons, it is extremely doubtful that the Japs could have even placed their artillery close enough to register.

Fighting was terrific and bloody in the Abucay area. There was much hand-to-hand combat. The highest tribute I can pay to the Philippine Scouts, who were officered by Americans and had been trained in prewar years as a part of the American Army, is, that I have never seen, nor do I ever expect to see, any better or braver soldiers than the Scouts. They were truly an inspiration.

There were many acts of heroism. The Japs attempted attack after attack, with numerically superior forces and every weapon at their disposal. They failed in every attempt. Casualties in the Scouts were high, but their determination and bravery was unsurpassed. They never complained, accepting whatever fate might bring them. They looked with disdain upon the Philippine Army. The Filipino considered the Scout with the highest of admiration. And the Scouts earned every bit of it!

It was at Abucay that we really began to learn something about the Jap and jungle warfare. Infiltration of individual Japs through the lines, dressed as Filipinos, became quite prevalent. They would anchor themselves in trees, behind the lines, camouflaged quite carefully so they were not visible, and would secure themselves by binding their bodies to the limbs. They would watch particularly for officers and noncommissioned officers, and would pick them off.

Some of these snipers, found after they had been killed, had in their possession a kind of drug, which evidently made them immune to hunger or anything that might deter them from their mission. The situation grew so bad, that it became necessary to organize combat patrols with the express mission of cleaning out snipers.

There seems to be a feeling prevalent among those in our Armed Forces, who are not Tankers, that whenever a situation develops, which cannot be coped with successfully, that tanks can do the job—whether it be walking on water or flying through the air. The attitude, in the Philippines, was no different.

Evidently because of the armor plate on a tank, request after request was made that tanks be employed in hunting out snipers. When a little thought is given to the subject, one can readily see that in order to hunt out snipers—the sniper, first of all, must be seen. Visibility inside of a tank is very limited, to say the least. To have complied with the requests would have meant, that the Tankers would have been compelled to get out of the tanks to find the snipers, thus making them the same kind of patrol which was already being used. The fact also remained that most of the terrain was impassable for tanks.

During a day of particularly heavy fighting at Abucay, I was ordered to report to an old Catholic Church in that town. It housed the command post of the 57th Combat Team. There I was to meet the Group Commander.

A consultation was in progress amidst heavy shelling by the Japs. I was immediately called into it with the urgent request that tanks be employed on the sniper mission. Explaining the fallacy of using tanks on this type of mission, a skeptical attitude prevailed. At this point, General Weaver arrived. After conferring with him, we both went back into the consultation, and in no uncertain terms, the General told them that tanks would not be used for snipers. He also explained why. This settled the issue.

While we were at the command post, the Japanese launched another of their vicious attacks. Shells, landing in the area, vomited and spewed death and destruction. Jap aircraft bombed and strafed. The din was deafening. The very earth, under our feet, shook with the intensity of that attack. The Devil's brew nearly succeeded in boiling over that day—but it failed! The Scouts turned the tide again, with acts of heroism, which made history. The wounded—mangled—shot through and through—uncomplaining—no whimpering! These were the Scouts—who also loved—and believed in—America!

The Japanese must have suffered tremendously that day.

The next day, I received an order from General Weaver, that tanks would proceed close to the area containing snipers, and that crews would then get out of their tanks and hunt for snipers! Why? I don't know. This was just one of the inconsistencies of the Tank Group Commander.

We sent some platoons into the sector and conformed with the order. However, we saw to it that the tanks were not taken close to where the hunt would take place.

At this time, the 194th Tank Battalion was also responsible for part of the beach defense on Manila Bay. For the most part, we assigned half-tracks to that mission. Jap aircraft hovered overhead almost all the time.

The crews worked out a system of baiting Jap planes. They used a large piece of white cloth. Each time planes were approaching, certain of the men would get out in the road and wildly wave the cloth in an effort to lure the Jap into flying low. It was somewhat like a bull fight. Sometimes, the ruse worked. The Jap does not like to "lose face" and, in quite a number of instances, would immediately dive and strafe the "toreadors" with a deluge of bullets and, sometimes, bombs. The half-tracks, carefully camouflaged, then went into action with their .50 caliber machine guns. Several Jap planes were brought down by this method. It proved to be quite a game, and a hot argument always ensued, whenever a plane was brought down, as to who was responsible!

During this period, orders were received from General Weaver, to send one company of tanks over to I Corps on the west side of Bataan. The Japs had made a push and had succeeded in breaking through our lines in the vicinity of Moron. An attempt was going to be made to close the gap.

Company "C", under command of Capt. Fred Moffitt, was sent on the mission. After arrival, they were met by General Wainwright and his staff. They were ordered to go north on a trail and were told that infantry would precede them. It was pointed out by Capt. Moffitt and the platoon leaders, that close infantry support would be absolutely necessary because of the thick jungle and the fact that the tanks would be unable to get off the trail. Attention was also called to the pie-pan mines with which the Japanese were equipped. While not able to blow up a tank, they could blow off tracks and idlers. The answer was that the infantry, preceding them, would be spread out in skirmish line for a long distance on each side of the trail, and would comb the jungle for any Japs that might be lurking there. The Tankers again urged close infantry support. One Jap in the jungle, near the trail, could toss or hide these pie-pan mines, in the path of the tanks and the damage would be done. However, no infantry was given for the close support needed. The tanks were ordered to proceed as per the plan. Wainwright was most impatient.

The infantry went forward. It was evident, later, that either the plan was not well organized or proper supervision was not given. The skirmish line probably did not extend more than 150 feet on each side of the trail.

The first platoon of tanks moving up the trail was suddenly stopped when explosions occurred beneath the two leading tanks. The very thing had happened against which the Tankers had warned. Japs had infiltrated behind the infantry from one or both flanks. When the infantry was out of sight, the pie-pan mines were laid in the trail and covered so they could not be seen.

Idlers and tracks on both tanks were badly damaged. It was impossible to proceed with the others until the damaged tanks had been repaired. Luckily, the infantry was successful in straightening out the line. My command post received an urgent call to send over the necessary parts. The fiasco drained my maintenance section of track links and idlers. We had no more.

The executive officer of Tank Group became incensed over

the affair and wrote a scathing report to USAFFE Headquarters at Corregidor. It was evidently approved by General Weaver. The report severely criticized General Wainwright for allowing such asinine use of tanks. Sometime soon after, the General saw this report. It did not improve the relations between him and the Tankers, particularly so after General MacArthur left for Australia and Wainwright become the supreme commander!

During the time the Abucay-Hacienda line was held, our primary mission was to be in a state of readiness to bolster up any part of the line where it might be needed. It was almost impossible to use tanks off any of the trails. From time to time we received calls to go to various points.

Once in the dead of night, we received an urgent call to take tanks to one of the command posts of a front line unit. The call stated that the CP was surrounded by Japs and that probably a break-through had been accomplished. No moon was shining. The tanks had to grope their way through the darkness. Progress was no faster than a man could walk. It was necessary to put one of the crew ahead of each tank to guide it, and another crew member behind each tank to act as infantry support, to watch for Jap infiltrators who might be lurking along the trail.

Arriving at the scene, they found the trouble already taken care of. A few Japs had infiltrated, fired several shots in the darkness, and then had disappeared. At about the same time, it was thought that Jap machine guns had opened fire on the command post. A favorite trick of the Nips was their use of firecrackers. They were equipped with bunches of them which closely approximated the sound of their .25 caliber machine gun with which the Japs were generously equipped. Infiltrators would set off bunches of these fire crackers, during the night, at various points, preferably behind our lines. It was particularly effective among Philippine Army units. The trick was used as an attempt to cause panic in the ranks of untrained troops. It was entirely successful in a number of instances. Fear of the unknown is a most terrible thing to witness among untrained and undisciplined troops. Sheer, uncontrolled panic is the result.

Our 155 mm guns were very effective in this area. The Japs hated them, with only the kind of hate, a Jap can display. It

was a frustrated hate, born of that all important characteristic—loss of face. Japanese airplanes continually sought these
guns out. They were extremely few in number and therefore
made it harder to find them. At the start of the war, I have it
from the artillerymen themselves, that only about 40 some
odd 155's were available in the Philippines. We had a much
lesser amount on Bataan. After the surrender, the Japs insisted
there were more guns than they found. They also insisted that
there was another battalion of tanks.

The usual procedure the Nips used, was the use of a reconnaissance plane. Every time he showed up, we knew what to
expect. We called this type of plane "Photo Joe." The plane
would circle lazily and leisurely over the area. When he
thought he had located a target, he would go into a half-
hearted dive. Almost immediately, three bombers would appear, from where they had been hiding beyond our ground
vision, and dive on the spot designated by Photo Joe, dropping a load of bombs.

Most of the bombing in Bataan was terribly inaccurate. I
have never seen them do any real dive bombing. It was simply a glide. The 155's were manned by Philippine Scouts under American officers and they nearly drove the Japs crazy.
It came to be a game of hide and seek. The bombers, after
dropping their load on what they supposed to be the target,
would no sooner get over the tree tops when the 155 would
speak again! And sure enough, Photo Joe would come back
to take another look. Sometimes it was possible to knock him
down. Knowing the Japanese as I do, there is no doubt in my
mind that the pilots of these planes, together with their crews,
either did a lot of propaganda work in their own behalf, with
their superiors, or else reverently bowed in the direction of
the Imperial Palace, the abode of the Son of Heaven, and
partook of the traditional belly slashing! They seldom hit any
of the gun positions and their frustration was evidenced by
the vicious return of the planes.

One afternoon, Captain Spoor and myself had made a detailed reconnaissance of the front lines in which there was a
great deal of heavy bombing. The Nips had dropped one
bomb in a grove of trees—evidently for luck as there was no
indication of troop activity. It happened to house a medical
unit. The bomb caused 19 casualties. Late in the afternoon,

we started back to the CP. The game of hide and seek was still in progress. It had centered on one particular gun and the Japs had concentrated on that one gun since about noon! It was apparent that they were at their wits end. The gun had been scoring hits all day. Bombs had been dropped repeatedly but had failed to reach their target.

The Japs had tried various tricks to locate the victim. The three bombers had separated and poised themselves at three different points. Photo Joe tried to hide himself by not flying directly over the area where he thought the gun was hidden. When his judgment told him he was right, he came in from the rear with his half-hearted dive. All three bombers came in like three dogs after a bone, and singly dropped their load—but the gun remained untouched!

The Japanese did not usually fly at night and we could tell when the last flight would be made. As Spoor and I rode down the trail in our Jeep, I remarked that probably there would be one more run by the Japs. It was almost impossible to move a vehicle down the trail without making a cloud of dust. The dry season in the Philippines (Luzon) is just what it implies. Except for a somewhat damp atmosphere at night, it is as dry as the proverbial bone. Just walking down that trail would raise the dust.

Sure enough, the Japs made another try. Photo Joe came over, circling leisurely, and suddenly went into a dive at our cloud of dust. The cloud hung in the air for some distance.

Spoor was driving and it was my duty to watch for planes. I yelled. "Here he comes!"

We were traveling at a very slow rate of speed. Spoor shut off the ignition and we dived for the ditch. "Joe" let loose with machine gun bullets which did not come anywhere near us. We expected the bombers to follow. They did.

They bombed, with all three planes, the cloud of dust, and missed us by almost a quarter of a mile!

CHAPTER 17

Between Outpost and Japs

THE JAPANESE HAD sustained such heavy losses in the Abucay area that they completely abandoned the attack. They also evacuated their area to the north. Our patrols verified the fact that the enemy was reorganizing. After the fall of Bataan, when we were reunited with some of our people who had been taken prisoner in the early stages of the war, we learned of the fatalism and fear, displayed by the Japs, during the siege of Bataan. Had not the huge second invasion force been sent in later on, there is no doubt, but what this original force, would have had to depend on starvation and disease, to accomplish their mission of forcing our surrender. Americans, who were prisoners, witnessed the actions and movements of Jap troops behind the lines. Those ordered to the front, went most reluctantly. Parties were held, at which the death of departing officers, was toasted. At least, on one occasion, a group of Japs was forced into the lines by their own gun fire in the rear! Many of the parties were hysterical with the usual Jap procedure of working themselves into a frenzy, tears being shed copiously, while drinking toasts to their death! They hated Bataan and the forces who occupied it.

Information, brought in by our patrols and from other intelligence sources, disclosed the fact that the Japanese were concentrating to the north of the left flank of II Corps. It will be remembered that this left flank was not physically joined with the right flank of I Corps, because of the heavy jungles and mountainous terrain, but was visited by our combat patrols from time to time. This left flank was the weak spot. The Jap is a past master in infiltration. A considerable number succeeded in infiltrating through this part of the line. They conducted no organized attack but satisfied themselves, for the present, with small harassing actions. However, it was apparent, that the threat was serious and could not be disregarded.

One of the Philippine Army organizations had been put

into position on our left flank when the line was first established, because it was felt that this portion of the line would have the least trouble and would be easiest to defend. Supplying them with rations was rather difficult, due to the terrain and the absence of adequate supply routes. Therefore, supply was not regular. The Philippine Army could never understand half-ration. All they knew was that they were hungry. Promises and explanations did their stomachs no good. They knew there was food somewhere and they wanted to get it. One day, no food whatever arrived. Many of the Filipinos left their guns in place and evacuated the position. They came to the rear for something to eat. Just like that! In all honesty, I am thoroughly convinced that they intended to eat, and then return and fight some more. At any rate, the Japanese were on the alert, walked in and took possession of that part of the line!

On the night of January 14th-15th, the 45th Infantry (Philippine Scouts) were ordered to move out from I Corps for the sector evacuated by the Philippine Army. After a most hectic and soul-trying march through the jungles, they arrived at the Hacienda on the night of 16th-17th. The 31st U. S. Infantry had also been ordered into the breach and, together with the 45th Infantry, counter attacked. The Japs were in very strong positions which were not difficult to defend. Fighting was extremely heavy and the enemy had strong reserves. Our forces were always sadly lacking in this respect. Part of the breach was closed with heavy casualties resulting on both sides. The Japs staged a counter attack on this part of the line but were repulsed very decisively. One soldier in the 31st Infantry was manning a machine gun. A group of Japs attacked. He sprayed them with the gun. They went down like flies. One Jap remained out of the entire group and was bearing down on the lone soldier, with gun and bayonet ready for the kill. By this time, the gun belt was empty and there was no time to reload. The soldier, without rising, reached for his pistol and very calmly shot down the onrushing Jap. It was found afterwards, that the group had contained 30 Japanese!

Because of the extreme precarious condition of the left flank, and the infiltration which had taken place, the high command decided upon another withdrawal. Orders had not been issued but it was evident they would be forthcoming before long. It was impossible to close the breach because of the strong position of the Japs. We had neither the men nor the equipment to do the job.

On January 22nd, General Weaver ordered a conference for the commanding officers and staffs of the 192nd and 194th Tank Battalions. At this conference, he stated that he had a plan in mind which should bring some good results. The general withdrawal order had not been issued but it would be; we would cover the withdrawal; we would then remain out in front of the new line and "raise hell with the Japanese by overrunning them as they moved up!" Captains Johnson and Spoor joined me in calling attention to the fact that the tanks would have no chance to operate except on the trails. We also mentioned that several stream crossings were involved, in which bridges would be blown.

The Tank Group Comamnder became incensed. He made a number of sarcastic remarks and added a bit of bellowing. The conference came to an end soon afterward with pointed instructions from the General to lay our plans. The three of us walked away.

"It's too damned bad we don't have a bottle of whiskey," commented Spoor, "then we could celebrate our suicide in advance!" He voiced the thoughts of all of us.

We talked the situation over among ourselves and tried to find some solution to it. We told no one else but the rest of the staff because we knew it could mean nothing else than complete annihilation of the entire battalion. We tried, in every possible way, to think our way out of the mess, but it was like the turning of a wheel—we always came back to the point from where we started. There was no solution.

On January 24th, the good Lord came to our aid. The withdrawal order of the high command was issued. It stated that a general withdrawal would be made to the Pilar-Bagac line during the night of January 24th-25th; that the main force would start at dusk on the 24th and would leave what is known as a shell, from each unit, on the front lines to cover up the evacuation of the main body; that at 3:00 A.M. on January 25th, the shell would withdraw to positions north of the Pilar-Bagac line, on Banibani Road, where it would serve as an outpost during the day, so as to allow the main line of resistance to be formed and organized; that on the night of January 25th-26th, the outpost would withdraw and *all* troops would be behind the main line of resistance (Pilar-Bagac) by daylight of January 26th; and that the tanks would cover all withdrawals.

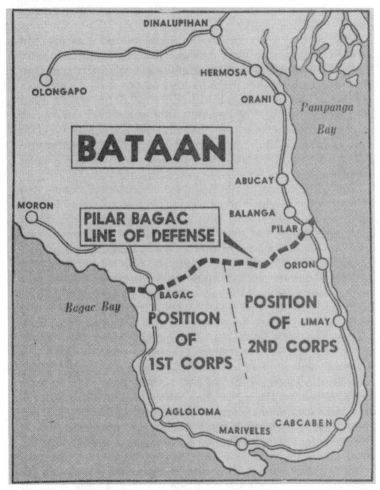

This order thwarted the efforts of the Tank Group Commander to keep us out in front after everyone else had withdrawn. That same day, he issued the following order:

The 192nd Tank Battalion was to cover the withdrawal of those forces in the Abucay area. The 194th Tank Battalion was to cover the withdrawal of all forces in the Hacienda area, or center and left flank units of II Corps. Also that I was to act as Clearance Officer and all shell commanders would report through me as they withdrew. We were told that further orders would be issued later in the day.

Some of the tank units of the 194th had been in position on the front lines for some days and had been pounded pretty badly. It was necessary to consummate a hurried reorganization which, under the circumstances was not so easy. Only two exits were available for the withdrawal of II Corps—the main road on the east side of Bataan, and a trail which was known as Back Road between Abucay and the Hacienda. We laid our plans and issued the necessary orders. The Clearance Point was set at the junction of Back Road and Hacienda Road.

The withdrawals of the main forces started at about 6:00 P.M., January 24th. The two exits were completely blocked. Had the Japs used even ordinary intelligence, there would have been a mass slaughter. Bringing out the Philippine Army was like herding a flock of sheep. It was a milling mob, totally unfamiliar with what was going on. Officers and non-commissioned officers—both Filipino and American—worked like mad to keep some semblance of military organization. The main body of the Philippine Army, anxious to please, only made matters worse. Eager to obey the half-understood commands, they only knew that it was desired they move down the road as quickly as possible. Trained troops know that it is all important to maintain road space and unit organization. The Filipino soldiers shoved and pushed—bent only on satisfying, somehow, the demanding voices of command. The result was a continual milling, sweating mass of humanity. Units intermingled with other units and became hopelessly lost in the mob. It was impossible to do anything else but keep the mass moving to the rear—praying—hoping—talking to yourself out loud—gesticulating—and trying to make yourself understood. It was a nightmare while it lasted. In the midst of one of these one-sided "arguments," I was suddenly aware that a Filipino soldier was standing close to me. I turned and saw that he had a long piece of sugar cane. He drew a knife

from his belt, cut off a generous piece and extended it to me:
"Here, sir," he said.

Taking the piece of cane, I impulsively put my arm around his shoulders and squeezed, then gently propelled him forward.

"Thanks, Joel!" was the only reply I could think of.

He grinned happily and rejoined the column, turned and waved, and was lost in the moving mass. He had exemplified the thing that prevailed among most Filipinos—implicit faith in Americans. As long as we were there with them, "everything was all right!"

An American lieutenant colonel, with the Philippine Army, was standing close by. He stopped in the midst of wiping the sweat from his face. "There she goes!" he said sharply.

Turning in the direction he was pointing, I saw a Jap flare. It was directly over our left flank. The dusk had deepened and night was falling rapidly. It was about 7:00 P.M. It developed that the enemy was attacking our left flank in force. Had their main effort been directed at the center of our line, chaos would have resulted. One of the shells left in that particular area had evacuated, soon after the main body had withdrawn. Their excuse was the usual one. They were looking for their "companions."

The left flank was being held by the 31st and 45th Infantry shells. Scouts and Americans joined hands to repel the attack. Jap infiltrators and 5th Columnists set fire to the sugar cane fields in the rear of the 3rd Battalion, 45th Infantry. It silhouetted the movements of the shell. Cane fields in the rear of the Japs were also set afire that night. The reason for this was never determined. Perhaps some of our people did it.

The initial attack of the Japanese was repulsed with heavy losses on both sides. The 31st and 45th had particularly suffered since taking over the flank a few days before. For instance, Company "L", 45th Scouts, entered the Abucay-Hacienda line with a strength of 131. After the withdrawal had been effected, there were only 79 left.

At about this time, I received additional orders from General Weaver that the 194th would hold the Clearance Point until all shell commanders had cleared; that the 194th would then take up positions along Cadre Road, which was only a short distance to the south of us and *north of where the out-*

post line would be formed; that we would occupy this position by daylight; that an infantry commander would meet me there with troops and together we would establish this temporary line in *advance of the outpost line.* The order also attached to me, one battery of SPM's (self-propelled mounts—half-tracks with 75mm guns) to help effect covering the withdrawal of the shells. I had this battery stationed at the Clearance Point ready to fire in any direction.

Heavy fighting continued that night on the left flank, with the rest of the line quiet. The Japs put their entire strength at this one point. The 31st and 45th shells were in extremely difficult straits, taking the full brunt of the Jap attack. As the night progressed, it became apparent that, unless something unusual happened to help them out, they would be unable to disengage themselves from the enemy. At about 1:00 A.M., a call for tanks was received. The moon was not yet up and it was very dark. How it was accomplished I will never know, but we succeeded in moving some of the tanks up the road to the left flank positions and placed them between the two shells and the Japanese. While they were moving up, the commander of the SPM's checked the range with me. We were not sure of anything but after deciding on a minimum range, we added a small safety factor and started firing. The tanks fired blindly in the darkness while the shells withdrew out of hostile fire to a group of Filipino buses which had been assigned to carry them to the rear. They were on their last legs and ready to drop in their tracks, but not too far gone to utter words of thanks. The tanks returned very slowly, firing as they came and the SPM's sprayed the evacuated area with shells. Firing by both tanks and 75's had been very effective. The Japs did not follow up.

It was now about 3:00 A.M. All shell commanders had reported except one. It was the shell referred to which had been in position on the center of the line. I was positive that it had withdrawn and the commander had failed to report. The executive officer of Tank Group reported to the Clearance Point at about the time that the 31st and 45th shells were going through. At about 4:00 A.M., I called his attention to the order for occupation of positions along Cadre Road and that we would be compelled to start immediately if we were to accomplish the mission. He agreed and stated that he would go direct to Tank Group and would tell them the situation.

We started for Cadre Road. By this time the moon was up, which helped somewhat, but it still was a difficult negotiation due to the trail's intricacies. One whole platoon, under command of Lt. Guinn, failed to make a turn on the trail and proceeded down another one. Had he continued, he would have run right into the Jap lines. Each time we made a turn on the trail, where there was danger of someone going astray, it was our practice to stop the entire column, throw out quick local security, checking vehicles and allowing a readjustment of road spaces. This was done and we found Guinn's platoon missing. Just as we were about to send a party to overtake them, his platoon came back. They had discovered their mistake in time. Everyone breathed a sigh of relief. We reached Cadre Road just as dawn was breaking.

The road was about 20 feet wide and ran east and west. There was absolutely no possible chance for any field of fire except for the width of the road. Dense jungle was on both sides. Why we were ever ordered into such a position will always remain a mystery. The best dispositions possible were made. We looked in vain for the infantry commander and troops the Tank Group Commander had mentioned in his order. I have never found anyone in higher headquarters, or lower down, who knew anything about any infantry supposed to be on Cadre Road!

Our kitchen trucks came up from the rear echelon and we had breakfast, which helped. There was little we could do, as far as local security was concerned, because of the jungle. We established listening posts and covered Back Road (the trail to the north) and Cadre Road. I then radioed General Weaver. He was not at headquarters. A message was left with his communications officer that we were in position, with no field of fire whatever, and with no infantry. No reply was received. I sent Captain Spoor south to the outpost line on Banibani Road, with instructions to tell the outpost commander just what orders we had received and to also ascertain whether or not it would be possible to have part of his force detailed to Cadre Road. Spoor reported back and the following is a gist of what occurred:

"What the hell are you doing up there in advance of the outpost line?" asked the commander.

Spoor explained that we were under orders to be there.

The commander then asked, "What damned fool issued any such orders as that?"

Our orders were then related in detail by Spoor, together with my request that part of the outpost force be sent up to support us.

The commander was blunt and straight to the point. "Tell Colonel Miller that even if I had the men to spare, which I have not, if I sent anyone to Cadre Road, I would be disobeying orders. This is the outpost line, beyond which, our troops are not supposed to be. According to your orders, General Weaver has disobeyed the general withdrawal order. I'd strongly advise you to pull your outfit back here on this line. Hell! Our own guns are liable to be shooting right into you!"

At about 1:00 P.M., having heard nothing from Weaver or anyone else, I sent in another radio message to Group Headquarters with the same information as the previous one. Still no reply. We knew both messages had been registered at headquarters because they were oral by way of the radio phone.

About 4:00 P.M., I received a message from Tank Group Headquarters stating that either myself or my designate would report at 6:00 P.M. for further orders. Lt. Spaulding, liaison officer, was sent, together with a verbal message from me inquiring about the two unanswered radio calls and also the complete absence of infantry.

Spaulding reported back about 7:00 P.M. with orders that the 194th Tank Battalion would cover the withdrawal of the entire outpost line on Banibani Road after dark, and then to conform to the general withdrawal order by being behind the main line of resistance (Pilar-Bagac line) by daylight the next morning, January 26th. Spaulding also reported on the verbal message I had sent. He received no answer as to why the radios had been disregarded. In answer to the inquiry relative to the absence of infantry, the general growled out, "Well, they were supposed to be there!"

It was fortunate for us that there had been no contact with the Japanese. Had the enemy struck, we would have been between his fire and that of our own troops to the south! From certain points of vantage that day, we had watched Jap bombers to the north of us and over our old positions. Evidently, the licking they had taken the night before had led them to believe our forces were still on the job, because they bombed those empty sectors all day long. As dusk arrived, we had every reason to feel good. If the Japs pushed tonight, they would be pushing against an unoccupied line and it was only reasonable to believe that they would reorganize before pushing on. This would take them, at least, until the following morning.

The night was very dark—almost pitch black. We were in position to cover the withdrawal of the outpost elements. Our SPM battery was still attached to us and also two or three units of the 192nd Tank Battalion. At about 1:00 A.M., January 26th, the last elements of the outpost had passed the Clearance Point. We could not trail them to the Pilar-Bagac line as progress was very slow due to the difficulties of driving tanks. Company "A" was at the northerly end of our column (the rear). About an hour after we had started, I received a radio call from the commanding officer of this company. One of his tanks had slipped off the side of a bridge in the darkness, until it hung on the very edge. They had tried to pull the tank across the bridge with tow cables, but it had slipped off the side and was now bottom side up in the bed of the stream. No one was in it at the time and therefore, no casualties. Knowing that it would be impossible to salvage it, I told them to fire a 37mm shell in it to set the gasoline on fire. This they did. The water in the stream was low at this time of the year and there was no difficulty in setting fire to the tank.

Once again we started down the road and had almost passed Banibani Road with the entire column when another radio call from Co. "A" came in. One of the last tanks had failed to make the turn in the darkness and had proceeded east a short distance when it went off the trail and lodged itself securely in the ditch. Halting the column, we waited for Co. "A" to give us the all clear signal. After a half hour had elapsed, a call came in stating that several tow cables had been broken trying to get the tank back on the trail. It would be impossible to do the job unless our 10-ton wrecker could be sent up from the rear echelon.

Knowing the General's extreme aversion to losing any tanks, no matter what the cause, and having lost one already tonight, I immediately put through a radio call for him in person. Finally the executive officer answered my call. I requested that he relay my message to the Group Commander. It related the trouble and recommended the tank be destroyed in view of the withdrawal order which stated that all troops were to be back of the Pilar-Bagac line by daylight.

He told me to hold on, and he would contact General Weaver who was sleeping. In a short time, Major Smythe, the executive, returned and said it was the General's orders that all Chesterfields be brought out. "Chesterfield" was the code word at that particular time used to designate tanks.

I called Smythe's attention to the fact, that as soon as daylight came—and dawn was not far off—Jap planes would be in the air searching us out and we would be like rats in a trap.

The reply was monotonous, "Bring out all Chesterfields." Then he asked me if I wanted them to send up our 10-ton wrecker. My reply blistered. I told him, in effect, that the 194th Tank Battalion wanted nothing from Tank Group! Then I turned off the radio.

CHAPTER 18

The Battle of January 26th

GENERAL WEAVER'S ORDER added fury to our helplessness. I wondered what the high command would have said had they known the true situation at that moment. I also wondered what would happen if the Japs spotted us at daylight with their planes, and who would be blamed for the fiasco, and whether or not the responsibility for disobeying USAFFE's withdrawal order would land on me.

Something which always fogged things up, and which was a constant thorn in our side, was General Weaver's insistence that Tank Group have direct radio communication with my combat elements to the exclusion of direct contact with my rear echelon. This was in direct contradiction to Armored Force doctrines. It always precluded the possibility of badly needed unification within my own battalion.

Sgt. Joseph Aaram, communications sergeant in charge of the rear echelon communications system, was one of the best in his line. He was considered such an expert by the Armored Force School at Fort Knox, Ky., that they tried to retain him as an instructor while we were in the United States.

He had listened to my conversation with Major Smythe. When I had turned off the radio in my half-track, he contacted me on another. I explained the situation and told him that we would be compelled to order the wrecker sent up so as to get the tank out of the ditch.

Aaram realized the gravity of the situation. On his own initiative, he took charge of direct communications. The period between this time and when the wrecker started out was one of utter turmoil. My rear echelon knew what I wanted. But Tank Group was insisting upon direct control. The situation became a stalemate of conflicting orders and indecision.

Sgt. Aaram attempted to smooth out the communication angle so it would function to our best advantage. Group was insisting upon its prerogative of taking things over. It resulted in a scrambling of the whole situation. It was similarly true in getting the wrecker on its way.

Tank Group gave my rear echelon the information that we did not want the wrecker! It was evidently because I had told Major Smythe, rather sharply, that we wanted nothing from Tank Group.

Realizing that we might be in this precarious position for some hours, we made disposition of the combat vehicles, in the darkness, as best we could. The column was on Back Road— merely a trail. There was very little cover in the area. We were stretched out about one mile—north and south—with the north (rear) end of the column resting on the junction of Back Road and Banibani Road. We put our battery of SPM's at the south end of the column, on a knoll, the highest elevation we could find. The intervening tanks and half-tracks were so disposed they could fire to either flank and front or rear. We threw out local security and prayed for the best.

At about 6:30 A.M., the wrecker had not as yet shown up. Dawn was just beginning to break. I radioed again to Tank Group Headquarters. Finally I reached Major Pettit, aide to the Tank Group Commander. I told him that no wrecker had shown up; that it was getting daylight; that Jap planes would soon be overhead, and that the whole battalion was being jeopardized for the sake of getting one tank out of the ditch. My urgent recommendation was that the outfit be ordered in immediately and comply with the withdrawal orders. Pettit said he would carry my request to General Weaver. In a short time he returned and I received the old parrot-like reply: "You will bring in all Chesterfields. Repeat—all Chesterfields." If my reply to Smythe had blistered, this one seared!

Daylight came, and with it hostile aircraft. They continuously circled over the area, but made no movement toward our column. Evidently we had better cover than we had thought.

We made another attempt, in the daylight, to get the tank out of the ditch, but failed miserably, after breaking two more tow cables. Nothing of any event occurred until about 10:30 A.M.

Suddenly one of the half-tracks, posted for local security on Banibani Road just a short distance west of the north end of Company "A", spotted a Japanese officer and a non-commissioned officer as they walked out on the road from the north.

The driver, Private Roy Nordstrom, was handling one of the machine guns and let them have it. Both were knocked down and out. Almost immediately from the west, small arms fire was received through our positions at the north end of the column. As yet, we did not see the enemy. We returned fire blindly—in the general direction from which we received it. I immediately radioed the south end of the column and told Spoor to be prepared to come to our aid as were being fired upon. Back came the answer: "So are we!"

It developed that the entire column was receiving fire from the west. They were returning the fire just as we were.

Lieutenants Spaulding and Fleming had come up to the north end of the column, a short time before the battle started, to find out why we had not shown up at a particular bridge to the south that they were guarding. They had been sent down the night before, so as to make certain that hysterics did not blow the bridge. They had come up in a Jeep.

When the fighting started, I ordered them to go back down to this bridge immediately and hold it until we came out. My inner thoughts were adding—"if we ever do."

I will never forget the sight they made as they went down the trail in that Jeep. Trying to stay out of sight of hostile aircraft, they slid, careened, and dodged their way in and out, and around trees at a speed that was miraculous. For the short time they were in sight of us, their antics looked like a thriller-diller stunt at the circus. The rest of the column saw the same sight, and one observer said he thought it surely was two of the fabled men from Mars riding Haley's Comet!

The entire column was now receiving heavy fire from the west. As stated before, the radio at Tank Group Headquarters was tuned in to the radio in my half-track. My radio operator naturally had informed them the moment firing started. From now on, there came a barrage of incoherent orders and instructions that should have been incorporated in a Gilbert and Sullivan comic opera.

These orders and instructions were almost child-like as well as incoherent. The radio operator was besieged with questions, which were followed by instructions and advice. These, he would be compelled to relay on to me.

The Tank Group Commander himself was handling the radio phone. A picture flashed through my mind of a movie I had once seen of Napoleon hovering over a map and directing the battle. Only this was by remote control.

The General would periodically insist that I come to the radio phone myself. This, I refused to do. Taking care of the operation was the only job I could handle at that particular time! I would be in the act of directing some phase of the operation, when I would be interrupted by the radio operator, shouting above the din of the battle that the General wanted me to do this or that.

One of the incoherent orders frantically radioed by the Tank Group Commander was repeated and repeated until it became sickening. "Infiltrate to the rear, bringing all Chesterfields" was the message.

Whatever was meant by "Infiltrate" I am still unable to fathom. The only place to infiltrate was right straight down the trail, with hostile aircraft overhead, and Jap ground forces pouring fire through us!

Finally the insistent heckling got the best of me. I walked over to the half-track, climbed up the side. Calling the operator by name, I yelled: "Tell that old sonuvabitch to go to hell, and turn that radio off!"

This the operator did with thankful alacrity. Turning to me with a much begrimed but grinning countenance he said, "Colonel, if you catch hell for this, I want to be a witness!"

It should be explained at this point just what we had encountered. We learned later, that on this same day, a landing had been effected by the Japs on the west coast of Bataan. The force we had encountered was part of a general plan of the Japanese to push in from the west, and straight down from the north with the objective of smashing through the main line of resistance before it could be properly organized on the Pilar-Bagac line.

The Japs had come down from the north in force, along the corridor, just to the west of us. We had not known they were in that area. And they did not know that we were in position along this north and south trail. We had every reason to expect contact with the enemy that morning but we didn't expect to have the whole column fired on at once. The Japs were taken completely by surprise and acted merely by instinct when our half-track fired the first shots. They far out-numbered us, but for the present, we had the advantage in armor plate.

Very shortly, the Japanese began to show themselves.

Our battery of SPM's could not have been placed in a bet-ter position for the action, had we been there in daylight, and planned it a long time before. In every available place along the entire line, wherever cover was afforded in which there might be Japs, they dropped their shells. The result was astonishing. The Nips poured out like fleas off a dog. As they appeared, they were picked off by the Tankers.

At one part of the column near the south end, a radio operator become very enthusiastic. He was armed only with a pistol. All the machine guns were in use. He could sit at his radio no longer, and climbed to the ground. He was an expert pistol shot. His first shot was seen to strike a Jap in the chest. Thereafter, he fired deliberately and calmly during the entire course of the battle. His name is Foley, and he is alive today.

Several of the Tankers, at the north end of the column, were out of their vehicles when the firing started. They grab-bed Tommy-guns and lay down behind mounds of earth and trees and returned the fire.

At about 11:30 A.M., the Japanese put their artillery in action. It evidently had been on its way down from the north as part of the support for their infantry. Also, by this time, a great deal of indirect mortar fire was dropping in our area. At first, this fire did not particularly disturb us because it was extremely inaccurate. However, as noon approached, it began to register uncomfortably close. One shell landed close enough to give our half-track a good bouncing. We had absolutely nothing in the way of mortars or high explosive shells to throw back at them. It would not be long before some of our vehicles would be hit.

As yet, there had been no hostile moves of enemy aircraft. They had been circling lazily overhead all morning. Liaison between the Jap ground troops and their planes must have been just about zero for which we were very thankful.

Shortly after 12:00 noon, I radioed the entire column that they would immediately start the withdrawal and would pro-ceed behind the main line of resistance, maintaining plenty of space between each vehicle. At this time there was no opposition from enemy infantry. All hostile small arms fire had ceased, but artillery and mortar fire was becoming increasingly heavy.

The vehicles started down the trail. Suddenly the enemy aircraft must have awakened to the fact that something had been going on of which they were unaware. As each vehicle moved down that trail, it was bombed and strafed. Our .50 and .30 caliber machine guns fired back at the planes as best as could be done while traveling at high speed. At least one plane was brought down.

No casualties resulted from the bombing and strafing. Several vehicles were struck by bomb splinters, but not bad enough to put them out of action. Many of the bombs did, however, come very close, and I did not hear anyone brag a great deal afterwards.

It was during this withdrawal that an event occurred over which we later had many a laugh. But it was not so funny at the time—to one man! Lieutenant Swearingen had started up with the wrecker, and had arrived at a point about one kilometer south of our column when the sound of heavy firing to the north was heard. Swearingen had the driver park the wrecker under cover, and then he proceeded north on foot. He had not quite reached the position when the withdrawal order was given. The vehicles moved down the trail at high speed.

Everyone was concerned with hostile aircraft, and nobody saw Swearingen. My half-track was the last vehicle out. We were firing at a plane which was diving at us. Above the roar of the guns and dropping bombs, a weird sound penetrated our ears. It came from the rear. We saw Swearingen running down the trail after our half-track as if all Billyhell was after him. He was bellowing at the top of his lungs: "Hey, you guys, wait for me!"

We stopped the vehicle and waited for him to catch up. He was entirely out of breath, but had a grin from ear to ear. It appeared he was not any too pleased at being left behind to take on the whole Jap Army and Air Force all alone! But he was certainly glad to have us wait. Thereafter, he was known as "Kid Marathon."

We found Spaulding and Fleming guarding the bridge and armed to the teeth. A crew of dynamiters were on hand. No prophet was needed to foretell that the bridge would remain intact until the clearance order was given!

One half-track had preceded the column on its withdrawal to protect it from any hindrance at the stream crossing. It had taken up its position well under cover. When the bridge was blown, one of the timbers flew through the air and struck Captain Fred Moffitt on his leg. He was hospitalized for quite some time. This was the only casualty we received from the whole affair.

Before finally retiring behind the Pilar-Bagac line, we shot final bursts of .50 caliber bullets northward into the general area where we had engaged the Japs. In passing through our lines, I fully realized what would have happened had not the battle been fought that morning. Our main line was still completely disorganized. Had the Japs been allowed to proceed with their attack, they could have walked right through, and there would have been no more Bataan. This was the last and only line which could be held.

After the Pilar-Bagac line was organized (there were no interruptions from the Japanese) many patrols were sent out from the American and Filipino forces. Verification of the Jap casualties that day went as high as 1,500. The lowest estimate was about 1,000. The patrols stated that the area was saturated with the stench of death.

I had heard no more from General Weaver after my rage over the radio. But our rear echelon radio operator was near the Tank Group radio half-track and heard the entire conversation. He told me later that the General slammed his fist down and bellowed: "Colonel Miller, I'll court martial you for that —I'll court martial you!"

Later confirmation from my rear echelon, depicted to me, graphically, the state of utter confusion in Tank Group when the battle started. Also the fight between Sgt. Aaram and Tank Group, when Group mixed up everything by tuning in after he had perfect contact with us. Aaram also was promised punishment.

Headquarters of Tank Group had heard the withdrawal order. As soon as we crossed the Pilar-Bagac line, we radioed the rear echelon to have a hot meal ready; and we told them it had better be good! We found it ready. It was plain; but excellent and greatly appreciated.

We then learned that General Weaver had ordered us to proceed southward into a new area. This was in conformity with the organization of the new line. Some of our rear installations had already been moved.

Finishing my meal, I started to the new area in a Jeep. On the way, I met General Weaver and his aide coming north. We stopped and I got out. Saluting, I prepared to catch hell.

Instead, he was all smiles, and congratulated me on the successful action. He insisted that I get in his vehicle and go to the new area with him. He did not ever refer to the radio incident or anything else except the course of the action. Before we reached our destination, he produced a quart of good Scotch whiskey and told me to drink long and hearty. *I did!*

The aide, as usual, produced his notebook as soon as we reached the new area, intending to receive a detailed report of the battle. However, I told him that I had other things to do and he could get it later. There never was any interview.

CHAPTER 19

U. S. Propaganda

THE NEXT DAY after the battle, January 27th, we learned that Major Smythe, Tank Group executive officer, had visited headquarters of I Corps on the west side of Bataan. This was General Wainwright's command. They had heard about the action of the day before and complimented the 194th Tank Battalion on the successful outcome. Smythe told them that the affair had been a carefully laid out plan of Tank Group! I Corps actually believed the story until the details came to light later in Cabanatuan Prison Camp. It was now that we also learned how we might have been fired on by our own artillery, while out in front of our own lines the day before. Tank Group Headquarters had failed to even notify our artillery, that we were still north of the Pilar-Bagac line!

The events of the battle were written up by Tank Group soon after. It took two pages of single spaced typewriting to complete the report. It was sent to the high command at Corregidor. I was never allowed to see the report. This is not surprising in view of the story Smythe told I Corps.

And now, I contracted something which was to be with me through nearly all of my future experiences in Bataan and in the prison camps. It was dysentery. For a period of about two weeks I was up and down alternately. Medical supplies were dwindling at an alarming rate.

The mission of the 194th Tank Battalion was to be as follows: We were to provide front line support for II Corps, and also to provide beach defense on Manila Bay, from the front line southward to Cabcaben. We were to work closely with II Corps in the defense of their sector, and handle the major portion of their radio communication. All this meant close liaison, to be effective.

Shortly after we had arrived in the new area, General Weaver gave me orders to stay away from II Corps Headquarters entirely. He said that all necessary orders would come from him direct, and that I was to take none from II Corps Headquarters.

To be denied personal contact with the very people we were supposed to support, was very difficult to say the least. Our effectiveness depended entirely upon close liaison. After thinking it over, I held a staff conference and we arrived at a solution. The Tank Group Commander's order had not specifically named anyone except myself. Therefore, other means of contact could be arranged to circumvent an impossible situation, even if it did lend itself to subterfuge.

Lieutenant Spaulding, battalion liaison officer, was called in, and I explained the mission. He was to go to II Corps Headquarters as the liaison officer and actually attach himself in that capacity. He would eat and sleep there, reporting to me periodically or whenever he deemed it necessary, so that we would be kept fully acquainted with developments. He was also told that it was a confidential mission. This was the only way out, to circumvent the asinine jealousy of the commander, which was always arising. This was the way we functioned until the fall of Bataan!

The Pilar-Bagac line was organized with greater care than had been shown previously. The left flank of I Corps was tied to the right flank of II Corps by actual occupation of troops. Positions were strengthened by clearing fields of fire, constructing earthworks, and laying simple, homemade mines in front of certain sectors. An attempt was made to conduct training of the Philippine Army which helped somewhat. The Tankers held schools with infantry, teaching them the fundamentals of infantry support when operating with tanks. Both basic and advanced training being taught with *the Japs pounding on the front door!* It was unreal—and yet—so was our predicament.

From now on, bombings and strafings were as common as fever and dysentery. The Japs made pushes against the line at various places. Two encounters, particularly bloody and terrific while they lasted, were fought in the I Corps sector. The Japs had forced a landing on the west coast of Bataan, referred to before, and had also driven in a wedge from the north. The enemy had thrown in crack troops—hari-kari—and the best that Nippon could produce. In both actions, it was typical jungle warfare, and the equipment of the Filipinos and

Americans, was most inadequate and totally unsuited to carry on the attack. But, they had to attack. Everything favored the Japanese defenders.

Intelligence had misjudged the enemy strength, and only after tremendous casualties on our side forced the issue, were sufficient forces brought on the scene. Even then, it was slaughter. Light tanks used had to slowly grind their way through the jungle, making of themselves a perfect target for anti-tank guns, mortar fire, and pie-pan mines. One tank was found filled completely with earth. The Japs had dug themselves in, and had hidden the earth in the knocked out tank. The four men of the tank crew were all dead, and buried under the earth in the tank.

The Jap Air Force attempted to drop ammunition and other supplies to their beleaguered landing force, which was not very successful. Finally, this force was driven back to the sea, where most of the survivors committed suicide by jumping over the cliff, landing in the water below or on the rocks. Those managing to land in the water were picked off. Papers and diaries of the Japs depicted their last moments. One diary in particular, displayed great emotion, and asked the Son of Heaven (the Emperor) to accept the profuse apologies of one so miserable, as to have failed to fulfill the imperial mission!

The wedge, driven in by the Japs from the north, was taken care of by reestablishing the front line and surrounding this force. It was then a case of going in after them, which was a duplication of the other action. When this affair was over, it was found that the Japs had excavated and constructed mounds of earth. It was at first thought that they had buried their dead in these mounds but after examination, it was found that the mounds contained artillery pieces and other materiel of war! Strange, indeed, are the ways of the Japanese.

Our tanks were equipped with short wave radios. At night, particularly, the crews would listen to the Domei news agency in Japan and also to KGEI in San Francisco. Shortly after the January 26th battle, they picked up a newscast from Domei which stated that the 194th Tank Battalion had withdrawn deeper into Bataan "with the rest of the rats to dig their own graves."

The broadcasts over KGEI, from San Francisco, were far from encouraging, at least, to us. They were of two types. One concerned itself with the tremendous production of war materiel in the United States, and how it would be used to crush our enemies. How we longed for just a little of that materiel! The other was a general theme built around direct taunts to the Japanese—they could not take Bataan—they did not have the guts to take Bataan—the defenders dared them to come in and take it!

We listened with mixed feelings—not realizing what it was all about. Literally, the seat of our pants was out, and we knew it! Later, in the prison camps, we came to realize that this propaganda, which was being broadcast all over the Far East, was just as much a part of the war, as were men and equipment.

The United States was working on the inherent weakness of the Japanese—loss of face. They were gambling on the assumption, that if they taunted the Jap long enough, he *would* come in and take Bataan. The United States also felt that the first invasion force of the Japanese had suffered so many casualties that it was too weak in itself to make much of an offensive. We, too, felt that this was the case, and if disease and malnutrition did not enter the picture too decisively, we could last until help arrived.

At this time, the Japanese were pushing an all-out southward offensive with the ultimate object of taking Australia. Had this been accomplished it would have denied the United States any bases in the Pacific west of the Hawaiian Islands. This, then, was the reason for the propaganda warfare we heard over KGEI. Somehow—the southward plunge had to be stopped.

One can only conjecture as to what the status of the war would have been had Australia been taken by the Japanese. At all events, it would have meant a much longer war and perhaps inevitable failure on the side of the United States.

Once in a great while, the Jap is capable of creating humor, but not very often. His humor, as a characteristic, is counterclockwise to the white man's. On this particular occasion, some of the men were listening to a broadcast from the Manila station, which was being used by the Japs for propaganda. The announcer stated that the next number was a transcription and dedicated especially to the "rats on Bataan." The number was recorded music. I do not remember whether my title is exactly correct but it was something about "Ships That Never Come In"! The piece was most appropriate. The ships we looked and longed for never did come in.

Periodically, the Japs would get out on Manila Bay at night and fire artillery pieces, from landing barges, at our beach installations. Damage was slight, but not to our nerves. We withheld our fire for the simple reason that we had nothing, on beach defense, that would reach them. Night operations (especially with inadequate guns and equipment) on the receiving end, causes imagination to run rampant. On one night, the Japs came precariously close to raising havoc with our command post. Their shells whizzed directly through the area and not very high in the air. It looked like a landing attempt but did not develop. Only once did we return the fire. This was in a segregated sector on the beach. Whether or not, it was a landing attempt, we were never able to determine definitely. The night was dark and the Jap barges, far out in the bay, were firing. It was thought that movement was detected out from shore and the defense, in this area, let loose. The firing continued for about fifteen minutes and nothing happened. We eventually came to the conclusion that these sporadic raids were made to harass us and also, to bait us into disclosing our beach positions and just what we had.

Patrols, both reconnaissance and combat, were constantly being sent out from our lines. These were composite patrols made up of both Americans and Filipinos. The 194th furnished its share for these patrols.

One of the maintenance sergeants of Company "D", whose duties kept him in the maintenance section, volunteered one day for one of these patrols. This was not in line of duty. It was clearly beyond the call of duty. My first reaction was to turn down his request because he was needed in the maintenance section and that was his job. However, he was insistent that his request be granted, and he was sent to report to the American officer commanding the patrol. The sergeant's name was Danforth.

The sergeant went one step further. He volunteered to take command of the "point" of the patrol. "Point" is just what the word implies. It precedes the patrol into enemy territory and is an extremely hazardous job. In this case, it preceded the main body of the patrol by several hundred yards.

The mission was to actually proceed into the town of Balanga, which was known to be in the hands of the Japanese. It was inside their lines. The information wanted, included details of enemy installations and their disposition.

Sergeant Danforth led his point into the town, under cover and unobserved. Three Filipinos and himself made up the point. He was equipped with both rifle and pistol. On rounding the corner of a building, he was confronted by four Jap soldiers. They were so surprised that they stood motionless and just gaped. The three Filipinos were a short distance to the rear, using cover so as to give the sergeant some protection. They didn't even get a chance to operate. Danforth threw his rifle up to fire. The gun missed fire. Dropping the rifle, he drew his pistol. It is quite positive that he killed two of the Japs and wounded a third. The fourth took to his heels and escaped. The Japs did not fire a single shot!

The point made a quick getaway and rejoined the main body of the patrol just south of Balanga. By this time, the town was a hot bed of aroused Japanese. They evidently thought it might be the forerunner of a general attack, and laid down an artillery barrage in the area which was occupied by the patrol. They were pinned down in this position until about 4:00 P.M., when they all returned to our lines safely. None of this story was related by Danforth. It was told by the three Filipinos in the point, and by the officer commanding the patrol. He recommended a decoration.

Citing the sergeant's actions in detail, I recommended him for at least the Silver Star and told him what I had done. He was very modest, and I sincerely felt that he deserved the decoration. The recommendation went directly to the Tank Group Commander who had the authority to award the Purple Heart and Silver Star decorations. My recommendation was returned with the notation, that this action did not warrant an award of the Silver Star for the reason that the sergeant had only done what was every soldier's duty. The Commander then went on to state that he would write a personal letter of commendation to Danforth.

This was done and the sergeant received the letter. He made no comment whatever, but slowly tore the letter into bits and dropped it on the ground. A day or so later, I had a personal conversation with the General, and brought up the subject of

Danforth. During the course of that conversation, I told Weaver that in my judgment, the sergeant's actions were clearly beyond the line of duty, and that, most certainly, no member of the maintenance crew, by any stretch of the imagination, was called upon to perform such duty unless the emergency existed when all personnel—no matter where assigned—might have to be used.

The General, however, would not retract his original decision, and passed it off by saying something to the effect that he might have considered otherwise had he known, in the first place, the sergeant came from the maintenance section.

We could never understand why, as long as the General had the authority to award the Silver Star, he did not reverse his decision. Had it been a matter of having to go through higher headquarters, admitting a mistake had been made, there might have been some reason for his decision. Sergeant Danforth died in a prison camp.

The forces on Bataan were greatly concerned over the food situation. It was very scarce. The half-ration dwindled below that level before many days had passed. Those in charge of kitchen installations used their own initiative in various ways.

Late in January, the mess officer of Company "D", together with some of the rear echelon personnel, ran across a carabao wandering around not far from the front lines. The carabao is used in the Philippines much as the white man uses oxen. A rope was promptly thrown around its neck and it was painstakingly led into the area. Everyone concerned was delighted at the thought of having a real meal.

The carabao was carefully tied to a tree, and it was decided that the execution would take place that afternoon. At the appointed time, most of the rear echelon personnel gathered to witness the event. The executioner drew his .45 caliber pistol. Standing directly in front of the animal, he pointed the gun, squeezed the trigger, and hit the carabao right between the eyes.

This taught everyone concerned a lesson. The carabao's head, at that particular point, is almost as hard as a rock. If an animal can have expression in its face—that one certainly registered surprise at the impact. Then he slowly began to wag his huge head. He let out a bellow, made a terrific lunge, and broke the rope. He tore off madly through the jungle.

The immediate reaction among the men was that of complete dismay. Then came wild activity. Some bolted through the jungle on foot in pursuit. Some jumped into half-tracks and followed while another group commandeered a Jeep. After much labor, the carabao was rounded up and killed. The meat was divided up with the rest of the battalion.

The 194th Tank Battalion had just about the only radio installations which amounted to anything in II Corps. Corps requested a conference on communications to which I sent Lieutenant Fleming and Sergeant Aaram. The result was that we were requested to set up a Radio Central to correlate both ground radio and contact with the Navy patrol boats operating in Manila Bay.

Fleming and Aaram were artists in the communication line. I have never seen two men who could gather and have on hand more odds and ends from which they could fashion radios. They had picked up a commercial panel truck on the way into Bataan. It was in this truck that they set up the Radio Central. By the time they finished with it, the inside looked like a Buck Rogers picture. This job not only handled everything desired by II Corps but also correlated Tank Group communications in its entirety. For some time it functioned very smoothly. And then one day Fleming was asked to report to Corps Headquarters.

He was called into conference with the Signal Corps at which he was told that they wished to have the Radio Central installations moved to Corps Headquarters and placed under control of the Signal Officer. Fleming remonstrated to no avail. He reported back to me and told the story.

It was completely out of the question to accede to the demands of the Signal Officer. It would have meant removing the tank communications system from our area. There was not enough radio equipment to send the Central to Corps Headquarters and still retain another installation for the tanks.

Fleming was told to go back and acquaint them with this information. I then asked him, frankly, what the reason was that they wished to move it in view of the fact that it was functioning entirely satisfactorily where it was. He then told me something I had not known before—that the original conference had not been quite smooth—that it was attempted at that time to set up the installation at Corps Headquarters under the Signal Officer. He said it was his opinion that the whole affair revolved around jealousy on the part of that officer.

This actually proved to be the case. Fleming went to headquarters as instructed and gave them my message and explained the reasons why. However, the Signal Officer had evidently sold his bill of goods to higher authority. An order was issued by II Corps that the Radio Central would be directly under command of that officer and that it would be installed at that headquarters.

The Central was dismounted, retaining our installations and giving all the rest to Corps. It was reestablished, after a fashion, but soon broke down and went out of use entirely. No attempt was made to reestablish it!

Captain Leo Schneider, senior medical officer of the 194th, and Lieutenant Hickman, junior medico, had set up an infirmary in our rear echelon area. We now had quite a number who were sick. The regular hospital areas were crowded and we tried to take care of the lesser cases in this installation. The men were up and down with malaria, dysentery, diarrhea, and dengue fever—and malnutrition was setting in. There were little or no drugs to work with. Quinine was very scarce. The medical unit made improvised beds with what they had at their disposal.

Captain Schneider was very ingenious. He was always inventing something. And he was more than handy with tools. Quite often he would surprise everyone by fashioning something out of nothing. Somewhere, he procured some powdered quinine. This is very difficult to administer due to the extreme bitterness of the drug. However, Schneider met the situation as usual. With the aid of the maintenance section, he invented and made a pill making machine. What he used to make the powder stick together is more than I will ever know. But he turned all the powder into pills.

Schneider was one of the senior medical captains in the whole USAFFE. Other captains, junior to him, were being promoted. Because he was fully qualified, I recommended to the Tank Group Commander that he be promoted to the rank of major. This was promptly turned down on the grounds that the tank battalion tables of organization would not allow medical officers above the rank of captain.

By endorsement on the communication, I pointed out that the medical corps was not a part of the Armored Force, that tables of organization listed them separately and that they were only attached personnel. While it was true that these tables did not allow us medical officers above the grade of captain, it was not the intention to detail these officers to the battalion, burying them with no chance for promotion. That was the reason why medical personnel was only attached.

The answer I received was that there was danger of the high command detailing a Filipino medical officer to our battalion in the place of Schneider if he actually received his promotion! This was not true. There were plenty of medical officers who could have been assigned, but once the General had issued a decision, nothing could change it. My arguments were of no avail. Schneider did not receive his promotion and was in the position of having to watch men less qualified and junior to him, receiving the grade of major!

The General did, however, recommend Lt. Hickman's promotion to the grade of captain, which I had recommended along with Schneider.

Captain Hickman, after becoming a prisoner of war, left us at Cabanatuan camp with a detail being taken to Palowan. We never saw him again. He died, we learned, on one of the hell ships.

CHAPTER 20

Hope — Bataan Airfields

MANY OF THE kitchens on Bataan were equipped with portable gasoline ranges. It was not long before the use of these ranges was prohibited, due to the shortage of gasoline. Already, the 12,000 gallons of aviation gasoline, which the 194th had salvaged from the dumps before coming into Bataan, had been eyed with envy by everyone who needed it. An expert was sent into our area by the high command to mix part of it with low test fuel so it could be used in vehicles other than tanks and airplanes. Some more of it was taken to be used in the two or three P-40's we had hidden in the jungle. We watched the supply diminish with reluctance but realized it had to be done.

Illness struck repeatedly during those strained and hopeless weeks and months on Bataan. One victim was a sergeant who was to die on the Death March.

Our communications section had set up a telephone switchboard in the area to give us direct communications between various sections, Tank Group Headquarters, and other installations outside the area. An operator was on duty 24 hours.

One night I was awakened, suddenly, by the General's aide. He told me the Tank Group Commander had tried to get the switchboard operator and had been unable to do so. The aide had been sent down, about 150 yards distant, to discern the trouble. The aide had found the board unattended. He reported back to the General, who instructed him to awaken me with orders that whoever had been on duty at the board would immediately be court martialed. I inquired of the aide if he had tried to determine why no one was at the switchboard. He said he had not done so. I told him to tell General Weaver that I would immediately investigate, and if the matter warranted a court martial, charges would be prepared. But if it did not warrant that procedure, someone else would have to prefer the charges. The aide was one of those souls that stick around like molasses, parroting the words that fall from the lips of their superiors. He was almost aghast at the fact that I did not, at once, summon personnel to make up the charges, and once more repeated his message. It was necessary to become extremely rude. He left, but not without meticulously saluting.

I investigated, and found that the man on duty, Sergeant Lang, had been taken ill and had been compelled to leave his post for a few minutes. He had a bad case of dysentery. The next morning, I sent a message to the General stating that the matter had been taken care of. It was never mentioned again.

Illness and fatigue, however, never caused us to give up hope. We had no knowledge, whatever, of the full damage inflicted on our Navy at Pearl Harbor. We fully expected to see that Navy in action.

Airfields had been prepared by the Engineers on Bataan—airfields built out of blood and guts—for the planes we never received. They were built, in the ever-living hope, that we would get air reinforcements. It was always the opinion that these planes would arrive, and that they would change the one-sided show the Japs were staging in the skies.

During the day, the Japs would bomb these fields, and at night, they would again be repaired. At times there was every indication to believe that aircraft was on the way. Oil barrels were placed around these fields, and inflammable material was placed inside the barrels. They would provide flaming markers when the planes would arrive at night. At times, the hopes of everyone on Bataan soared sky-high. At these times, the oil barrels were lighted. The planes did not come, and dawn brought fresh disappointment, but not despair. They would come—we knew it!

I have talked with higher commanders and a great number of Air Corps personnel—both officers and enlisted men. They have told me that orders were actually received that on such and such a night, aircraft reinforcements would arrive.

As far as I can ascertain, there never was any such intention or plan in the overall picture!

One of these airfields had been prepared when we held the Abucay-Hacienda line. It was located on the east side of Bataan and just north of the new Pilar-Bagac line. One day, after we had retired to the new line, a Japanese plane was hit badly by our anti-aircraft fire and was forced to land on this field.

Our artillery, what little there was of it, did miraculous work. The observers were constantly on the job watching for any target of opportunity that might present itself. To say that they "raised hell" with the Japs would not even begin to tell the story. Any movement in Japanese lines was scrutinized very closely.

They did *not* shoot at everything that moved. Like the Bunker Hill days of "don't fire until you see the whites of their eyes," they waited until they really had a target. The observers evidently watched the smoking plane and traced its course until it landed on the field. Almost immediately, one of our 155mm guns opened up and scored a direct hit on the plane. The enthusiasm in the artillery, after this, was intensified. It is seldom that an artillery piece has a chance to shoot at a plane.

On another occasion there seemed to be a great deal of activity in an old church, behind the front lines of the Japs. The observers, after watching this activity for some time, came to the conclusion that some kind of an important conference was about to be held. They noted, what they thought to be, many Japanese officers arriving.

They waited until all activity had ceased. Then they fired an intensive barrage of 155mm shells on the church, demolishing the building completely. Our patrols later brought in the information that the artillery observers had guessed right. Few, if any, of the Jap officers had escaped.

Our artillery had carefully surveyed the area on Bataan. It was seldom necessary for them to fire any registration bursts—so carefully had they done their work. This applied not only to the 155mm guns but also to the 75mm guns. At the surrender, the Japanese insisted there were many more guns than they found evidence of, so potent were the few we had.

Many times at night, the Japanese would attempt to bring in troops and supplies down the main road on the east side of Bataan. Our artillery was always on the alert. Invariably the enemy would expose the movement by flashing a light or allowing the lead vehicle to travel with dimmed lights. Their losses were terrific, but they never seemed to learn. How they hated those guns!

There was a great deal of difference between American artillery methods and those of the Japanese. American artillery will generally fire one burst for registration. If they are over the target, they adjust by resetting the range, and firing another. This might be short. The next burst fired would be corrected so as to actually land on the target.

The Japanese battery was composed of four guns. The whole battery would fire in rapid sequence. In a short time, one "boom" would sound from the American lines. Invariably, the next return of fire from the Jap lines would be three "booms" in rapid sequence. Then another "boom" from our lines, followed by "boom-boom" from the Japs. Without even attempting to observe, we could always tell what was happening. Our artillery was picking off one Jap gun at a time. This was true even though Japanese artillery, being more modern, outranged ours. They never changed their system.

Air Corps personnel on Bataan was used, to a great extent, as infantry. This was necessary in view of the fact that they had no planes, and because of the acute shortage of American soldiers. They were hastily organized as per the tables of organization of the infantry.

Their's was a pitiful plight. Air Corps officers, trained to pilot an airplane, suddenly found themselves in the role of infantry officers commanding men. Enlisted men who had been trained as airplane mechanics, or such, found themselves as non-commissioned officers or privates of infantry. Infantry cannot be trained overnight, any more than can other branches. It takes a long time to properly train the doughboy. In addition to this, Air Corps personnel, due for promotion, was denied the jump in grade. The high command ruled, that inasmuch as they were soldiering as infantry, they must abide by the tables of organization of infantry and could not be promoted unless an actual vacancy existed! Such was the reasoning of people indoctrinated with hidebound Army Regulations—even on Bataan!

By the end of February, the forces on Bataan were visibly weakening. Morale and mental attitudes were of the best but physique was declining rapidly. Malnutrition made itself quite evident. Men would become dizzy, with black spots appearing before their eyes. The majority had contracted all of the diseases heretofore mentioned. Malaria was very persistent. I have been told by medical authority, that Bataan was only second to an area on the island of Mindoro, for the world's worst place for contracting the dread disease. We had very little quinine to fight it. Our meager stock of the drug had to be rationed. Only enough was available to keep us on our feet—and very wobbly limbs that supplied those feet.

By this time all of the carabao had been cleaned up. Horses and mules were also slaughtered and eaten. Company "D" from Kentucky, had the Kentuckian's deep love for horses. Whether they actually knew that part of their miserable ration was horse meat stew, I do not know. In all honesty, I do not believe the majority did know. Whenever meat appeared in the ration not many questions were asked. We were thankful to get it. After the horse meat had disappeared, and it was generally known that it was horse meat, some of the Kentuckians said they did not know it, and if they had, they would never have eaten it. Knowing them as I did, I am thoroughly convinced they meant what they said!

Our nights were filled with the weird howls of the "wailing" monkey—something we could never get accustomed to. It was somewhat akin to the howling of the Japs. Some of the men stated, with downright positiveness, that the Jap had descended directly from this jungle occupant—and not so long ago! There was also a small type of monkey. Some of them made friends with us and would perch themselves nearby and chatter incessantly. There were small and large lizards—some four to five feet long—which were caught when possible and used for food.

About this time, we heard over the short wave radio from KGEI at San Francisco, that the famous Sergeant York of World War I had requested he be allowed to head the boys of his county and come to the aid of the Bataan defenders. Hopeless as our situation had come to be, we could still put humor in the absurdity of the newscast. From that time on and through the prison camps, whenever a rumor was heard relative to our troops making a landing (and there were literally thousands of those rumors) the stock remark was: "Sergeant York and his boys have landed!"

During the siege of Bataan, approximately 200 or more Japanese planes were knocked down. One day on Corregidor, anti-aircraft guns knocked down seven at one time. The burst landed squarely in the middle of a Jap formation. Whenever a plane was brought down, everyone on Bataan knew about it almost immediately. A certain unmistakable, congratulatory yell had automatically developed with the advent of the first planes knocked down. How and who started it, will probably remain a mystery forever. The fact remains that whenever that yell started, it was repeated and relayed all over Bataan, and everyone who heard it knew that another Jap plane was out of business. Only once, to my knowledge, was the yell premature!

Early in March, 1942, quite a number of us were able to send a short message to our loved ones in the United States. The messages were written out and taken to the island of Cebu, which as yet had not been captured by the Japanese. A radio station was still operating. Ironically, my wife received my message that all was well, the day before Bataan fell in April!

It did not help that empty feeling in our stomachs, to get the truth of one of the stupid situations that had arisen, back in the early days of the war.

The Sikiano (French Indo-China ship) was captured by the United States shortly after December 8, 1941. It was manned by Japanese and lay in Mariveles, Bataan, until about December 20th, while the high command negotiated with the State Department of the United States, to ascertain legal status. The ship was loaded with gasoline, kerosene, and—what was most important—2,000,000 pounds of flour which was so badly needed. Finally, about December 20th, official permission was granted to unload the cargo. About 400,000 gallons of gasoline was unloaded in drums. Then the Japanese bombed and sunk the ship. The cargo of flour and everything else was lost! How that flour could have been used on Bataan!

Our orders from the Tank Group Commander became more and more bewildering. He issued a lengthy order stating that our tanks would be used as pill boxes on the front lines. The order gave detailed instructions as to just how they would be dug in. Protests did no good. The decision did not help the morale of the outfit any. We played an ace in the form of a little underground work. Two days later, an order came out from USAFFE which stated, among other things, that the tanks would *not* be used as pill boxes! That was that!

A little later, at a conference, the General made a statement that if II Corps did not conduct an offensive against the Japs in our sector, the tanks would. In the first place, the physical condition of the troops precluded the possibility of such an offensive. In the second place, artillery and other supporting weapons, necessary for an offensive, were practically non-existent.

Informally, all this was called to his attention, which apparently made no impression. He outlined a tentative plan, from his map, for an offensive by the tanks. The plan was nothing more nor less than the running of his finger over the map, in a circle, in front of our main line of resistance. The tanks would take off—following the circle—with the mission of overrunning and shooting up the Japs. How we were to travel over the area involved will never be known. Some of it was impossible to traverse without wings! This plan, however, never materialized.

Another plan that he had in mind was to turn the Tankers into Infantrymen, which he said could be done in 24 hours. We had a heated argument over this and the Tankers won. It was the first time we had won an argument with him. Nothing more was said along those lines.

And yet another master plan was concocted by Tank Group. The scheme was to go north of our lines, during the night, and stretch a cable diagonally across the road down which we knew the Japs were bringing trucks. The idea was that the trucks would hit the cable diagonally and then would be thrown off the road into the ditch! Whether or not this plan would have defeated the Japs can only be left to the imagination! We never tried it.

Despite the turmoil of these hectic days and wild plans of operations, the forces on Bataan retained their humor. We called ourselves names, coined either from ideas heard over the short wave radio from the United States, or thought up on the spot. Among us were MacArthur's Magnificents, Wainwright's Warriors, Wainwright's Worriers, Battling Bastards of Bataan, Orphans of the Pacific, and Doug's Doddering Dullards!

Propaganda, in the form of leaflets, pictures, etc., was dropped on us by Jap planes. It was directed mostly to the Filipino troops, although one piece of propaganda was meant for the

Americans. It pictured a skeleton—depicting the American soldier—holding out for a lost cause. The other propaganda dropped contained pictures of nude women and also peaceful pictures of Filipino women with their children in the safety of their homes. The Jap way of thinking was, on the one hand, to play upon the sensuality of the individual if he were so inclined, and on the other, to create a yearning for loved ones—all in the hopes of starting wholesale desertions. Always, in the batch of propaganda, were two other pertinent pieces of literature. One was a badly written indictment against the United States and why the Filipino should not espouse our cause. The other was a safe "pass" into Japanese lines. It instructed the recipient, that with this pass, he would be received with all due hospitality and would be conducted back to his home and loved ones. All he had to do was to lay down his arms and "come over" and everything would be forgiven! Very few Filipinos took advantage of that "generous" offer.

One night, we were startled to hear a loud speaker emanating from Jap positions. It exhorted the Filipino and all others to give up and end the useless, hopeless resistance. The voice was just getting warmed up to the point of shedding the proverbial Japanese crocodile tears, when our artillery slammed the position with a short but very effective barrage. We never did hear the loud speaker again!

Captain Spoor brought me two pieces of paper one day. He had picked them up in our headquarters. On each was scrawled a poem, the authors of which were unknown. The first was complete. The second was half finished. For want of something better to do, I finished it:

Be My Valentine

While the bombers soar above
Come and be my jungle love
Here beneath the absent moon
We'll enjoy a flashlight spoon
Safe? from burst of bomb or shell
Be my Val— Oh! What the hell!
You're 10,000 miles away
Feb. fourteenth is just a day!

Stranded on Bataan

They sent us to the Philippines
We thought it a vacation
This visit to the land of dreams
Proved our complete ruination.

Soon after we had landed here
The Japs came down to meet us
With planes and bombs and tanks and guns
They all came down to greet us.

Our tanks were rolled from Stotsenburg
Down to Batangas Bay
From there we hit Lingayen Gulf
Then to Bataan to stay.

We covered all withdrawals too
In the darkness of the night
No infantry for close support
Though we howled with all our might.

The Agno River line was held
With thirty M-3 tanks
Five and twenty good, long miles
Along the river's bank.

No other troops available
To help us through the night
Our weapons mighty useless
Not even could we sight.

The tanks were always last to leave
The active scene of strife
Our orders late or none at all
This was our daily life.

So here we sit, in old Bataan
Just waiting for our aid
We listen to the radio—tell
How much U. S. has made!

CHAPTER 21

"Help Is on the Way"

INTELLIGENCE REPORTS, coming into Bataan about the middle of February, indicated that something big was going to happen. From that time until early in April, the Japs were pouring troops and materiel of war into Luzon. As time went on, it became apparent that the Japs were landing a second invasion force. As was evidenced later on, it was a huge one. United States propaganda had won. The Japs were going to save face.

Enemy air activity increased. The tempo gradually mounted. One day 78 bombers flew over us. We thought an attempt might be made to land paratroopers on our airfields, and we took special precautions for any such possibility. However, nothing of the kind materialized.

Plans were laid to erect some kind of shelters, in the event we could hold out until the rainy season started. We knew, if this came to pass, that the Japs could not conduct much of an offensive, for the reason that it would bog down. If disease and malnutrition could be kept at bay, we might last until help arrived. Normally, wet weather would start about the first of May, but if luck was with us, it might come in April. Thus we reasoned, and thus we hoped.

Two newspaper correspondents, quartered on Corregidor, visited headquarters of the 194th one day. I had the opportunity of talking to them for about two hours before they had to take the boat back to the Rock. This boat made the run daily between Corregidor and Cabcaben, Bataan. The return trip was made after dusk each day. During our talk, they confirmed a persistent rumor I had heard for some time, relative to the censorship conducted by General MacArthur. They stated that all censorship was handled by MacArthur—personally—across his desk, and that all communiques were written by him. This accounted for the dramatic wording of those communiques we had heard relayed out of San Francisco over KGEI!

On March 12, 1942, it was made known that General Mac-Arthur had left for Australia under orders of the President of the United States. We heard it by rumor at first, which was soon confirmed by official orders. The reaction among officers and men, was at first somewhat bitter, but after time had been taken out for a little reasoning, Bataan defenders on the whole, did not retain that bitterness. They realized that the order, without doubt, had been issued by the President for the good of the war effort—that the location of the commander of the United States Forces in the Far East, should be wherever he could best function. There were some who held their bitterness and still do, but the vast majority did not. The lasting criticism held against MacArthur has nothing to do with this incident. It relates itself to his indecision, lack of proper and practical planning, and failure to prosecute WPO-3 (War Plan Orange No. 3) during the prewar days, and during the period of war up to the time we retired to Bataan.

Two schools of thought now generated discussions.

The first argued that MacArthur had been taken to Australia to organize reinforcements which were there waiting for us—both troops and supplies. Also that we could not expect help until someone, who knew the true situation, arrived on the scene to direct it. It must be admitted that this school had documentary evidence to back up its reasoning. This evidence was in the form of two releases from Corregidor before MacArthur left. The first (both were in mimeograph form and required to be read to the troops) was while we were still holding the Abucay-Hacienda line:

Hq.
USAFFE
Fort Mills, P. I.

January 15, 1942

Subject: Message From General MacArthur

To: All Unit Commanders

The following message from General MacArthur will be read and explained to all troops. Every Company Commander is charged with the personal responsibility for the delivery of this message. Each headquarters will follow up to insure reception by every company or similiar unit.

Help is on the way from the United States. Thousands of troops and hundreds of planes are being dispatched. The exact time of arrival of reinforcements is unknown as they will have to fight their way through Japanse attempts against them. It is imperative that our troops hold until these reinforcements arrive.

.....................; our supplies are ample; a determined defense will defeat the enemy's attack.

. . . .

(Signed) MACARTHUR

CARL H. SEALS, Col. A.G.D.
Adjutant General

The second release came sometime in February, when we had retired to the Pilar-Bagac line. It was contained in the mimeographed news sheets officially issued by USAFFE. It was quite a story, written by a newspaper correspondent, who had accompanied a convoy from the United States to Australia, and lent support to MacArthur's foregoing statement. In essence, the correspondent described the convoy as being the largest ever viewed by man. He did not give the composition of the convoy, but according to him, it really was huge, and to the beleaguered defenders of Bataan, it meant a great deal. Coming from USAFFE, it meant everything!

The second school of thought argued that if all this were true, the best place for MacArthur to do the directing, would be right where he had been—on Corregidor. They opined that there was no chance for reinforcements reaching us in time. That was the reason why MacArthur had been taken away. If supplies were ample—where were they? We desperately needed them now!

Once again, it must be remembered that we had no idea how badly we had been hit at Pearl Harbor. Also that a drowning man will always grasp at any straw. Those talking for the latter viewpoint were always glad to be out-argued.

My own personal opinion was somewhat inconsistent. I argued with myself continuously, and would favor one side and then the other. I think this was true of most of us. I know that I never gave up *hoping*. Faith in Uncle Sam kept the spark alive.

Anyone who ever has, or will, under estimate the enlisted

man, is due for a rude awakening. His eyes and his ears are always open and nothing escapes his attention. In fact, enlisted men, by the very nature of their existence, may be more alert at times, than the officer. They live by their wits, indulge in many and varied discussions, and are always trying to evaluate the future. The officer, naturally, is in a more confined status, and while he also evaluates the future, he is more concerned with the responsibility of immediate problems, with which he is specifically charged. Those who have served in the ranks know, that if you wish to ascertain the latest "scuttlebutt"—find out what the men are thinking and talking about.

Sometime before MacArthur left for Australia, the men in the 194th were discussing a rumor to that effect and the possibility thereof! I had not heard it before even if I had been "around." Walking into the S-1 Section of my headquarters one day, I found a group of the men gathered together, reading from a sheet of paper. They were laughing quite heartily. Joining the group, I asked what it was all about, and one of the sergeants handed the paper to me. It was a poem to be sung to the air "The Battle Hymn of the Republic." Who wrote the poem, no one knows—or, at least, I have never heard. I only know that many others, in different outfits, had seen this poem *before* MacArthur's departure. This literary effort is very derogatory to him. It is not for this reason that I set it down on paper. My only reason is to depict, with clarity, just what went on in the minds of the men of Bataan, and how they most forcibly evaluated the future. The story cannot be told without incorporating the details. Anyway—here it is:

USAFFE Cry of Freedom

Dugout Doug MacArthur lies a shaking on the Rock,
Safe from all the bombers and from any sudden shock
Dugout Doug is eating of the best food on Bataan
And his troops go starving on.

Dugout Doug's not timid, he's just cautious, not afraid
He's protecting carefully the stars that Franklin made
Four star generals are rare as good food on Bataan
And his troops go starving on.

Dugout Doug is ready in his Kris Craft for the flee
Over bounding billows and the wildly raging sea
For the Japs are pounding on the gates of Old Bataan
And his troops go starving on.

We've fought the war the hard way since they said the fight
    was on
All the way from Lingayen to the hills of Old Bataan
And we'll continue fighting after Dugout Doug is gone
And still go starving on.

Chorus:
Dugout Doug, come out from hiding
Dugout Doug, come out from hiding
Send to Franklin the glad tidings
That his troops go starving on!

When MacArthur left for Australia, Major General Jonathan Wainwright was given command of Luzon, including Corregidor. It was MacArthur's intention to still exercise command by remote control. Who changed it, I do not know. But soon after, Wainwright was promoted to lieutenant general, commander in chief of the troops in the Philippines. As far as I could ever ascertain, the order came directly from Washington and without the knowledge of MacArthur. Thereafter the term USAFFE was dropped, and by order from Wainwright we became USFIP (United States Forces in the Philippines).

About the time of the change in supreme commanders, our "Air Force" staged an offensive of their own against the Japs. We had picked up two or three P-40's. They were used from time to time for reconnaissance. The Japanese had taken over Subic Bay and shore installations when we had retired to Bataan. The Air Force had fitted these P-40's with homemade bomb racks. They waited until the Nips had gathered quite a large concentration of shipping in the harbor. Then, they took off, loaded with explosives, and came in low and fast. Considerable damage was done and the P-40's came safely back but cracked up when landing on the airfield near Mariveles. Bad luck seemed to follow us no matter what we did. It helped our morale though, when we listened to Domei

News Agency broadcasting from Tokyo, relative to the raid. The announcement stated that Subic Bay shipping had been attacked by a large fleet of B-17's (somewhere in the neighborhood of 30) and that about half of them were shot down!

I Corps, on the west side of Bataan, was now commanded by Brigadier General A. M. Jones. Major General Parker still commanded II Corps on the east side. Wainwright had kept his headquarters on Bataan until Washington gave him the command of USFIP, after which, he headquartered on Corregidor. He placed Major General Edward P. King (our old friend of Stotsenburg) in command of the Luzon Forces. That automatically put King in as commanding general of Bataan.

Intelligence reports, during the latter part of March, included pertinent information that the Japs were concentrating in front of II Corps. G-2 estimates, of the original enemy invasion force and the new landings of the second invasion force, placed Jap strength since the start of the war at 300,000 to 400,000—all on Luzon! They were fully equipped, well fed, and in addition, were veteran troops.

Jap planes dropped many demands for immediate surrender. They were all addressed to Wainwright and implied a dire threat if no answer was forthcoming within three days. There was no reply made.

Enemy long-range guns were now set up across Manila Bay, east of Corregidor. They poured heavy concentrations on Corregidor and the little island fortresses of Drum, Frank, and Hughes. Most of our armament could only be fired out to sea. The designers had never contemplated a situation in which it might be necessary to fire in any other direction! With what was available, the enemy fire was returned. However, this artillery was further handicapped by the fact that we had no air observation. The Japs, of course, did.

New types of enemy bombers were making their appearance. Small but fierce localized attacks were being staged on the II Corps line. They were all repelled but casualties were heavy. We knew what the Jap was trying to find—the right spot in the line for an all-out offensive against us. Our patrols were meeting with stiffer resistance which increased as each day went by. There could be no doubt that II Corps would be hit and hit hard. And there was nothing to do about it. Troops and materiel of war were not available to strengthen any part of the line. Gasoline supplies were so low that most vehicles had to be laid up. That meant the line of supply, what little we did have, was almost a nonentity. A major attack now would mean complete disaster. Men were becoming too weak even to repair simple earthworks damaged by enemy fire. And still, hand to hand combat was, and would be fought.

On about the last day of March, the Japs bombed one of our hospitals. It was plainly marked and there could be no excuse. Over the radio, the Japs announced their traditional "so sorry" speech. It had been unintentional. Between then and the fall of Bataan (9 days later) they bombed the plainly marked hospital areas two more times to my knowledge! The casualties were heavy.

At 3:00 P.M., April 3rd—Good Friday—the Japs launched their all-out attack. They had brought up a tremendous concentration of artillery, mortars, anti-tank guns and tanks to within range of a portion of the II Corps line. They poured into this sector a vast deluge of high explosive shells. All their efforts were directed at this one sector. At the same time, Jap bombers also concentrated on the area. Our line was, absolutely and literally, blown right out of the ground.

By Saturday afternoon, Holy Saturday, April 4th, their long-range artillery was reaching well into Bataan. Rear areas were being pounded as well as front lines. After that terrific shelling and bombing of this sector, Jap infantry, with supporting weapons, moved up and took possession of the blown out portion of the line. Then they worked toward the east—Manila Bay. It obviously was an attempt to roll up the front lines.

Late Saturday afternoon the Tank Group Commander appeared at my command post and gave me the latest information. In substance, it was what we already knew. He said the Philippine Division under General Lough would make an attempt to close the gap by counter attacking. I would proceed with one Tank Company into the area to aid that attack. He also said that the company I would take from beach defense, would be replaced by one company of the 192nd Tank Battalion which would remain attached to my outfit.

I designated Co. "C", and shortly after dark started out with them on the trek. Canby was left in command of the

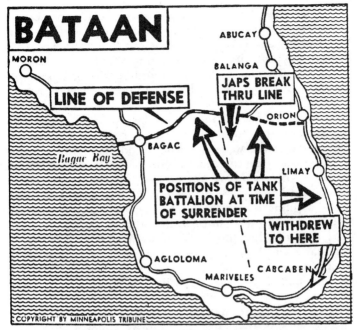

rear echelon and Johnson in command of the combat elements. Spoor accompanied me. We reached an area which could be used for bivouac and left the company there. Our next job was to learn the latest developments and find the Philippine Division.

Spoor and I very nearly took ourselves and our Jeep into enemy occupied territory that night. By mere luck, we stumbled into the 31st Infantry. They were in bivouac and had arrived a short time before, and were in very poor physical condition. In coming up, they could march for only about ten minutes and then had to rest. They would take the offensive the next morning.

The whereabouts of Headquarters, Philippine Division, was not known. Things were in a state of flux. Positions and headquarters were being shifted geographically, continuously, to meet the ever-changing situation. Where they were a short time ago, did not hold good now. Spoor and I traveled up and down trails all night. About 7:00 A.M. Sunday—Easter—we located the headquarters.

The Japanese had made much progress and had succeeded in establishing themselves firmly in the sector through which they had broken. Our forces to the east had refused their left flank to the Japs, and were attempting to hold that flank. The Philippine Division was trying to formulate some type of plan for the attack, that might have a little intelligence attached to it.

So much Japanese strength was pitted against them, that the situation seemed hopeless. The 45th Infantry (Philippine Scouts) was to the west of II Corps, and mountains separated us. After much consultation, pulling plans apart and putting them together again, it was decided that the 45th Infantry would attack, early the next morning, north on Trail 29. It would attempt to turn the Jap right flank, which if successful, would cause the Japs, in turn, to withdraw northward out of the breach they had forced. We would take our tanks over the mountains and join the 45th in the attack. The plan was almost hopeless from the start, but was the best that could be brought out of the bag under the conditions which prevailed.

Spoor and I drove over the mountains, arriving at Trail 29 about 4:00 P.M. that same day—Sunday. Colonel Doyle, commanding officer of the 45th, had arrived a little earlier with two battalions of his regiment. He told me they had been ordered over from the west that day. Trail 29 was in I Corps area. He stated he would attack at 6:00 A.M. the next morning, April 6th. We laid our plans, and at about 7:00 P.M. Spoor and I went back to pick up Company "C" still in bivouac.

The trail over the mountains was jammed with traffic. All of these trails were just what the word implies—just *trails*. They were hewn out of the jungle by the troops, after we had withdrawn behind the Pilar-Bagac line. In many places it was impossible for two vehicles to pass. Many wounded were being evacuated. The whole thing was in a state of intense confusion.

After much difficulty we reached the bivouac. The company was prepared for movement over the mountains and we started. If we thought we had had a hard time coming over in one lone Jeep, it was "duck soup" compared with the job we now had to perform.

A good share of the way, we had to almost literally bring our men up and either lift vehicles off the trail or shove them off with tanks. In addition, our tanks were in very bad shape. We coaxed, cussed, and hauled. How can one live so long in just a few, short hours? It seemed like years, and when I recall that night—six and one-half years later—it still does! All vehicles containing wounded going to the rear, had to be taken care of. Still we had a mission to perform.

Heat lightning on the horizon made me think of naval battles—*our Navy*—arriving with the help we had prayed so hard to get—*guns—planes—men—to drive the yellow bastards back from where they came! Why didn't they come?*

My reverie came to an end abruptly. We were at Trail 29 and the time was 6:10 A.M.—ten minutes late. Moving up the trail, we found the 45th moving northward steadily. It was not until 9:00 A.M. that the Japs were encountered and the meeting engagement took place.

There was no place for tanks to operate except on the trail. Dense jungle loomed on each side of us. With Colonel Doyle and his staff, we discussed the situation and decided to develop the attack so as to use the tanks at most advantage.

The Japs were using explosive bullets a great deal. This is a bullet that proceeds on its path of travel until striking an object. It then explodes. It was one of the tricks of the Oriental mind. Many of the bullets would reach to the rear of our line before striking an object that would cause it to explode. It gave the impression that infiltrations of the enemy had occurred, and that we were being fired upon from the rear.

Not much progress could be made by either side, due to the dense jungle. The situation had not developed to warrant the use of tanks.

At about 3:30 P.M., Colonel Doyle and I went into a huddle. He was extremely concerned with the fact, that he had been unable to make contact with other troops of the I Corps to the left. Nor had there been contact with any troops on our right. That indicated that the Japs were in full possession to the east. We expected that, but the burning question was—how far south?

The Philippine Scouts were doing the best they could. Jap mortar fire was heavy. The Scouts had to take it with none to throw back. During the day, I had the opportunity—and honor—of witnessing the mettle of these Scouts.

After the battle had opened in the morning, Colonel Doyle had sent a patrol of Scouts, out to the west, to make contact with our forces. This patrol never returned. All in all, five patrols were sent out in that direction during the day. When the first patrol failed to return, everyone knew what had happened.

As each succeeding group was called up to receive instructions and orders for patrol duty, every last man took his orders with no trace of reluctance or fear whatever. There was only explicit obedience in the job they had to perform. They knew the seriousness of the situation which confronted them, and I marveled at their soldierly qualities. They knew that death undoubtedly awaited them, but the last patrol went just as eagerly as the first.

All during this day, many wounded Scouts were brought to the rear. Not once did I hear one whimper of pain or an utterance of complaint.

Now, as Colonel Doyle and I talked the situation over with a view of developing the Japanese positions, I asked him if he had any trench mortars. He replied that he had only one, and the supply of shells was very limited. He called on S-4 to determine exactly how many shells were available. The S-4 reported that the regiment had ten! We then decided to set this one mortar up in position and attempt to have direct observation. Five of the shells would be spared for the operation!

The plan was to fire them at 5:00 P.M. in an attempt to dislodge part of the Jap line, so that the tanks could follow up and put the Nips on the run.

The mortar was set up and direct observation was obtained. Now, the enemy received a taste of the medicine they had been dishing out all day! The five pathetic shells were expended with miraculous results. Direct hits were made on the Japanese line. That portion of the line not only evacuated, but left their guns and equipment as they ran! Perhaps they were taken completely by surprise. The Scouts immediately followed up, killing many Japs on either side of the breach, and putting the rest on the run. This was accomplished before the tanks could even make their way up the trail!

This later proved to be a most fortunate occurrence. In following the Scouts up the trail, I found that the Japs had placed their vicious pie-pan mines not only on the trail, but also in every locality where a tank could possibly travel. Had our tanks proceeded as to plan, the thing that we were always concerned about would have happened. The tanks would have been knocked out.

I pointed this out to Doyle. He was one officer with whom we came in contact, who at all times, was cognizant of the limitations and capabilities of tanks. Doyle and his Scouts consolidated the position obtained. It was growing dark, so we laid plans for the continuance of the attack the next morning. He was still greatly concerned about the vulnerability of his flanks, not having made contact all day.

His executive officer, Lt. Colonel Wright, and myself went back to the rear echelon of the 45th, to try to contact by field telephone, the headquarters of the Philippine Division for further orders and to ascertain the situation.

It was *situation perilous!*

CHAPTER 22

The Fall of Bataan

SHORTLY AFTER WE arrived at the rear echelon of the 45th Infantry, headquarters of the Philippine Division was reached on the field telephone by Colonel Wright. He told them what had happened and asked for further orders. Briefly, we were to consolidate the gains and attack early the next morning. No information was available as to the situation on our left, but it was thought that the Japanese were not active but were merely holding and not making much of an attempt to push. The situation on our right was deteriorating very rapidly. The Japanese had consolidated their breakthrough and were advancing steadily. Casualties were high on both sides, but apparently, the Japs had men and equipment which knew no bounds. The command post of the division had been forced to change position because of receiving small arms fire from the enemy. This meant that the Japs were in full possession of the regimental reserve line of the sector in which they had made their initial thrust. How far south of that line they were—no one knew.

After taking care of other details, we were just starting to leave when the field telephone rang. It was Division Headquarters with other orders countermanding the one we had just received. II Corps had come up with other plans.

The 45th Infantry and supporting tanks were to proceed over the mountains to the east, that night, to the vicinity of Trails 6 and 8 in the II Corps area, and go into position on the high ground north of Trail 8. The 57th Infantry (also Philippine Scouts) would go into position immediately, in that vicinity. We would be on their left. There would be an attempt to establish a new line of resistance, extending from the refused flank of the forces to the east, southwesterly across the breach which the Japs had made. It was felt that the pocket, already consolidated by the enemy, could not be recaptured at that time. To save the flank of our troops on the original line was of paramount importance.

Just as the conversation was terminated, a voice came over the wire in perfect American English: "Curtains for you, Mr. Doyle!" It was a known fact that the Japs had tapped our field lines before, but it was not very comforting to have them tell you about it!

We went forward in the darkness and acquainted Colonel Doyle with the new orders. My men reported to me that they had been fired upon at dusk, evidently by snipers. It had been too dark, and the jungle so thick, that they had been unable to do anything about it except to return the fire in that general direction. No further hostile fire was delivered.

We formed the column on the trail and brought it southward to the junction of Trails 29 and 8. There, we met General Lough, commander of the Philippine Division. He stated that the situation to the east was flux—*period!* And he did not have a great deal of confidence in being able to carry out the new orders to completion.

General Lough was an individual who was always determined to know the situation from first hand information. He constantly kept his staff on edge by remaining too close to enemy lines. To capture a division command post means almost chaos within the division. The head of the body is gone. Each unit of that division functions piecemeal until it can be reorganized. The General never would move his command post until it was absolutely necessary, and he did come close to being captured. Therefore, I knew he was making his statements from personal knowledge and not from reports. He also said that at least a part of Trail 6, which ran north and south, was in the hands of the Japanese that afternoon. For that reason, he wanted to move over the mountains very slowly and not get the whole outfit in a trap. What a prophet he proved himself to be that night!

It was decided that a portion of the 45th and two of my tanks would act as the advance party, as it were. We would proceed over the mountains. If everything was in order, the rest of the outfit would follow and go into position. If we met resistance, we should turn the column around and report back. Lough reasoned that if resistance was encountered, the Japs must be there in force.

Two tanks were placed at the head of the column. Scouts were sent out in front, on foot, to act as "feelers." The 45th had marched a long distance the day before over mountainous terrain, had fought all this day, and now were on a mission that would have been rough, even for fresh troops. Once again the mettle of these superb soldiers came to the front. During that night, and the events which followed, I never heard one word of complaint, only extreme attention to duty!

At the end of each 50 minutes, we halted for ten minutes, to give the foot soldiers a rest. As we approached the proximity of Trails 6 and 8, it so happened that the 50-minute period had elapsed and the lead tank, setting the time and pace, stopped for the usual 10-minute rest. I was riding in a Jeep directly behind the second tank. My driver had swung to the extreme right of the trail.

Just about the time we stopped, the Scouts in front of the leading tank came running back. It was fairly light as the moon was up. They were about even with the first tank when they called out: *"Japs!"*

Almost simultaneously, a shot was fired from an anti-tank gun located at the junction of Trails 6 and 8. The shell was armor piercing and went directly through the turret of the first tank. It came close to the head of the tank commander, Lt. Frank Riley. Almost immediately, heavy caliber machine guns opened up, together with other anti-tank guns.

The second tank had stopped on the trail just behind the first, but was located in just enough of a depression, so that the top of the turret was barely exposed. At least one, and perhaps more, Jap shells hit the top and bounced off. The driver of the first tank received particles of metal in his eyes but not too serious. Other than the severe concussion Lt. Riley had received, there were no other casualties.

The crew of the first tank evacuated it after firing a burst in return. Then, with the crew of the second tank, they backed it toward a bend in the trail to our rear.

Meanwhile, the Scouts had formed a line to our rear and fired blindly in the direction of the Japs to cover our withdrawal. That is the only thing that saved us. Their actions that night would have been more than a credit to the best trained and bravest soldiers in the world.

Shells followed us the 100 yards or so, in withdrawing to the bend in the trail. They blew sand and gravel into our skin, and we picked it out for days after, but we arrived intact. The two occupants in the rear of my Jeep, one of which was Colonel Wright, we never have determined their fate. I have never seen them, but did hear that Wright dove for the jungle, was wounded, but came out alive. My Jeep received a direct hit on the right side.

Under cover of the fire being delivered by the Scouts, we turned the vehicles, which had accompanied us, to the west. The general withdrawal of the column was covered by our one tank. I talked with two of the leaders of the Scouts who had been in the "feelers." They told me that they had discerned shadowy forms as they approached the junction, and had just been on the point of challenging when they heard a voice say plainly: "Here comes Doyle and his gang!"

By now, the physical condition of the Scouts we had with us, was near complete exhaustion. On the return march, we saw quite a number of Philippine Army soldiers who had thrown away their rifles and were evacuating to the rear. The Scouts were different. Often one would drop in his tracks. It was only by shame that we could get their exhausted bodies to stumble on. We would look at them and say: "Are you Philippine Army or are you Scout?" Without exception, they would stand as erect as possible—and then plod on. I love them and I am not ashamed of it!

Our column finally reached the junction we had left the night before—Trails 8 and 29. It was about 8:00 A.M., Tuesday, April 7th. Having sent a message to General Lough, on the way back, we found the balance of the 45th Infantry had been ordered out of the area to another assignment. The balance of my tanks were waiting for us. They had received no further orders other than to hold the trail junction. We had a reunion on the spot. They had heard several stories ranging all the way from our capture to our deaths. That morning, they had stopped a Japanese tank attack down Trail 29 from the north, knocking out two Jap tanks and discouraging the rest.

One of our tanks, in the engagement, had one of its cylinders blown out. The tank commander said the engine had been acting up before, but after the cylinder was blown out, the engine seemed to be running more smoothly! He was careful, however, to keep the motor idling.

Shortly after we arrived at the junction, a radio message

was received from General Weaver. It ordered me to leave the company there, and to return to the 194th on the east side of Bataan to take direct command again. I was to stop at Tank Group Headquarters for further orders on my way through. Leaving Captain Fred Moffitt in charge, I started back. There was no possible route open except to go west and thence south along the west coast of Bataan.

I met Colonel Doyle on the way out and acquainted him with my new orders. I asked him to keep an eye out for Co. "C" as there was no one at the junction to help them in event the Japanese pushed their attack on Trail 29 again. He promised he would—and he did.

During the day, Japanese bombers and strafers pounded unmercilessly. They came over in veritable clouds—wave after wave. At times the sky was almost black with them.

Reaching Tank Group Headquarters, I reported to the commander. He was very friendly that night and I sincerely wish I could remember him that way. He told me that the situation was extremely precarious. It had been impossible to organize, in any way, the high ground in the vicinity of Trails 6 and 8. The main line of II Corps had been forced to give and it was being rolled up. He had ordered our rear echelon into an area further to the south, as it had been bombed heavily that afternoon. He told me to take direct command again of front line tank support and beach installations.

Driving north, I found the road clogged with traffic coming south. This was the only road we had. After battling against odds for several hours, I met the head of our rear echelon column on its way to the new location. This was just to the west of Cabcaben airfield. Japanese bombers had raised havoc with our old area that afternoon. We arrived at our destination about 4:00 A.M., Wednesday, April 8th.

With ever increasing pressure, backed up by unlimited reserves of men and equipment, the Japs were rolling up the main line to the east. Thus they forced that portion of the line to become ever narrower. Lack of an adequate road system precluded the possibility of throwing in anything effective enough to stop the push—even if we had had anything to throw in.

Headquarters II Corps had called on the 194th Tank Battalion for a conference the day before, which Captain Johnson had attended as my representative. The conference was for discussion of a plan for the operation of a company of tanks on Trail 2 and 10 and in an area at the front. Upon arriving at headquarters, Johnson was shown the plan by the G-3 of II Corps and Lt. Colonel Smythe (just promoted from major), executive officer of Tank Group.

The plan was in detail, even to the extent of being plotted on the map. It called for the use of tanks as "road patrols" on the trails, without any support whatever. Johnson was asked to give an opinion. He told them frankly that if they wanted an honest opinion, the plan was lousy! Trails were very narrow, hostile aircraft were overhead bombing and strafing all trails, Jap anti-tank guns and artillery covered all trail approaches, the tanks could not get off the trails, and no supporting infantry was available. Other than that, the plan was excellent!

A modified plan was then agreed upon. It was submitted to General Parker, commanding II Corps, who approved it after a wait of two hours. Capt. Johnson returned to the 194th command post and made ararngements for Co. "D", under command of Capt. Jack Altman, to go forward.

As later developments proved, even the modified plan could not be consummated, due to the confusion which existed in that part of the sector. What had been points of resistance literally became points of enemy occupation within a few minutes. Most of our meager artillery had been either put out of action or captured. There were no supporting weapons, nor what might be termed as supporting troops.

The break-through had been complete. The Japs had brought everything in—almost including the proverbial kitchen sink! Our tanks, sent up on the trails, were not only bombed heavily and quite a number knocked out, but those that survived, were bogged down on these trails by disabled Filipino buses and other vehicles, which blocked all movement.

Our beach defense units, Company "A" of the 194th, and Company "A" of the 192nd (attached to the 194th) were still in position and in the path of the Japanese advance. One of our half-track crews on Trail 10, equipped with radio, performed excellent and meritorious service, in submitting first hand information to II Corps, during the last two days of fighting—April 7th and 8th.

The Japs attempted a landing through our beach positions. They used smoke to cover their advance, but the wind was such that the screen was more of a hindrance to them than value. They made no progress and finally withdrew.

The new site, which we moved into, had no value whatever. Thick jungle and deep ravines were on each side of the trail. The best we could do, was to move into the area immediately adjacent and along the trail.

Late that afternoon, April 8th, I received orders to move the echelon into another area further to the south near Tank Group Headquarters. Also included in the orders—our combat units would hold their positions but would withdraw that night so as to be in the Tank Group area before daylight the next morning, April 9th.

The movement was made. We picked up Co. "D" and put them in the column. Military police stopped us several kilometers north of our destination. They stated that existing dumps of munitions were to be blown in a short time and all traffic was to be halted during the operation.

Capt. Spoor and I were in a Jeep. As we sat waiting, I told him to shut off the motor so that we could conserve the gasoline. He replied that the motor had been shut off. What then was causing the vibration? Climbing out, my feet, on contacting the ground, conveyed the same tremor I had felt while sitting in the Jeep.

It increased in intensity until it became quite rough. I had to grasp the side of the vehicle, to keep my equilibrium. It was an earthquake. Even Mother Nature seemed to be turning against us. Shortly after, the dumps of dynamite and other explosives were sent skyward, belching flames high in the air, with a roar that seemed to come from the devil himself. Our feelings were numbed. We knew then, that here was the beginning of the end of Bataan.

After that, we were allowed to proceed to our area. Further orders were awaiting us there. If I received a message from Tank Group Headquarters with the one word *"blast"* in it, we were to immediately destroy all vehicles, guns and ammunition.

Elements of the 200th C.A. (AA), who had been bombed

out of their positions April 8th and who had turned themselves into infantry, together with elements of the 194th Tank Battalion, fired the last shots against the Japanese on Bataan on the night of April 8th-9th. By 6:30 A.M. of April 9th, the 194th in its entirety was in the area to which it had been ordered. At 7:00 A.M., I received a message from Group Headquarters.

It contained the one word—*"Blast."*

Black Thursday had arrived!

We placed our vehicles in segregated areas, broke off the gasoline valves in the crew compartments of the tanks so as to flood them with the aviation gasoline, and set fire to the interior. We also fired 37mm armor piercing shells into the tank and truck motors. Gasoline was dumped into the cabs and bodies of the trucks. The armor plate on the tanks was subjected to such intense heat that it was made useless except for scrap iron. There was not much left of our vehicles. Small arms and machine guns were completely stripped. Parts were tossed into the blazing vehicles, gun barrels were bent around trees, and stocks of rifles and Tommy guns were broken. We tossed the remains far out into the jungle.

Then we sat down to await developments!

Capt. Clinton D. Quinlen was sent with a detail of men to visit the Quartermaster Rationing Distribution Point with the hope of getting food for the outfit. After some time he reported back with a fair amount of food—but he virtually had to steal it. He was met with refusal to give out any food or cigarettes on the basis that the Quartermaster had no authority and would have to await orders! This, even in view of the fact that everyone knew that Bataan had been surrendered early that morning!

Quinlen used his initiative. He and the detail took the food, plus cigarettes, even while being threatened with court martial. The same procedure took place at another point. The officer, who was trying to draw the rations was told that he did not have an authentic strength return with him, showing the number of men to be fed. It was impossible, naturally, for the officer to have a strength return, inasmuch as this particular assembly area had been picked by the high command where withdrawing troops were to report. No one knew, nor could it be foretold just how many troops would come into the area. The Quartermaster officer in charge was still hidebound with regulationitis. He could not understand that an emergency existed for which there were no regulations! I was quartered in the same building with him at Cabanatuan Prison Camp for a short time. He was still regulation bound!

We took all the food we had in our outfit and divided it up equally among all our personnel. We had more to eat that day than we had had on any occasion since the start of the war. That was also to include a future period of nearly three and one-half years, but we didn't know it then. Our menu on April 9, 1942, included canned fruit.

The result of the Quartermaster's ridiculous stand was that the Japs reached the food dumps first—and destroyed them! Some of my men were sent on work details back into Bataan at a later date and saw the dumps. Canned goods were scattered all over the area. Each can had a hole punched in it by a bayonet or other sharp instrument!

Later in the day, we learned that negotiations had been made that morning, at about 5:00 o'clock, for the surrender. Also that General Wainwright had told General King that he would not surrender. King replied that there was nothing else to do. If he did not, he would be responsible for the annihilation of the troops. Wainwright replied to the effect: "There can be no surrender."

No Japanese appeared in our area on April 9th, although we knew they were close by. Officers and men of the 194th remained close together in the bivouac. Some partook of much needed rest. Some took part in poker and crap games. In our immediate vicinity, we had a crap game. I have never participated in a game of chance which meant so little as that one. We did not know what was in store for us. We did not know whether the winner could make use of his ill-gotten gains. We only knew that we had to kill time—somehow!

Our supper that night was a feast—corned beef hash and canned peaches. We cleaned it up. Everyone went to sleep with a full stomach. We dreamed of home and loved ones.

Though we did not know it then, those dreams were to be with us for weary months and years to come. We were to taste the torments of hell itself—the Death March—the hell ships—the stinking prison camps—starvation—disease—abuse—*death!* *Why?*

CHAPTER 23

The Japs Take Over

IT WAS ABOUT 7:00 A.M., Friday, April 10th, that the Japanese came into our area. They moved along the trail in column and were accompanied by a well-groomed interpreter who appeared to be very well educated and spoke precise English.

The column was composed of infantry and artillery, and evidently had been marching a long time. The soldiers looked as though they had had a rough time of it. The interpreter stopped while the main body of Japs moved on up the trail.

It was here that we witnessed an incident, characteristic of Japanese brutality and savage instinct, we were to see and experience for years to come.

One of the Jap soldiers fell down from sheer exhaustion. He apparently could not rise to his feet. He was immediately exhorted in sharp commands by a Jap sergeant. This failed to arouse him. The sergeant then slapped his face several times, almost hard enough to draw blood. This was followed by repeated kickings in the body by the sergeant.

Finally, with the aid of two privates, the man was put on his feet. He was shoved into the column. He stumbled forward on his nerve, face contorted in agony. Not a sound did he make.

The interpreter told us we could take whatever we could carry. Naturally, not knowing where we were going or how, we loaded ourselves quite heavily. Prior to this, I had destroyed my movie camera and all the films I had taken since the start of war. To be quite frank, I found myself somewhat tearful, when the destruction was completed. It all seemed like a bad dream. I am quite sure that almost everyone else felt the same way.

Addressing the interpreter, I inquired if transportation of any kind would be furnished. He replied that we would only have a short distance to walk and that we would then be picked up and transported to Mariveles, which is on the south tip of Bataan.

I asked him where we were going to be taken from there. He shrugged his shoulders and said he did not know.

On my person I had a wrist watch and a pocket watch. The interpreter was very much enamored with the pocket watch and wanted to know if I would sell it to him. I told him I did not care to dispose of it. Then he told me to get all the officers and men in column, which I did, and we moved up the trail.

A short time later, he asked me again if I would sell the watch to him. Before I could reply he asked how much it was worth. I told him that it had sold for about thirty dollars during the 1920's. After thinking the matter over, I decided to sell him the watch if he asked me again. He had stated that cash money would come in very handy later on.

Sure enough, he repeated the question: "Do you want to sell your watch?" I said, "Yes," and handed him the watch. He pocketed it, telling me he would pay for it as soon as we reached Mariveles, as he did not have the cash with him at the time.

We reached a point up the trail about two kilometers from where we had started. We were halted and the interpreter instructed me to fall the column out alongside the trail, and to remain in the immediate vicinity. This was done.

The place where we had halted seemed to be a sort of headquarters. A Japanese major was in command. He was fat and arrogant—about forty years old. Jap soldiers procured a chair for the major and placed it in the shade. Here, I witnessed the "caste" system in all its glory. As the sun shifted, His Highness would laboriously hoist his posterior, emit a few grunts, and a Jap soldier would move the chair into the shade again. This process was repeated as long as the major remained in the area. His map was held by two other soldiers, at a level with his eyes, so that he would not be compelled to bend over his fat belly. Military courtesy deluxe!

The major called me over and showed me the maps of Bataan with which the Japs were equipped. He did not speak English, but conversed through the interpreter. *The maps were exact reproductions of the best topographical maps our Army had in the Philippines!* The only feature which did not appear on the map was the main road on the east side of Bataan. I had the opportunity of examining the map minutely. My profession in civil life is that of engineer and I examined that map with the eye of an engineer.

Some time during the morning, the major left the area. Soon after, a Jap brigadier general made his appearance on horseback. He evidently found something wrong, because in the usual Jap way, he howled and grunted out gutteral commands, and a lot of scurrying took place. I was seated under a tree and noticed that he was looking me over pretty closely. Several times, the non-commissioned officer with whom the general was conversing, looked as if he would be coming over to requisition me for something or other, but each time, the General restrained him and nothing happened.

A little later on in the day, one of the Jap sergeants became quite ill. Another sergeant, who could speak fairly fluent English, came over and asked me if we had a doctor in the column. Captain Schneider was nearby and attended the sick Jap. What he did, I do not know, but one of the things he called for was hot water. Inside another hour, the Jap sergeant was on his feet, feeling much better. He, and the other non-com, who could speak English, came over and conversed for quite a time with Schneider and myself. They were both nearly six feet tall. We learned that the sick one had been attending college in Tokyo when the war broke out. He had been through the Malayan and Singapore campaign, and then had been with the Jap assault forces that took the Dutch East Indies. He hoped the war would be over soon so that he might go back to school. Apparently, the Jap high command had told the troops that the war would soon be over. Both the sergeant and his pal stated, with the utmost conviction, that Bataan ended the war. I told them that Corregidor had not surrendered as yet. They expressed amazement which was followed by disappointment. In a short time they brightened up again with the statement that Corregidor was the only thing left. After that, the war would be over. These two Japs were of a different breed than the bandy legged apes with whom we were to make our home for three and one-half years. True—they had the counter-clockwise Oriental mind, and all the Japanese characteristics—but in spite of that—they were different.

The sergeant showed me a small sack which he had tied to his belt. I looked inside and saw *human fingers*. The other

Jap explained that these were little fingers cut from the hands of five dead Japanese soldiers, close friends, who had been killed in the last few days of fighting!

The conversation finally got around to prisoners of war. They expressed their sympathy, but not in the white man's way. They indicated that because we had fought bravely, we never should have surrendered. When confronted with the fact that there was nothing more we could do, in the face of the odds against us, they shrugged their shoulders and calmly said that we should have gone on fighting anyway. When asked why we should invite complete annihilation which would have accomplished absolutely nothing, their reply was that the Japanese army would have admired us very much, because the Japanese did not surrender! I pointed out that we had taken about 400 Japanese prisoners during the campaign, and that they were either in the hospital or in the stockade, to the south of us. The sergeant interpreter looked at me in silence. Finally, when he had digested my statement, he turned to the other and a long conversation in Japanese ensued. At the end of it, the interpreter turned to me and said, "The Japanese do not surrender!" Before I could reply, they both scrambled to their feet and made off.

We stayed in this position until about 7:00 P.M. No food was furnished by the Japs. We did, however, get a little to eat. Most of us had saved some canned food. It was pooled together and redistribution made. It proved to be a godsend.

The column was formed and we prepared to move. The Japs placed me in command. In the column were the 194th Tank Battalion, elements of the 192nd Tank Battalion, Air Corps personnel, and other casual troops. Two guards were assigned with me at the head of the column. Both men were of the same type, as the two with whom we had had the interesting conversation, previously in the day—big, and approaching close to six feet. One spoke just enough English to make conversation possible. They were very courteous to me.

But, instead of going to Mariveles—we went north, in the opposite direction.

Needless to say, I never saw the interpreter again, with my watch.

I explained to the guards that the officers and enlisted men in the column were in a much weakened state, and that the

great majority were sick. They took recognition of this condition and allowed frequent rests that night. Every time we stopped to rest, the two Jap guards would find a suitable place for
me to sit down. At one of the stops, I threw myself on the
ground, most thankful for the brief respite. The guard, who

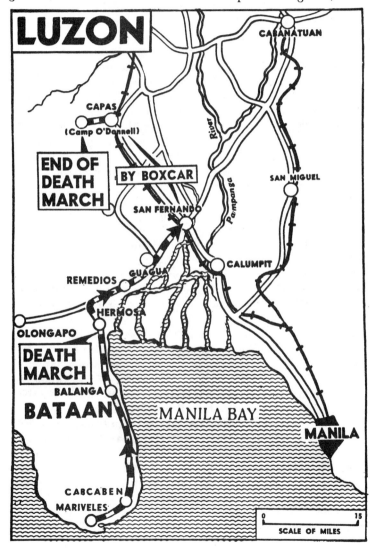

could not talk English, shook me by the shoulder and jabbered. I rose to my feet, and he pointed toward the other guard.
Looking in his direction, I saw him motioning to me. He
had found a box and had placed it on the shoulder of the
road for me to sit on! Then he produced a cigarette for me
and lit it. What I had yet to learn was, that the Jap was capable of both kindness and cruelty, a Doctor Jekyll and Mr.
Hyde, tears and sadism.

On the march that night, the guards said that they understood trucks would meet us further up the road, and that we
would be taken to Manila where we would be given adequate
quarters. I have never doubted their veracity in telling me
this. They, undoubtedly, had been told that by higher authority. Japs are like that. Details mean nothing. We were to be
the witnesses for three and one-half years of orders coming
down, which were continually being misinterpreted and details lacking. The Jap is incapable of coordinating details. I
am sure that these two guards were told that trucks would
meet us, and that their orders were to take us up the road
until that occurred. The originator of the order, without
doubt, had no idea where we were going except that he had
been told to take us north. That is hard to understand from
the white man's point of view. But, that is the way the Japanese, to a large extent, fought the war. It is extremely fortunate
that they were incapable of coordinating details in the American way. Otherwise, the war might have ended much differently.

From these guards, and other Jap personnel in the area
where we had been quartered that day, we gained a great deal
of information, as to the composition of the second Japanese
invasion force. I began to get the picture of just what the
propaganda had been all about that we had heard over the
KGEI short wave radio station at San Francisco.

The Japanese had fallen for the bait. And the characteristic of saving face—so common with the Japanese—had brought
results which was the one big mistake they made in the entire
war. The propaganda of the United States, in stating flatly
that the Japanese could not take Bataan, and that the defenders dared them to take it, had gone all over the Far East.
They actually stopped their southward plunge towards Australia and thus saved America their only base. They brought

the cream of the crop, back to the Philippines, from the Dutch East Indies and from Singapore. They even brought them from China and the mainland of Japan itself, in the evolved determination to show the world they could take Bataan and Corregidor. They took no chances, but brought in everything.

As late as the latter part of July, 1942, the Japs were still taking this force out of the Philippines to continue the southward plunge. But, by that time, it was too late. *The Japanese never were able to take the offensive again, on a major scale.* Had they continued the offensive as their time table planned, and by-passed the Philippines when their first invasion force failed, there is no doubt whatever but that Australia would have been in the hands of the Japanese. *There were hardly any troops to oppose them.*

Evaluating this information, meant a great deal of good for our morale. Hope sprung anew! We realized then, that we had played a big part in the war, and that our defense of Bataan had been a major effort. It helped!

At about 3:00 A.M., the Jap guards called a halt and allowed us to rest for about an hour. We were in a much exhausted state, and the belongings we were carrying, weighed heavily. But we were loath to part with them, because of the belief that we would meet the trucks.

At about 4:00 A.M., we continued the march, and at various times, stopped to rest. We reached Lamao at about 8:00 A.M., April 11th. Here we were allowed to forage for breakfast. The Japs produced no food, therefore very little was available. At about 9:00 A.M., we continued the march and reached Limay at about noon. It was here that our troubles started.

Our two guards, after much courteous leave-taking, departed. The marchers were in a pitiful state. No food was available, and very little water. The Japanese, here, seemed to be under hardly any control. They ran rampant in the area, looting, searching baggage at shakedown inspections, and taking whatever they wanted. I took off my wrist watch. Then I took the watch, what money I had, and several other small articles that I wished to keep and secreted them in both shirt sleeves, folding them up my arm above the elbow.

An order was passed down for all colonels and lieutenant

colonels to report to Japanese headquarters, which was in a schoolhouse. I reported with Colonel Williams of the Signal Corps.

As we were to learn later, the scene which we saw was characteristic of the Japanese. Everything seemed to be in an utter state of confusion. No one seemed to know why we were sent for. It was the usual Jap brainstorm. Colonel Williams and I finally engaged the attention of a Jap interpreter who, without any doubt, had been born in the United States. He was most arrogant and impatient, to say the least. The language he used was typically American.

Colonel Williams explained the physical condition of the prisoners. He was careful to drive home the point that we were not only exhausted but were malnutritioned and ill. And that it was mandatory that either transportation be furnished or that an area be set aside in the near vicinity where recuperation, of some sort, could be had.

The interpreter jabbered to the officer in command. After a minute or so of palaver and grunts, he told us it would be impossible to furnish transportation, and that we would wait outside.

As far as the 194th Tank Battalion is concerned and those other elements with us, Limay was the start of the Death March. Up to this time it had been tough, but no one had been treated too badly.

After waiting outside the schoolhouse, for about an hour, witnessing the mob spirit which prevailed among the Jap soldiers, all colonels and lieutenant colonels were lined up. We were then ordered to get into a truck. I just had time to contact Captain Muir and tell him what had happened, when we were whisked off.

It seemed to be that the further toward the rear we proceeded, the treatment became worse. I have thought, perhaps, that some of the Japs in the rear areas, were remnants of the first invasion force and did everything possible to kill us off. This may not have been true. We were to experience the same kind of brutality from Japanese who had never been in contact with us before, and in Japan itself.

We were taken as far as Balanga where we were ordered out of the truck and told to get in line, in what proved to be, another shakedown inspection. Other prisoners had preceded us to this spot, and the line was quite long. It was impossible to see what was happening up ahead.

However, I did hear several cries—and then silence. When I had advanced to the location of the shakedown, I saw a mass of blood on the ground, but no evidence of a body. Afterwards, I heard the story. Japs had found something in the belongings of one of the prisoners and had taken offense. They had clubbed the individual, and then bayoneted him.

It was a shock to all of us. A prisoner of war is totally unarmed and at the mercy of his captors. Also the fact remained that most of the prisoners were emaciated and completely helpless from a physical standpoint. We were to learn, that offending a Jap, is probably the easiest thing to do in the world. For instance, the five pointed star is the symbol of the Japanese Army. The soldier wears it on the front of his cap, and it appears on other paraphernalia. The rank of our brigadier general carries with it one star as the insignia. At least one brigadier was beaten by the Japs for wearing the star.

A thorough shakedown was held at this point. Many articles, including cigarettes, were taken by the inspectors. We had been told that we would get something to eat here. But after the shakedown, we were ordered across the road and into an open field where we were formed into columns.

By this time, there was no semblance of units. Everyone was all mixed up. Luckily, I happened to find Captain Quinlen, and we stayed together for the rest of the March.

The arch of my left foot had broken down and I had extreme difficulty walking. Captain Hickman, our medico, earlier in the day, had dug out enough adhesive tape to bind the arch as best he could. If it had not been for this, I would have been unable to continue the March and would not be telling the story.

After waiting for about an hour, we were told, bruskly, there would be no food. The march was continued. Guards were very brutal and needed only the slightest provocation to display that brutality.

All during this day, and the rest of the march, we witnessed the might of the Japanese Army and its equipment. We marvelled at how it was possible even to have stood up for one week, against the enormous war machine that had been brought in. Our thoughts continually dwelt on a comparison of our own pitiful and inadequate equipment with that of the enemy; the tremendous reserves of manpower they had thrown against us, and the healthy condition they were in. When compared to the physique of our own people, it was brought home to us, just how futile had been our hopes that eventually we could turn the tables.

As far as I am concerned, personally—and I know this to be true of all the rest—I will never know how that march was completed. It was divided into what might be classed as three phases, the first of which we were now taking part. This first phase was forced marches of from 100 to 153 kilometers, depending in which part of Bataan troops were located when the surrender occurred. A kilometer is ⅝ of a mile.

Those who could not keep up were simply killed by clubbing, shooting, and bayoneting. Almost all of the prisoners were in a mental state which can only be described as foggy. As one American doctor who made the march commented: "The prisoners made the Bataan-San Fernando march on the marrow of their bones!"

The Death March was conducted strictly at the point of the bayonet. No distinction was made between officers and enlisted men. Very little or no food was ever given, and when it was, only a few spoonfuls of rice were available.

A thought kept chasing itself through my mind on that march. I wondered why the human body should struggle for life when it would have been much easier to die. And I thought of the time when a cat of ours had kittens, and there was no way to dispose of those kittens except to drown them.

After the children had gone to bed, it became my unpleasant duty to act as executioner. I drew a pail of water and went out in the back yard. Then I took the kittens one by one, and held them under water until life expired. I will never forget how those newborn kittens struggled for life.

And as I marched along that night, I could feel those kittens struggling for life again. I actually seemed to feel their squirming bodies. Strange thoughts to have.

Never again do I wish to feel anything which is alive, struggling for life, in my hands!

CHAPTER 24

March of Death

WATER WAS A paramount issue. It became something to think about, then to yearn for, and finally to dream about. The guards did not allow any halts, that night of April 11-12, 1942, near water.

But in the darkness, when an artesian well was approached, men would dart from the column with a cup. They would scoop up some water, and share it with companions. If the guard was close, it meant death for some. I made one dash that night and came very close to receiving a blow that would have crushed my skull. What nearly came to be my undoing was, that I had first taken a long drink and then filled the cup. I heard a bellow of rage that could only come from a Jap. Instinctively ducking low, I ran for the shadowy column. I felt the swish of the gun butt and heard it strike with a terrific thump. Then came the screaming of the frustrated Jap buzzard and more thumps. The water had revived me enough so that it had given me strength to make the getaway. I wondered why no pursuit had taken place, and then realized that the additional thumps I had heard, meant that someone else had made a dash for the well. Whether or not they were successful, I do not know.

Some of the men had reached a state of mind closely bordering insanity, from the lack of water. In desperation, they would scoop it up from stagnant pools in the road ditches. In the tropics a stagnant pool is virtually alive with dysentery germs. Even open streams are dangerous in this respect. But the fact remains, that even our pores cried out for water.

While moving through a small barrio (settlement or village) the part of the column, to which Quinlen and I were attached, became separated from those ahead of us. We stopped—not knowing which way we were to go. Knowing that the guards needed little or no excuse for acts of violence, we maintained our column carefully and sat down on the road. Some Filipinos appeared and we called them over and asked for water. A miracle took place. The Filipinos brought buckets of it and we drank until we could hold no more. They had just disappeared with the empty buckets when a party of Jap guards arrived on the scene. Jabbering among themselves for some time, they herded us to our feet and started the march once more. We chuckled to ourselves as we thought of how we had had our fill of water in spite of the Japs. When the human body becomes a captive, the brain is continually at work, devising schemes to outwit the captor, and exulting when it does. For a time, we thought of nothing else except that we did get the water.

Later, that night, a short but violent rain storm came down. I can truthfully state, that never have I been so cold in my life. It struck to the very marrow of our bones. Then it stopped, as suddenly as it began.

A couple of hours after the rain, we were again sorely in need of water. Our dehydrated bodies had soaked up the supply we did procure, just like a sponge.

Each time we made a halt, and we only had two of brief duration that night, our leg muscles would stiffen. Walking became torture. Every step we took seemed to be the last. But the brain kept signaling a message to take just one more step. That led to another, and somehow we kept on. Often, shots would be heard, followed by cries of pain. Sometimes there was just a shot and silence afterward. Bayonets themselves make very little sound, but the cries accompanying those diabolical thrusts, are different from any human sound I have ever heard. And we heard many of them that night—also the unmistakable thud of rifle butt against flesh and bone. The Japs are most proficient with bayonets and gun butts, *if* the other fellow is unarmed!

At about 4:00 A.M. Sunday, April 12th, we arrived at Orani and were herded into a barbed wire enclosure. We could smell the stench long before we arrived. In order to get inside the barbed wire, it was necessary for us to close up in a packed formation. There were many other prisoners in the enclosure. Then, we were ordered to sit down. There was not room enough to lie down. We stayed in this position until about 7:00 A.M. By that time, the guards seemed to have relaxed somewhat, and we started to move around.

That was probably the worst scene, of anything I have ever

witnessed in my entire life. The enclosure was crowded to the point of not being able to move without rubbing against someone. It had evidently been used as a prison bull pen for some time. Human waste was on the ground.

A pit had been dug, earlier, in the corner of the pen for toilet purposes. In the tropics, human excrement, if left exposed for only a short time, becomes alive with maggots. The pit itself, and the area around it, seemed to be moving. It was absolutely and literally covered with a constantly moving sea of maggots. The fact that we had nothing in our stomachs, was the only reason why most of us did not vomit at the sight—or even the thought of it.

The sun came up like a blazing ball of fire. There was not one tree in the area. It was like sitting in the center of a hothouse with no air or water. We were soon to learn that we were to be given the sun treatment—one of the forms of cruelty at which the Jap is most adept. The only head gear most of us had (if any) was the oversea's cap which afforded no protection from the sun. As it rose higher, the filth dried into our skin. During all that day we were kept in the enclosure. The Japs allowed only enough water to cool the tongue and bring a real thirst. That was part of the sun treatment.

Americans and Filipinos alike began to grow delirious. After much shouting and spasmodic thrashing around, most of them would drift off into coma. Then, sooner or later, would come death. Whenever some one started to babble, you knew another life was on its way out.

There are some men who cannot remember ever arriving at Orani. The march had numbed their sensibilities to such an extent that they were walking dead men—Zombies—incapable of thinking and devoid of all feeling. Some of them survived.

Towards the latter part of the afternoon, the Japs brought in some rice. It amounted to about three tablespoons per man. I took one mouthful, but could eat no more. Violent hiccups developed as soon as the rice had been swallowed. Many of the others were affected the same way. I gave the rest of my rice to Quinlen.

If the sun had stayed up for another hour, I am convinced that I would have started to babble; my mind was beginning to have spells of blackout. I did more concentrating, in that last hour of sun treatment, than I have ever done before or since. It was a grueling task—and what a subject to concentrate on! I took each calendar month, day by day, and tried to remember birthdays—holidays—any day that had a special meaning. That concentration must have been deep, because by the time I had reached September, the sun was no more, and the cool of the evening was upon us. And my mind was intensely alert. That lesson helped me many times, in the months and years spent in Jap prisons! The body may be imprisoned but *not the mind!*

It is my opinion that the normal body could not have taken the abuse of the Death March. Some of our American doctors who were on that march, state perhaps, is was a good thing for those of us who survived, that our bodies were not normal when we started the march. They base their opinion on the fact that the body was more readily able to accept the abuse, than it would have been otherwise, with so violent and abrupt a change. Probably it was also a good thing that our mental state was foggy. Much of the march remains only as a bad nightmare. But many of the details, and those I relate, are stamped indelibly on my memory, and are just as vivid as a complete photograph.

It was not a strange thing to see dead men. That was simply taken for granted. Many died in the enclosure that day. They lay just as they had died. The Japs would not permit them to be moved.

And now, as during our later experiences as prisoners of these savages, we found ourselves calmly awaiting the answer to one question—when would we be next?

At about 7:00 P.M., we were again lined up in column and started on the trek. We marched all that night, which was just about a duplication of the night before, and would serve no purpose in setting down a repetition here. Shootings, bayonetings, and skull crushings continued. Quinlen and I were still together.

Shortly after daylight, I saw a Filipino soldier sitting on the side of the board. He was in an exhausted state. A Jap guard ran at him, his bayonet leveled. The Filipino got to his feet, and hobbled as best he could off the side of the road and into a rice paddy. The Jap closed in and knocked the Filipino down. The guard calmly thrust his bayonet through the man's stomach.

Other guards alongside the column, had their guns leveled. It would have taken but one small incident for mass murder to have occurred.

Jap troops were being transported in trucks southward. It was an endless stream. We heard quite a number, shouting insults at us in English, and a goodly percentage of those voices, came to us in American English. I can still hear one of them:

"For cryin' out loud! Git your heads up—you sons of bitches!"

One Jap, leering evilly, leaned out from the truck in which he was riding. He was holding his rifle by the barrel. With both hands, he swung, smashing the butt of the stock against the bowed head of an American soldier, on the outside of the column. Brave people—these Japs!

We began to see Filipino civilians along the road. They were very sympathetic, noting our misery. They risked death, by covertly tossing raw turnips to us. Quinlen and I each caught one.

It was along this particular stretch of road that we saw something which was most horrible to behold. It was a body, held semi-upright by the strands of a barbed wire fence. The body had been a Filipino soldier. The abdomen had been slashed open, and the bowels ripped therefrom, and hung on the wire! The reason for this barbarity, was merely the Japanese way of telling everyone to be good!

In the early morning of this day, we came to Remedios, the site of our night battle with the Japanese. This was the first time we had seen the place in daylight. It was then that I clearly understood why the Japs had not had a chance against us that night, by their frontal attack.

It was one place in all the area in which we had battled, that contained level ground on both sides of the road—ground that was without jungle or rice paddy. There was a perfect field of fire to the front, with no obstructions. The only chance for dislodging us that night, would have been by an envelopent on either or both flanks. This they had failed to do. And this was the reason for their complete defeat that night.

I tried to concentrate on thinking of other things rather than my own physical discomfort. But it was getting to the point where it was impossible. The arch of my left foot had been giving me more than considerable trouble, all through the march. It was from here to Lubao that was probably the hardest part of the march for me, as far as walking was concerned.

Quinlen's feet were a mass of huge blisters that had started to break. Some were as large as a silver dollar.

At one of our infrequent halts, I saw one man with his shoe off. His face expressed utter misery. From the heel to the ball of the foot, the whole under-skin was hanging loose. It appeared to be like the worn sole of a shoe—hanging limp, and flapping.

It was apparent that Quinlen and I could not go much further. I could hardly bear any weight, whatever, on my left foot. I even tried walking on my toes and heels. That was just about as bad. Quinlen was in the same shape, walking in excruciating pain.

We made up our minds, as we hobbled along, that we would try to make Lubao. And then, we agreed, let happen what would. If the turn of life's wheel meant that our number was up, it was all right with us. We knew that we could not go on in the condition we were in. Our minds were steadfast, on that. It is most fortunate that the human mind has the ability of adjustment, both to varied conditions and shock.

After what seemed to be tortuous years, we entered the town. The Japs called a halt. The column, as one man, slumped down into the gutter. We were so completely exhausted that the very filth and dirt of the street felt good to us.

The halt was *not* made because the Japs wanted to give us a rest. It was a reorganization point and we stayed there for at least half an hour.

As usual, the Japs were operating in a sheer state of confusion. There was a great deal of the now familiar high-pitched gibberish and lots of running around. *Then the miracle occurred.*

Quinlen and I both were definitely convinced we could go no further. That was, at least, until we could obtain quite a rest. We had discussed the possibility of creeping away into some of the ruins and secreting ourselves so as to get some rest. But no opportunity had presented itself.

Suddenly a Filipino bus came clattering down the road, from the direction of Bataan. In it were quite a number of

Americans. The bus stopped close to us. The Americans said they had been picked up in southern Bataan and had been ordered by the Japs to get into this bus, and told the driver to go to San Fernando.

Why the Japs ordered them to ride is more than anyone can understand. It was just one of the innumerable quirks of the unpredictable Japanese mind. No one could tell what they would do next. They might give you a cigarette one minute, and put a bayonet through you the next!

The idea seemed to be born simultaneously in the minds of both Quinlen and myself—*to get on that bus!*

Quinlen climbed on and found a seat. I started in after him when one of the Jap guards hit me a stunning blow on the jaw with his gun butt.

It is very difficult to explain our mental status to normal people. The blow I received should have floored me. But at that time, I did not even know whether it hurt or not. Later reactions told me it must have. Since then, my jaw has given me considerable trouble by wanting to go out of joint, if I have my mouth open, unusually wide, to yawn. That has not stopped my yapping, however! The latest developments have occurred in the form of excruciating aches in my left arm, together with extreme numbness in the left hand, caused from the pinching of a nerve by the neck vertebrae, as a result of that blow.

I paid no attention to the guard, but simply climbed in the bus alongside Quinlen. The guard grunted, and walked off. The only explanation I am able to produce is, that the guard thought I was trying to leave the bus when it stopped. And so he hit me with the gun butt to get me back inside again!

It was a miracle from the Lord Almighty and I have always regarded it as such.

The bus moved off. It was driven by a Filipino. After much slow traveling and frequent halts (which Quinlen and I most enjoyed) we arrived at San Fernando. Here we were put into another barbed wire compound and seated in rows. It was a continuation of the sun treatment. This compound was a duplication of Orani, filled to overflowing with sick, dying and dead Americans and Filipinos. They were lying in filth and maggots. Flies by the millions were crawling over them. This compound had everything in the book! No water was available. Filipino collaborators were in evidence, shouting in English and herding the prisoners. I recognized one whom I had seen in San Fernando prior to the war. He had the same heavy cane, which I had seen him with in those sleepy days. I did not see him use it on any of the Americans, but he pounded ferociously on the heads and backs of Filipino soldiers. I marvelled at their stamina and indifference to pain. Not one sound did I hear out of them.

Sometime after midday, we received approximately four tablespoons of rice. At the first mouthful, the same thing happened again to me—violent hiccups. By this time, our bodies seriously needed salt. We had been streaming sweat for so long that there was simply no more sweat to come. I sat down, with my head hunched between drawn knees, preparatory to another period of concentration. Barely was I settled when a furore started at the main gate.

The Japs were starting another column. Quinlen and I joined it. Perhaps we would have been clubbed into it anyway. At all events, we reasoned, anything was better than the sun treatment. The rest, we had obtained, brief as it was, gave us a new lease on life, if it could be called a lease.

The column was marched to the depot, where we found Filipino box cars lined up. These cars are much smaller than the American. They measured about six feet wide by eighteen feet long. True to fashion, the Japs piled as many prisoners into each box car as it would hold. 110 men were packed in our car and a comparable amount in the rest. This was less than *one square foot per man!*

Some, after they climbed in and were backed up, sat down. Their knees were drawn straight up under their chins. Others stood up. Whatever position you happened to take, proved to be the only position physically possible for the entire trip. Legs could not be moved—arms, barely. Quinlen sat down. I was debating with myself as to standing or sitting, but had my mind made up for me by the press of humanity, which left me standing.

Soon the train was loaded. The heat was almost unbearable. Then the guards came alongside and closed both doors. It was like a furnace, crammed and packed solid, with human bodies. After an interminable delay, the train gave a jerk and moved off. Those nearest one of the side doors, managed to rip it open. This gave a little relief but not much. The air we breathed seemed almost to burn our throats.

There was no help for the dysentery and diarrhea cases. They were compelled to live in their own filth—and everybody else lived with it. Nausea with resultant vomiting was common among many. The stench was foul beyond belief.

In our cramped positions, there was barely no movement whatever. Limbs would ache almost to the point of causing mental instability. Then they would go completely numb. The heat became more intense—if that were possible—as the ride lengthened. Men died where they were with no protest. Their nearest neighbor would be completely unaware of what had happened. Or perhaps their sensibilities were so numbed, they were incapable of comprehending.

I know that my sensibilities were numb, to the point, where I was living in a bad dream.

The ride lasted for more than three hours. At some of the towns through which we passed, crowds of Filipinos were on the station platforms. They risked Jap violence, and even death, by trying to throw rice cakes and fruit into the cars. Very little found its way to the target. But it made us virtually love them.

Some of the other carloads of prisoners were unable to open their side door during the trip. They were in worse shape than we.

Finally the train stopped at what proved to be Capas. We were ordered to detrain and form into columns. It seemed as if I were walking on stilts. It was a long time before I was able to have any feeling, whatever, in my legs, from the knees down. This was followed by excruciating pain, when they came to life.

While we were in column at the depot, quite a crowd of Filipinos had gathered. We noticed that they carried paper bags. As we started to march away, the Filipinos tossed the bags into the column. They contained rice cakes and fruit. Then they darted away from the screaming, chasing Jap guards. As far as we could determine, none of our friends were caught. My stomach rebelled at the thought of food and I passed up my meager portion. I was to learn later, that if one wished to live, he would eat any and all edible things, that might be classed as food—even if he could hold it down for only a few minutes.

We now knew that we were on our way to Camp O'Donnell. Soon the camp was to be notorious as the infamous "Camp of Death"—offspring of Hell.

CHAPTER 25

Camp O'Donnell — Offspring of Hell

CAMP O'DONNELL was in the process of being built, prior to the war, for the Philippine Army. It was not as yet completed. Buildings were under construction, many of them having no roofs. The name of this camp, strange to relate, came from the Spanish. The land originally belonged to a family by the name of Odonel—hence O'Donnell. It was about five kilometers from Capas.

As we stumbled down the road, we could see pails of water which had been set outside of each Filipino house. There was no one in sight. There was no sign of life. This was their way of getting water to us. Otherwise it would have been impossible. God bless them!

Some of the pails had been tipped over by the Jap guards. Some were still upright. When the guards were out of sight, the Filipinos stole back and refilled the pails. This continued all the way from Capas to O'Donnell.

Men on the outside ranks would dip a cup as they passed. Each man, as far as I could see, received a drink. The Japs here, did not pay much attention to the dipping. However, if anyone faltered, the same procedure as in the past, took place.

There was no halt called, in this phase of the gruelling march. It was about 6:00 P.M., Monday, April 13th, when we finally entered the gates of Camp O'Donnell, out of which many would never return. As I passed through those gates, I numbly wondered how many would survive.

Quinlen and I were extremely fortunate in getting to O'Donnell as soon as we did. We had been on the march from Friday night to Monday night. I had had nothing to eat in that time except a couple of small raw turnips. Many others, who were yet to come, were on that march and given sun treatment in stages, for 13 days and more!

We were taken into an open space within the camp. Then we were lined up for a shakedown inspection. Here we received our first initiation in the underground among prisoners. A whispered warning permeated our ranks, passed from rear to head. It came from other prisoners who had arrived earlier, and who had, somehow, passed the word on to us:

"For God's sake, get rid of any Jap money or other Jap stuff—*quick!*"

I had a Jap five peso note which had been brought in Bataan by one of the Filipinos engaged in smuggling operations. The note was one of the many printed by Japan, long before the war, and for use in the Philippines, whenever the war would start! They flooded the islands with this worthless currency. I had been saving it for a souvenir. Quickly, I extricated it from my sleeve, scooped a little hole in the earth with my foot, and buried it. I was none too soon, and from what I found out afterwards, God certainly must have been with me.

An interpreter stopped in front of me. He was probably about twenty-three or four years old, well built, perfectly groomed, and very arrogant. He talked with me for some time, asking where I was from in the States. He did not tell me, but it was unnecessary to tag him as an American-born Japanese. His English was just as American as mine. Displaying my meager belongings, I tried a trick that had worked before. I showed him a leather bound folder which contained the pictures of my family. Japs are keenly interested in pictures and especially in family pictures. In the years to come, I was to use this folder in many a predicament. The interpreter took the pictures like a piece of iron is drawn to a magnet. He asked questions about ages of the family, how long I had been married—and on and on. Finally, he handed back the folder and inspected the other things. It was only cursory, however, and the only thing he took was my safety razor and the two old blades in the kit. I had used these two blades since coming into Bataan and had kept them sharpened by stropping them on the heel of my hand. I asked why I could not keep the razor. He replied that it was orders to pick them all up. He passed on to the next man and I heaved a sigh of relief. My foot was still standing on the spot where I had buried the Jap note—*and I kept it there!*

After the shakedown was over, we were made to stand and face a small box. The commandant of the camp, a Jap captain, mounted this box. He stared at us evilly. He was one of the ugliest mortals I have ever seen. He breathed the very essence of hate. He roared at us, stopping only when he was out of breath. Then the interpreter would enlighten us. Meanwhile, the commandant would fold his arms and glare until the interpreter had finished. This gibberish lasted for about fifteen minutes. The captain literally frothed at the mouth.

We were all so nearly gone that very few of us retained much of what was said. However, afterwards, we all agreed on the last words. He told us that we were not prisoners of war. We were captives and would be treated as such! We were an inferior race. The Japanese would win the war. Then he reached his climax.

. "You are our enemies," he screamed, "and we will fight you and fight you and fight you—for 100 years!"

This was the first time we had come into contact with the 100-year phrase, that we were to hear, so often, in the future. The Japanese meant by that phrase, that this was only *one* part of their program to eventually rule the world.

If this phase would fail, they would open the next phase as soon as possible and never would cease—even if it took 100 years to do it. We found that the Japanese actually believed in what they said. There could be no defeat for Japan. They might suffer reverses, but a reverse would be only a temporary stopping point. It would not be the loss of a war, such as western people consider it.

We listened as if in a dream. I wondered if the savage drivel would never end. All we wanted was to be left alone—to lie down somewhere in peace. Our bodies were near the end of the rope. Our minds kept us erect. The expression of the Jap bastard, as he delivered his ape-like harangue, reminded me of an idiot.

Finally we were dismissed. The Americans who had arrived earlier than we, assigned us to our miserable quarters. They had set up a sort of kitchen. The only things to cook with were huge pots and old oil barrels in which to boil rice.

There was a slim ration of rice available that night. But I found that after the first mouthful, violent hiccups occurred again. It was impossible for me to eat. I crawled in my assigned space, stretched out on the bamboo floor and tried to sleep. The bamboo was laid crosswise to the way we had to sleep and was spaced about two inches apart. The fact that if left marks on our bodies for a long time to come, was not the reason why most of us could not sleep that night. We were too exhausted to sleep. It was impossible for us to relax. We lay still like mummies, and the bamboo ground our flesh against the bones. We didn't mind it because we could not even feel it!

It was this night that I realized fully, what dehydration meant. Everyone else had the same experience. The terrific urge to urinate would come. Actually, only a bare teaspoon of urine would be forthcoming. The pain accompanying it was almost unbearable. To illustrate just how dehydrated we were, I can normally just circle my wrist with my thumb and middle finger. I now found that I could circle my wrist with the tip of the thumb touching the first joint of the middle finger!

During the period of the Death March and after arrival at Camp O'Donnell, an abnormal time elapsed before bowel movements occurred. I went for nine days without one. Some of the prisoners went as long as 14 days!

Other groups of prisoners arrived daily. We watched them come in, and go through the same procedure as we went through. Reunions took place, with much hand shaking and congratulations for having survived thus far.

Gradually, both the 192nd and 194th Tank Battalion personnel arrived. We managed to segregate them generally in one area. The Tank Group Commander and his staff had been brought to Camp O'Donnell by motor transportation.

The water situation was very bad. Most of the time only two spigots were available for the approximately 8,000 Americans in the camp. Long lines would form. It was entirely possible for many to stand in line all day and still not get to the spigot. Every little while, the water pumps would break down. The Japs tried to repair them in the usual Jap way, which meant that no progress was made. Finally, they ordered the Americans to detail their own personnel on the pumps. From then on, the situation was a little better. Eventually, this detail rigged up more spigots. But for the first two weeks in O'Donnell, water was at a premium.

In one of the later groups to arrive, were some of my men. One of them gave me a small piece of brown sugar he had picked up on the march. This sugar was molded in small cakes and was common in the Philippines. I have never experienced such a reaction before or since. It hit with a great deal more force than a big drink of whiskey on an empty stomach. It only lasted a short time, but while it did, I could feel a glow throughout my whole body. Strength seemed to flow into me. Later, I was to experience the same type of reaction at various times, but never quite like this one.

We set up a mess for the Tank Group personnel, and served the rice out of old oil barrels. Rice was all we had with very little salt. I forced my first meal down. It stayed about fifteen minutes. Gradually, I succeeded in overcoming the nausea to the point where I retained the meager ration.

American medical personnel set up a so-called hospital. Most of us were sick, including the new arrivals, and all were in various stages of starvation. The "hospital" was located in a rambling, half-completed building. Part of it had no roof, and that part which did, was full of holes.

There were little or no medical supplies. Dysentery, malaria, dengue fever, and malnutritional diseases were rampant. Requests were made of the Japanese, to send a detail back into Bataan and pick up what drugs had been left there. This was promptly refused.

Those who were the most sick, were moved into the hospital. There was room for only about eight to nine hundred. Patients had to be laid shoulder to shoulder on the board floor. Most of them had inadequate clothing and some were naked. In the tropics, temperatures of 80 degrees or lower, are cold, even when fully clothed. The blood has been thinned so that the body can withstand humidity and heat. Those of us outside the hospital suffered with the cool of the nights. Patients shook as if with the ague. When the hospital was filled to capacity, much of the overflow was put beneath the floors and stretched out on the ground. In order to qualify for the hospital, the patient had to be near death. As it filled to overflowing, even that qualification had to be forgotten.

The Japs provided no medicine whatever. The water situation was so bad that there was not even enough to wash the human waste from the sick and the dying. Many, afflicted with dysentery, never left the latrine area, but lay all around it until they died.

A report was drawn up and presented to the Japs. It depicted a thorough analysis of conditions. At the time this report was made, Colonel Sage, who had commanded the 200th Coast Artillery from New Mexico, was the senior officer in the camp and it was he who made the report. The only answer he received from the Japanese was that we were captives and not prisoners of war. Therefore, the Japanese had no responsibility!

Each day at 11:30 A.M., conferences were held by Colonel Sage with the senior officers present in the camp. As senior officer of the Tank Group, at that time, I attended those conferences and knew what was going on.

It would be impossible to adequately describe the hordes of flies in Camp O'Donnell. They buzzed around by the millions and droned all day long. They bred out of maggots and were carriers of disease, settling alternately on human filth, and then upon the rice we ate. It was standard operating procedure to eat the rice with one hand and rotate the other over your mess kit. Even then, the flies, like dive bombers, would hurl themselves into the rice. One afternoon, for want of something better to do, I made a crude fly swatter out of a piece of bamboo. I sat in one spot and in the space of 10 minutes killed 520 flies! I counted them.

Starvation was evident in all prisoners. Ribs could be counted at a quick glance. We were living skeletons, and that is the way we were destined to remain for the duration of the war. Buttocks sagged—loose skin—devoid of flesh or muscle. Men asleep, might have been dead. There was no difference. We found ourselves, on waking, looking at others still sleeping—wondering whether they were alive.

The medics tried to segregate cases as much as possible, but this did not help a great deal. We attempted to separate weaker men from the others, so that they would not be sent out of the camp on work details. In this, we were somewhat successful, and probably saved some lives.

It was in this camp that we had our first real lesson in black marketing. Working details were taken out of the camp for short or long periods. These details, when coming back into the area, always tried to smuggle things in. They were more or less successful. A can of sardines sold for twenty pesos (ten dollars). Other things were of a comparable price. We thought this outrageous, but as time went on, the price went up. It must be realized that two salient factors entered the black marketing. In the first place, the outside price had to be paid, and that in itself was excessive. In the second place, the smuggler had to take tremendous chances in bringing things in. Sometimes, the Japs would only give a cursory shakedown of the work details. At other times, it would be minute. On other occasions, there might not be any inspection. No one knew what to expect. The Jap was unpredictable. Anyhow, we were initiated into the inner circles of the law of supply and demand.

The officers of the 192nd and 194th Tank Battalions pooled their money and had working parties attempt to pick up drugs outside and bring them in. They were not always successful but did procure a small supply. Money was not plentiful, and the price was high. For instance, it cost 65 pesos for one bottle of dysentery pills. That is equivalent to $32.50 in our money. There were only about 50 or 60 pills to a bottle and they were not very effective; but they did some good. Officers of the 200th C.A. did the same as we.

Very little quinine, to combat malaria, could be picked up. It was horrible to watch the violent shakings of those afflicted, as they had their periodic "spells," and to wonder when your next one would arrive.

The Japanese at Camp O'Donnell paid little or no attention to us inside the barbed wire enclosure. The death rate was startling, even to the prisoners who were rather calloused to death. A few days after we had entered the camp, the death rate among Americans was from 15 to 20 per day. It increased until the peak was reached, which was about 58 per day. About 1,500 Americans died in this camp in less than two months. Filipinos were in a separate enclosure, across the road from the Tank Group. Day and night—continuously—the parade of dead Filipinos went past our area, carried to their "graveyard" down the road.

The Japanese seemed to pay the Filipinos more attention than they did us. Collaborators were hard at work, aiding the enemies of their own people. Several forms of torture were devised, one of them being the extreme form of sun treatmnt.

A long pole had been rigged up in a horizontal position, high enough so that when a man's arms were raised over his

head—the hands crossed above the pole and lashed securely—
the tip of his toes would just scrape the ground. Bare headed,
he was compelled to maintain this position in the sun for
many hours at a time. Of course, no water was given him.

From what I could determine, quite a number of the Filipinos were civilians who, probably, had been a little too
patriotic, to suit the Japanese.

In both enclosures, it was like a perennial parade, only the
marchers carried lifeless figures, instead of banners. And the
marchers were almost lifeless too.

The men assigned to dig graves were in such a weakened
state and sick, and the soil was so hard, that it was impossible to scoop out much more than six inches of earth. The
American cemetery in Camp O'Donnell was known as "Boot
Hill." It was named after an old cemetery in the southwestern
United States, which had its beginning in wild west days when
men died with their boots on.

The graves registration division at this camp did wonderful work. They kept record of the deaths and of where each
individual was buried, in so far as possible. Much credit is due
any personnel who accomplished deeds, beyond that of keeping themselves alive. It must be remembered, that no one in
the camp was healthy. Everyone was disease-ridden in some
form or other, and everyone was struck with malnutrition.
First Lt. Fred W. Koenig, Graves Registration, was largely
responsible for this splendid service.

The chaplains, in my estimation, did a marvelous piece of
work at O'Donnell, for the mental well being of the prisoners.
Both Catholic and Protestant services were held regularly. I
can say, personally, that it helped me a great deal. Memorial
Day was particularly observed, by religious services. Strange to
relate, the Japanese did not interfere.

During this period, we were able to get some black market
salt. I obtained one spoonful and ate it as greedily as I would
the best candy I had ever tasted. For some unknown reason,
all through our existence as prisoners of war, the Japanese
never issued enough salt.

Malnutritional diseases showed up quickly. We learned rapidly, how some bodies could store up more vitamins than
others. Some of the men began to swell up and would be un-
recognizable. This was not confined to the face alone, but

also to the limbs, especially the legs. They would swell to the point where the skin would actually burst.

This we found to be the wet type of beriberi. We also knew the dry type, which would cause the limbs to go to sleep. Beriberi is caused chiefly from lack of vitamin B-1. It generally started with the feet. They would go completely numb. Both forms of beriberi would progress through the body until it reached the heart. Then death would occur. I never contracted the wet type, but did experience the dry.

Shortly after I had my first evacuation, dysentery visited me again. This time it sought to kill. Dysentery dehydrates the body very rapidly. I learned another important phase of prison life which took the lives of many.

The thought of food, and especially the insipid rice we got, was exceedingly repulsive to the dysentery patient. If the individual fails to eat, the germ has nothing to work on but the gastric juices of the stomach. Then it is not long before death takes over.

Many refused to eat anything. It became a case of making up your mind, whether you wanted to hang on, or let go. The mental state was all-important. The patient simply had to have the will to live. I do not mean to infer that everyone would have lived had they had the mental urge. I have known many who died, who probably had more of the mental urge to live than did some who actually came through. I merely wish to point out that having the mental urge helped a great deal.

From the moment we entered Camp O'Donnell until the end of the war, rumors were our bread and butter. We lived on them. Some were sublime, some were ridiculous, and some had a great deal of truth in them. They came from many sources.

With a few of the prisoners, these rumors did some harm, but not so with the great majority. As far as I, personally, was concerned, all through my prison life I liked to hear all the rumors. It helped my state of mind. Despair was the worst thing that could happen to anyone—and it was very easy to despair. Without the proper mental outlook, and a certain amount of optimism, the will to live skidded down to the zero point.

The Japanese would draw pictures of ships on the ground

and would intimate that Roosevelt and Tojo were shaking hands and that we would go home soon. One rumor, coming like a flood, had it, that we were to be exchanged for certain Japanese civilians in the United States.

Then there was the one about ships in Lingayen Gulf that were being painted pure white with a large American flag on either side. The information was that American prisoners were doing the painting. Coupled to this was another rumor that ships were in Manila Bay. Then came a rumor that we would be moved to Fort McKinley, for processing, prior to going home.

We were to learn that some of these rumors emanated from the Japanese themselves. The Japs are past masters of sadism and all forms of torture. They would deliberately give out what was supposed to be authentic information, in hopes that our morale would be raised to the point where they could observe the adverse mental effect on us, when we discovered the rumor was not correct. However, it taught us self control in the mastering of our emotions, and, I am convinced, helped to build up our faith. We never gave up hope, although hope was a forlorn item in those days after the fall of Bataan. Keeping the spark of life flickering through the nightmare of starvation, disease and abuse, gave us a renewed faith in America, and in the determination of outlasting our sadistic, unprincipled Jap captors.

Even with the population of Boot Hill ever increasing, we never lost that faith. It was exemplified in a poem written at O'Donnell by 1st Lt. Fred W. Koenig, Graves Registration, and dedicated to those who died in this infamous Jap Hell:

The Vanquished Speak

Here on this sun-scorched Hill, we laid us down
In silence deep as in the silence of defeat.
Upon our wasted brow, you placed no laurel crown,
But neither did you sound the trumpet for retreat.
Mourn not for us, for here defeat and victory are one,
We cannot feel Humanity's insidious harm;
Our strife with Famine, Pain, and Pestilence are done,
Our compromise with Death laid by that mortal storm.
Though chastened, well we know our Mission is not dead,

Nor are the dreams of victory we dreamed in vain.
For lo! The Dawn is in the East! The night is fled
Before an August Day which will be ours again!
So rest we here, dear comrades, on this foreign Hill.
This alien clay made somehow richer by our dust
Provides us with a transitory couch, until
The loving hills of Home enfold us in maternal trust.
We are assured brave hearts across the sea will not forget
The humble sacrifice we laid on Freedom's Sacred Shrine,
And hold that Righteousness will be triumphant yet,
And o'er the Earth again His Star of Peace will shine.

CHAPTER 26

Administration by Remote Control

FOR THE FIRST two weeks at Camp O'Donnell, rice was the only food we could obtain. Then it was supplemented by about two to four ounces of camotes (native sweet potato) per day. A few times we received a small amount of mongo (native) beans—similar to our dried peas. About once a week, Carabao meat was issued on a basis of about $\frac{1}{8}$ to $\frac{1}{4}$ ounce per man. As an example, our particular mess was feeding 900 men. We received our weekly meat ration. It consisted of 18 pounds of carabao ribs! There was ample food available but the Japs were deliberately starving us.

The leaves and bark from guava trees proved to be an aid for the lesser cases of dysentery. These were boiled, and brewed into a tea. It did help those who had minor attacks, but had little or no effect on the more severe cases. It was also taken as a preventive. Whether or not it accomplished the desired end, I am unable to say.

Diseases common during my two months stay at O'Donnell were malaria, dengue fever, dysentery, diarrhea, malnutrition, beriberi, yaws or tropical ulcers, and Guam blisters. The ulcers appeared externally upon the body and became ugly, open sores. The blisters appeared as a severe rash in which the skin became almost raw. Yellow jaundice also made its appearance.

One day, an American prisoner (patient in the hospital) grew delirious and wandered out of the hospital area. Somehow, he got outside the barbed wire. Instead of trying to get away, he simply roamed about in the open. The guards picked him up. Americans in contact with the Japs explained the prisoner's delirious condition. However, he was flogged unmercifully. Then, they lashed him up by the wrists and gave him the sun treatment the balance of the day. This was done in front of Jap headquarters. The next day, he was flogged again and given the sun treatment. No one ever saw him again after this.

Sometime during the month of May, all the generals and full colonels were taken out of the camp. Before leaving, Major General Edward King, former commander on Bataan, talked to each group of prisoners in the camp. I will never forget his fortitude and soldierly bearing in the face of adversity and humiliation. He was always an inspiration to me, during my years of prison life.

He came over to visit us before his departure. In his talk, he took full responsibility for everything that had happened. He was that kind of officer and gentleman. He told us to keep our spirits high, and he let us know that he was certain it was not always going to be this way. He tried his best to cheer us up.

All the men in the Tank Group stood at respectful attention when he came and when he left. I saluted him for the Group, and I knew that I was saluting not only the rank but also the man. All of us, that day, had a deep feeling of admiration and respect for General King.

The day before leaving, General Weaver announced that, although leaving the camp, he was not relinquishing control, but would administer to the Tank Group "by remote control, through my staff." I am still wondering how he expected to accomplish that as a prisoner of war! Perhaps he was emulating MacArthur.

The next morning I was standing in front of General King's quarters, talking to both King and Weaver. It was only a few minutes before they were taken away. General King turned to Weaver, and asked him who he was leaving in control of the Tank Group.

He replied, "Lieutenant Colonel Smythe."

General King asked, "Is Colonel Smythe senior to Colonel Miller?"

The reply was short, "Yes."

I am still under the impression that King looked rather queerly at Weaver. I said nothing, for two reasons. First, the generals were ready to take off, and actually did, a moment later. Secondly, the situation was too ridiculous and childish for even the suggestion of an argument, under those conditions.

The following day I had a talk with Colonel Sage, who had been left by King as the senior American officer. Sage asked me whether or not I was the senior of Smythe. I told him I was. He then stated that he had always assumed that to be the case, and he had been surprised when Weaver had designated Symthe. He told me to let things rest for the time being, and he would take care of the matter.

Within twenty-four hours, Colonel Sage sent for me and officially presented the arm band which carried the designation of Tank Group Commander. I asked him if he had had any unpleasantness with Smythe. He said he had not. He had merely asked Smythe if he was the senior, to which Smythe replied he was not. The only reason I could ever attach as to why General Weaver designated Smythe, was because of the spirit of the old school tie. Both were West Pointers.

We were able to keep ourselves informed as to the status of Corregidor. The Japs, of course, were using Clark Field. It lay about 13 air miles to the south of O'Donnell. Each day we could observe Jap bombers circling for altitude, above Clark Field, to take off for the bombing of Corregidor. After May 6th, the periodical flights ceased. We knew then, that something must have happened. We were well aware, that to hold Corregidor, Bataan must be held. The Japs had moved heavy artillery and placed it in position at elevations on Bataan, looking down on Corregidor. With this kind of direct observation, it was a simple matter for them to pour in a deadly and continuous fire. Nothing comparable, to throw back, existed on Corregidor. No thought had been given, in the prewar years, to an attack on the Rock from Bataan, although completion of topographic maps years before, had raised the issue in army circles. Both Bataan and Corregidor should have been fortified. To argue that no steps were taken, because of the decision of the United States not to defend the Philippines, and then to suddenly reverse that decision a year or so before war came, is not a sound argument. In the days when that defense was definitely a part of the war plan, *nothing was ever done, nor was anything done about it, in the time at our disposal, in 1941.*

By the latter part of May, many work details had been taken out of Camp O'Donnell, for parts unknown. A large number of the Tank Group was included. Speculation, as to destination, was rife. Farewells were spoken with much bantering:

"See you in Frisco, Bill!"

"Hope you get a potgut out of this trip!"

"Pick up your fanny, or you'll be making three tracks!"

And more.

There were some of the incoming prisoners who, evidently, had not received the warning about having Jap money on their person. They were immediately segregated from the rest and brutally beaten. They then disappeared and were never seen again.

Haircuts at O'Donnell were good, fair, and bad. We were not organized to the stage of barbershops as yet. We cut each other's hair with whatever we could find to do it with. I had managed to keep a pair of fingernail scissors secreted in the lining of my musette bag.

Russ Swearingen let himself in for something one day when he said he would like to get his hair trimmed somehow. I volunteered to do the job and Russ agreed. Secretly, I had always wanted to try my hand at this game but had never had the chance. Suffice it to say, this was my first and last one. Methodically, I went to work, starting on one side of his head and working around to the other side. It was botchy without doubt, and one side had been cut higher than the other.

Capt. Muir standing nearby, offered sage advice, "Why don't you put a chalk line on it, Colonel?"

"Get a bowl!" someone else remarked.

Estimating the difference between the two sides, I set to work again, but cut off too much. There was a repetition of this operation several times. Finally, only a small island of hair was left on the top of his head.

"Cut it short!" Capt. Ed. Johnson suggested.

I did! Russ was not *too* displeased! Feeling of his head, he drily remarked, "It's a good thing you weren't cutting out my appendix!"

Mosquitos were bad at this camp, but not as bad as we were to experience later. There was no protection whatever. Those who had fought off malaria were now almost sure to get it from the malarial mosquito.

Many bets were placed as to when we would be free men again. The release dates ran all the way from within six weeks to the end of the war involving years. The majority of us could not go along with the "years" business, the main reason being, that we would not allow ourselves to think in terms of years. It probably was a good thing.

For quite some time we had heard the rumor that the most of us would be moved to another camp. This rumor was coupled to the Fort McKinley processing point, in preparation for going home. Then, Cabanatuan entered the conjectured list of possible destinations.

On June 1st, lists were drawn up. We would move by groups of 100. My name appeared as company commander of one group. It was apparent, that no longer were we going to be allowed to stay together as an organization. My group was composed of all officers. We were ordered to be ready to leave the next morning at 5:00 o'clock.

At the appointed time, we assembled into column of fours and moved off. Without incident, we arrived at Capas and were loaded into the all too familiar box cars. This time, Jap guards were placed in each car with us. It was a godsend. They saw to it, for their own comfort, that the cars were not so heavily loaded as before, and that the side doors remained open. I, as did many of the others, had a terrible case of dysentery. However, with the doors open and with helping hands, we were able to handle the situation fairly good.

As before, Filipinos were gathered at some of the stations, with offerings of fruit and rice cakes, which they threw into the cars as we passed. The guards in our car made no effort to stop it. Once again—unpredictable!

As the train traveled further south, we could not help but hope against hope that the McKinley rumor would prove true. However, after passing through Calumpit and proceeding south a few miles, we switched over to the Cabanatuan route. Then we knew for sure which rumor was correct. No one would ever admit he had believed the McKinley story, but secretly, many of the prisoners did.

Our ride consumed the better part of the daylight hours. At about 6:00 P.M., we arrived at Cabanatuan, and were bivouacked in an open yard behind a Filipino schoolhouse. We were given some rice. And then came a miracle dish. It was a cupful of onion soup—nothing else but onions and water. But it was more delicious than I can ever describe. And there was salt in it!

Other prisoners had used the same area. There were no

latrines dug. Human waste lay on top of the ground at the rear, with the usual maggots.

The next morning, at about 6:00 o'clock, we lined up again in column, and marched to Cabanatuan prison camp. It was about nine kilometers from the town. We arrived at about 11:00 A.M., had the usual shakedown, and were assigned to quarters.

This camp was better in many respects than O'Donnell. It, too, was a Philippine Army camp, in the process of being built prior to the war. Some of the buildings had not been completed.

The water supply was more plentiful and the food was better. We had the opportunity of breaking up our messes into smaller groups. There is no doubt, but what the fact that work details were organized in this camp, provided a little better ration.

One part of the area, separated from the rest, was organized by our medicos into a hospital section. Here, it was possible to segregate dysentery and other communicable diseases. From the time I arrived at Cabanatuan to November 4th, when taken to Japan, about 2,500 Americans died. June and July were the heaviest months—about 2,000 deaths. The great majority of the deaths were attributable, directly, to dysentery and malaria. They were coupled, of course, with the ever present malnutrition. Starvation, nutritional and actual, was the real cause of the majority of the excessively large number of deaths, that occurred during prison life.

The Medics had set up part of the hospital area into what was known as the Zero Ward. Very seldom did anyone ever come out of that ward alive. Actual conditions, in the matter of housing, for the patients were little better than at O'Donnell. They lay on the bare floor or ground with no protection from flies, mosquitos, or cold. Drugs were at a premium. Later on, underground contacts were made with Filipinos on the outside, and the drug situation picked up.

Diseases, in addition to those contracted at O'Donnell, were, for the most part, due to lack of vitamins. They included pellagra, scurvy, blindness (partial and total), eye ulcers, pneumonia, tuberculosis, dobe itch, worms, and diphtheria (about 300 cases of which about 100 died). The diseases experienced at O'Donnell and Cabanatuan, followed us more or less throughout our entire prison life of three and one-half years.

During our early stay at Cabanatuan, I made a personal investigation at one of the so-called dispensaries, when it was reported to me, that an American doctor had refused to give quinine to one of our men who had malaria, and was in bad shape. The doctor allowed me to examine his stock of drugs. He had a small bottle with, perhaps, what amounted to about three teaspoons of powdered quinine. This was for 500 men in his area! Comparable amounts of other drugs were on hand. The victim in question died about three days later.

The first nutritional deficiency observed in our prison life seemed to be beriberi. It occurred generally about three months after the departure from a balanced diet. Pellagra and scurvy followed this, but several months later. Scurvy would disappear rapidly if fresh fruits, such as limes and tangerines, could be procured. Another nutritional deficiency manifested itself during the hours of darkness. We called it night blindness. A large number of prisoners displayed this symptom of vitamin lack to a greater or lesser degree. Terrific urinating followed us for the entire period of captivity. Twenty-four times in twenty-four hours was by no means uncommon.

It was a strange thing to observe just how each individual was affected by malnutrition. Some died rapidly; some lingered on—living in death; others should have died, but didn't. Two men living side by side, and under the same identical conditions, would have different symptoms.

From the time I arrived at Cabanatuan, until about the first of August, I was continually up and down with dysentery and dengue fever. In the absence of any drug for dysentery, our medics strongly advised getting ashes and charcoal from our kitchen fires, and eating it. Many of us tried this, and it helped to a certain extent. At least, it slowed down a little; but gradually, I became worse.

About the middle of July, some of the enlisted men of the Tank Group came in from a work detail that had taken them into Bataan. It was the practice of the Japanese to shakedown each work group as they came in. They would confiscate any unauthorized articles. Drugs and medicines were on the list. The individual concerned would generally receive punishment in the form of a beating. By a stroke of fortune this particular detail was not shaken down very carefully, and they brought some drugs into the camp. I don't know yet what they gave me. But for several days they administered these drugs. By the first of August, I was on my feet once more, and feeling as good as possible, under the conditions.

Black marketing was rampant in this camp. Some food-stuffs were smuggled in from the outside by work parties. Others made contact with Filipinos, and would either negotiate with them through the barbed wire at night, or would actually climb the fence and make trades, returning with their precious wares. It was possible to go through the fence at night if conditions were absolutely right.

We had quite an education in the law of supply and demand. If a certain something was needed, and it was scarce, the price went up accordingly. A regular stock market soon developed.

Where did the money come from? It came from several sources. Some still had funds from Bataan, which they had succeeded in hiding from the numerous shakedowns. The only way to stop the human brain from plotting, in regards to smuggling, is to strip the individual of all clothing—and then you cannot be sure. False bottoms in sacks, and bags, and pockets, were contrived. Articles were tied about the waist, under armpits, on ankles, and even suspended from the crotch. I saw one man go through a Japanese shakedown, and appear later with 26 smoked fish! They weighed approximately sixteen pounds! Two of the fish were concealed in the top of his hat.

Another source of funds was through the underground. A goodly number of the Americans had had connections in Manila before the war, in civilian status and otherwise. Truck drivers, pressed into service by the Japanese, and also Filipinos, acted as intermediaries. Messages, some food, and money reached certain of these Americans.

The United States Government also supplied some funds—unknowingly. Before the fall of Bataan, the Finance Department of the Army had destroyed or buried huge sums of paper currency (pesos). At least one member of a detail, sent back into Bataan to work, stumbled on one of the caches. He came up with more than 30,000 pesos and managed to smuggle it into Cabanatuan Camp. He loaned a good portion of it out to prisoners, and accepted a promissory note, or handmade check in return. All notes and checks were to be honored upon return to the States.

About August 1st, the Japanese announced that we were no longer captives, but were prisoners of war! We could never understand the difference, as the treatment remained the same. However, they did announce that we would now be paid according to international law. I stayed there until November 4th but no pay was forthcoming.

One night in August, at about 9:00 o'clock, the barracks leaders were suddenly called to headquarters. There it was announced by the Japs that their foreign office had submitted conditions to the American state department concerning our release. Our return home now, so they said, was up to the United States. We never knew what this meant, nor did we ever hear any more about it.

A group of Americans, who were engaged in smuggling activity through the fence, ran afoul of an outside Japanese patrol one night. They were caught as they were making their way through the fence. The Japs had laid a trap for them. That night, they were beaten terribly and tied up. The next day, they were given the sun treatment—still tied up. Periodically throughout the day, Jap soldiers would walk by and hit them with clubs and gun butts. After a couple of days of this treatment, they were taken out at the edge of camp, more dead than alive, and shot.

The Japanese divided us into groups of ten. If anyone in the group escaped and was not caught, the balance of that group was summarily shot. To escape, meant placing your fellow prisoners in jeopardy.

The ten man group idea originated with the Japanese high command. All prison camps and work details were put on the same basis. Even the Filipinos were organized on the same lines. The mayor of each city or barrio was made responsible for the conduct of the inhabitants. If something displeased the Japs, it would be pinned on some particular group and mass murder resulted.

The commander of Camp Cabanatuan was Lieutenant Colonel Mori. We discovered that he had operated a bicycle shop in Manila up to the time war actually came! The brigadier general I had seen in Bataan on horseback, the day when the Japs came in to get us, was familiar to me. I have searched my memory ever since, but cannot remember where I saw him before the war. There is no doubt but what it was in the Philippines.

Two of the 194th men, on separate details outside Cabanatuan, were shot because men out of their groups escaped. They were Earl G. Smith, 20900751, July 16, 1942, and Howell A. Emley, 39378201, also on July 16, 1942.

A number of escapes occurred at Cabanatuan. I know of no one who retained their freedom, while I was at that camp. Each time an escapee was caught, he was paraded through the camp by the sadistic Japanese. A large sign was hung on the front of him. It portrayed what was apparently supposed to be Jap humor. It did not even make sense. After a fairly long period of this, the escapee would disappear. We never saw him again nor did anyone else in this world.

During his public parade, the prisoner's hands were bound tightly behind his back. A rope was attached to his middle which was held by the guards surrounding him.

In the building next to mine, were quartered another group of lieutenant colonels. They were prisoners from Corregidor. Among them were Lieutenant Colonels Biggs and Breitung. They, together with Lieutenant Gilbert, United States Navy, tried to escape and were caught before reaching the outside of the barbed wire.

They were beaten that night. The next day, they were tied up outside the headquarters and the beating continued—day and night. The morning of the second day, they were taken to the main gate of the camp and were tied to posts. Each man was entirely nude. Japs that passed by, added to the beatings. Any Filipino citizen who passed, was compelled by the Japs, to strike the prisoners. If they did not strike hard enough to please the Sons of Heaven, they in turn received a beating.

On this day a terrific typhoon struck the area. The victims, helpless as they were, had to face the elements. Their naked bodies were battered and bruised from head to foot. Blood streamed down in little rivulets. They hung from their posts like Christ on the Cross.

The next day they were thrown into a truck, taken out of the area, and killed. An eye witness states that Colonel Breitung and Lieutenant Gilbert were shot. Colonel Biggs had been extremely defiant. He was beheaded, because the Japanese believed, that the soul cannot enter heaven, if a beheading occurs before death.

At a muster in the hospital area, the Japanese discovered that two patients were missing. They immediately accused each ten man group with an escape in their ranks, and ordered an execution of the remaining patients. The hospital organized an intensive search of the area, and just before the execution orders were carried out, the two "escapees" were found in the long grass within the enclosure. Both were dead. One had reached the stage of almost unbelievable delirium.

He was found with a dead rat clutched in his hand. Part of the rat—he had devoured!

CHAPTER 27

The Hell Ship

As a general thing, the Japanese did not bother us a great deal, on the inside of Camp Cabanatuan. True enough, there were periodic inspections and shakedowns. But there was not a great deal of inside heckling. The Japs seemed to be content to allow us to administer ourselves, more or less.

At Camp O'Donnell, I instigated thinking, among both officers and enlisted men of the 194th Tank Battalion. That thinking pertained to what had happened in the Philippine campaign. There were still some missing links in the chain of events, which could only be supplied by the local participants in each case. Most of these blank spots were eradicated, and I knew that unless I set the events down, they would escape my memory as time went on. It was at Cabanatuan that I actually started taking notes, using scraps of paper, labels on tin cans, or what-have-you—abbreviating, key words, simple sentences—*flags*—that would trip my mind and make me remember. Also, some depositions were taken. I procured a small wood tobacco box, in which the notes were kept to protect them from the dampness of the tropics.

I bought an old, dirty, stained, individual mosquito net from one of the prisoners taken on Corregidor and arranged the folds so that the box was hidden. Whenever the Japs came in for a shakedown, I grasped the net in one hand so that I was holding the folds containing the box. Raising it high above my head, the net fell to the floor, apparently disclosing—just the net. The ruse worked every time I had to use it. Often, I thought of how I had tried to perform sleight of hand tricks, in the prewar days, and failed miserably. Now, through desperation, I succeeded with a trick so simple, that as I look back on those days, it seems incredible.

The death rate at Cabanatuan slowed down a great deal after August 1st. The chief reason was that the weaker ones had already died. Also, we were able to handle the sanitary situation a little better. Latrines had been dug and enough

rough lumber purloined, to build seats over the open trenches. Considerable difficulty was experienced with the rainy season, which allowed the trenches to fill with water. Also, we
could find no way to confine the maggots to the trenches. But
the human body was receiving adequate water and a little
better food. Then, too, the hospital area was larger than at
O'Donnell and segregations could actually be made.

Rations, here at Cabanatuan, consisted chiefly of rice in
larger issues than previously. About four ounces of vegetables
per day appeared—egg plant, camote (native sweet potato),
some corn, or sweet potato tops. About once each week, one
ounce per man, of carabao meat, was issued. A small amount
of cucumbers was available for about one month. It gave each
prisoner a slice, about one-quarter inch by one and one-half
inches in diameter, twice a week for that month. Once a week
or so, two ounces of cocoanut was issued. A few bananas appeared for about a month.

Sometime in August, I contracted beriberi. It was of the dry
type. It started with my feet, and by the early part of September, my lower limbs were asleep, up to and including, the
knees. Both dry and wet beriberi was on the increase at an
alarming rate. The deficiency was primarily B-1 vitamin.
Yeast contains that necessary element. Someone at Cabanatuan evolved the idea of fermenting rice. The medics approved the idea and nearly all the kitchens saved enough
from the ration to dispense a small amount to those suffering from beriberi. It helped a great number, including myself.

Once in awhile, a little flour came in. Ingenious prisoners
built ovens out of old oil barrels. The cooks took advantage
of every opportunity to change the everlasting diet of rice
and water. Some of the concoctions they turned out were masterpieces of the culinary art—or so it seemed under those conditions. At any rate, they deserve a great deal of credit.

Japanese radio broadcasts and other mediums of propaganda related that American prisoners were being fed chicken
and eggs. That was true. On one occasion we received chickens
for the camp, on the basis of five scrawny chickens for 500
men! On another—50 eggs for 500 men! All went into the
soup.

Quartered in the same building with me, were members of

the staff of II Corps, which the 194th had supported on
Bataan. One of them passed the remark, that they did not
see much of me at their headquarters, while on the peninsula. I replied by saying that we always seemed to know what
II Corps wanted, to which the answer was:

"That's true. But how did you know?"

I told them of the orders I had received from General
Weaver and how a bad situation had been circumvented. The
staff, without exception, volunteered the information, that
the Tank Group Commander was "in bad" with every headquarters on Bataan for the asinine attitude he had taken.

For the first week or so at Cabanatuan there was no way
to wipe away the human waste after a bowel movement, unless the individual was lucky enough to possess a few scraps
of paper. Earth had to be used. We had been more fortunate
at O'Donnell. Leaves, kogon grass, and some paper had been
available. The Japanese never issued anything for toilet paper
while I remained at Cabanatuan. As work parties came and
went, some paper accumulated and we managed to get along.
We utilized it almost to the extent of using both sides! However, many of the prisoners, and especially dysentery cases,
had to resort to earth in the final analysis. There were no
trees or bushes to furnish leaves.

Rumors were more prevalent at Cabanatuan than at O'Donnell. In fact, it seemed as though a rumor factory had been
set up. Mass production, on the assembly line basis, could not
have surpassed the stock we always had on hand.

Any time a new arrival showed up in camp, or a work detail
would come in from the outside, rumors would start flying.
Some would start from half-heard conversations. Others would
come from embellishments of the original report, or from
repeating the report, one to the other. Some of the rumors
were wild and contained no truth whatsoever. Many gave us
considerable information. It became a game to evaluate these
rumors, and piece together, the progress of the war.

Radios were forbidden to the Filipinos, except when direct
supervision could be exercised by the Japanese. However, this
did not deter Mr. Filipino. He, like the Americans, was always
scheming to beat the hated Jap. Many actual radio broadcasts
from the United States were picked up by our friends, and

relayed to us via the underground. The information was generally given to our work details.

We actually received a report on the Midway battle. It was so authentic that it almost caused a wild celebration. It was the kind of tonic we needed.

What must have been Jap inspired, was the rumor on about July 1st, that on the 4th, we would receive good news. Openly, or secretly, everyone was hoping that the impossible would happen and that we would be freed. However, most of us were immune, by this time, to disappointments. Nothing whatever, out of the ordinary, occurred on July 4th. There had been a great deal of interest on the outcome of the heavyweight championship bout on this day, and much conversation had centered around it. Shortly after the 4th, we received a rumor that Joe Louis had been knocked out. This was one rumor that was in reverse!

A rumor, quite persistent at the time, declared that we were going to be exchanged—somehow or other. This rumor said we would be taken to a neutral country and kept there until the end of the war. Several countries were named, but the one most frequently quoted was Ecuador.

As to how some of the rumors started, can be explained by an account of the one which came out of our quarters. One day, we were discussing the various rumors. It had been reported that Americans were fighting with much success in Europe (this was the summer of 1942). One of our group remarked that, according to the rumors," the Americans were going to town in Europe." Soon, a rumor started that we were to be exchanged and would be sent to some town in Europe. This came at the time when exchange rumors were most prolific. By a coincidence, this rumor was traced down to its source. It had spread like wildfire all over the camp. It developed that when the above conversation had taken place, an enlisted man had been passing by our quarters and had heard the tale end of the statement. He interpreted it to mean that we were going to some town in Europe. It was repeated with the assurance that it must be true because it came from the "brass"!

The Japanese spread Manila newspapers over the camp several times during the period when Rommel and his mechanized forces were closing in on Cairo. It looked bad until we happened to notice a very small item on the inside page, which stated that a strong American mechanized force had landed in the Middle East. Our hopes went soaring. It meant to us, that at last, America had fighting forces in the war zones.

Lieutenant Colonel O. O. Wilson, nicknamed Zero, was the morale raiser. He organized and took part in the camp entertainment which generally was staged just before sundown. The talent he produced was nothing short of marvelous. The evening performances became something to look forward to, and to take the mind off the sordidness of prison life. It also helped to give us something to talk about in daily conversation. It helped the mental attitude a great deal. Prisoners found themselves laughing heartily in spite of themselves. The program was interspersed by songs—both old and the newer ones we had learned before war came. The songs brought memories, and instilled new determination, to out-live the hell we were in. One of the songs we sang quite regularly, was accepted as the theme song of Cabanatuan Prison Camp. The melody was "Happy Days Are Here Again," and the words were written by First Lieutenant Bill Burrell of the Army:

> Happy days will come again
> Let us sing a song of cheer 'til then
> It will soon be said—"Remember when"
> As we feast on steaks and beer.
> 'Frisco lies just o'er the hill
> The U.S.A. will be there still
> With what it takes to fill the bill
> When sailing day draws near.
> So chins up—everyone
> A smile will get it done
> We'll all be home Thanksgiving Day
> We'll see the lights of old Broadway
> Until then a song will speed the day
> Happy days will come again.

Religious services were held, both with and without, Japanese permission. Depending upon the mood of our "hosts" they were held openly—or secretly. But they were held! As a general rule, chaplains were denied the right to officiate when deaths occurred. As far as I ever observed, the only way in which they might be present at the so-called funerals, was to worm their way on the list of the burying details. No one ever knew why the Japs refused us the last rites.

Flies were just as bad at Cabanatuan as at O'Donnell, if not worse. I can still hear the drone of those millions of flies—the insistent crawling over our flesh—the continual flailing of arms to drive the bastards away—their dive bombing attacks as they buried themselves in our meager rations of watery rice. God deliver me from flies!

Mosquitos were much worse here than at O'Donnell. They came with the night—silently—different in that respect from their northern cousins—and they pestered. Many times, sleep was out of the question. We wrapped our faces in rags, or whatever else might be available, and lay down, only to awaken half suffocated. We welcomed the dawn when the mosquitos would leave, and the brief respite between then and sunrise, before the flies would descend upon us.

About November 1st, names were being drawn up for the formation of a 1,500 man detail, to leave Cabanatuan. The persistent and undisputed rumor said that the destination was to be Japan. My name appeared on the list.

A great deal of sentiment was shown whenever a detail was about to leave for parts unknown. Friends who were left behind, would always try to contribute something or other. No matter how small in intrinsic value it might be, it was most gratefully received.

One of the 194th men who worked in our kitchen, gave me some extra rice and soup the night we were to leave. I knew it came out of his own rations, but I could not have turned it down without insulting him. It would have been like slapping his face. Another man quietly handed me a can of sardines which he had picked up on an outside work detail. Three others presented me with a stout cane they had fashioned, to aid me in the night blindness I had become afflicted with. Still another group lined up silently outside my quarters, in perfect military formation. All stood at salute as I came out—and unashamed tears spilled down my cheeks unchecked. There is no greater comradeship than that born in the hell of war. Most of those men are now dead.

The Japs announced that we would carry our breakfast

with us and that there would be an extremely large ration of meat for each man. Breakfast consisted of a smaller amount of rice than usual—and the big, extra issue of meat.

This piece of meat averaged in size, for each man, about two inches in diameter and about a quarter of an inch thick. The Japs had not lied; it *was* a great deal bigger than we had received so far in the seven months we had been prisoners!

Needless to say, the majority ate their breakfast on the march to the town of Cabanatuan, before it was time to do so. Most of us had adopted the policy of eating any food issued—immediately. Then we knew it was ours for keeps! It took me the better part of an hour to eat my meat because of its toughness; but, at least it kept my jaws moving.

We left Cabanatuan Prison Camp at about 3:00 A.M., November 5, 1942. Arriving at the town, we were herded into the hated box cars. Ninety-eight of us were in the car I was assigned to. This gave us a little more room than we had had before, and by organizing ourselves, it was possible to shift positions during our day long ride.

An old, wizened Japanese colonel, more closely resembling an ape than a human, made a speech to us. Through his interpreter, he talked in true Jap fashion. He almost shed a few crocodile tears, and told us that we must guard our health. How often we were to hear that phrase in the years to come! Then he told us that we were to be taken to Japan, where we would receive better treatment and lots of food. After a little more of this drivel, he finished, and the train moved off.

Whether or not we stopped at stations enroute, the blessed Filipinos were on hand to throw foodstuffs to us. At one station where we stopped, they had brought buckets of a kind of fruit drink. It was delicious. Very strangely, the Japs did not bother anyone at this station. The populace also served us with a kind of fruit-rice pie. There was not a great deal for each individual, but, once more, the Filipino stock soared high in our estimation.

We reached Manila at about 5:00 P.M. and were marched through the streets to the port area. Straight down to Pier 7 we went, the same pier at which we had landed in September, 1941, with high hopes in our hearts.

During this march through the streets of Manila, we constantly saw Filipinos quietly placing their hands to their faces.

The index finger and the one next to it would form a V! It is an actual fact that some children were murdered by the Japanese for displaying the V sign which they had learned, earlier in the war. One old lady stood watching us, crying silently, the tears running down her cheeks unchecked.

We stayed that night on a cement floor adjoining Pier 7. Quite a stock of uncured leaf tobacco was piled up on the pier, evidently meant for shipment out of the Philippines. We never knew whether or not the Nips realized who took it; but a considerable quantity was taken by us and secreted in our belongings. I fastened two bunches of the leaves on the inside of each trouser leg.

The uncured tobacco, without a doubt, was the most terrible stuff I have ever smoked. Inveterate smoker that I am, it gave me the hiccups. We had not, as yet, learned the art of curing tobacco. After we reached Japan, we learned. There, we displayed the leaves openly, telling the Japs that we had been allowed to bring it from the Philippines. True to form, they saved face by ignoring it, which pleased us immensely.

We were kept at this one spot until about 5:00 o'clock the next afternoon, November 6th. Then we were herded onto a boat and down into the hold.

The boat was the Nagato Maru, a weather-beaten old freighter, which apparently had been in use for about 40 years. There were three holds. I was quartered in the forward hold. The first deck below was occupied by Japanese troops.

We were in the hold, below that, right against the bottom of the ship. The quota for this one space was 600. All around the sides, had been built double deck stalls, with wooden flooring.

The prisoners were herded down into the hold like a flock of stumbling sheep and were packed in as tightly as they could be jammed. Finally, the Japanese themselves had to admit, that not even the Imperial Mind, could possibly cram 600 human bodies into the space. However, between 550 and 560 were jammed in, like pickles packed in a jar.

There was just barely room to sit down, with the knees drawn up tightly under the chin. The heat was almost unbearable. During that night, some were allowed to step up on deck. We gained brief respite in this manner.

The other holds on the ship were packed in the same way.

1,500 of us were on the boat with a comparable number of Nip troops.

On the morning of November 7th, we set sail. Everyone was ordered down into the hold. It brought sharply to my mind, movies I had seen, depicting the lives of prisoners on the old Spanish galley ships. It was almost unbelievable that such a thing could be happening in our age.

There were only two latrines on the ship for the prisoners. One was on each side of the top deck. Dysentery and diarrhea were rampant—and it was to get worse. It soon became apparent that the two latrines would never handle the three holds with their cargo of 1,500 humans.

Urinations were abnormally frequent due to dehydration and the diet. Water was very scarce, but due to the soup we received, we were in better shape than men on some of the other prison ships, who were to take this journey later in the war.

To reach the latrine, you had to actually walk on other men's bodies. You simply stepped on a human form as you picked your way. We procured two tubs which were placed at the bottom of the steps in our hold. These were for the worst dysentery cases.

The space allotted each 10 men in the hold of this ship was four feet, nine inches by six feet, two inches. Unbelievable? Yes—it was unbelievable to us also!

No medicine was aboard the ship. We were allowed to set up a so-called sick bay on the open deck, in the midst of coiled ropes, cables and other paraphernalia. In reality, there was nothing we could do. We watched each other get weaker and weaker under conditions that defy the imagination. A number of deaths occurred; the bodies were buried at sea—no ceremony—simply a soul passed on.

Two or three areas in our hold had a little more room. These were coveted spaces. Here, five men were assigned—and the space measured six feet by five feet!

The severe cases of dysentery had to sit on the stairway, or as close as possible to the buckets during the entire voyage. Dysentery hits with sudden and agonizing griping in the intestines. Then the victim becomes so weak he can barely move—perhaps not at all. Men would stumble, crawl, and actually roll down the stairway like sick animals, to reach

those buckets. Volunteers were available to help the sick. But
the volunteers were in almost the same condition, or were
rapidly becoming so. Spirits weakened. I found myself wondering if it wouldn't be easier to die.

The conditions were protested, but to no avail. The Jap
attitude was "so sorry"—and that was all. There was nothing
they would do about it. The Jap interpreter on board was
drunk for almost the entire voyage. He was most abusive. Our
only hope was to make Japan without further delay.

Men, tottering from sickness and disease, were beaten and
kicked by the Jap troops. On going to the latrine on deck, the
stairway led up through one side of their quarters. The abuse
occurred as prisoners made their painful way to the toilet. It
seemed that their shoes sometimes scraped against the metal
steps, and disturbed some of the yellow bastards. After the top
deck was reached, you joined the long line of fellow sufferers,
and awaited your turn.

After a trip to the latrine had been made and you descended
into the lower hold, it was as if someone struck you a heavy
blow in the face. The wave of stench and heat was nearly
more than the human could stomach.

Armistice Day, November 11th, we arrived at Takao, Formosa. Very few men were allowed on deck. Here we stayed
until November 15th when we were, at last, under way again—
but not for long. Arriving at Mako, Formosa, we stayed until
November 18th. The Japs claimed a bad storm was the reason for the delay.

Sometime during the voyage, there was much excitement
among the Japs. We could feel the explosions of depth
charges, and the deck guns on our ship went into action. We
never knew just what occurred. We only knew that if a tor-
pedo or bomb hit the tub we were on, we were trapped with
no possible way to escape.

As is always the case with Americans, even when faced with
extreme adverse conditions—and death, there are always those
who can resort to humor. The voyage, therefore, still had some
humorous angles. Wise cracking was just as prevalent, or perhaps more so, than under normal conditions. Songs were sung,
and some of them were very uncomplimentary to the Japs.
Men even talked over plans of what they would do when the
war was over. Going to the toilet one night, inadvertently I

stepped on what happened to be the face of one of the prisoners. Instead of being angry, he simply wiped it off on his sleeve. Looking up, he cracked:

"Mister, 'The Face on the Barroom Floor' didn't have anything on me!"

On the trip we had become terribly lousy. These parasites added to our misery. They were to be with us for quite some time before we could rid ourselves of their unwelcome presence. There was nothing to be done about it now except scratch—if you had the room to scratch.

The terrific searing heat stayed with us until we were several days out of Japan. Then the weather turned cold. It seemed to clear the air a little down where we were.

The Nagato Maru pulled into the harbor of Moji, Japan, late in the afternoon of November 24th. Here we stayed until about 5:00 P.M. of the next day. It seemed to all of us, that we were older by many years.

As I look back on that boat trip, I sometimes find myself doubting that such a thing could have occurred. For 19 days and 19 nights more than 95 percent of the prisoners on board that ship had to sit in cramped positions, or simply stand up. Those sitting took turns with others who had been standing. You shared and shared alike.

We had no apparel but tropical clothes, consisting of either light shirts and trousers, or a Filipino light denim suit. The great majority had no socks or underwear. Some were without shoes.

It is miraculous that we were able to take the abuse, we had taken, for the almost three continuous weeks of that voyage. And now—we were to undergo another test—one we had not, as yet, experienced.

The weather at Moji was freezing. That temperature was hard to take. Our bodies were miserably under weight, malnutritioned and diseased. Our blood was thinned by the tropics—like water. The wind and cold cut like a knife—and we shook, and shivered, as if with the ague.

This winter, and the ones to come, brought us just a little closer to the Spirit of Valley Forge.

CHAPTER 28

"No Man Has Really Eaten Until He Has Starved"

As WE STEPPED off the boat, two Japanese, with tanks and spray guns, disinfected our exteriors. Whether they believed this would kill the germs inside of our clothing and on our bodies, was another sixty-four dollar question. That's the way the Nip does things.

It was dusk, and word was passed down the line to form in a column of fours. Then a voice, in good straight American, came piercing out of the semi-darkness:

"All right," it said. "Snap out of it and get the lead out!"

It came from a figure that was dressed in the latest American style. Later, we were to know him as Fuji Moto San. He looked as if he had just walked off Fifth Avenue, New York City. His physical proportions gave the impression that he was taller than was the actual case.

I became fairly well acquainted with him at two different camps, that is, as well acquainted as one could with the Jap. He never admitted it, but I am sure that he was born in the United States, and had been in the employ of the Japanese, part of the time at least. In fact, a friend of mine from California, during the course of conversation with Fuji Moto, trapped him into admitting he had known a certain contractor on our west coast, and had viewed one of his construction jobs near Salinas, California. The only job this contractor ever had in that locality was at Fort Ord, and the job started in 1941!

We received a most welcome surprise. Little wooden boxes were passed around which contained rice, seaweed, pickled daikons (similar in texture to the turnip but watery like a radish), and wonder of wonders—a slice of tangerine. There was also a tub of hot tea. That small piece of tangerine was like salt placed in an open wound. Because of the scurvy, nearly all of us had, the acid bit into our mouths and tongues like red hot needles.

After our most welcome repast, we were transported by ferry to Honshu (main island of Japan), after which, we entrained in coaches. This luxury somewhat lifted up our depressed thoughts on what we had just seen. While waiting for the train, we had seen General Electric, and other up-to-date American equipment, in use by the Japs on their railroads. We all knew, before the war ever started, that Japan had this equipment, and also had hired our engineering experts to put it into operation. But actually seeing it in the hands of these devilish people, was another thing altogether.

The next day dawned—November 26, 1942—Thanksgiving Day. Most of us had thoughts of the previous ones at home—of the good things to eat, and the warmth and cheer which we had never truly appreciated. Our people must have felt those thoughts!

We rode all that day until late afternoon, making frequent stops enroute. Our course had taken us through the immense industrial area of Japan. And it was immense! As far as the eye could reach, there were huge smokestacks. Everything was in full operation. We realized just how much the great majority of Americans had underestimated the strength of Japan.

Finally, we arrived at Osaka. 500 of us were taken to an empty space, which was a part of the big railroad station. Here we waited until well into the evening, when we were loaded on trolley cars. After about two hours ride, the cars stopped and we formed into column once more.

Many in the group were in very bad shape. Everyone had a severe hacking cough. Some were on the verge of pneumonia, and a goodly percentage were suffering from beriberi, manifested mostly, by deep-down aching feet. By helping each other, and walking as slow as the guards would permit, we reached our destination. Fortunately, it only took about 45 minutes.

Our column was made up of 178 officers and 322 enlisted men. The Japs had designated me as company commander and had placed me at the head of the column. One of the guards asked if we were hungry, to which I replied that we were very hungry. He then told me that we would get a good meal when we reached the camp. Needless to say, we did *not!*

At about 10:00 P.M., on this Thanksgiving night, we reached Tanagawa Prison Camp. It was a new one which had been built only recently. The setup was typical.

The buildings were of flimsy, rough lumber. The outside was coated with a sort of stucco, made by using the earth at hand and mixing with a little cement and water. The cold, icy wind howled through the huge cracks and openings. On the inside, double decked stalls had been built on both sides with a narrow passageway down the center. This passageway held rough, narrow tables with benches on either side. The floor was earth. The lower bunk decks were elevated about two feet above the earth floor.

Quarters were assigned and we were each given five thin cotton sheets. There was no heat in the buildings. Down the center of the aisle were two concrete pits in which charcoal could be burned for heat—if you had the charcoal. We bedded down in twos and threes so as to pool the sheets and take advantage of body heat. But hardly anyone slept. We shook and shivered until routed out the next morning for muster.

Breakfast was tea and a slim portion of lugao (watery rice).

We immediately did everything we could to organize the camp and better our conditions as much as possible. A conference was held with Fuji Moto in which he stated that camp regulations would soon be forthcoming. A picture of the condition of our people was presented together with the request for medicine, supplies, better food and a segregation of the more severe cases. He promised that he would take all this up with the commandant, a captain. However, he said, that the captain would be leaving soon and we would have a new commander. Fuji Moto was always courteous to us.

We had an outside water rack which froze solidly every night. Water then had to be carried in buckets from a long way outside the camp. To have put the water pipes below the frost line, with a shutoff and drain that could be operated each evening—was too much for the Imperial Mind to comprehend. Each morning was a repetition of the previous one. The Japs would come out and open the faucets. Naturally, nothing would happen. Then the jabbering started. More Japs came slithering out of their quarters clad in warm, padded kimonas. More jabbering—scratching of cropped slopeheads—calling for the American Duty Officer. Pretending to make a minute inpection, they soon tired of watching him and melted away. When the temperature had risen and the pipes thawed out, he would report to the Jap office that everything was O.K. Leaks developed and the rack became a shower bath. Whether or not the pipes were ever buried, I do not know. For the period I was there, nothing was done. Fortunately, water for breakfast was always drawn by our kitchen crew the night before.

Fuji Moto San stayed at Tanagawa for about a week or so. He called in the barracks leaders and myself for a conference with the commandant one evening. We tried to explain our needs and the condition of the prisoners. However, he was not particularly interested in that subject and dismissed it with words to the effect that everything would be taken care of. We soon learned the reason for the meeting.

Japanese are as curious as we have been led to believe. Until they get nasty and mean, their questioning is almost childlike. The queries that night were only an initiation to the many of the future.

What are your impressions of the war?

Why did the war start?

Who did we think would win the war?

What did we think of the Japanese soldier?

What did we think of the Japanese artillery?

When did we think the war would end?

And many more of this same type of question.

Some of us had begun to evaluate the Japanese way of thinking, and to realize that we could not negotiate with them on the basis of Western standards. Many of the prisoners never seemed to be able to get this through their heads.

If you were too servile, you were liable to be picked upon and beaten. If you were too straightforward, it was considered as an insult, and you were beaten. A happy medium was the best course. Each situation had to be treated separately. Japs always liked compliments if they were not too obvious. The right kind of compliment, at the right time, caused them to puff up with self esteem. It might even gain some concession for the prisoners. The Jap definitely has an inferiority complex. This, together with his counter-clockwise way of thinking, presents a very difficult problem in dealing with him.

Most of us, at the conference that night, tried to steer our answers so that they did not deviate from the center line. We must have been successful, because there were no repercussions, and the commandant did not fly into a rage as is so common when the Jap is displeased.

Fuji Moto left us with the announcement that he would be back in a couple of weeks. Before he left, he did several things for me that caused me to wonder if he was everything he pretended to be. I had been up and down with dysentery and what I thought to be flu. Several times, Fuji Moto came to my quarters. It was always when no one else was around. He gave me aspirins and told me not to give up, but to get well. To crown this startling event, he brought over some recent newspapers printed in English. They were Japanese propaganda papers which they were sending out all over the Far East. However, they contained news from which we could do a fair job of separating lies from the truth. We never saw Fuji Moto again until near the end of the war. I have always wondered if he could have been one of our agents in Japan. I heard, after the war, that he had been tried by the War Crimes Commission and given a sentence. This would have been the natural procedure, whether or not he was our agent, so as to protect him from the Japanese populace. It does not necessarily mean that he is serving that sentence. Some day, I hope to find out.

The commandant of the camp soon left, and a sergeant major took over. Also, a new interpreter arrived. His name was Takagi and he was mean all the way through. He spoke fairly good English. We found that he had been in England when war broke out and had been interned in a concentration camp. His repatriation came on the first shipload of diplomatic exchanges. He hated us intensely, especially the officers.

Something which effected us adversely, was the Japanese language. It is impossible to express oneself coherently in Japanese. For instance—to read a Jap newspaper, about 5,000 characters must be memorized, and even then, different meanings are construed from the same group of characters. Even orders coming down from the higher command were constantly being misinterpreted by Nip subordinates. This meant that in a conversation, relayed by the interpreter, a totally different meaning might be construed from what we had actually said. *And,* if the interpreter so desired, he might convey the misinterpretation deliberately, without incriminating himself. This, Takagi did frequently.

The sergeant major was a true son of Nippon—suave—"so sorry"—full of promises and crocodile tears—unethical.

We soon learned that this was to be a work camp. Using this as a leverage, the sergeant major, on December 22nd, issued overcoats to us, and also caps. The caps were summer headpieces made of straw, with a thin piece of cloth covering the exteriors.

I was designated as American Commander, being the senior officer in the camp. It was agreed upon that we would be allowed to administer ourselves to a great extent. However, this agreement—as were all agreements with the Japs—was voided almost as soon as it was made. An agreement meant nothing to them. One of the stipulations was, that I would have full charge of the kitchen which was being operated by our men. This was extremely important in the life of a prisoner in the hands of the Japanese.

"Starvation plays peculiar tricks with human behavior and the human mind."

Each group of prisoners had good and bad among them. When faced with adversity, some had no code of ethics. Others were weak. We found that education and our higher civilization did not help much, as far as honor was concerned, unless the individual had character in him. When the veneer was stripped off, you were sometimes surprised to find what was underneath.

It was necessary to have only the most honorable men in the kitchen. Otherwise, trades were made and some bellies filled at the expense of the main group of prisoners. I immediately placed a second lieutenant in charge of the galley (for some reason or other, we accepted the Navy term "galley" almost from the start of our imprisonment). This lieutenant was most highly respected for his integrity by all officers and enlisted men of the camp. Then, I announced that the original galley force would be kept intact until if and when any one of them went astray. The whole camp, with the exception of a very small group, was well satisfied.

This arrangement lasted for about twenty-four hours. The Japs fired him. On making inquiry, I was told that the Japanese did not have mess officers in their army. When reminded

that an agreement had been made, that fact was calmly brushed aside and their argument reiterated. It was like talking to
a stone wall.

The Japs set up two rations. One was called the worker's
ration. The other was the non-worker's ration. The first called
for 500 grams of rice per day, while the second was 250 grams.
The sick were classified under the non-worker's ration! The
Japanese theory was, that if you did not work, you did not
need the food. This applied also to the worker on rest days
(about one in every ten). If a Japanese holiday came along
and no one worked on the regular detail, the rations were
automatically cut! Another morale destroying factor was the
issue of food. It was always short. Rice sacks coming into camp
were invariably pilfered by Japs on the outside. As much as
ten pounds might be missing from a 100 pound sack. This
made no difference. It still weighed 100 pounds and that is
what we received and were charged for. Japs, inside the camp,
would steal from us again, after the food had been issued. We
couldn't win!

To be eligible for the worker's ration, the individual had
to perform manual labor. And it had to be on a Japanese recognized project. This ration of rice for a twenty-hour hour
period was slightly less than one pound, two ounces. The non-
worker's ration of 250 grams was slightly less than nine ounces
for the same period. Try this procedure some day—weigh out
the worker's ration of rice. Then take more or less away from
it because of the pilferage we constantly encountered. Cook it
up and add a little pinch of salt—not enough to season it, because that would not be a fair test. Eat nothing else for twenty-
four hours except a small portion of meatless, watery soup.
Then, and then only, will you get some idea of what the
ration was—*if you were on the worker's ration*. I am not asking you to try the other ration. Perhaps this will explain why,
ex-prisoners of war *hate* to see any food wasted, picked over
by a supercilious individual, and left on the plate to be
thrown away as garbage!

"No man has really eaten until he has starved, or been
clean until he has felt the nibbling of lice, or has lived until
he has felt death."

Our bodies were not normal. They were already malnutritioned, diseased, and seriously ill. Please try the above recom-

mendation. If you do, I can assure you that your griping (if you have griped) about America, will cease!

Officers in Tanagawa Camp were worked inside the area on various jobs—all the way from pick and shovel work, to tilling the soil on an adjacent plot for the camp garden. Even though the officers performed this manual labor, they were classified as non-workers, and received that ration. In the matter of soups, even this meager portion was divided. The workers received all the solids. The officers were allotted the liquid. Naturally, because of the cold weather, hunger was intensified.

After much argument and cajoling, we were allowed to use one barracks as a "hospital." We placed therein, the most severe cases. Very little medicine was available, but segregation meant better care. Each day, we argued with the Japs regarding the status of the patients. Sometimes we won and sometimes we lost. During the time I was a "guest" at this camp, a little over one and one-half months, 37 officers and enlisted men died. This number did not include others who were near death, who, for some reason or other were taken out of the camp by the Japs. We were given to understand they were being taken to the hospital in Osaka. This was only a part of the Japanese "face saving" gesture. I have proof that the majority of this group also died.

Every time a death occurred, the Japs always asked the same question: "What is the procedure in your country? Do you bury the body or do you cremate it?" Always my answer was the same: "We do not cremate unless it is a specific wish of the diseased. We bury them." The result was always the same—an order would come out that the body would be cremated! And so it was.

Each time a death would occur, we would request that we be allowed a certain time to hold prayers over the body. In nearly all cases, the order for cremation would come so quickly, that prayers had to be said as the body was being taken to the crematory. On several occasions, prayers had to be said as the remains were being carried through the door to the cart we used.

Prisoners, at this camp, were required to salute all Japanese regardless of rank. Failure to do so, meant a severe beating. I questioned Fuji Moto about this, and he replied:

"You have been used to doing things different in America.

You are now in Japan. Do everything you are told to do. That is your only salvation."

All prisoners slept with every stitch of clothing on, due to the severe cold weather. Rags and pieces of paper were used as underwear and socks. Each night we hoped that the next day would be sunshiny.

At Tanagawa, we called our latrine the "wind tunnel." It was the recipient of the cold, icy blasts which never seemed to abate at this camp. The construction was of such a nature that there was little or no protection. Due to vitamin deficiency and the watery diet, it was common to be compelled to urinate from 10 to 12 times during the hours of darkness. Many times, these excursions occurred 15 minutes apart. Sometimes, we would be so numb with the cold that it was extremely difficult to take care of ourselves properly.

Morning and evening musters were held by the Japanese. The former was held outside in column of fours, while the latter was inside, standing at attention alongside your bunk space. Counting had to be done in Japanese, each prisoner counting off in sequence. The barracks leader had to make a report in Japanese, just before ordering the occupants to "Bango" (Count Off). Interminable checking nearly always took place. If someone had been put in the "hospital," it was always reported to the Jap office. The same was true of any personnel on duty, by order of the Japs, but not actually present for muster. However, this only confused the Nip, and a long drawn out conference had to be held each time muster was held, and an explanation given over and over. The Sons of Heaven truly have one track minds.

Tanagawa Camp was listed as No. 1 among 13 other prisoner of war camps in the Osaka area. Each prisoner was given a number painted on a small piece of wood which he was required to wear on his outer garments. Failure to wear the tag meant a beating.

Opening ceremonies were held in which the commandant made a speech. This speech making was common practice among the Japs. They puffed, and surged, and blowed. At the end of each phrase, the orator would fold his arms on his expanded chest, glare at his audience, and nod his head emphatically, as the interpreter translated. I do not know, whether this way of giving a speech is characteristic of the

Japanese, or whether they aped the delivery from Mussolini. I remembered movies of Mussolini in all his glory, and it seemed to me that the Japanese must have admired and adopted his style.

There was intense hatred for American officers here. It was evidenced, not only by the rations we received, but by the general treatment as well. Humiliations were in order for all officers.

In the early part of January, 1943, I went into the office on one of my numerous trips to argue for more food. I met Takagi, the interpreter. He asked me what I wanted. I replied that I had come in to go over the food situation. No one else was in the office, except the regular Jap clerical staff. I had hoped that the sergeant major would be there.

Takagi bristled and said that we were getting plenty of food. This was the one time that I made a very foolish mistake. My reply was pointed and without any varnish on it. He had a pencil in his hand and he jabbed the point viciously into the cheek of my face. I still carry the scar. The office force came forward as reinforcements. Takagi told me never to come in again and ask for food. My first reaction was to kill or be killed. The latter was a foregone conclusion. Something bigger than I intervened and a calmness settled on me that I cannot explain. All I did was to turn and walk out.

This incident did not deter our requests for more food. We made them, but not to the interpreter. The sergeant major became the target. Takagi became much worse, after I left this camp. It is interesting to note that he was tried for war crimes and sentenced to hang. Can I say I am sorry?

CHAPTER 29

The Session on Food

THREE DAYS BEFORE Christmas, the Japs announced that a Red Cross individual food box would be issued—one to every three men. They produced Red Cross post cards, which accompanied the boxes. These cards had a space provided for signatures so as to prove the individual had received the box. All of us signed these cards.

The day before Christmas the Japs made the issue. But instead of one box to every three men, we received the following: Eleven 12-ounce cans of corned beef, 11 small chocolate bars, 11 eight-ounce packages of cheese, about 12 raisins per man, a very small portion of sardines and salmon, two hardtacks per man, and a small supply of powdered milk. *All this for 500 men!*

With the exception of the corned beef and milk, which was turned over to the kitchen for the soup and tea, each man's share could easily be placed in the palm of one hand. There was quite a stock of Red Cross food in the storehouse, but the Japanese *refused* to issue it. Dividing up the miserable stipend was not only a real job, but a ceremony as well. Each raisin had to be counted. A poll of the camp had to be taken as to whether the individual wanted a bit of cheese or chocolate. He could not have both. The decision was momentous. Men were carefully chosen, for their integrity, to do the dividing. Others watched with drooling mouths. To the normal person, this perhaps sounds asinine and childish. We were not normal. We were abnormal—starving—and it was most important to us.

Christmas was a Japanese holiday, but not because of the birth of Christ. It so happens that December 25th is a national holiday of Nippon. There was no work, and with a Jap holiday, it means food as well. Everyone received the non-worker's ration because he did not work!

The night before Christmas, I was down with malaria. The camp had requested permission to sing Christmas carols and to have a bonfire in the camp compound. The unpredictable Jap granted the request. I listened to those carols with mixed feelings as the voices drifted in from the yard. Thoughts of other Christmas Eve's in America swept through my mind. I turned my face to the wall.

The last song was spontaneous. I can still hear it in its sudden burst of harmony, coming like a stupendous message of cheer. It was "God Bless America!" Something moved me to crawl out of my bunk, and I stood at attention, spine tingling. Violent repercussions were expected. None came. The Japs made no sign, whatever, that they recognized the song!

New Year's Day is another Jap holiday, but not because it is the start of the New Year. They have a great ceremony, and it made our stomachs feel like churning. Their usual procedure, among other things, is to congregate and Banzai three times, lifting their arms toward the direction of the Imperial Palace.

They lined us up in the yard that morning with instructions that we would Banzai with them. Everyone went through the motions. But the word "Banzai" did not come forth. Some were saying, "God bless America" as they howled. Others were turning toward the direction of the Imperial Palace, which housed the Son of Heaven, and hurled verbal insults. It was obvious that the Japs, who were screaming at the top of their lungs, did not hear our utterances. It was extremely fortunate for us. To have insulted the Emperor in their presence, would have meant instant beatings and death.

We were terribly infested with body lice at this camp and there was not very much we could do about it. The weather was so cold and clothing so scarce, that we could ill afford to strip ourselves so as to boil our apparel in water. The next best thing, if the sun came out, was to take off one garment at a time and institute an intense, but very rapid search. This helped some but not a great deal. The parasites multiplied in untold numbers and our bodies were raw from scratching.

No games of any type or description were allowed in the camp. Everyone, not actually outside on a work detail, was compelled to take strenuous calisthenics, learn Japanese commands, and drill the Japanese way. Many of the seriously ill were made to partake. Part of the treatment (supposed to make us well and healthy) was to double time around the compound while in formation. Anyone who failed to keep up, regardless of sickness and inability, was beaten. Protests only brought more beatings.

We actually succeeded in getting a hot bath at Tanagawa. Japs believe in the mass bathing method. A huge concrete vat is provided in which hot water is supplied. The procedure to be followed, calls for bathing the body under a water tap or shower first to remove the dirt, and then to soak in the tub. The vat will accommodate as many as can crowd into it. Several requests had been made for the bath, and much to our surprise, it was finally granted. Needless to say, we did not bathe first under the water tap. It was almost ice cold.

The camp was staggered in ten minute periods for each group. The scum on top of the water in the vat, deposited by the filth of our bodies, was scooped off by each new group. Regardless of that side of the picture, it was the most luxurious feeling I have ever experienced. The warmth was felt clean down into the very marrow of our bones. It was the first bath in two months, and the first heat for our bodies, outside of the sun, since we had encountered the freezing weather in Japan. Reluctantly, we climbed from the tub when our time was up. For hours we tingled with the feel of it. The last group through protested, that those preceding them in the vat, must never have had a bath in their entire lives, and said they could prove it by one look at the water. Appeasement was in order, and it was ruled that the order for bathing would be reversed when the next bath came around!

Realizing it was impossible to do anything with Takagi, in the matter of food, I wrote a letter to the sergeant major, using a different line than had been followed before. This was a work camp and the Nips were intensely interested in just that. Generally speaking, I told him that our health was very bad before coming to this camp and that unless we received more food and vitamins, we would not be able to perform on the work details efficiently. The letter ended by requesting a conference with him, and also for permission to allow my barracks leaders to attend it. The opportunity for delivering it came when Takagi left the area one day and when I knew the sergeant major was in the office. Walking in, I laid the letter on his desk before him. It was a lucky day. He seemed to be in good humor and replied in his pidgin English, "Soon."

This was a word used a great deal by Japs. It might mean just what it implied, and it might mean never. But at least, the message reposed with the highest authority in the camp, and the prisoners knew it had been done.

A few days after, much to my surprise, Takagi sent for me and stated that the sergeant major had set 3:00 o'clock that afternoon for a conference with the barracks leaders and myself. He did not refer in any way to his order to me a week or so before.

At the appointed time, we were ushered into the presence of the All Highest, and seated before him. A cordial spirit seemed to pervade the office. We were even given a cigarette!

We had rehearsed just what we were going to talk about and how it would be presented. Our American doctor was with us. Facts about the human body were presented—vitamins—calories—everything in detail. The Japs asked multitudinous questions and took copious notes. The conference lasted for about two hours. Judging by Western standards, we had made a touchdown. Our case had been presented in its entirety. We left the office feeling highly elated. The sergeant major had promised he would do what he could. He had said the food would get better. Optimism saturated the camp.

Jap activity was observed in the storehouse. We received—in addition to our regular ration that evening—*one-half raw carrot per man!* We had stipulated in the conference that carrots contained vitamin A, which was good for the eyes.

As we were to learn, the asking of questions and the taking of notes, was just part of the game. Giving us the raw carrots—the Japs considered they had done their part.

We also learned the next day, *that the carrots had been brought into the camp for the working ration soup. When the galley force asked for the carrot ration, they were calmly told that it had already been issued the night before and we had eaten it!*

Our score was exactly *nothing!* There is no such thing as negotiating with the Jap when he has the upper hand. Even normally, he will calmly ignore his just obligations, if they interfere in any way. He has no ethics.

Uniforms of the Japanese were generally ill fitting, especially their britches. The seats were unusually large. I could never determine the reason for this. It certainly was not be-

cause of the extra largeness of their rears. Officers' britches
particularly seemed to be accentuated in this respect. Most of
them, when viewed from the rear, displayed the amusing picture of the crotch of the britches just about reaching the
backs of their knees. One of the prisoners explained that the
largeness was to hide their tails!

Shortly before I left Tanagawa Camp, a new commandant
arrived. His rank was that of a second lieutenant. He was
about six feet tall and well proportioned. I had no opportunity of knowing anything about his administration, but was
told by others, who remained after we left, that he was not
as bad as the average Jap we had encountered thus far.

On January 14th it was announced that 100 officers would
be taken out of Tanagawa and transferred to another camp.
My name appeared on this list. The commandant called me
into the office and announced that I would be in charge of the
group. He also produced a map and showed me where we
were to be taken. This much information was very unusual to
be getting from the Japanese. Our new destination was to be
Zentsuji Prison Camp. It was located on the next island to
the south—Shikoku. I asked when we would be leaving and
he replied that it would probably be that day. There would
be an inspection before we left. Inspection meant shakedown.

About the middle of the afternoon, word was passed down
from the office to form for inspection. We hurriedly shook
hands with those to remain behind, gathered up our belongings, and formed ranks in the compound. As the one designated to be in charge of the group, I deposited my belongings
ahead of the first rank. I was ordered to accompany the inspecting Japs.

I had a few bad moments. My ragged and dirty mosquito
net reposed on top of the other articles, where I had placed
it, so as to be grasped and held aloft as per the regular ritual.
The box of notes was hidden, as usual, in the folds. There
were several Japs making the inspection. I thought that my
articles might be inspected while I was away from the vicinity.

I constantly kept an eye out for any Jap who might be making for my pile. We had made approximately three rows of
prisoners, when I noticed one of the guards apparently heading for it. Quickly, I headed him off and pointed toward my
pile. Then I pointed to the guard whom I had been accom-

panying. I shook my head, and managed to get across to him the idea that my belongings had already been inspected.

To my utter amazement and peace of mind, he nodded his head. All this took place in silence and in back of guard I was with. There was no search of my effects.

We all thought that we were leaving that day, immediately after inspection. But such was not the case. In true Japanese fashion—it had merely been a "dry run" and we were allowed to go back to our barracks. It was announced that we would leave the next day. Another shakedown was expected at that time but there was none. You could never predict what the Jap would do. You could only guess.

At dusk, we took the trolley to Osaka and detrained in the big station. We were taken to an outside shed to await our train. We saw preparations outside the station which cheered us immensely. The Japs had started to sandbag certain areas. That meant that they were getting ready for bombings. Had we known that it would be more than two years before those bombs became reality, our optimism would not have been so keen.

While we were waiting, another group of prisoners appeared. They numbered thirty, and proved to be a part of the group who had been separated from us when we first arrived in Japan. Capt. Johnson (194th S-3) and Capt. Burke (C. O. of Co. "A") were in the group. We had a reunion and exchanged rumors—authentic and otherwise. They had been held at another camp in Osaka and had been accorded the same treatment as ourselves.

After riding all that night on the train, we loaded on a ferry boat. Dawn was just breaking as we crossed the Inland Sea. Arriving at Takamatsu, we loaded on another train, arriving at the town of Zentsuji without incident. After marching a short distance, we were herded into Zentsuji Prison Camp. It was located in the town and in the midst of a huge army training area. We arrived at about 10:00 A.M., January 16, 1943. For nearly two and one-half years, this was to be our home.

Another shakedown was in store for us. This time, I was allowed to stay with my belongings. After an interminable delay, the inspecting started, and in due course, the party stopped in front of me. Like a trained animal, I went through my ritual, nonchalantly grasping the tattered and stained mosquito net, at just exactly the right place, raising it above my head so that the end of it touched the ground. Inwardly, my prayers were fervent that the deception would pass again. It did! Viewing the net with disdain, they confined their efforts to the small pile on the ground. After grunting and some jabbering, they passed on. Almost caressingly, I laid my good friend, the net, on top of my possessions.

Zentsuji War Prison Camp had been set up originally by the Japanese as their propaganda camp. They had taken many pictures (some movies) of the prisoners which appeared in propaganda newspapers and magazines. This propaganda had found its way into the United States and the Red Cross printed some of the information. This was the only camp, to my knowledge, that was exploited by the Japs for propaganda purposes. Americans, taken on Wake and Guam Islands in December of 1941 had been brought to this camp about one year before we arrived. Their treatment had not been too bad. The International Red Cross Representative had been allowed to visit the camp—also for propoganda purposes. This man was a native of Switzerland, had resided in Japan for years, and was married to a Japanese woman. It should have been unnecessary to use propaganda on him! At any rate, all other prison camps (according to the Jap version) were like Zentsuji. The camp also housed Australian and British officer prisoners who were taken in the early stages of the war at Rabaul and other actions in the Southwest Pacific.

The American prisoners from Wake and Guam had the camp well organized. Because of the camp's propaganda status, it was possible to work on the face saving characteristic of the Jap, and gain more concessions than was possible in the other camps.

The galley was staffed by hard working and efficient men from the Navy and Marines. A sick bay had been established with American hospital orderlies assigned to it. Lt. Commander Van Peenen, navy doctor, was allowed a great deal of leeway in treatment of the sick. The Japs had allowed Red Cross library books to come in. Prisoners had been given permission to subscribe to a limited number of the two Japanese propaganda newspapers, printed in English—the Nippon Times and The Mainichi. Also a limited number of subscriptions had been permitted to the Nippon Times Magazine and to Contemporary Japan—propaganda publications printed in English.

The Japs had insisted that these original American occupants of the camp have maps of the Far East posted on the walls. They had even helped in keeping the maps posted. This was at the time when Japan was expanding in its plunge for power. They were flushed with success and bloated with optimism.

Food had not been too bad. It was not good, but it was not serious either. Some Red Cross food had been allowed to come in.

Our arrival was the signal for a change in all this. Treatment and food deteriorated rapidly. Maps were ordered destroyed. Japan was getting hurt.

We were assigned to quarters, segregated from the rest of the camp's occupants, and quarantined for two weeks. It was during this period that the Wake and Guam prisoners showed their mettle. The things they did for us can never be paid for. Our debt will last as long as we shall have life.

The galley force was instructed by them to deduct certain amounts from their own rations and give it to us! They had been allowed to bring quite a quantity of their own clothing from Wake and Guam, and from this stock, they helped to clothe us. Our sick, who were unable to care for themselves, were taken over by them. They fed us vitamin pills that had been procured. They took our lice infested clothing and boiled the articles to kill the parasites. Sometimes it was necessary to repeat the operation, but they did it with no complaint, and finally rid every one of us of the hellish affliction. They badgered the Japanese into giving us some Jap clothing and to replace the overcoats that Tanagawa authorities had taken away from us. The overcoats were short and flimsy, but they were something to cover our bodies, eternally shaking from the cold. They secretly visited us, bringing offerings of bits of food and tobacco, much of which was smuggled in from the outside by work parties. They gave us what news was available. Checkers, cards, acey-duecey, and other games were allowed, and they gave us much of their paraphernalia. Every possible thing that could be done for us, was done!

Zentsuji was a bonanza, as far as keeping notes was concerned. Paper was more plentiful due to the supply the other Americans had accumulated. There were multitudinous places to hide the notes. Captain Wilson, American Army Signal officer, who had been detailed to Wake Island shortly before war came, even supplied me with a Jap fountain pen and ink! I went to work.

Saving face was quite apparent with the Japanese authorities here. The personnel, evidently, had been selected to perpetuate it. Even though treatment and food deteriorated, it was always accompanied by face saving methods.

Before we were assigned to our quarters, the commanding general of that particular district made a speech to us. A Japanese speech is quite a ceremony. There must always be something for the speaker to stand on. Invariably, a table is placed in front of him. The table is covered with a white cloth. This speech was no exception. The Jap staff assembled attired in their best clothes and equipped, as they always were, with their swords. The Japs are very proud of their swords and caress them constantly. These swords are not merely for show but are meant to use—and the Japs used them!

We were lined up before the table when the dignitaries arrived. The General took his position. To the Western mind, the scene would normally provoke laughter, because it resembles a comic strip. However, we did not laugh! A tall Jap lieutenant of about six feet, slightly stooped, and probably fifty years of age, acted as adjutant. This individual was attached to the camp permanently. He had been given the name of "Sake Pete" by the Americans who had made his acquaintance first. The name was quite appropriate as he was under the influence of sake more often than not. Saturday nights were observed most religiously, more than any other time, by "Pete" and his sake. He was an awkward individual and was constantly falling over his own feet. He shuffled, as did all Japs, but his shuffling was different. We always knew who was coming when his trompings fell upon our ears.

Sake Pete stood in front of us. Evidently, his duty was to make the presentation. He faced the General and saluted snappily—that is—snappy for him. Then he reported in Japanese. The General returned the salute, after which, Sake Pete again saluted and attempted a brisk *face right*. Either he had one foot pinned down by the other, or his mind did not co-

ordinate with his feet. Anyway, he lost his balance and all but
sat down in place. Recovering, he started off to the right but
stumbled just as though he had been tripped, and was unable
to stop at the line of staff officers. This did not bother him,
however. His face never changed its expression, and he shuffled back into place.

The speech was monotonously the same as the others we
had heard. It was interpreted by an American born Jap, who
had been nicknamed "Buttons" by the Wake and Guam prisoners, because of the funny uniform he wore when they first
saw him. It resembled a bell hop's attire with a generous
array of buttons.

In essence, the General gave us his full title, and that he was
in command of this district. He stated that we were prisoners
of war—being taken care of by the generosity of Japan, which
was guided by the spirit of Bushido—that Japan was winning
the war, which should be apparent to us by now—that we
must obey all orders and regulations or be severely punished—
we must guard our health—the war would be over soon and
we would all go home. And more prattle of a like nature.

While in quarantine, I read one of the issues of the monthly propaganda magazines "Contemporary Japan" in which I
found a lengthy article by the Japanese government, which
outlined the reasons for Japan going to war.

One of these reasons stated that the 194th Tank Battalion
had landed at Manila on September 26, 1941, fully equipped
with tanks and so forth. It said that we were a National
Guard outfit and therefore could be sent to the Philippines
for one reason only.

That was to make war on Japan!

In other words, the article went on to explain, we were a
reserve component of the Army of the United States, and that
it was the intention of the United States to make war—
otherwise we would not have been sent to the Philippines!

The 194th was the only outfit mentioned in the article as
one of the reasons why Japan went to war!

CHAPTER 30

"Donald Duck" Becomes Sick

WE WERE THE first prisoners from the Philippines to arrive at Zentsuji. The Japs were most curious about us. One day, during the quarantine, we were allowed outside in a segregated area for fifteen minutes. Captain Hosatani, executive officer of the camp, interrogated me with the aid of Buttons, the interpreter. Hosatani had been a school-teacher before the war. The questions were about the same as the usual ones asked by the Japs. He volunteered the information that the Japanese considered the Filipinos as being the lowest class of people they had encountered in the Southwest Pacific. Inwardly, I was elated. It simply meant that the Filipinos, as a whole, were remaining loyal to the United States. The Americans knew this anyway, but to have such expressions made in Japan itself, cinched our faith and belief.

During the period of the quarantine, we were weighed. This, we learned, was a monthly event. Why they weighed us, no one ever knew. If the camp showed a loss from the previous month, which was invariably the case, the Japs would explain it by stating that "it was seasonal and normal." If the camp average remained the same as the previous month, it was good and proved that we were healthy. Sometimes the camp would show a gain. This was caused, for the most part, by water being retained in the system such as wet beriberi. The Japs, however, always credited it to the food! It was possible for the individual to weigh several pounds, plus or minus, on the same day, depending at what time the weighing took place. There is no doubt but what the difference could be accounted for, by water. Enormous quantities could be retained by beriberi.

All personnel was being paid, at this camp, at the rate of their respective rank in the Japanese Army. The senior officers were allowed 50 yen per month, and the junior officers 40 yen. The balance of the pay due, the Japs told us, they were placing on deposit. Paying the prisoners was a part of the propaganda to prove they were abiding by international law.

A sort of PX had been set up. Whenever anything came into the camp for the prisoners to buy, it was proportioned out to each group on the basis of the number in each. Most of the stuff was almost worthless. It included bamboo forks and spoons, bamboo cups, straw skivies (sandals), straw hats, a powder that tasted somewhat like horseradish when mixed with water, another type that we called fish powder, a very weak red pepper, some paper, a few pencils, and various kinds of pills. Once, the Japs brought in a quantity of red and yellow colored liquid which was supposed to make a pleasant drink. It probably would have, if sugar had been added. We didn't have the sugar, so we made ink out of it.

Toward the last part of our stay at Zentsuji, a supply of Hoshi powder was brought into the PX and sold to the prisoners. We never did find out just what it was but were given to understand that it came from rice polishings or some other process connected with rice. It was edible and not bad tasting—at that time—when mixed with water. However, it gave most of us violent "runs."

The Japanese are a nation that thrives on pills. As advertised, they will cure any and all things. I remember one brand of pill that carried the advertisement, among other things, of curing crying at night!

We were so constantly hungry that we bought anything that came in that might fill the stomach. We also carried the forlorn hope that, maybe, somehow, a pill might contain some form of vitamin that we needed. I, personally, never had any pills on hand. As soon as they arrived, I would eat them. Nearly all of the pills were edible, but without doubt, worthless. However, they created no adverse effects except, perhaps, to increase the tempo of the "runs," which we had anyway. I suppose under normal circumstances the pills would be offensive to the taste. But most of us had no objection to the taste as long as it filled a portion of that boundless vacuum in the stomach!

We were quite positive that the Japanese officials at this camp conducted a "racket" on the things that were sold. Nothing of any value ever came in. The area was combed by the Japs for all worthless articles which were then sold to the prisoners. This was also in line with the face saving characteristic of being able to say they had paid us and were allowing a PX stocked with needed articles. Needless to say, had we been turned loose in an American ten cent store, at that time, we undoubtedly would have bought everything in sight! We used to dream of those stores.

Shortly after we arrived at Zentsuji, the food took a tailspin. On paper, the cereal ration consisted of 390 grams per person per day. Pilferage and other losses brought it down to about 300 grams. Many times it was much less. It probably averaged about ten ounces per day or less. It was composed mostly of rice sweepings (with plenty of grit and this and that), combined with wheat, millet, maize and such. In the early part of our stay, we received small issues of soy beans along with the rice, but it was not long before this disappeared. We received a soup which consisted, mostly, of hot water and inferior greens. The great share of these greens could be likened to weeds that grow wild almost anywhere. We also experienced daikons and cucumbers boiled into soup.

For one period, that ran into months, we received nothing but unedible stems of some kind of weed, which had been salted down in the fall, in a salt brine. It was the same as chewing straw; the more you put into your mouth and chewed, the more pulp you got. It simply could not be chewed up. Sometimes, burdock roots were brought in to take the place of greens. Naturally, this diet created and aggravated dysentery and diarrhea.

The American naval doctor, Lieutenant Commander Van Peenen, performed miracles. He should, in my estimation, have bestowed on him the highest honor the United States can offer.

Even though sick and malnutritioned himself, he worked day and night, with little or nothing, to alleviate the ills and discomforts of the prisoners. The heroism and the great spirit of the man is apparent when I make the statement that he was not an optimist, as far as the end of the war was concerned.

He always believed, right up to the end of the war, that it would continue for a much longer time. The easiest thing for Van to have done, under those circumstances, would have been to travel a path a great deal less burdensome. He would have received no criticism whatever. At times, we tried to show Van our appreciation by taking up a collection, throughout the camp, of cigarettes. He would accept these offerings in great humbleness, and then we would find him acting as host, giving them to others whom he knew were "dying" for a smoke! And he enjoyed smoking himself.

Van all but killed himself, in his efforts to make life just a little better for everyone else. He had the work party smuggle in drugs which he cached in hiding places. He forever fought with the Japanese for medicines and better treatment of the sick. In some of these efforts, he was successful. But he was constantly being stymied by the Jap doctor assigned to the camp—Dr. Saito.

This doctor was well educated, but was one of the most sadistic Japanese with whom I came in contact. As is the custom in the Japanese Army, Saito took his turn as Japanese Duty Officer. He was very vindictive toward the prisoners, particularly the officers. He was another who was sentenced to a long term of imprisonment.

Van Peenen, all through the long winter months, shivering and shaking with cold, as were all the prisoners, continued to treat the suffering. He was handicapped further, by multitudinous chillblains. In my humble opinion, there was no greater hero in all the war than Van Peenen. He was a continual inspiration to all of us.

Tobacco was another of our everyday problems.

Once in awhile we were able to procure cigarettes from the Japs. Sometimes, the work party was able to smuggle in a small supply of what we called "hair tobacco." We could never ascertain just what the stuff really was, but were given to understand that it is barley straw, finely chopped, and saturated with a tobacco juice extract. It was vile and bitter. The Japs smoked it in their tiny bowl pipes. Not over two whiffs and the pipe was smoked!

Tobacco was always at a premium. We smoked tea leaves, eucalyptus leaves, fern leaves, tops of plants, and anything else that looked like it would smoke. We would also mix small portions of real tobacco with the rest of the abominable mixture. Those who did not smoke, claimed the smell was terrific. I do not believe there is any doubt of that!

It was common for one prisoner to turn to the other, early

in the day, and inquire: "What are you smoking today, rope or pine needles?" Then they would exchange mixtures—for variety!

The Japanese were constantly attempting to catch some of us with black market tobacco. One day, one of our most troublesome interpreters, whom we had nicknamed "Donald Duck" because of his continual quacking and heckling, came into the room where I was smoking a pipe. I always tried to be very careful when I had black market tobacco, loading the pipe and then hiding the supply.

Donald Duck was very friendly and sat down alongside me. He asked for the makings of a cigarette. I had a can of an abominable mixture consisting of tea leaves and other leaves. This was what he was offered.

He examined the can very carefully, smelled of it and asked what it was. I told him it was a mixture I was then smoking, and he was most welcome to try it. He could not help but know that I was smoking tobacco. Luckily, the fire was deep in the bowl of my pipe and there was not much left.

In traditional Jap fashion, to save face, he rolled a cigarette and lit it. He took several drags and inhaled deeply, but even his face saving could not stomach it. He laid the cigarette down and walked rapidly from the room as though he had suddenly thought of something he had to do.

We watched him through the window. He went directly to the benjo (latrine). I knew then that he wanted to be sick—and he was! Several of the prisoners were in the benjo and watched his performance. He was probably more sick after the war—for he is now serving 40 years at hard labor.

Donald Duck was a well educated Jap, speaking several languages. But all the prisoners agreed that he was "cracked," because of the many things he did—things even that were at odds with the Jap camp authorities. We strongly suspicioned that he was a member of Kempei Tai (Jap secret police). They were known by the prisoners as Kempies.

Whenever possible, the outside working party would smuggle uncured leaf tobacco into camp. They picked it up from bundles on the docks where they worked. It was brought in, generally, concealed underneath their clothing. One man constructed himself a belt from which he could suspend articles. The belt was secured around his waist and next to his skin.

Suspenders of a sort were attached so that the articles hung down along his legs. In this manner, he was able to bring in quite a number of "hands" of this tobacco.

Whenever any group of Americans are together, someone in that group has a knowledge of what you wish to know—no matter what it is. I have never seen it fail in the prison camp. That is the real test of American pioneering, resourcefulness, and initiative. Sure enough—we found someone who knew how to cure tobacco.

Posting our own guards to watch for the approach of Japanese guards, we would set to work. Each leaf was smoothed out separately. Tea water was sprinkled on each leaf. Sugar in the tea water would have been better—but we did not have the sugar—and if we had, we would have eaten it! This operation was continued, smoothing each leaf on top of the other, until quite a pile accumulated.

Two of us would then roll the small bundle of leaves together, as tightly as it was humanly possible to do. Therein lay the secret of the cure. We rolled the leaves so tightly and with such concentrated effort, that our bodies streamed with sweat.

The next operation took a piece of rope which was wound around the entire roll of tobacco, much like you would splice wire, covering the roll completely, and as tight as it could be wound. It was then secreted in a cache, and left for about a week or longer—if you could withstand the temptation of getting a smoke.

After this waiting period, the rope was removed. The result was a compact plug of tobacco which could be cut off into the grade or slice desired. It was really good tobacco!

Several times, the Nippon Times and Mainichi propaganda newspaper were stopped and no issues were made. We learned, through our underground, that the Japs thought we were learning a little too much. After durations of a couple of weeks or a month, they were allowed back in. Each time, the face saving characteristic won out, and the issue of papers started again.

Most of the propoganda was fairly easy for us to interpret. We learned to evaluate Jap phrasings, terminology, and reports. We felt that we were fairly well informed, in spite of the adverse news reported by the Nips.

It was amusing to read the "Hero" stories that were printed. Beyond the shadow of a doubt, the Jap is the biggest braggart on earth. Literally, according to the stories, the Jap warrior—imbued with the spirit of Bushido (code of the warrior), made the wild elephants of the jungle do his bidding; he came to crocodile infested rivers and finally crossed on the backs of these reptiles; he slew ferocious tigers with his bare hands; he invented the airplane; a Jap Zero fighter was being attacked by American fighter planes—he was out of ammunition—had a ball of rice he had not eaten—threw it back at one of the pursuing planes where it hit the propeller—the plane crashed and burned—the Jap Zero returned to his base unharmed! And much, much more of the childish drivel!

As one of the prisoners remarked: "They even have lightning on their side!"

We kept the score on the number of American warships the Japanese claimed they sunk. Within a month, the score could not even be verified by their own newspaper reports! And, they had sunk a total of more ships than we had to start with, plus more than could ever have been possibly built since the start of war!

Much space was taken up in the propaganda papers with the Co-Prosperity Sphere. P. T. Barnum should have been alive to read that build-up. It was *the* fairy tale personified. In true Jap style, they built their population from 80,000,000 Japs to 100,000,000. They had the scheme all worked out—for Japan.

The Song of the National Vow appeared in the Nippon Times. We had heard the Japs sing this song many times, while on the march, but never knew the words. Jap singing was more closely akin to the croaking of bullfrogs. I have never heard one yet who could carry a tune. Here are the words to that song:

"At sea be my body watersoaked;
On land be it with grass overgrown;
Let me die by the side of my sovereign;
Never will I look back!"

Many Jap poems appeared, which sometimes threw the camp into uproars. As an example:

"Is that the dew
On the sleeve of the seeker
Of pleasure at late hours
Or the tears that fall
From a heart in mortal pain?"

I read this aloud from the paper. A voice from the other side of the room said: "Nuts! The slant-eye just wiped his nose—that's all!"

About the time of the second front in Normandy—June, 1944—all newspapers and propaganda magazines were stopped. They never were allowed again. We developed our own news bureau from that time on until we left Zentsuji in June, 1945.

The outside work detail at the dock area made contact, and managed to secure an average of about four Japanese language newspapers per week. They were smuggled into camp. Prisoners were divided up by rooms and divisions for muster purposes. Several prisoners could read Japanese. We had also organized the American group, secretly, for any contingency that might occur.

Certain individuals, who could take shorthand notes, were appointed to act as newscasters. The system became so efficient that as soon as the newspaper arrived in camp, it was usually read, translated, the shorthand people had their notes, and the newspaper destroyed—in as short a time as 30 minutes.

The newscasters then returned to pass out the news. Guards were posted as each room was visited. Secret maps were kept, and the progress of the war was charted fairly accurately.

To my knowledge, the Japanese never uncovered this method. However, they did know that somehow we were getting news. Eventually, Colonel Kondo, camp commandant, decided to save face. Several times, he called the Division Leaders into conference, and proceeded in true Bushido spirit, to hand out the news.

On one occasion—the invasion of the Philippines—he pointed to a large wall map and stated, through the interpreter, that the Japanese had allowed the Americans to land on the island of Luzon. This we already knew from our news sources.

He then observed that the Japanese had allowed the Americans to gain possession of the Central Plain of Luzon, but that the Japs had full possession of the high ground and mountains, and were now proceeding to exterminate the Americans.

I asked the interpreter if the Colonel would allow any questions. The Colonel gave his permission. My question was merely one of curiosity to see how he would react to it. After explaining that the Japanese had invaded the Philippines in 1941, exactly as the Americans had now: "Is it not true that whoever has possession of the Central Plain, has possession of Luzon?"

The question was interpreted. The Colonel jabbered very impatiently, as if he were talking to a child. He pointed to the map again, and raised his arms high and then lowered them almost to the floor. The interpreter explained once more that the Japanese had *allowed* the Americans to land and to occupy the Central Plain; that the Japanese had complete possession of the high ground from which all Americans would be exterminated. Then he dismissed that part of the war.

He next went on to say, that part of the Japanese strategy was, to use their Air Force against our shipping. He emphasized the fact that America had to transport troops and supplies by water, and that it took only one airplane and one bomb to sink a ship. Therefore, he stated, we could not build ships fast enough to keep up with the sinkings!

I asked the interpreter another question: "What significance is there, in relation to the end of the war, in the many American B-29's that are coming over Japan?"

The Colonel smiled almost benevolently. He said that this was just what the Japanese had been waiting for. That part of the strategy was, to draw American aircraft over Japan, so they could be destroyed and end the war. Then we could all go home!

He turned quickly to me, and through the interpreter, asked how many Americans the United States would be willing to sacrifice. My reply was that the United States was prepared to sacrifice all Americans. Then I asked him: "When will the war be over?"

"Not until the Americans surrender," he replied slowly.

There was a slight pause, and then he added, "I do not expect the Americans to surrender, and therefore the war will be endless."

At another "news" conference, the Colonel explained to us that the Japanese had enticed the Americans to land on the Sulphur Islands (Iojima) and were exterminating them to the last man. The Nip staff, who always were present at these conferences, revealed a Japanese characteristic that is difficult for the western mind to comprehend. The Jap does not always smile and laugh for the same reason as the white man of the western world.

The Colonel spoke one short sentence to the interpreter, stating that his dearest friend was in command of the Sulphur Islands, and in the thickest of the bitter battle.

Immediately, every member of his staff laughed heartily!

The only explanation, as far as I could determine, and I tie it in with similar experiences in three and one-half years of contact with the Japanese, is that by laughing, the staff expressed their pleasure in complimenting their commander on the fact that his dearest friend was in danger and fighting gallantly for the Emperor!

CHAPTER 31

"War" Conferences with the Japs

SEVERAL TIMES, while we were at Zentsuji, the Japanese ordered certain officers to attend sessions, which we called "War Conferences." The individuals concerned would be assembled in a room and seated. They were interrogated at great length on a number of asinine questions.

At one of the sessions, which I was ordered to attend, the Japs had present, the executive officer of the camp, a civilian, and a member of the military police. The MP was without doubt a native born American. If you closed your eyes you were listening to an American. He was an excellent physical specimen and very well educated. He asked questions at the instigation of the civilian, who also appeared to be very intelligent.

These questions ranged all the way from types of weapons we were not even familiar with, to our impressions of the war. Some were quite childlike. We could never see any rhyme or reason to these conferences. We had been prisoners and out of the game for a long time.

They asked us if we belonged to any secret or political societies; what we knew of anti-Jewish societies, the National Labor Party, the White Shirts, the Silver Shirts; if we were communists, editors, writers, radio announcers, playwrights, commentators; production of America—airplanes, pilots, munitions of war; production in Germany; economic situation of South America, United States, Germany; what our chances were of taking back Java and the Philippines; efficiency of the American supply lines *and Japanese supply lines;* enmity of Britain and Russia; Indian Campaign; are American women efficient; women's organizations; could our women fly planes and how much could they contribute to the war effort; the second front; was Russia going with our help or her's alone; independence of Burma, and on and on.

This conference took place on April 17, 1944. I often won-

dered whether they expected us—prisoners of war for years—
to be able to supply the answers!

They were very curious about our welfare organizations,
whether we were married or not, and they even wanted to
know about our family life.

Our answers to all these questions, if the answer would
boost the stock of America, was to lay it on as heavy as we
could. Particularly did we paint the picture of our women and
their part in the war effort—and we knew, that anything we
said on that score, could be well justified!

At one point in the conference, the civilian instigated the
question: "What do you think of Japan's resources for winning the war?" The question was directed at Major Bidgood
who flashed an immediate reply.

"If Japan is in the same shape as my stomach, she must be
all in!" he stated emphatically.

Much to my surprise, the MP said very politely, "Perhaps
Japan has a different idea than that." He did not relay Bidgood's reply. Whether or not the other Japs understood, I do
not know.

There was one question always asked at these sessions,
which always drew the stock answer: "What do you wish
most?"

The answer was always the same and it came from all the
prisoners, even though it was directed at one individual:
"Food!"

These "War Conferences" made us more and more amazed
at the Japanese mind. Somehow, the questions asked us,
seemed so stupid in view of the fact that we were prisoners of
war, and had been out of circulation for a long time. It vin-
dicated the belief I had had for a long time, that the Japanese were unable, as a people, to coordinate information. It is
a fact, that many of the top people in Japan, discounted much
of the information given them, by the very people they had
sent to the United States to acquire that information. They
did not even believe all of the facts brought to them by Japs
born in the United States. It was inconceivable that America
could gear itself for war, with such a late start. It was inconceivable that Japan could lose! And such is the workings of
the totalitarian mind.

As time went on, I was very happy that I had never told

the Japs what my true occupation had been in civil life. Questionnaires were circulated a number of times inquiring into our private lives. One of the questions always related itself to our civil occupation. I always answered it by stating that I was a clerk in an office. Thus, I was relieved from being questioned, or used, on any specialist knowledge whatever. If I had answered that my occupation was engineering, there is not the shadow of a doubt but what I would have been assigned to work of that nature.

Returning from these conferences, each individual who had attended, was expected to tell the other prisoners just what happened. Just as soon as you reached your humble domicile, you were greeted with something like this:

"Well, what did the August Noodle want today?"

"Did you tell 'em that Uncle is going to check up on his nephews soon?"

"Here today and here tomorrow!"

"Should we worry, or should we say 'The Lord will provide'?"

"Hurry up, Uncle!"

"Shut up, you birds! Don't get your bowels in a turmoil!"

Then you sat down and related the details as well as you could remember them. Questions were without end—because the western mind was trying to grapple with Oriental reasoning.

There was no heat whatever during the winter months. Snow and ice covered the ground, long periods of the time. The temperature, at night, went as low as, from 10 to 18 degrees below freezing. The only relief was the sun—and we longed for it—always! Chillblains would form, particularly on the ears, hands and feet. The first indication would be violent red spots. Then, they would break out into open sores. They would remain until summer arrived once more. On the succeeding winter, you could be assured that you would have the same ones—sooner—plus others. They were especially bad in the early morning, after a night of comparative inactivity. We are destined to carry these "weak spots" as long as we live.

Tea water and the hot watery soups did a double duty. We warmed our hands on the containers. If felt sublime—believe me.

The summer of 1944, I collected rags—anything I could get.

With an old needle, and threads picked from the rags, I steadily sewed—all summer. Many were the jibes I took from fellow prisoners.

"Hell! The war'll be over before next winter!"

"Have you joined the pessimist's ranks, Colonel?"

And one day came the finishing touch to the jibes—except that this was all seriousness. It came from a confirmed pessimist. He watched me for some time. Then he said, very slowly:

"Colonel, with you doing that, after what you have said, the war must be going to last a long, long time."

My reply was, "————, what I have said, I still believe. But when I was a youngster, I was a Boy Scout, and the motto has always stuck in my mind—Be Prepared!"

He sighed, and went away.

What was I sewing? A pair of booties, mittens, and a raggedy-hellish-looking all-colored blanket! And I certainly used them that next winter! It was not pessimism either. It was something else to do, and it was "Be Prepared."

We had a definition for a pessimist, and it was something like this: "One who cannot enjoy the sun when it shines, because he is afraid it will rain, and when it rains, he is sure the sun will never shine again."

One of our most confirmed pessimists was a most intelligent person. He was a graduate of the United States Naval Academy. After the war was over, and we were celebrating at our last prison camp, I saw him, far back in the shadows. Approaching him, I asked why he did not join the celebration. "Colonel," he said, "I guess I am the man who will never smile again!"

And thus it is, with some of the prisoners of war. We, who can "smile again" are most fortunate. After all, three and one-half years is a long, long time!

The Wake and Guam prisoners at Zentsuji had initiated practically all of Yankee ingenuity. They had hung weights on the doors, suspended by grass ropes so that they would close automatically. This never failed to intrigue the Japs.

They had made a hand operated lathe, which was kept beneath the flooring. Where they had accumulated the parts—the Lord only knows. It was operated by two men. One turned the product out. The other operated the rope around the

pulley. The rope was endless, and the operator just kept pulling, hand over hand. Their specialty was pipes. I still have
one bowl that was turned out there. For tools, they gathered
stray spikes and nails. These were flattened out for chisels, by
using rocks, or pieces of iron for hammers. Rocks were used
for filing and sharpening. Spikes and nails were also twisted
and sharpened for drills. It was almost unbelievable. The Japs
never caught up with the contraption. They saw the pipes—
and wondered where they came from. But, not being able to
offer an answer, and in the traditional face saving characteristic—they never said anything!

Since being a prisoner of war for three and one-half years,
I can readily understand, how some of the things happen in
our own prisons, at which the public is amazed. The human
mind becomes very active in prison life. Probably, this is because physical activity is channeled or curtailed. Ingenious
schemes, which otherwise might go unborn, are thought up.

Necessity is truly the mother of invention. We took particular delight in beating the Japs at anything—legally or illegally.

One of our interpreters, Asabuki by name, had been educated in Cambridge, England. He came from the aristocracy
of Japan and was always very courteous. He never did anything to add to our discomfort, and I always felt that he hated
the war. He sent for me one day and said that the camp commandant wished me, as senior officer from the Philippines, to
write my impressions of the campaign there. My first impulse
was to refuse. On second thought, I decided to do it for
propaganda. The Japs were throwing propaganda at us.
Why not try it from our angle? I told Asabuki I would do it
but would need quite a bit of paper. He said that paper was
very scarce, and then asked me how much I would need. I
told him the job would take about 12 to 15 sheets. He sort of
sighed but produced the amount.

After a couple of days, I came to him again and said that I
would need more paper. My excuse was, that the impressions
had to be written up in the rough, and many notes made so
that the finished product would be comprehensive and read-
able. Reluctantly, he procured more paper. Before I finished,
I had accumulated a stock of 24 sheets besides the ones on
which the article appeared. I have a copy of the article in my

possession, which was made and buried with the rest of my notes, before leaving Zentsuji. Also, before submitting the document, I had several other prisoners read it.

Although rather brief, I played up the highlights of the campaign. Every battle was a complete victory for us. It was propaganda plus, but not enough so as to cause suspicion. In the last paragraph, I stated that we were very much surprised that it took so long for the Japanese to take the Philippines in view of their vast superiority of manpower, food, weapons, and equipment. Also, that we had surrendered by a general surrender order, with the knowledge that further resistance would have been futile and unnecessary, due to the fact that we had accomplished our mission of delay and diversion of the enemy forces.

Cambridge Joe (Asabuki) thanked me for the article when I brought it in. Then he asked me a question:

"What is it like to be at the front?"

As best I could, I told him. He pondered a little, and said that he had never been on the battle line, and wondered what it was like. As though speaking to himself, he said:

"If I have to go, I wonder how I will react?"

Next, he asked me a question which made me cagey:

"Are the Japanese as brave as the stories we hear?"

My answer was non-committal, which might either have been taken for the affirmative or the negative. He slowly shook his head and replied—apologetically:

"Of course, all I know is what I read in the newspapers."

Captain Hosatani walked in at that time and our conversation ended.

One had to be a confirmed pessimist in a prison camp, to stay in the doldrums very long, regardless of the discomforts and privations. If a graphic chart could be produced, showing the mental attitudes of the individual prisoners, the lines would travel up and down—some more—some less. War news caused the spirits to rise. Fits of depression would cause them to sink low. Good American humor brought them up again. Regardless of our darkest hours, humor was always there, and it caused many to rise up out of their despair.

One prisoner came in one day and asked me if I would like to join a new club his roommates had formed. I inquired what the club was.

"Kumnitchawa Club," he replied.

"What in the hell is that?" I asked.

"Well," he explained, "when we get back to the States, we have all agreed that we will travel the streets uttering the word '*Kumnitchawa*.' If anyone looks like he might understand—sock 'im!"

I understood that the originator of the club was Major Yeager, now an instructor at West Point. Yeager was never without humor.

The Catholic Chaplain, Father Turner, an Australian, was accosted one day:

"Father, this certainly is an ideal place for a Catholic."

"Why do you say that?" Father Turner asked.

"It's a Lenten Paradise—Fast and Abstinence!"

On another instance, one of the Catholic prisoners wishing to go to confession, walked up to Father Turner and asked:

"How about reading my meter, Father?"

Padre Turner was known as the Bishop of Zentsuji.

Rising in the morning, seeing the same old faces, sometimes for years, was not conducive to very good relationship—early in the morning—in some cases. Nerves might be very much on edge. We tried to set standards of gentlemanly courtesy. Hence the morning salutations. I must admit, that at times, it was a great deal easier to frown than to smile. One morning at Reveille, one of the occupants of our group, knowing that the morning salutations were about to start, shouted:

"*Good morning to everybody!* Now, let's shut up about it!"

Rumors were always with us. The great majority wanted to hear them. Someone came in and loudly whispered, "Hot rumor!"

Everyone gathered around. In a lower whisper he said, "Germans are in Berlin!"

Another, with the same approach, "Rumor! We're on the right side in this war!"

More, "Hear the latest rumor?" "No, what is it?" "It's still in the making!"

And, "A rumor in the camp says there's a rumor, but no one knows what it is!"

Greeting a fellow prisoner with "How do you do," sometimes was not taken in the spirit of a greeting. It was taken literally by some who proceeded with a long dissertation of ills and woes. We soon learned who, and who not, to make that greeting to.

At various times, while at Zentsuji, other groups of prisoners came in. They included Americans, British, Australians, Dutch, and Javanese. As each new group arrived, we obtained more information of the war and of other prison camps. Sometimes we received news of men from whom we had become separated. Some of these prisoners were from the American Air Forces, who had been knocked down after Bataan and Corregidor. We derived still more information from them.

One of the later arrivals, was a lieutenant in the National Guard Artillery outfit, that had been destined for the Philippines. War had broken out and they had been landed in Java. It was there that they were captured. They had been brought to a camp in northern Japan. One of the party had rolled up one of the latest radios in a bedding roll. They actually succeeded in getting the roll into their camp without the radio being discovered by the Japs. Quickly, it was installed beneath the bunk deck, and was tuned in to short wave radio broadcasts from KGEI in San Francisco. It was equipped with ear phones. The lieutenant had memorized pertinent broadcasts, including some of President Roosevelt's speeches. At various times, he secretly appeared among the groups of camp, and gave us the story.

Another arrival was 1st Lieutenant Fred Garrett, a pilot, who had been knocked down in the South Seas. His leg had been amputated by the Japanese—close to the hip. There was no need for any amputation if proper medical attention had been given at the time. Nor was there any need to amputate in the hip locality when they did go to work. The Japs told him that they were amputating so that he would never fly again.

Before the amputation, he had been allowed to lay in a cell in his own filth. Maggots hatched in his wound. His story has appeared in the Reader's Digest under the title, "The Silver Bracelet."

This youngster was a source of optimism to the rest of the camp. Up to the time of our release as prisoners of war, his wound was still draining. He had a pair of homemade bamboo crutches. No one in the camp ever saw Fred Garrett without a brilliant, infectious smile on his face and an ever-ready greeting. When we started to feel sorry for ourselves, and saw Fred Garrett, the feeling did not last very long! His determination was, that he would fly again!

Some Red Cross supplies, including food, came into this camp. There was some clothing, medical supplies, thread, and similar articles. Much of the food was allowed to remain in storage, for periods of longer than a year. Much of it was spoiled. Some was stolen by the Japs and diverted to their own use. At the end of the war, great stocks were destroyed by bombing and burning, all over Japan. The Japs had stored what they did not want.

Red Cross clothing was not issued in the cold weather. It was given us (what we received) when the warm weather would start. Whenever Red Cross foodstuffs were issued in the camp, it was a heyday. One taste of the coveted food, struck the body like a big swig of liquor landing on an empty stomach. A rosy glow followed. The body, especially the face, swelled to grotesque proportions. It could be described, as a food jag. You could feel it from the bottom of your feet to the top of your head. Words are almost useless to describe that feeling, but it was a wallop!

Food was always the chief topic in a prisoner of war camp. Never could you find a conversation that did not swing into the subject of food. You would find yourself listening to, or dissertating yourself, on how to make a simple dish—even the preparation of the lowly hamburger. This should be readily understood. The body was denuded of all normal taste, and was most deficient in vitamins. It was far below it's normal weight. Real hunger causes the individual to do curious things. I actually made up a poem on food—and believe me, that poem honestly represents the truth. Here it is:

A POW's Dream of Food

The food, at night, in dreams I see
Throws me into ecstacies;
The table piled with dainties rare—
Oh, wondrous, *wondrous* bill of fare

Is almost more than I can bear—
    And thus I dream.
There's steaks and chops and breads galore;
Candy bars are by the score.
Pumpkin pies and cookies too,
Doughnuts, bismarks—thick, rich stew,
Mugs of coffee—more to brew—
    All this I dream.
Piles of cheese and vats of cream,
Bowls of nuts and salads green.
Pots of beans and peas and corn,
Golden honey, fresh as morn,
Dates and figs and grapes adorn—
    My dreams.
Biscuits, fresh, with crisp brown tops,
Chicken gravy—steamy hot.
Strawberry shortcake, jams and jells,
Popcorn—ice cream in canals,
Pastries—more than I can tell—
    Oh! Dream of dreams.
Peanut butter, ham and eggs,
Waffles, hot cakes—by the keg.
Syrup dark and syrup light—
Sausage, bacon, fruits so bright.
Coffee cake. Oh! What a sight—
    It's all a dream.
In all my dreams I've nearly died
To get a taste, a bite—*I've tried!*
Somehow, my dreams, they always lack
A taste, a smell, a little snack.
My belly gets an awful whack—
    In all my dreams.
Sometime I hope my wish comes true,
Before I wake, to have a chew.
I'll grab and gobble things I see
With gusto and alacrity!
I'll be as full as I can be
    Before I wake!

One of the chief pastimes of camp—any POW camp—was
the writing of recipes. Some of them, as I look them over to-

day, sound most foolish. At the time they were written, they were very serious. Whatever the individual hankered for, dominated the recipe. That, of course, is understandable. One prisoner, I recall, after relating what he would like to eat, always and forever, topped it off with cherries! If it was mashed potatoes and gravy, cherries were added!

CHAPTER 32

POW's Go Over the Fence

OUR HUNGER WAS SO great, at all times, that a pain was perpetually present in the stomach. The little rice that we received, was digested in a period far less than two hours. Sometimes food was saved, so as to have one belly-filling meal in the future. I tried this a couple of times and then stopped it. It is a fact that the stomach actually shrinks from lack of food. I found myself more hungry, after it had been stretched out with a "big" allotment, than I had been before I started. Thereafter, I ate things as I received them.

Here are a few "screwball" recipes that were concocted from the imagination born of starved bodies and minds:

Peach Delight: Ice cold peach halves. Fill with peanut butter, melted O'Henry chocolate bars, and chocolate sauce. Pin halves together and put into cups. Pour thick chocolate syrup over and chill. When chocolate is hard, cover liberally with thick whipped cream and marshmallow sauce. Sprinkle with ground peanuts and other nuts. Add scoop of ice cream with cherry on top.

Sweet Potato Divine: Boil and mash sweet potatoes. Mix in casserole with raisins, peanuts and other nuts, marshmallows, melted O'Henry chocolate bar, plenty of sugar, chocolate syrup, and Sherry wine. Top with Sherry and bake.

Screwball Special: Corn meal and wheat flour. Make into dough. Roll flat and cover liberally with corn and peas. Add layer of half-cooked pork sausage. Strips of favorite cheese, bacon, and ham over top. Roll and bake.

Delectable: Peas, corn, fried diced lean pork, corned beef, diced ham, mashed sardines in tomato sauce, potatoes, onions, and garlic. Simmer in enough water for stew. Make up pork gravy. Pour gravy in stew and mix thoroughly. Serve on hot toast saturated with melted butter.

Dream: Boiled beans with lots of salt pork, fried lean pork diced, crisp bacon diced, suet, mashed sardines in olive oil, sugar, and molasses. Add desired amount of onions and garlic. Enough water for stew. Cook thoroughly.

Directly next door to the camp, and on the other side of the high board fence, was a shrine where the Japanese held ceremonies, and frequently would lay gifts of food on the altar. It was an offering to their gods. In a number of instances, our people went over the fence at night and purloined the food. It was brought into the camp. No one was ever caught. It undoubtedly would have meant death. I have often wondered what the Japs thought when the offerings to their gods disappeared!

We had outside guards and inside guards. After closely observing their schedules, it was possible to time the approximate appearance as they made their rounds.

After one of these escapades had been successfully consummated, and the food eaten, one of the culprits was heard to say:

"Stomach! Get ready for the famine!" After a short pause, he added:

"When, and if I get home, I'm going to carry a lunch with me wherever I go!"

The Japanese have an aversion to allowing anyone to look down, from a height, upon either shrines or dignitaries. Whenever ceremonies were being held in the shrine, blackout curtains were ordered drawn over the north side of the buildings on the second floors. The orders also included the strict stipulation that no one was to look out of those windows. Sometimes, the order came to vacate the second floor entirely, during certain hours.

When a dignitary was in camp, the same order was put out as for the shrine. Needless to say, many peeks were made. We ascertained there was nothing secret going on. It was merely the Japanese way of thinking.

On one occasion, when shrine ceremonies were being held, one of the prisoners was observed bowing. The following conversation took place:

"What are you bowing for?"

"To also give my greetings to the Imperial ————!" came the reply.

"You're bowing the wrong way."

"I am not! Check the direction of my rear!"

A voice at the other end of the room was heard:

"He's right. Face away from the Imperial Palace when you bow, so you can see eye to eye with him!"

On each December 8th (7th U.S. time) it was always observed by the Japs as Imperial Rescript Day, and was declared a holiday. All newspapers—English propaganda and otherwise—printed the original proclamation of the Emperor on the front pages. Each year, the commandant of the camp made a speech to the prisoners, or to their representatives. I relate, herewith, the speech made by the Jap commandant at Zentsuji on December 8, 1943. The wording and punctuations are an exact copy as received from the interpreter:

"By now you must be well aware of the fact that since the outbreak of the war, the Japanese empire has been obtaining magnificent achievements in Burma, or the successive victories being won in the south sea region which is unprecedented in the world's annals of war.

As time passes on, the firmness of solidarity has been greatly strengthened. Not only within the empire, but among all the countries of greater east Asia. Relating to the development and exploitation of raw materials for production necessary for the execution of a long-termed war is steadily being progressed, by which I presume you have perceived the utter invincibility of Japan. After all, as the Anglo-American countries aimlessly increase their impure and ambiguous devouring ambition which leads to this war, the Japanese empire rose in determination with the sword of justice in their hands to liberate the one billion people of greater east Asia. Thus because of this noble object for war it is only natural and proper that the aforementioned war results were obtained. You who are the victims of this ambiguous ambition which caused the war and who here observe this day of anniversary, undoubtedly have deep emotions within your hearts. (Turning to the state of affairs within the camp:) If you have in general observed the various regulations and are endeavoring to display the desired spirit of self-discipline to which I express my respect, nevertheless there have been a few regrettable cases; for instance, there were several successive cases of punishment inflicted on those who wrongfully conducted themselves for some who received repeated warnings from the Japanese duty officers and their members of the camp. Those are some of the regrettable cases; therefore it is wished, for the sake of the honor of your countries, you should be discreet in your deeds and admonish your fellow prisoners in order to exterminate any repulsive incidents from happening both during work and in the course of normal camp life. As the second anniversary of the war is here greeted and while the home front is still being more strengthened, and the determination to carry out the war is affirmed anew. I strongly desire that you will further heighten and display the spirt of self-discipline. By this, I end my address."

True to form, the "so sorry-crocodile tears" attitude of the Sons of Heaven, was evidenced in his speech with relation to punishments. The first part was merely an echoing of the propaganda we read daily in the newspapers allowed us at that time.

This speech was read to the prisoners by the room leaders. Reaction, in general, was displayed by the following remarks made in our room:

"I'll bet the Nips are deeply moved by the August Imperial Rescript."

"If they are, I'll bet they got a physic first!"

"Let's all sing that little ditty—We Wonder *When* the Rising Sun Will Set."

Beatings were continuous, but probably were not quite as serious as in some other camps. They increased in volume as the war progressed. Other forms of punishment were comparable. Standing at attention for hours; kneeling down with toes pointed to the rear; divested of clothing in the summer time, during the hours of darkness, in the brig, or in segregated areas, so that millions of mosquitoes could feed upon the naked body; placing prisoners in the brig in the winter—snow and ice on the ground—with no overcoats or blankets, and sometimes without any shoes—these were common forms of punishment for minor, and in the great majority of cases, imagined and trumped-up violations.

Seven officers were put into the brig one morning by Donald Duck. He had accused three of them of not saluting the Jap commandant when he left camp by car. The officers said they did salute, and knowing their veracity, I know they did. Four other officers backed them up. The Duck grew incoherent and ordered all of them into the office. After much abuse, he finally dismissed them. Before they could get out of the office, he arrested them for not bowing properly—accused them of disrespect to the Emperor!

It would be impossible to enumerate all the cases of abuse, nor would there be any point to it. Therefore, a few samples are given.

Major C. F. Maynard, over 60 years of age, was beaten, almost unconscious, because he had to relieve himself during an air raid alarm. He would have died had he not feigned unconsciousness. This was at a time when the Benjo (toilet) was connected with the room we were in and permission had been granted.

Lt. Tom Griffin was beaten and kicked so that he had to have medical attention after his punishment. The reason? There was none whatever. He was made to stand at attention by Dr. Saito from 4:30 P.M. to 8:00 P.M. Try this sometime—for only a few minutes!

An Australian lieutenant was on night guard in a building (we were ordered to maintain such a guard). He was kicked and slugged, and had his glasses broken by a guard, because an electric light had burned out in the hallway!

When prisoners were placed in the brig, only a little rice was allowed. Water or tea was disallowed. Suffering was intense. Rooms in the brig were so made that the individual had to sit or stand. There was a small, open window in the back of the cells, next to the high board fence. Calculating the time schedule of the inside guards, it was sometimes possible to pass some food and water to the prisoners inside. There is no doubt but what many lives were saved by this procedure.

In order to go to bed in your bunk when sick, it was necessary that the patient have a high fever—102 or more. He was then awarded a bed tag which allowed him to use his bed covers and lie down—but he had to crawl out and stand the lengthy morning and evening musters—and even then, he was not immune to abuse.

In one case, a sergeant of the guard, severly beat an enlisted man because he did not get out of his bunk and stand at attention, when the sergeant entered the room. This man was down with pneumonia, was actually in the Sick Bay, and had

had his climax only an hour before! It was humanly impossible for the man to even crawl out of his bunk.

Protests were continually lodged with no results.

In spite of the abuse, humor was present among the beaten. One victim reported back and said:

"The Bible says something about 'an eye for an eye and a tooth for a tooth.' But there's no damned reason why they have to give me a whole new set of teeth!"

And another:

"That's what I like about this place—all the attention I get!"

Religious services were held more thoroughly, at Zentsuji, than at any of the other camps we were in. This was due to better facilities. Both Protestant and Catholic chaplains were most faithful in their duties. When allowed to do so, Father Turner held Mass every morning, even in the dead of winter, when the inside of the place allowed, was exactly the same as the inside of a refrigerator. The chaplains did a world of good for the spiritual and mental welfare of the prisoners.

Service chaplains—anywhere—any place—can do a vast amount of good for everyone concerned. Those people simply *have to believe* in their faith. I know from personal experience, that the treating of spiritual hunger, in the camp, did more good in the pinches, than if we had had plenty of food.

John May, Protestant Chaplain of the Australian Army, composed one of the most beautiful poems I have ever read:

Lines for a Birthday

Long and so long is the span of miles
Between my love and me;
Wide and so wide are the Leagues of the Deep,
The deep dividing sea;
Slow, oh, so slow do the long days go
That keeps my love from me.

Strong and so strong is the love that binds
My own love's heart to me;
Far and so far do my thoughts take wing—
Oh, joys of memory!
Close and so close are my thoughts to her,
That—almost—I am free!

On the other side of the camp, beyond the high board fence and on the opposite side of the shrine, was a Japanese bake shop in which hardtack was made for the Army. For quite a long period, prisoners from the camp would time the inside guard, go over or under the fence, and raid the place. They obtained quantities of sugar and hardtack. The cache would be in various places.

The enlisted men had built-in a most ingenious set of trap doors. One went through the bunk deck, and the other, directly below, through the floor. It was impossible to detect them unless one knew where they were. This allowed access to the area underneath the flooring. This was the place where they cached all "hot" articles, and particularly, the sugar.

The "thefts" actually reached the point, where the Japanese were accusing each other, in the bake shop, of raiding it. They were not far off the track, at that, as Japs will steal from each other with no qualms of conscience.

We were particularly afraid that if this sort of thing continued, the Japs would bring severe penalties upon the whole camp. We tried to discourage it for that reason.

However, as hunger was the paramount issue, more and more of the prisoners were willing to take the chance. It became apparent that someone would be caught. And so it was.

One night, an enlisted man was caught outside the fence. There were quite a number of prisoners outside the buildings, illegally, at the time, but were on the inside of the compound. They, too, had either been on the other side of the fence, or were about to go. When the alarm was given, everyone was able to get to their bunks except the man outside. This incident occurred at about midnight.

The Japs immediately aroused all the prisoners, and we had to stand muster. It lasted for over an hour. They were checking to see if anyone else was outside. Dr. Saito was the duty officer, and he was very displeased that some of the officers were not missing.

The enlisted man, following the usual custom, was beaten and tossed into the brig. After that, he was taken out of the camp. I heard several rumors concerning his fate, but never learned definitely just what happened.

The next day, in the middle of the morning, the Japs made a shakedown inspection. It occurred without any warning whatever. This was one time, that our underground did not function efficiently enough to get the danger signals out in time.

We were all herded outside the buildings and on the road, in our regular muster positions. I had no chance to hide anything. In my possessions was a can about three-quarters full of black market tobacco. Other prisoners also had comparable amounts which they had no chance to hide. One had a considerable amount of Japanese yen, which he had accumulated unethically. This individual had no code of ethics, and was forever driving "deals" with other prisoners who were abnormally weak. For instance, he would trade upon the weakness of those who smoked. He did not. Therefore, his allotment of cigarettes and other tobacco, would be hoarded until such a time as the camp was devoid of all tobacco. Then, he would dangle his stock before the others, and collect his "pound of flesh" from the weaker ones. He also accepted rice from their meager rations.

It became necessary for me to issue an order, putting a stop to these practices. I had no legal right to issue such an order, as prisoners of war lose all command status. However, I was Division Leader, and had instituted a Board of Investigation—secretly from the Japs. This Board investigated all cases and recommended court martial—after the war—for those individuals found deserving it. This Board helped a great deal in keeping most officers in line, and showing them the error of their ways.

The Captain, who had the large wad of yen, was a graduate of West Point, and most certainly should have been the last one to engage in such unethical dealings. The Academy teaches duty, honor, country—to the last degree. His brother "Pointers" did everything they could to keep him in line, but finally gave up in disgust. However, the individual was so smooth about his dealings, that no specific charge could be made against him—or, at least, none ever was. His profession should have been that of the shady money lender—the ilk that manages to stay within the law, but who should be associated with something that crawls out from under a rock.

Anyway, he knew that the Japs had been trying to catch prisoners with an unwarranted amount of yen. They knew that black marketing was going on. It was obvious how much we had purchased of the worthless stuff brought into the so-called PX. They had issued orders against gambling. Therefore, it was only a matter of simple arithmetic to arrive at what each prisoner should have in his possession.

When the order came for us to form outside, he dropped his wad into a receptacle used to collect refuse, intending to retrieve it after the shakedown. What happened to it, I do not know, but it was not there when he came back to search for it! He even had the nerve to circulate a request among the prisoners for its return. Everyone in the camp rejoiced!

Forming in our various divisions, we lined up on the road. The Japs went through our possessions in the building. We could hear shouting and considerable noise. Boards were ripped loose in an attempt to find hidden caches. Finally, they came outside and proceeded to search each prisoner separately. When that started, I suddenly realized that I had a small tin of "hair" tobacco in my pocket.

The Jap supply officer—"Little Emo," or "Junior," as we called him, stood in front of the divisions. Obviously, he was attempting to watch so that no one would empty his pockets and throw something away. He was standing almost directly in front of me. I was in front of the American officers' division. I knew that if I had to submit to a search, the hair tobacco would be found. Then, I thought of the advice humorously given me, sometime before, when our underground gave us warning of an impending shakedown. I was trying to find a hiding place—quick—for some of my notes I had been working on:

"Put 'em in the middle of the floor, and then the slant-eyes won't see them!"

It was good advice. They never could see what was before them. I did not take it literally in the case of the notes. But I did take it literally that day in the road.

"Little Emo" had already issued the order, through the interpreters, "Keep your hands out of your pockets!" Nonchalantly (on the surface) I slightly turned toward my divison, and at the same time, quickly slid my hand into my pocket and withdrew the small can. Turning to the front, I removed the cover by clasping my hands in front of me. Little by little, I sifted the contents on the ground, until it was finally emptied. Then, it was a simple matter to mix it with the dust.

"Junior" was not aware of what had occurred—for which, I
was very thankful! I heard someone whisper behind me:

"I'll never trust you again, Colonel!"

Someone else whispered: "Wonder if the bastards will search
our beards?"

And above all, at this particular time, I heard another
whispered conversation going on. Why they were talking
about that subject—no one will ever know. Perhaps we were
as unpredictable as the Japs:

"About time for the primary elections, isn't it?"

"Not for us, big boy—not for us!"

It developed that the Nips were searching for crumbs of
hardtack in the pockets of the prisoners. They went through
the ranks. Their search produced nothing but suspicion. Five
officers were found in that category. In order to save face, they
picked those five and put them in the brig. Whether the five,
or any part of them, actually went over the fence, I do not
know. I do know, that none of the other prisoners I talked to,
could actually state that they did. These victims were kept in
the brig for about one week. They were questioned quite a
number of times during that period, but none broke down.
Their suffering was most severe. We protested but met with
no success.

We were then permitted to reenter the buildings, and found
our belongings scattered all over. My can of tobacco was gone!
A short time later, the interpreter entered the room and told
me that Capt. Hosatani wanted me in the office. He left, and I
shook hands with my roommates. I knew I was to enter the
brig.

Reaching the office, I found Hosatani and the interpreter
seated behind a desk. My can of tobacco, along with some
others, was on top of the desk.

The interpreter started out by telling me that I had the
largest division in the camp, and therefore my responsibility
was great. He said the Japanese were having more trouble
with my division than with any other division.

He asked me what I knew about the fence episode. My
reply was that I knew nothing whatever.

I was asked how I could be a division leader and know
nothing about it. I told them that it was not my duty to know
those things, that, as a prisoner of war, I had no control what-

ever and no command status. I said my duty, as division leader, was merely to communicate Japanese orders to the division, and to act in an administrative capacity only. And I ended up by stating that the Japanese had never agreed to our request, that we be allowed to administer our own people.

After further questioning, I was asked if I had heard any stories. I replied that I had heard many rumors about all sorts of things. Curious by nature, they wanted to know what sort of rumors I had heard.

I told them that I had heard the Japanese were winning the war and that I had also heard that the Americans were winning the war. They were extremely anxious to know where I had heard the rumors, to which I replied that they were all over the camp, ever since we came in.

All this time, I was wondering when they would confront me with the tobacco. Suddenly, they expressed complete disgust at my ignorance and told me to return to my quarters. They did not even mention the tobacco!

Later, I learned why. In true Japanese one-track mindedness—they had found the tobacco in various rooms, and had placed it in the hallways until they were through with the shakedown. They had failed to spot the place where they had found it. It was a typical Japanese method of avoiding loss of face. They completely ignored all the tobacco they had **found!**

CHAPTER 33

Japanese Way of Thinking

THE JAPS WERE constantly trying to put us on work details outside of the camp. We, just as constantly, kept protesting that it violated international law. Our argument was, that we were willing to work on agricultural projects that might augment our food supply, and also to give us needed exercise. We kept reiterating, however, that exercise without food, would result in complete physical breakdown. The Japs always came right back and said, that anything we raised would be used to augment our food supply. It actually worked in reverse. The more we raised, the more Bushido cut the regular ration. In addition to this, they stole a good portion of what we raised. When confronted with this, the Jap solved the matter in one of two ways. Either he tried to save face by promising to increase the ration to make up for what he termed "borrowing," or he was insulted and one or more received a beating.

It finally reached the point where we knew it was useless to try to bargain with them. We were licked before we even started. An agreement would be reached which was perfectly understood by both sides. Then the Nips would completely violate it and we would protest. Surprise would be registered, in which the "apes" would work themselves into the "crocodile-tears" frame of mind, that *we* should have misunderstood the agreement, kept so carefully by Japanese.

After taking a canvass of the camp one night, we decided to put up a solid front and refuse to volunteer for work. The Nipponese interpreted the word "volunteer" far differently than we did. Our decision was communicated to the Jap office. The next morning, an order was issued for us to form by divisions in the road. There, an order was read by an interpreter, which emanated from the commandant. He wanted to know how many would volunteer for work. A poll was taken and the answer was "none."

This information was carried into the office, and we waited.

Soon, the interpreter appeared again. He said the Superintendent did not believe that the prisoners would not volunteer for work, and had therefore ordered an individual poll on the matter. Once again the answer, "none," was forthcoming. Once again, the interpreter disappeared within the building. After some delay he reappeared ordering all division leaders into the office.

The Jap Colonel was truly in the Jap mood—stating that the Imperial August Mind had dealt generously with the prisoners. They were still alive, and in good health by virtue of the Bushido spirit. The prisoners did not appreciate Japan's generosity. Why did they not volunteer?

A lengthy discussion ensued in which the word "volunteer" was carefully explained by the division leaders. Finally, the commandant grew very impatient, and ordered that the prisoners *would* volunteer for work. Someone said: "If that is an order, backed up by the bayonet, it is not volunteering." The commandant, through the interpreter, verbally kicked everybody out, by stating emphatically: "It is my order!"

We formed ourselves into work details under protest. The protest was written, and lodged with the commandant. Our work was cursory and heckled the Japanese to no small degree. It meant daily beatings for some, including the brig, but we never weakened. That is the way we continued until we left Zentsuji. The Japs retaliated by lowering the quality (if that was possible) and the amount of our miserable ration.

Sweet potatoes were planted. When it came time for the harvest, we found that most of them had been gathered by the Japs. For the greater part of our efforts, we were allowed to gather up the vines for our soup! Many could not eat the mess because of immediate nausea and severe diarrhea. We protested, as usual, with the usual results.

This time, the Japs promised we would get a replacement of what had been taken. They had not been stolen, explained the slope heads. We would be repaid. *We were, but the rice ration was cut accordingly!* When we protested that, we were told quite calmly, that Japan was at war, and the potatoes took the place of the cereal ration. It would be illegal for them to give us both! When it was pointed out, that we had been denied what had been promised in the first place, and which we had produced ourselves, it was blandly pointed out that higher authority had ordered the ration cut a few days before, but because of "borrowing" our potatoes, the local camp authorities had realized their obligation and had forestalled the cut until then! Therefore, we had been paid back! Such is the Jap way of repudiating any promise they may make.

In spite of the dire situation and low spirits, one could walk throughout the entire camp and meet with humor. With reference to the sweet potato soup, made with only water and the vines:

"That damned soup sure made me sick."

"Not me—too many things grabbing at it when it went through my alimentary canal!"

"We'll be good connoisseuers of hog slop, by the time we're out of here—if we ever are!"

"That soup hasn't any character whatever!"

"You said it! It shall be known as gastric masturbation!"

"The proper way to get the spirit of **Bushido** before you eat, is to tighten your belt!"

"How would you like a nice, juicy T-bone steak?"

"How would you like a sock in the puss?"

"Cut out the light talk and have some of our nice, hot, wet tea."

"Tea drinking is illicit!"

"No, it ain't! Have some and exercise your bladder!"

"I'm going to teach my wife economy when I get back. We're going to mow the lawn and use the grass for soup. When we have coffee or tea, we're going to save the grounds, wring 'em out, and sweep the floor with 'em. Then we'll put 'em in the sun to dry, after which—I'll smoke!"

"My belly has grown fast to my backbone. I can't even straighten up!"

"You sure look like it, Humpy. You'll be an old man before you know it."

"Take a look at yourself! You're no arrow—that is, to shoot at anything and hit it!"

"What a terrible way to speak to a man in my condition!"

And thus it went—no matter how dark the outlook might be.

In the winter time, beriberi was at its worst. Excruciating aches occurred in the feet. The only relief was to plunge them in ice cold water. I suppose this numbed the feet to insensibility. The aches were especially bad at night. For the most part, the dry type of beriberi was experienced at Zentsuji. Through the efforts of Dr. Van Peenen, and his loyal staff of helpers, the dreaded disease was kept in as dormant a state as possible.

Washing clothes in winter was a trying ordeal. Plunging chillblain covered hands into the cold water, was enough to deter anyone. Perhaps much of the washing would have been foregone had it not been for the high standards set by the Wake and Guam prisoners. True, they had not gone through the rough experiences of the Philippine prisoners. But, even then, it would have been very easy for them to forsake some of those standards. They did not. They had set the pace, and we kept it.

A limited amount of soap was issued and used most sparingly. Most of the prisoners remained clean shaven. It was a hard task. The Japs issued one razor blade each month, from Red Cross stocks. Sharpening the blade was done by stropping it on the heel of the hand. There were a few glass sharpeners, which succeeded, mostly, in helping to dull the blade. Sometimes, it was almost like tearing the hair out by the roots, but we kept at it. Individually, every other day, we kept half of our hot cup of tea to shave with.

Probably two of the world's most unfortunate men were in our midst at Zentsuji.

The first was "Pappy" Dunsmore of the U.S. Navy. He had been serving on Guam. His tour of duty had just about expired, and he was waiting for the relief man to arrive. This man was actually on his way, and on the high seas when war broke out. "Pappy," of course, was taken prisoner when Guam fell, a few days after hostilities started. His relief was on the Cruiser Houston. This ship engaged the Japs in the waters around the Dutch East Indies. It put up one of the most valiant fights of the entire war, but was doomed before the battle ever started. Eventually, it was sunk. The "reliefer" was one of the survivors, and in company with some of the others, was brought by the Japs to Zentsuji. "Pappy's" relief had arrived! We learned the story after we had arrived, and emulated the other prisoners from Guam, by congratulating Pappy on the fact that the Navy had kept its word!

The second unfortunate was a civilian, H. P. Hevenor, who was connected with the Bureau of the Budget in Washington. He had been on an assignment to check on the construction job at Wake Island. He had flown in by Clipper from Honolulu. The Clipper was moored down in the water within sight of where H. P. was housed. The Japs came in and unloaded a cargo of bombs which missed the Clipper completely but raised havoc with the shore installations. Shortly thereafter, the Clipper took off for Honolulu, like a duck that has been shot at in supposedly placid waters, leaving H. P. to face the future. He did, in a style that imbued every one of us with complete admiration. He was an example to us all, as to what a true gentleman should be.

Both of these valiant prisoners were optimists!

The Wake prisoners had a story they loved to tell. It was one of asininity and irony, so common in every branch of the service in those early days of war.

About one week, after war had begun and the defenders were heavily engaged with the terrific onslaught of the Japanese, a radio message was received from the Medics at Honolulu, with sage advice to have the men wear long trousers and shirts to protect them from bomb burns! Another radio message came in from Honolulu, that permission was granted to move into the uncompleted barracks, and to board up the windows as there was no glass available and probably would be difficult to get them any! All this from Hawaii, while the Nips were bombing hell out of Wake, and attempting landings!

Sounds like a silly symphony? It did to the defenders of Wake, also!

Each day that went by, added to the volume of my notes. Fingers, stiff with chillblains and freezing weather, made it a tedious job. Sometimes, it was almost impossible, because of my constant day dreaming of mountains of food.

Due to reorganizing divisions of the prisoners, and partly because I was a senior officer, my place of abode was changed six times while at Zentsuji. The first thing to be done, as each change was made, was to establish hiding places. All in all, I made five small trap doors for access under the bunk decks, three secret shelves, and a false bottom in a Japanese face powder box. At times, it was impossible to get at the secret hiding places, with the exception of the powder box. Pieces of paper were cut to fit the box. The scraps were saved for other notes. A number of times, at shakedown inspections, the Japs would pick up the box, which I kept in plain sight, and look inside. It always contained some powder which I had procured from the PX. Never did they even so much as put a finger in it. Grunting, they would disdainfully put it aside and pick up something else. Although elated, I never felt like bragging—then!

The Japs, and especially Little Emo, always acted as our barometer when the war news was bad for Japan. Repercussions always followed, and Junior's face was a dead giveaway. It became downright livid. Our news sources always verified it. Naturally, the Jap could not interpret the news, as to its full meaning, in the same true sense as we could. Their totalitarian minds were regimented to accept propaganda explanations, emanating from the high command. They knew, sometimes, that the news was bad but were generally unable to evaluate it properly. Little Emo believed, way down deep, that Japan was invincible, and that it was unthinkable for any nation to challenge her sovereignty. He spent sleepless nights listening to the radio, when he took his turn as duty officer. At the morning musters, he would strut as pompously as his fat, little body permitted, eyeing us with disdain and hatred. His sword was almost bigger than he. As one prisoner remarked:

"He even struts when he sits!"

An enlisted man, on the dock detail, brought me a pocketful of wheat one night. He had purloined several pocketfuls on the wharf. The method used was unique. He carried a piece of bamboo, sharpened at one end. It was short enough to be secreted in his clothing, and long enough to accomplish the desired end. Leaning nonchalantly against a pile of bags containing rice, wheat, beans or anything else comparable, he would manipulate the bamboo so that the sharpened end penetrated the bag, and the other end rested in his pocket. In this way, any number of pockets could be filled in a short space of time. The bamboo, of course, was hollow. It was possible to steal with the guards looking on.

The wheat was soaked in water for a few hours, until softened somewhat, and then eaten. It was very good, and most welcome.

In all prison camps, we nicknamed the Japanese in attendance. These names were chosen primarily because of physical characteristics. Here are some of those names, in addition to the ones already mentioned:

Creepy, Sportsu, Humpy, Paddlefoot, The Snake, The Squirrel, Goldtooth, Bundle of Love, Gobo, The Wine Merchant, Bushido, One Armed Bandit, The Kendo Kid, Fat Stuff, Peg Leg, Gimpy, Duck Butt, Horse Face, Leather Wrist, White Fist, Iron Fist, Shufflefoot, Smiling Jack.

As each American holiday came around, it was remembered, and observed in some way. On July 4, 1943, the American prisoners in Room 26 had an appropriate program at their meager evening meal. The usual precautions were taken to watch for Jap guards.

The Flag of the United States was reproduced on scraps of paper. These flags were pasted to slivers of bamboo. The paste was made from rice and water, taken from the ration. The program consisted of short stories and anecdotes appropriate to the occasion. Lt. Jack Bradley, National Guardsman, from New Mexico read a poem he had written:

> In the twilight of calm meditation
> 'though prisoner's lot is mine,
> I partake of Freedom's Sweet Ambrosia
> Nectar mellow and divine.
> Through the placid haze of memory,
> I discern a banner there,
> Symbolic of a nation, a land
> Unknowing to despair.
> Her treasured presence is denied me here,
> Denied to outer eye.
> But She waves freely in my heart;
> Her radiance lights the sky!
> May God bless Her white girt', crimson glory,
> Her placid field of blue.
> May God bless Her time-cherished story
> Of a people born anew.
> Long may She wave o'er that thrice blessed soil,
> Long may Her children thrive!

> She stands a symbol of humanity
> In Her, our hopes survive.
> And though they hold me prisoner,
> Before me but a wall,
> That flag flies ever in my mind,
> In memory's hidden hall!

The ceremonies ended by the whole room singing, "God Bless America."

That day, one Britisher remarked, in a good-natured, bantering conversation:

"You call it Independence Day. We call it Thanksgiving Day!"

An American, engaged in the conversation, replied:

"Well, Redcoat, it took you from 1775 to 1781 to decide that!"

Discussions were always going on, among all prisoners, as to the progress of the war. Commander Keene, U.S. Navy, was arguing with Lt. Colonel Scott, British Army. It centered around the island of Peleu in the Southwest Pacific.

"Do you think, that with ten United States Navy carriers, able to operate against Peleu, that it would not be reduced?" asked Keene.

"Well, don't forget that Malta has been attacked continuously, since the start of the war, and is still O.K.," replied Scott.

"My dear sir! The United States Navy did not attack Malta!" was Keene's answer.

And a little later on, the discussion centered on the merits of the U.S. Navy versus the Army. It ended up as follows:

"The Army may be the senior service, but the Navy is the first line of defense!"

To which came the reply:

"Only because they happen to be where they can't get out of the way!"

At Zentsuji, we were pestered by bedbugs, fleas, mosquitoes and flies. The bedbugs were probably the worst offenders. They were nested in the woodwork by the millions. The only relief from them was during the cold, winter months. However, the first day of warm weather, brought them out. Sores developed from the combination of bites and scratching.

It was very difficult to heal any sores due to our physical condition. The flies were not as bad as we had experienced in the Philippines, but they were bad, nevertheless.

We conceived the idea, in Zentsuji, of organizing the United States Zentsujians, so as to keep contact with our fellow ex-prisoners of war, if and when we were released. We also sold the plan to the other nationalities in camp. We were to organize by nations in separate groups. Our tie would be the exchange of any publications, addresses, and so forth. The Americans organized. The others only went so far as to take lists of names. Whether or not, the British, Dutch and Australians perfected anything after the war, I do not know. Our organization is alive and functioning. We drew up a constitution and elected officers secretly from the Japs. On the day that we made the final draft of, and accepted the constitution, we were gathered in one of the rooms. Each State had elected delegates for that purpose. The Japs allowed no congregation of prisoners. Therefore, if we wished to hold a meeting, the occupants of that particular room would move out and occupy the quarters of those individuals that wished to hold the meeting. The Japs never discovered the ruse.

Our emblem, which appears herein, was the result of much discussion and many ideas. It was finally adopted, and the drawing was handed to me, as national president, for safe keeping. Lt. Fred W. Koenig was requested to write up something, exemplifying the emblem, that would be appropriate. He submitted the following, which was adopted:

Emblem of Zentsujians

I am the lucent emblem of adversity o'ercome;
I am the eternal symbol of fidelity retained;
I am the immutable echo of friendly voices dumb;
I am the boundless wings of faith unchained.
I am the star you fashioned in thraldom's night,—
When pagan frenzy challenged an unwary world.
I pierced the opaque clouds with blessed light,
And succoured hopes in bondage hurled.
I am the shield of valiant brotherhood,
Which shared the fates of pestilential years.
I am the buckler of your honor which withstood

The maligning stain of miscreants weak tears.
I am your scroll unfurled for man to read—
A tenet—scriven with the blood of noble men,
For future flagging years to wisely heed,
Lest all you brooked shall wiley rise again.

CHAPTER 34

Christmas at Zentsuji

THE WIDTH OF THE bunk space allowed each prisoner was about thirty inches. The width of a man is about 22 inches. More space was available, but the Jap system was to crowd everyone into as small a space as possible. There were a few prisoners who had more space than this, but only because the bay allotted did not have enough personnel to fill it up. Living under crowded conditions was not very conducive to promoting harmonious relations with bunk mates. Squabbles arose that would have been considered childish under normal circumstances. But to the everlasting credit of the prisoners, tolerancy was always the rule and not the exception.

Requests were made several times, in writing and verbally, for the Japs to turn over the Red Cross supplies to a prisoner committee. Each time, it was turned down on some pretext or other. The last time, they showed their true colors. The reply was, in essence, that the Japanese were responsible for it coming into the country, and would be responsible for its distribution.

So bad did the salt situation become, that we were having bad cramps in our limbs. These occurred mostly at night when most activity ceased. It was sometimes necessary to massage and stretch the muscles for as long as an hour at a time.

From the second story windows of our barracks, we could observe activities in the school yard, a short distance from the camp. At school time in the mornings, all the children were formed into groups. They faced the schoolhouse steps, bowed and chanted at the direction of what must have been the school head, who was posted at a loud speaker. Periodically, they had military formations and passed in review. The ages ranged all the way from kindergarten to about 14 years. The school yard was also used for the assemblage of the local populace, both men and women, who participated in military drills. This, evidently, was the home guard.

One of our interpreters, Mauriama, was talking to Commander Keene one day. He was always serious and sober faced. He told Keene that he had some news for him. After much delay, he said: "Bad news for America. America losing and losing and losing every battle more and more!" Reporting back, Keene gave us the "news."

Trying to run our schedule by Japanese time was an impossibility. As an example: one night, we had to set our time up ten minutes to conform with the Nip bugler for muster. At taps, one hour later, it had to be set up five minutes more. The next morning, the time went back five minutes for muster. By noon, the bugle went back twenty minutes. There were three clocks in the Japanese offices. At no time did I ever see them the same.

Generally speaking, Japanese lips are not fitted to sound the bugle. It was always so bad, that we became "acclimated" to sour notes, cracks in tone, and unfinished calls. It was amusing at first but soon became a part of our existence.

Military terms, used in official communiques, were always the subject of much conversation and witticism. Some of those terms were as follows: Annihilate, mainstay, bleeding tactics, according to plan, inner flank strategy, near hits, body crashing tactics, self-blasting, thunder sunk, five layer enemy positions, detaching movements, elastic withdrawals, and elastic compression movements. Prisoners' comments:

"This paper says they withdrew because it was of no further strategic value."

"Yeah! They aren't there any longer!"

"Here, they're talking about an artillery patrol. What's that?"

"It's one of those shells that follow you about!"

"There'll be some belly slashings tonight!"

One day, the Nips proudly announced that they were killing two goats which would go into our soup that night. They killed the goats—and promptly stole nearly all of the meat. Conversation at mealtime:

"I thought we were supposed to get goat in our soup tonight."

"Can't prove it by me. I didn't get any."

"Well, if there isn't any goat in the soup, I'll swear that somebody washed their dirty underwear in it!"

Another one, muttering under his breath:

"Damn it! Worms in the rice again!"

"Just kick 'em off," replied someone.

"Save 'em for me. I need proteins!" offered another voice.

"Not a good recommendation for the hotel, is it?" asked the room leader.

One good soul, wanting to take his mind off the worms, offered a bit of gossip:

"The Nips say we must conserve on water."

"Hell! We've had more rainfall this year than last!" said the worm hater.

"They need more for the soup," explained one of the prisoners.

"Do not talk so about the Imperial Water!" answered another.

And the optimist added his bit:

"Each day that passes is one day closer."

"Closer to what?" asked the pessimist.

"I'll bet a hole could be bored right through your head and come out with bone shavings!" said the optimist.

"Well, I've been drilled by experts!" returned the pessimist.

At various times, lectures were held within groups. These lectures ranged all the way from the Malayan Campaign to Dunkirk. Naturally, the Japs were kept in ignorance of what the lectures were about. They were always told that the lecturer was going to talk about some subject entirely foreign to the war. If the Sons of Heaven were in a good mood, the lecture went on. If permission was denied, the lecture went on anyway. In this manner, we learned much about the experiences of others.

For the benefit of the inside guards who prowled about, the listeners would adopt positions around the room so as not to arouse suspicions. The lecturer would seat himself inconspicuously and the program would start. Certain prisoners posted themselves so as to be on the alert and still hear the lecture. Early in the game, we used the word "Tally Ho" to signal the approach of the enemy. Finally the Japs found out what the expression meant. Several beatings occurred and an order was put out by them that the word was taboo. Thereafter we adopted "Forty-four," which was used successfully.

The lecture was going strong one night and it was exceedingly interesting. Our people, who were on the alert, became a little careless. A Jap guard was in our midst before we knew it. Luckily, the lecturer was looking in the right direction and saw the guard come in. Without even faltering, he began to talk about Chicago:

"Chicago has a hotel capacity for 400,000 people."

Immediately, a voice in the back of the room said:

"Holy smokes! What a building that must be!"

Spontaneously, everyone roared. The guard grunted and walked out!

The speaker, unperturbed, continued with his lecture.

The topic assigned me, for lectures, was the Philippine Campaign. The audience was composed of both officers and enlisted men. Getting warmed up one night, I pointed out some of the flagrant mistakes made by the high command; that they must assume the blame for not making use of those things which they had at their disposal. Pausing a moment, I was interrupted by one of the men who, very seriously, spoke up:

"Colonel, they can court martial you for calling a superior an SOB, but if you can prove it, you'll be acquitted!"

Groping your way to the benjo (toilet) at night, in complete darkness, was a trip fraught with both peril and humor. Jagged holes had appeared in the flooring and these had to be by-passed by the sense of touch. One could hear conversations on almost any subject. Perhaps the ears were attuned more acutely because it was dark. I heard one conversation regarding the status of the war in the Caribbean. The first speaker evidently had had service in Puerto Rico. He finally ended up by saying:

"Puerto Rico is the watchdog of the Caribbean."

Chuckling, the other unknown voice replied:

"Hope they fed him better than they did the watchdog of the Pacific, or he's probably so weak he can't bite his own fleas!"

Coming back, I heard a minor commotion near the water spigot. Someone asked:

"Let's go, Bob. What the hell are you doing?"

"Trying to clean my false teeth. Dropped the upper plate and I can't find it," was the answer.

"Well, get a move on before the Japs come along. Sounds like you're taking an inventory in a hardware store!"

From the Caribbean to false teeth—all in one trip to the benjo!

Verily, I have heard all types of snores that ever could be produced—except my own. One of our bunk mates had a snore which I have never heard matched. It was not loud, nor was it what could be termed as soft. It had a sound, that slow but sure, would invade your dreams. I awakened in the dead of night, at the insistence of the snore, and heard someone say:

"How do you shut off this radiator?"

The answer came quick:

"When he starts to gurgle, cut his throat!"

On November 9, 1944, when the national elections were being held in the United States, a straw vote was taken among the Americans to see how they felt about Roosevelt and Dewey. This vote was taken by Lt. Tom Foy, without the Jap's knowledge. We knew the two candidates were running, from propaganda appearing in the Nipponese newspapers. The result was very interesting. We had been prisoners for about two and one-half years, and had been fed Japanese propaganda during that period in which Roosevelt was always blamed for the war. The result of the ballot was: Roosevelt 334; Dewey 37.

The first air raid alarm occurred on July 4, 1944. We learned later that this raid took place on the island of Kyushu, to the west of us. It was an experimental raid by B-29's. The Japs were extremely nasty that day.

Every time an air raid alarm sounded, all prisoners were herded into certain rooms. The purpose probably was to have us under closer control. If a bomb had struck our place of assembly, the prisoner populace would have been eliminated in a hurry. We tried to convince the Japs that we should repair to our own quarters at each alarm, but we did not get very far with that idea!

Jap personnel of the camp always climbed to the top of the galley roof when air raids were on. Always, they had their swords, and always, the swords were drawn. Eventually, they built a platform on which to stand. Whether or not, their intention was to smite the hated American airplanes with their Bushido swords, can only be left to the imagination.

Birthdays were religiously observed at Zentsuji. Someone

always remembered. Greeting cards were contrived with whatever might be available. Humble gifts were exchanged. That gift might be in the form of a cigarette saved for the occasion, or it might be a between-meal snack provided by saving a part of the meager ration of the meal before. Any gift meant a sacrifice by the donor. One gift I received on my birthday will always remain vivid in my mind. We had received an individual Red Cross box sometime in June of 1943. Much of it was spoiled because it had been kept in storage by the Japs too long. Each package contained, among other things, two packs of Roy cigarettes and one packet of George Washington pipe tobacco. Naturally, it did not take long to get rid of the tobacco, and as a consequence, it was worth almost a fortune. My birthday came on September 15th. On that day, Russ Swearingen visited my quarters, congratulated me on my birthday, and presented me with a package of George Washington tobacco! Russ enjoyed smoking as much as I did. He had deliberately saved the pipe tobacco from his box from June to September to give to me! It was probably worth about ten cents in the United States at that time. In the prison camp, it was worth more than its weight in gold, plus the sacrifice it entailed. An act of that kind could not help but restore faith in human nature. If that spirit pervaded the world today, there would be no cause for worry about war!

Never, do I expect to find the Christmas spirit anywhere, that was displayed at Zentsuji. It is almost indescribable in its beauty and its sheer strength. It was a spirit fashioned by men who had so little with which to work—a spirit that was close to Christ. We felt His presence.

The Wake and Guam prisoners had fostered this spirit in 1942. They had convinced the Japs and had laid the ground work. That spirit was so strong that even the Sons of Heaven, with all their vindictiveness, failed to oppose our celebration of Christmas. And so infectious did the spirit become, that they actually procured extra food for that day!

We pointed toward it for weeks, working up programs which we hoped to present. Naturally, permission had to be granted by the Japs. I suppose it was a face saving gesture, but we always received the permission. Christmas carols were practiced diligently. Dicken's "A Christmas Carol" was chosen by the Americans for presentation. Lt. Fred Koenig took the part of Scrooge, and he left nothing to be desired. Hymns were rehearsed, and also Ave Maria for both Protestant and Catholic services on *the day*. The best singers in the camp were recruited and put through their paces. Nothing was forgotten.

Old newspapers were gathered up and cut into long ribbons to be fashioned into rings, pasted together with rice taken out of our rations. We even wangled some paste from the Japs! A spoonful or two of our precious rice made up the difference. We mashed it up with water to make more paste. The newspapers were colored with Jap shoe polish, leaves and other products of Mother Nature boiled in water, liquid we were using for ink, and what-have-you.

Almost miraculously, some artistic talented prisoners produced works of beauty. They used Nip tooth powder which was mixed with water. They set to work on the windows of the camp. The mixture was applied so as to give a frosted effect. Typical Christmas scenes appeared thereon—the traditional church—bells—snow flakes—Santa Claus and his reindeer! Pitiful? It was beautiful!

Old tin cans were salvaged and scoured to brightness—cut up and made into shining chandeliers—tin stars and twisted bits of tin, suspended by a jealously accumulated stock of odds and ends, that could be used as string. Pieces of wood, rocks and smuggled scraps of iron—used to bend the tin into shape. Pieces of white string that had been hoarded, colored as closely as possible, to the traditional Yuletide red and green—to tie up a meager gift. Old pieces of cardboard were resurrected from the dumps to be made into stars and covered with tinfoil, hoarded for months. Wreaths appeared, fashioned from small limbs of pine trees gathered on the return trips to camp, by outside working parties—bound together with tough weeds. The magic letters, made from anything at hand, spelling out *Merry Christmas* and *Happy New Year,* hanging from the chandeliers, or suspended from the walls. A coveted mirror cleverly arranged so that it caught the rays of the sun, or the feeble glow of the 30 watt light bulb—reflecting the light on a shiny star. One room succeeded in talking the Japs into letting them use empty Red Cross cartons, from which they constructed an almost real fireplace.

Christmas cards and New Year's greetings were made out

of anything that was available. Some attempts were crude but just as beautiful in spirit as they were crude in the visible portrayal. Others were masterpieces, drawn in freezing weather by the chillblained hands of artists, whose fingers became numb and almost lifeless, even as they worked.

On Christmas Eve, a program of carol singing by the camp choir was conducted. To nearly all of us, it was the most beautiful music we had ever heard. Perhaps it was because of our surroundings, and the deep loneliness we felt at that time of the year. But, for whatever reason, there were few dry eyes at that program. We sat in the darkness, listening, thinking of loved ones at home, and silently weeping. To not have done so, under those conditions, one would have had to be bereft of any soul whatever.

Rice was hoarded from the day before, so as to contribute toward the group parties to be held on Christmas Day. In many instances, some precious tidbit from a previous Red Cross issue would make its appearance, to flavor the party rice.

Christmas morning, the very air in the prison camp was charged with cheery greetings. The spirits of everyone were high. So infectious was it, that even the sour-puss Jap guards actually managed the trace of a smile. Griping was taboo, not by any rule, but by the Christmas spirit itself. Squabbles were forgotten, and men seemed to be born anew. Catholic and Protestant services were held. The camp choir, composed of all religious faiths, sang at both services. Chaplains had pointed to Christmas Day and it seemed as though, they too, had just a little bit more to offer.

Each building had set up a service to deliver all "mail," which had been deposited in a certain place on Christmas Eve. The delivery was made early the next morning. It included cards of greeting from one friend to the other, and "gifts" such as lone cigarettes, a pair of shoe laces, a homemade handkerchief fashioned from a rag, small bits of soap and so forth—all saved meticulously for the purpose of giving, on this day of days.

After church services, the parties would start. Greetings and handclasps would begin all over again—as though we had not seen each other for years. Hot water was available from the galley in which we might brew tea, and we sat around and reminisced—and smoked—if we had the smokes. We lingered over our hoarded snacks of rice, making it last as long as possible. Jokes were told and wisecracks made that we had heard a dozen times before—and we laughed heartily. It did us good to laugh. Programs were arranged at the parties at which certain qualified prisoners performed.

The night before Christmas in 1943, one of the enlisted men from the work detail on the docks, smuggled in some Scotch whiskey. It was prewar stuff and very good. The Japs conducted no shakedown of the work party as they came in that night. The detail had guessed there would be none, and had secreted much booty in their clothing and lunch bags. One question that we never asked was, "Where did you get it?" The man brought me an untouched 5th of the whiskey. On Christmas, the 194th Tank officers at Zentsuji had a party. At the proper time, I produced the bottle. For a moment it seemed that everyone stopped breathing, and eyes just about popped out of their sockets. However, no one asked where it had come from. Carefully removing the seal, we measured out the drinks, sipped, and drank toasts. Probably none of us will ever offer toasts quite as deeply sincere as we did that day. If we do, it will have to be under similar conditions!

On Christmas night, both 1943 and 1944, the Americans staged "A Christmas Carol." It was a distinct success each time and the audience was truly appreciative. It had been rehearsed quite carefully. Even the Jap interpreters, who, under camp regulations had to be present, seemed to enjoy it. And thus the day ended.

Without doubt, none of us ever experienced a Christmas such as that, before or since. The expensive gifts were missing, to be sure. But in their place was the real spirit of Christmas. It was a spirit, exemplified, in the small, homely offerings from one friend to the other—the shedding of arguments and petty dislikes which come to people living too close together. The important part was, that the spirit of the Christmas Child Himself was present, in that prison camp.

New Year's Day was also observed, but not to any such extent as Christmas. Greetings were exchanged together with some cards. Room Number 1 sent out a unique folder on New Year's Day, 1945. The drawing appearing on the face of the folder is shown in this book. On the second page is the following poem:

> We hope you'll recall, in lines of rhyme,
> We sent you greetings at Christmas time;
> Again by this means, we strive to convey,
> All that our hearts prompt our lips to say:
> The *happy* we use is full of meaning,
> Omnibus word with good wishes teeming;
> Wishes Prosperous, Healthy, Wise,
> Each in full measure within it lies;
> Reunion, Liberty, Freedom, Peace,
> These too we mean its use to release:
> So may '45 be a year without peer,
> For *all a* really *Happy New Year!*

CHAPTER 35

Our Chief Is Dead!

EACH DAY OF imprisonment, I added to my notes. Believe me, when I say that sometimes, it seemed useless. In spite of optimistic viewpoints, there were periods when the outlook was most black. Little invisible devils, creatures of adversity, were constantly trying to undermine the will to resist the hopelessness of despair. No matter how optimistic you were, your make-up was that of human clay, and you succumbed for longer or shorter stages of despondency. Then, the sun would shine again, and your conscience would smite, pointing the finger of scorn with shameful accusation. Finally, the cycle of human weakness would wear itself out, with inevitable remorse and self-inflicted penance.

Generally speaking, I always took precautions when working on notes. On one occasion, I was either careless or too preoccupied. Bent over the crude table, I suddenly became acutely aware that I was being watched. Looking up, I was confronted by a Japanese guard, who was peering down intently at the scrap of paper on which I had been recording a beating of the day before. The mind either works quickly, or it doesn't work at all under circumstances of that kind. Something bigger than I, prompted me to do what I did. Still looking at him, I grinned and shoved the paper in his direction. It was a matter of bluffing or of being caught. There just wasn't anything else to do. The guard grabbed it and held it close to his beady eyes. After an interminable period, he threw it down, turned around in the opposite direction, and bellowed in Japanese at one of the prisoners on the other side of the room. Then he slithered out, in the same manner as he had entered. Without doubt, he could not read English and the bluff had worked.

On another occasion, the Jap colonel, commanding the camp, made an inspection. We knew it was coming but expected it to be only cursory. Regardless of whether or not we guessed it to be routine, we always tried to hide those things the Nips should not see. I had had no chance to cache my notes for several days. Therefore, I used the pieces of paper that fitted into the bottom of the powder box. They were securely in place with the much used and soiled powder on top. The box was in plain sight.

We heard the inspecting party approaching. At the door of our room, they held quite a confab, jabbering in Japanese. Not a great deal of attention was paid to anyone until they arrived in front of my bunk. It was then that I caught the true significance of the inspection. The colonel had a Jap general along with him. He was from the Prisoner Bureau in Tokyo. His strutting emulated that of Donald Duck, and he had the strangest set of whiskers I have ever seen. Only the movies could duplicate that caricature. The whiskers were thin and wispy, and very scarce. The colonel, through the interpreter, had me put all of my possessions on the foot of my bunk. They examined everything meticulously, even to the point of unfolding a few old rags I had accumulated. The powder box, I placed directly in front of them. The colonel picked it up and took off the cover. Showing it to the general, he jabbered and then tossed it carelessly back into place. Some of the powder spilled and I nearly had heart failure. Remembering O'Donnell, I reached down and brought up the folder containing my family pictures and handed it to the colonel. Sure enough, that became the center of interest. After a lot of confab, the colonel handed it back to me, bowed, and the party left the room! I will never know why the party searched my belongings. Perhaps it was thought that I had something they wanted. Perhaps it was only curiosity. The fact remains, that I was the only one searched in the entire group. After they had left, I kissed the old powder box.

The inevitable wisecracking started:

"The only zoo in the world where the animals come to see the visitors!"

"If Whiskers had tail feathers, he'd look like a peacock!"

"He must have copied his style from his illustrious monkey ancestors."

"Yeah! But there must have been a billygoat in it somewhere!"

"They all look like apes, but that one is a dead ringer!"

"Well, don't just stand around with your teeth in your mouth—you may lose 'em one of these days!"

"Right, my low-browed friend. Let's all sing the Japanese anthem—When Its Daikon Time In Nippon!"

After the inspection that day, one of our friends, from the other side of the camp, came bursting into our room. He was out of breath from hurrying and climbing the stairs. For a moment, he panted—and he really was breathless. It didn't take a great deal to put us into that condition. Some had to make two or three attempts before they could climb to the second floor of the barracks. The limbs just refused to function. Any exertion, out of the ordinary, would almost leave the lungs in a collapsed state. Our visitor wore a luxurious beard, and per usual, caused the standard comments:

"Well hello, Flathead! What flavor is your beard today?"

"How long since you dusted it, Breathless?"

"Don't shake it out in here! We've got enough of a menagerie as it is!"

Our guest, still breathing hard, surveyed his hecklers and then remarked:

"You birds are so full of wind, you'd be an asset to the Navy!"

After more of the bantering, we learned the reason for his hurried call. For want of something better to do, he had originated a "hot" rumor among one of the groups in the next building, and then had come over to our quarters as fast as he could, to see how long it would take for the rumor to reach us! I do not remember how long a period elapsed, before the event occurred, but it did and it was not very long!

The first direct view of a B-29 I received, was early in March, 1945. It was flying high and came in from the southeast. Vapor trailed for a long distance behind it. Straight for our camp it came. When just about directly overhead, the plane swung to the southwest and faded from sight. The trail of vapor hung in the sky and formed a perfect V!

Whether or not this was intentional, only the crew of that plane can give the answer. But it certainly created a great deal of enthusiasm in the camp.

From this time on, B-29's were numerous. Bombings were frequent and the Japs hated them. Often the raids were so close that the camp buildings shook and quivered. A perpetual smoky haze settled over the landscape, and the sun's rays did not seem as warm as we had experienced before. How we longed to be in those planes! Literally, it meant only a few thousand feet between us and freedom!

At about 3:00 P.M., April 13, 1945, Colonel Kondo announced the death of President Roosevelt. He had caught the news as it came over the Jap radio and could hardly wait to give us the depressing message. This was the kind of news the Sons of Heaven were very enthusiastic to dish out. True to form, the commandant offered his sympathy of "so sorry"—Japanese sympathy—permeated with the sadistic curiosity of observing how low our morale might sink.

The morale did sink to a very low level. Our Chief was dead. We wondered how it would affect the American people and the war effort. Were our national affairs in such shape, that the next man could take over without a costly delay? Jumbled thoughts filled our minds. The news came as a stunning blow and it numbed us.

The next day, optimism again started to climb. No one man could possess the ability to wage a war, on a scale such as this! To be sure, his death would be deeply felt, but America's war effort was in high gear and depended on no one individual! Thus we reasoned, and thus our faith and optimism came back—quick!

Smuggled Jap newspapers played up the President's death as a sure sign of victory for Nippon. Perhaps they really believed some of the things they wrote. Naturally, they reasoned in the same manner as they would have done, had the Emperor died. To them, the Emperor was the Son of Heaven and they literally worshipped him as such.

The next day, we requested the commandant for permission to hold memorial services for the dead President. The request was granted. The service was short, with prayers by the chaplains, and a brief memorial address given by Lt. Verity, United States Army. The address was built around "The Chief" and not F. D. R. as an individual. It was dignified by its simplicity and respect for the President who had gone West.

While on a garden project one afternoon, we witnessed an incident of brutality among the Japanese themselves. The project was on quite an elevation and we could see into the valley below. A number of recruits were undergoing bayonet practice with a sergeant in command. One of the recruits evidently did not go through his paces in a manner to suit the master. All activity stopped, the recruit came to order arms and stood at attention. Then the sergeant stepped over and slugged him in the face repeatedly. The only movement of the victim was from the blows he received. To top it off, the Bushido Spirit manifested itself when the sergeant kicked the man as hard as he could. The other recruits looked on impassively! Then the drill went on.

One of the prisoners in the work party remarked:

"Hope the so and so don't pick on me. The bedbugs did last night and I'm anemic!"

"Well, there's two things about it—either we'll be picked on or we won't!" replied another.

For sometime, our underground had been circulating a persistent rumor that we were to be moved to another camp. There was much conjecture as to where we were going.

Jap military police began to be more active. A whole company of them came into camp and nosed around for about half a day. It appeared to be a conducted tour. They did not disturb us however. It was a relief when they left.

By the first of June, I came to the conclusion that we were really going to move. Everything pointed to it. My notes had developed into a voluminous bundle. There would be no possibility of carrying them with me.

First of all, I procured two fairly large tin cans with tight lids, in which had come some Red Cross powdered milk. Into these, I carefully packed the notes. Over the open tops of the cans, I spread the lining of an old toilet kit, that had somehow found its way into the camp. It would help to keep moisture out of the cans. Over this, the lids were secured.

The next step was to select the time and place for burial. Arrangements were made with several prisoners, to participate in some form of activity in the area, to attract attention of any prowling Japs in that direction. The place for burial was selected just behind the east trash bin. The activity decided upon was reading something or other and rehearsing part of a show program. This was to take place in front of the trash bin. This bin was about four or more feet high and allowed cover to screen the burial.

Procuring a shovel, we timed the inside patrol of the guards. Barely had they turned the corner past us when the action started. A small garden plot was between the bin and the high board fence. Therefore, taking the shovel out to that spot was a natural act if anyone was watching me. I had selected the exact spot prior to the time and started to dig feverishly. I had not counted on its being so hard. The ground was packed solid with an almost cement-like hardness. It was just about impossible to go deeper than about ten inches. Hastily placing the cans, I tamped the material back as hard as possible, using the shovel handle and my feet. After puttering about the garden for a short time, I called the activity off and replaced the shovel. No one had appeared to disturb us! I slept much easier that night. The accumulation of those notes was made under the most adverse conditions possible. To have lost them to the Japanese would have meant a trip to Tokyo and the end!

From that time to the end of the war, I still kept notes. However, they were brief and merely a record of daily events. The main project had been completed. These notes were very easy to cache on my person.

About the middle of June, 1945, the Japanese announced that we would be moved to other camps—by nationalities. For the next ten days, dates were given, several times, as to when we would depart. Each time, nothing happened and we began to doubt if we ever would be moved. However, other pertinent things pointed to the opposite viewpoint. Undoubtedly, the delays were due to American bombings which were raising havoc with transportation.

In the late afternoon on June 23, 1945, those of us who had been previously designated by the Japs to be company commanders for the movement, were called over to the office. A big Japanese lieutenant met us, together with an interpreter. As usual, he made a speech. We would move the next day. We would form so and so at 3:00 P.M. We must be careful not to excite the Japanese civilians. They did not like us. So on and on.

At the appointed time on June 24th, we formed. The unending "Bango" (count off) went on for at least half an hour. Jap guards, with their one track minds, never did have any intelligent system for checking the number in each company.

Prisoner companies were always formed in groups of 100. Then the surplus numbers were added. On the second count, the guards with my company "found" one extra man for whom they could not account. There actually was no one that came in that category. The guards were simply mixed up, which was standing operating procedure with the Nips. One prisoner muttered to the man next to him:

"Why in hell don't they put him in the spare parts kit?"

Finally, after more bangoing, we were off. Farewells were called to the other prisoners who had gathered to see us go. Bantering was the order of the day. Sentiment was covered up by jibes, all given and taken in the spirit of the occasion. A British lieutenant colonel stood on the sidelines. He had a stiff knee and had undergone a great deal of adversity. We had learned to know and admire him. His name was Brigdon. One of his American friends called out:

"Is it true, Briggie, that they are using the fog in England for a smoke screen?"

Brigdon replied with a wide grin and a wave of the arm.

One of the enlisted men came alongside and slipped me a tangerine he had brought in while out on a work detail. He walked with me as far as the gate. I immediately ate the tangerine, peelings and all. As I gulped the last mouthful, he took his leave and said:

"That's the Japanese spirit, Colonel. Don't throw anything away!"

We marched through the town to the depot. Many Japanese civilians watched us. If they, or any others, were hostile to us on that trip, they were Houdini's in concealing their emotions. We knew, from our underground, that the civilians were extremely anxious for the war to cease. But we also knew, that only the Emperor could actually call a halt.

The Japanese lieutenant, in charge of the movement, had told us we could take whatever we could carry. So weak were the prisoners, that almost as soon as the gate was cleared, odds and ends, that had been accumulated, were thrown away. Those odds and ends consisted of everything from empty tin cans used for eating and drinking, to rags that had been saved. We were lucky to carry ourselves. Arriving at the station, we crammed ourselves aboard the train. Day coaches were furnished but they were crowded almost as bad as the Philippine box cars. Arms, legs, and bodies were an intermingled mass.

While it was still light, we arrived at Takamatsu and detrained, preparatory to taking the ferry across the inland sea. More civilians watched us with apathetic indifference. We were much heartened by this display, because it meant verification that the war must be nearing the end.

Boarding the ferry, after dark, we were herded into the hold, and after an unventful passage, we debarked on the main island of Honshu. After a short journey on the train, we arrived at Okayama, and were packed into a room in the station. There were large crowds of civilians here who also regarded us with that same apathetic indifference. Much to our surprise *and delight,* we received the same box luncheon as in 1942 when we had arrived in Japan. There was not room for all to recline, either sitting or lying. At stated periods, we exchanged places. Everyone was in high spirits, however. We had been fed! We stayed in this room all night—335 of us with about as much room as on the hell ship.

Twenty-four hours later, this railroad station was blown to bits by American bombers!

During that long night, one of the prisoners reminisced:

"We're graduates of Zentsuji International War Prison College. We have BA, MT, and DR degrees—Bachelor of Abstinence—Master of Tolerance—Doctor of Resourcefulness! What's the next one?"

Just as one prisoner was being relieved from the standing position, to assume the coveted sitting posture, he was interrupted by another unfortunate:

"Take off your pants if you're going to sit down!"

"Why?" asked the fortunate one.

"Because you're in Japan. You'll wear 'em out!"

Another bit of conversation took place which is worthy of relating:

"Joe, your shirt is dirty."

"How do you get that way? I washed it only yesterday."

"Well, your washing sure shows tattle tale black!"

And a second lieutenant next to me reminded:

"Colonel, you've smoked everything there is. But, please don't start on the roof tonight. We may need it!"

Early the next morning, a miracle happened. *We were fed*

again from the little wooden boxes! Comments were profuse. The Japs were losing the war and they knew it! We would be treated better from now on! Red Cross boxes would be awaiting us on arrival at our destination! Utopia!

Can you blame us for being so optimistic?

Shortly thereafter, we boarded day coaches and the train pulled out. It was over the same route as in 1942—but what a difference!

Before leaving Zentsuji, we were especially warned that no maps would be taken along. However, Russ Swearingen took the chance and carried two detailed maps of Japan, which he had purloined from one of the propaganda publications we had been allowed to read while at Zentsuji. He carried them next to his skin, underneath his shirt. Thus, we knew the route as we progressed.

We traveled from Okayama to Osaka, a great part of the industrial district of Japan. Wooden blinds were drawn on the windows, and the orders of the Japanese were, that no one would attempt to look out of the cars. Posting our own guards, which by then was standing operating procedure, I broke a corner of the blind and peered out. The other side of our coach did the same thing. Afterwards, when we compared notes, probably every section of the train did the same thing! In 1942, we had seen a tremendous industrial area with smokestacks rising to the sky. We had seen this with sinking hearts. Now, we saw what the Japanese did not want us to see.

As far as the horizon, there was absolutely nothing standing except, now and then, a lone smokestack. Civilians were "dug in" with roofs of any and all things. It was a ghost area, all the way to Osaka. Afterwards, we were to learn that the B-29's only dropped a minimum of high explosive bombs. The great majority were incendiary. The bombers would drop the variety of bombs. Then the fighter planes would come in, circle the area for the necessary length of time, keeping fire fighting equipment at bay, and then leave. As a result, there was no control by the Japanese.

It was not the atomic bomb that won the war. I am willing to admit that it saved many lines—ours most certainly. Had the Emperor willed that the war would go on—it would! But it did not win the war! The war had already been won. The industrial giant of the Japanese had been exterminated. The atomic bomb had merely helped the Emperor to make up his mind a bit faster.

That night, we arrived in Fukui, which is close to the west coast of Japan—west and slightly north of Tokyo. We hiked across town and were put into trolley cars. After riding for some distance, we detrained and started up the mountains.

Fred Garret, on crutches and with an open wound, was in the column. Every so often, we prevailed on the guards to stop, and put in a call for that worthy individual. Each time, the answer was relayed back that he was O.K. and still coming! Another lieutenant, whose name I have forgotten, but who should receive the highest honors, was afflicted with an extreme case of beriberi. He could hardly navigate, when we left Zentsuji. He was with Fred. No two men in history, have ever undergone more torture than those two men that night. Every step was *up*—pitch dark—with rolling stones under foot! The distance has been debated, but we settled with it being between seven and ten kilometers!

At about 4:00 A.M., we arrived at our destination. The best of us were "all in" and we waited for the tail-end of the column. Fred Garret and his companion hobbled through the gate! The prisoners spontaneously cheered!

We had arrived at Rokuroshi!

CHAPTER 36

The War Is Over!

IT WAS NOT LONG before we had located our position on the maps which Russ Swearingen had smuggled in. We were about twenty-five miles east of Fuki. This was west and slightly north of Tokyo, and probably about thirty miles inland from the west coast of Japan.

Rokuroshi was a bad camp, to say the least. It was an old Army cantonment that had not been used for years. Instead of 30 inches, for bunk space per man as allowed at Zentsuji, we were allowed only 22 inches here. Those, who had to be quartered in the loft, overhead, did not even have that much. Much of the ground floor space did not have bunk decks. Old, filthy blankets were issued that stunk to the high heavens.

Wonder of wonders, we received rice, and a watery soup made from fish heads. To us, it was a Thanksgiving dinner. At first, we thought perhaps the change in treatment had come. Not very many hours after, however, we knew our thinking was all wrong. *The Japs deducted what we had received, from our ration allowance of the next couple of days!*

Soon after our arrival, one of the interpreters assigned to the camp, visited us. It was Fujimoto San, whom we had first met on the docks at Moji, and last seen at Tanagawa. This time, he was dressed in Japanese clothing. His hair was cut in Nip style—closely clipped. He was friendly and asked numerous questions relative to our experiences, since we had seen him last. During our stay at Rokuroshi, we frequently talked with him. I received the impression that he wanted to carry on these conversations. There were times when he was most aloof, but this was always during the periods when Jap personnel of the camp were particularly mean.

The fleas, here, were more terrible than I could ever hope to describe. Some of the prisoners were not bothered a great deal. They could feel them but received no bites. Most of us were almost eaten alive. My back, from the shoulders down to my ankles, became like a raw piece of hamburger. The fleas would bite mostly at night. Scratching was inevitable which caused infection. As time went on, it was impossible to sleep. All throughout our imprisonment, we had been pestered by vermin, but never like this. I wondered, seriously, just what the end would be. And even more than three years later, the scars caused by those damnable fleas, are still visible.

Rokuroshi quickly proved to be much worse than Zentsuji, in the matter of both food and treatment. The usual shake-down was held on the same day that we arrived. However, this time, I did not worry much. The few notes I did have were easy to conceal.

The Japs had a plan to work us on an agricultural project. It was the same old propaganda—whatever we raised would be used to augment our rations. It was a constant fight to circumvent such plans as much as possible. Our people were rapidly deteriorating, in a physical way, more than had been experienced before. It was impossible to rise from a sitting position, without grasping something for support, until the blackout and dizziness had temporarily subsided.

Faces were haggard and drawn. Hollows under the eyes became more accentuated. It was evident that our bodies would not be able to take much more of the abuse.

I had a private conversation with Dr. Van Peenen and asked him his opinion. He replied that according to American medical standards, we all should have been dead a long time ago. It was his estimation that if conditions did not become better, the end was in sight for all of us. He said, that at all events, we could not hope to go through another winter.

Even with this knowledge, Van Peenen worked all the harder for the welfare of the prisoners.

The only soup we were getting was hot water and wild plants, growing in the mountains. Each day, details would go out and gather the plants. The rice ration was supposed to be the same as allowed at Zentsuji. More times than not, it was far less. Horse bones came in on one occasion for our soup. They were covered with maggots. These were cleaned off and the bones dumped into the soup. Afterwards, the bones were divided up among each group where they were pounded, scraped and eaten! What few snakes we encountered were caught and roasted, as was the larvae from wasp's nests. Any root that could be chewed was eaten. **Our only aim was to live!**

One morning, we refused to go to work on the agricultural project unless more food was immediately forthcoming. The Japs retaliated by cutting the rice ration still more, and refusing to allow details to gather wild plants. They also made all prisoners stay inside the building. This was even worse than their physical treatment, which became very nasty. The compound was exceedingly smaller than at Zentsuji. A fence had been built around the camp, just a few feet from the edge of our barracks. It would have been bad enough to have confined us to the compound. But to be kept inside was almost unbearable.

Two days later, August 5th, we awakened to find that two officers had escaped, Lieutenants Dillard and Smith. The Japanese were thrown into a furore. All doors and windows were nailed shut, with the exception of one door, that led to the latrine. No games of any kind were allowed. Several officers, sleeping near the escapees, were taken to the Jap office for questioning. Naturally, they could give no information. Therefore, they were made to stand at attention, all day, in the sun.

The next day, Dillard and Smith were captured and returned to the camp. Their hands were tied behind them, and they were made to reenact just how they had escaped. They had to rehearse their route and go into exact details. After this, they were mistreated and taken away.

About twenty-four hours later, a Jap officer from headquarters at Osaka arrived, and all the prisoners were lined up to listen to his speech. In effect, it was that we should not try to escape. We would be caught, he warned, because Japanese civilians had no sympathy for us and would help to hunt us down. All Japanese were helping to win the war, and so on and on.

After the speech, some of the doors were opened and we were allowed into the small compound. An announcement was made that we would be given the worker's ration if we would continue on the agricultural project. Soon after arriving at Rokuroshi, we had agreed to work four hours per day, voluntarily, if the ration was made adequate. The majority of us felt the war could not last much longer and that our salvation lay in food. When this latest offer was made, a consultation was held with our medicos. Their advice was to accept the offer, and to give the work project just as much lip service as possible. We went back to work—half of the camp in the morning, and half in the afternoon. Rations became a little better but not much. Attempts to better the ration got us exactly nowhere. We were told that we had no rights; that Japan was going to win the war; she would be responsible to no nation or group of nations.

On August 8th, a secret poll of the camp was taken, as to when each prisoner thought the war would end. I decided to choose my birthday, September 15th. The mean of that poll gave the date as November 11th. The most optimistic date submitted was August 9th, the next day! The extreme pessimist verdict was for just about one year later.

We made a token effort at working, which was just about all we could do. Young fern stems and buds were gathered and eaten by the handful. However, too much of it made us sick.

On August 15th, the Japs became overly vindictive. We were in a quandary but reasoned that it must be because of some setback of the war. True enough, it was announced, later in the day, that the repercussions were in retaliation for the inhuman weapon used by the United States. We did not know it then, but the atomic bomb had been dropped. The treatment was protested in a signed communication to the commandant. There was no reply.

Early in the morning on August 17th, a Jap order was issued that there would be no work until further orders. We set our underground to work and were soon in possession of the information that the commandant had been called by long distance telephone, to come to Osaka.

The air was tense. It really *was* something for the Jap to call off all work. Most of us felt that the war was over, although we hardly dared to believe too strongly. The guards relaxed to a great degree. We were allowed complete freedom inside the compound. Food became a little more plentiful—at least, it was not cut because we were not working!

The days passed slowly and we anxiously awaited the return of the commandant. Short walks were organized, with the permission of the Japs, and quite a number of the prisoners participated. Morning and evening musters were the opposite of what they had been. The Japs hurried through them, with none of the unpleasantries of the past. We awakened, on the morning of August 21st, to hear the American Reveille being sounded on a bugle. It was the first time we had heard it since early December, 1941. Investigating, we found one of the prisoners, standing near the Jap guardhouse with the bugle in his hands. Guards were standing around—most affable!

On August 22nd, the commandant returned. Soon after, he sent a message to our barracks, stating that he wished to talk to the senior officers in their quarters. The place happened to be the room in which I was located. In a short time he appeared, accompanied by Calibata, the interpreter. We closed the door. He stood there, facing us, with the usual stolid, impassive countenance. Then quietly, through the interpreter, he began to speak—very quietly:

"Japan has shaken hands with the world, which is good for all of us," he solemnly pronounced. His manner was very serious, and there was no sign of the usual arrogance. The announcement came calmly and without expression, except for an almost imperceptible downcast note.

We asked questions pertaining to the immediate future—how we would be liberated, food, and many more. He replied to the effect that he did not have all the details as yet but would communicate them to us as soon as received. On the matter of food, he said that he had already made arrangements for the delivery of fruit, beans, flour and meat. He would make every attempt to have other foodstuffs delivered as soon as possible. Jap clothing on hand in the camp would be issued immediately. *Utopia!*

The commandant had one more thing to tell us, before he left the room. Instructions had been given him at his headquarters in Osaka, that large PW letters were to be painted on the roofs of the camp buildings. American planes would be coming, to drop food and other supplies by parachute. He wanted to know whether or not we wished Jap personnel to do the job! Imagine our feelings, if you can, being asked what we wished, after doing things at the point of the bayonet for three and one-half years! We told him that our personnel wanted to do that job! He then bowed and left.

Fujimoto San had accompanied the commandant on the

day that he had left for Osaka. He had not returned to Rokuroshi but had been retained at Jap headquarters. We never saw him again. As stated in an earlier chapter, I hope, some day, to find out the truth surrounding that individual.

We opened the door of our room to repeat the announcement to the rest of the prisoners. It was our intention, to send out word for them all to gather in this part of the building. *That was unnecessary!* They were waiting in mass formation.

As the door opened, we saw them. Everyone stood there— rigid—like men of stone. I swear that no one was even breathing. The silence seemed to reach out and strike, until it was more terrifying than noise.

That was *the moment*—the end of an era of hell—the beginning of an era of hysterical joy!

The announcement was made to the prisoners, in short terse words. Before any reaction came, and it could have been but a split second, a voice was heard—in typical American fashion:

"Who won?"

That did it! All hell broke loose!

Prisoners screamed and danced and wept and prayed. They shook hands and pounded one another on the back. They whistled and stomped. It was stark pandemonium. You talked to yourself, to everyone else—and the Lord. You tried to sing "America" and a lump in your throat knocked the tune apart. But it was there just the same. And so was "Praise God From Whom All Blessings Flow" and the heartfelt thankfulness of men who knew the true meaning of thanksgiving.

And through it all was the common expression that leaped from prisoner to prisoner: "Boy, we made it! *We made it!*"

Impatience started immediately thereafer. When would we get more food? When would the planes come? How about tobacco? When would we be liberated?

Should we be censured for this impatience? I think not. We had waited for this day from the very start of the siege of Bataan. The earth-hell had been traversed from beginning to end—in every nook and corner. The bitter dregs of adversity had been swallowed to the last drop. I think it was our privilege to be impatient!

The next day, the letters PW were painted on the roofs.

We scanned the skies for airplanes until our eyes ached, and only until dark did we give up the search.

I had a talk with Calibata, the interpreter, and asked him about Tojo. His reply clearly indicates the Japanese way of thinking:

"Tojo is a bad man. He is a war criminal!"

"Why?" I asked.

"Because he did not win the war," answered Calibata. Then he added, "Tojo is ashamed. He has fled to Manchukuo."

This must have been the story put out by the high command. Tojo did not flee to Manchukuo. He could not have left the country without permission of the government. He simply went into seclusion in the Tokyo area when he was dethroned in 1944. However, there would have been no point in arguing with the interpreter. He believed in what he said and that was that!

After more conversation of no importance, he slowly shook his head and said:

"Japan is sad in her great victory."

I had no comment!

The Japanese made an issue of cigarettes. Quantities of rice and wheat and meat came in. Enough fruit, mostly grapes, was issued by the Japs—enough to give each person in the camp 17 pounds! A quantity of melons came in. We were told that the melons were a gift from the school children in a nearby town. The Nips announced that the townspeople were baking rice cakes for us. They did! Flour and beans rolled up to the galley!

We had the runs, but no one cared. We just went back and ate more!

Commander Harrington, United States Navy, actually brought out an American flag! He had carried it, throughout his imprisonment, secreted in a bundle of old rags! It was hung in the barracks. We looked and adored!

The camp did not forget to pray in thanksgiving. A special service was held out of doors, in the quiet of the evening. It was simple but most sincere, and the participants meant it.

We ate grapes, and walked around the compound with lighted cigarettes, or pipes crammed with the cigarette tobacco. It was impossible to absorb the true meaning of the war's end in its entirety. Subconsciously we were still prisoners.

We would find ourselves suddenly awakening to the fact that the war was over. A warm glow, completely satisfying in its intensity, would saturate the body. This process of re-awakening would come and go, in a steady series of reactions for a long time yet to come.

The average loss of weight below normal in the camp was about 50 pounds per man. My waistline measured 25¼ inches. Normally, it is 34 inches. Everyone was down to skin and bones—human skeletons.

It was interesting to watch how the body consumed food. In nearly all cases, an unbelievable amount of gas accumulated. Belching was of such nature, that I could hardly believe it possible in the human body.

The individual might be lying in a prone position, taking a nap, and would find himself violently awakened by a terrific heartburn. The gas would not expel itself except by belching, and then only in an upright position. It was some time before the food reached the bowels. True, we had the runs, but mostly from chronic diarrhea and dysentery, stimulated into unusual activity by liquids, probably from the fruit.

Nearly everyone protruded in the stomach area to such an extent that the figure was funnily lopsided. The bulge was much higher than is the case of a pot belly. You howled at the sight of others, until you realized that you looked exactly the same. Visualize an almost skeleton torso, with "pipe stem" arms and legs—and a "high" belly. What we wouldn't have given for a camera, during those first days of stomach liberation!

The body needed food so badly that the stomach refused to allow the natural process to the bowels.

Perhaps some medical men will be much amused at this layman's description of the human body and its reactions. Perhaps some will disbelieve. But as Dr. Peenen once told me:

"Remember that our stories will be judged by American medical standards. Perhaps you would not believe some of those stories had you not participated. The human body could not take the abuse it already has taken, under those standards."

Everyone wanted *bread*. We could readily understand why

bread is called the staff of life. We decided to use some of the flour and bake a batch of bread. Each prisoner had a tin can in his possession. It was what we used for our soup.

The cans were taken to the galley, and the cooks mixed up the dough. A share was placed in each can. There were no ovens. The cooks did the next best thing, and placed the cans in the fire boxes next to the open fire, turning them from time to time. Eventually, all the prisoners had their taste of "bread." It was downright pasty inside, but the best bread, by far, that I have ever eaten!

Each day, we looked in vain for the promised American planes to fly over the camp. So intently did we screen the skies, that not even did a bug or bird, within the range of vision, escape our scrutiny.

At about 9:00 A.M., September 2nd, a piercing cry brought the prisoners out of their quarters on the run. A plane had been sighted far across the valley, weaving its way around the mountain tops. It circled and then headed straight for Rokuroshi. Staring dumbly and open mouthed, we watched the approach. It "buzzed" the camp at a low altitude and it galvanized us into action. Wildly waving our arms we "talked" to it as loud as we could howl. The crew of that plane must have surely felt our pent up feelings. It was a B-29, the first we had ever seen at close range. Tingling shocks played up and down our spines. Here was reality bringing with it *the proof*. We laughed and we cried, almost hysterical with emotions that wanted an outlet.

The huge craft winged its way out of sight, but we knew it would be back. And back it came with other planes following in its wake. Circling the camp several times, they dropped about 100 parachutes bringing to earth American food, clothing, smokes, and medical supplies.

Several of the chutes did not open. The result was, that cans of peaches and other fruit burst open on contact with the ground. Prisoners scooped up whole handfuls of peaches and dirt, pushing it into their mouths until faces looked like kids in a jam jar—U.S. style.

Some narrowly missed being killed by these loads. I was so intent on watching this miraculous sight, that I failed to notice a parachute coming near me. I felt a gentle nudge against the right side of my body, and turned to see a 50-gallon oil drum, filled with food, as it gently but firmly deposited itself beside me.

As soon as we could get some order, everything was brought to a central spot and sorted out, after which it was issued. Both cigarettes and pipe tobacco had been included, and wonder of wonders, I received a can of my favorite brand—Briggs. Loading my cracked and patched up pipe, I smoked, and felt like a king!

From that time on, day and night, prisoners would be individually eating, concocting dishes, satisfying tastes—and running for the latrine between times!

One of my best meals was at 3:00 A.M. I had lain down for a nap at about midnight. Awakening, I suddenly remembered that the war was over—*and, that we had food!*

Berating myself for not making the most of it, I arose from my bunk, sliced a big pan full of potatoes, onions and bacon, and cooked it. Everyone else was either eating or cooking too. It was with a deep feeling of reluctance, whenever one had eaten his fill. Your insides kept begging you to eat more, but you were unable to hold it.

DDT powder had also been dropped with the supplies. We knew nothing whatever as to the merits of this powder, but the instructions said it was good to combat insects.

Ever since it had been announced that the war was over, I had not attempted to go to sleep at night, because of the fleas. We could now keep lights burning all night, and I worked with my notes.

I was very much amused when I returned to the United States to read an article on DDT powder in which it partly dealt with whether or not the powder was harmful to the human body.

I can testify that it is not! As soon as we had procured a can, we rubbed the powder on the open sores of our bodies. Then we rubbed it into our blankets.

From the time we began using the powder, either the fleas died, or they vacated! There were no ill effects whatever from the "bath" we took with DDT.

CHAPTER 37

Freedom!

ON THE SAME MORNING that our planes dropped the supplies, September 2nd, the Japanese commandant announced that a radio program of formal ceremonies would be broadcast that afternoon, and that immediately thereafter, we were to take over the camp. These orders had come from headquarters at Osaka.

In preparation for the "taking over," we selected a tall tree and felled it. Trimming off the branches, it was erected to act as a flag pole. Rope was produced by the Japs, when we requested it, with the utmost of alacrity.

The broadcast was made by an American voice, and it announced the surrender of Japan. The voice then ordered all prisoners of war to immediately disarm the guards and take over their respective camps.

This was what we had lived and prayed for, and yet, now that it was here, full realization came slowly. Our nightmare of prison life was still as much a part of us, as our arms and our legs. Just as it is difficult for a drowning man, after rescue, to describe his thoughts, so is it difficult to describe the mental gropings of the mind, after peace had blacked out the horrors of hell. Those mental gropings sought to shed the mantle of darkness, under which we had existed for three years and five months. It should be readily understood, when I say that we found ourselves somewhat dazed for a time.

There is an end to everything, and so it was with the war. But the end of the war, to us, meant the beginning of something new.

It meant new life, new hopes, new thrills. It meant the newness of trying to become accustomed to things that once were normal, but now were part of a dream world.

It seems, even now, that those last days at Rokuroshi, were on a moving screen. Scenes still flash before the eyes—scenes of outstanding activity, that were a living part of the change from war to peace.

The flag pole was a scrawny thing, but the best we could find. It was soon to hold the symbol of free men—*Old Glory!*

The Japanese commandant was notified officially that we were about to take over the camp. Prisoners were lined up in formation, by branches of the service, in front of the pole. The stolid Jap guards, without arms formed to our right, also facing the pole.

Old Glory, in all her beauty and majesty, was slowly raised, as an American sounded "To The Color" on a Jap bugle.

The Japanese commandant and the guards stood at rigid attention. They saluted as the flag went skyward, her folds spreading out to silently greet the clear skies above, and to gesture a token, that all was well, to the upturned prisoner faces below. Among those faces, there were few dry eyes.

I thought of words, that had been stamped indelibly on my memory, during those years of prison life—words of Old Glory could she but speak:

"I swing before your eyes, a bright gleam of color, a symbol of yourself. My stars and my stripes are your dream and your labors. They are bright with cheer, brilliant with courage, firm with *faith,* because *you* have made them so, out of your hearts. For *you* are the makers of me, your flag, and it is well, that you glory in the making!"

When the ceremony was over, all was pandemonium. Hand shaking, back slapping, and tears were intermingled in wave after wave of massed emotion. Men can display their souls along with tears. Naked souls were displayed that day.

All rifles, sidearms, and sabers were turned in by the Japanese. Distribution was made to the prisoners, by drawing lots. I must confess that I obtained the duty officer's saber, not by drawing lots. I have that saber in my possession today, together with one of the rifles. They are memories of the totalitarian force that kept me in captivity, and will serve to remind me, to be humbly thankful for the blessedness of America.

The next day, September 3rd, Colonel Marion Unruh (an air officer knocked down over Rabaul) and myself moved into the Jap commandant's private quarters. He, and the rest of the Nips, moved into old buildings on the outskirts of the camp. The radio voice had also stipulated, that our captors would be held responsible for the welfare of the prisoners.

Therefore, the Japs had to stay on. Probably the worst punishment that could be meted out to the commandant, was the necessity for him to report to us in what had been his own domicile. This, he did, punctiliously, bowing and standing at attention, until he was told to sit down.

In no way were we discourteous. Any attempt for revenge on the Japs at Rokuroshi was discouraged—for two reasons. First of all, we were not yet "out of the woods." Anything might happen if the wrong kind of incident occurred. We realized that the Japanese had adopted the subservient attitude, only because the Emperor—The Son of Heaven—had told them to stop fighting. They worshiped in his direction, but human nature was human nature and they might forget the Emperor's orders. Secondly, we were Americans, and we knew, even without definite knowledge, that prisoners of war in the hands of Americans, had been treated as per international law; that the code of Americans, precluded taking undue advantage of the under dog. It may be surprising, that the great majority of the prisoners, wished only to see the guilty punished, *but by legal process*. That, to me, speaks well for the code of ethics of Americans. There is no doubt but what I probably would have killed, had I come in contact with some of the Japs that took part in my past. The same can be said of other prisoners. I believe we could have even had a clear conscience afterwards, because of the absolute inhumanness of those individuals. However, we did not meet them here.

On September 4th, a Jap officer from headquarters at Osaka arrived. His mission was apparently to formally surrender arms, installations, and so forth. At first, he wanted to consider swords as the personal property of the individuals entitled to wear them. He based his request on the argument that swords were a part of the uniform and highly revered by the Japanese. We pointed out, in no uncertain terms, that the sword had been used by the Japanese as a weapon and that no consideration to the request would be given. By this time, we had learned that the Jap respected a firm attitude. He accepted the decision almost immediately and bowed his way out.

Since the surrender had been officially announced, we had been too busy eating, smoking and waking up, to think about any kind of mass celebration. However, on the 6th of September, we planned a huge bonfire for that night. What the program would be—no one knew. The fact remained that the hated wood fence around the compound was still in place. It was decided to use the damnable affair for the fire, plus anything else that would burn—outside of the buildings. Some of the more enthusiastic even suggested that we put the torch to the buildings also!

It was no chore to round up enough personnel to rip the fence from its moorings and put it in place for the fire. At about 8:oo P.M., we gathered and the light was applied. Japs, in the far shadows, stole up to view the sight. Impromptu speeches were made with plenty of catcalls from the audience. Songs were sung which included—*always*—"God Bless America." That was the only serious note. Everything else was hilarious with no restraint. The party broke up gradually. Sooner or later, someone became hungry and wandered off to cook himself up a mess of onions and potatoes and bacon, or to satisfy his unsatisfied taste of something else. I remember that I had a hankering for flour gravy. I took some flour, mixed it with water to the proper consistency, put bacon grease in the pan, and set it on the fire. Hastily remembering my beloved onions, I hurriedly cut one up and dumped it in the mess. What I finally ended up with, was stew, if normal reasoning can be that tolerant. It was good and it was satisfying!

Daily, we listened to the radio announcements. The American voice reiterated instructions, that recovery parties were being sent as rapidly as possible, urging all prisoners to remain in their camps until that occurred.

On September 7th, we commissioned a Jap truck; gave Major Bill Orr a mission together with our blessings, and sent him on a reconnaissance, to gather all information possible. Bill was a West Pointer and the soul of honor. We knew, that if anyone would stick to that kind of a mission, it was Bill Orr. In the wee small hours the next morning, he was back and reported in. The recovery party would reach us on the morning of the 8th.

Sure enough, at about 9:oo A.M., we spotted the party making its way up from the valley below. The whole camp viewed its progress, impatiently awaiting the deliverers.

As they neared the gate, the prisoners swarmed down to meet them. Uniforms and equipment received the most minute examination. The prisoners reached out, touching first and handling afterwards. It was all new to us and we marvelled. We literally swarmed all over the G.I.'s. Accompanying the party were two doctors and two nurses. The prisoners actually paid no attention, whatever, to the nurses. They stood on the sidelines—watching. Finally, during a lull in the buzz of conversation, one of them called:

"Don't we count at all?"

I don't believe any of the prisoners were exactly shy, nor was it our intention to slight the nurses. We simply had been out of circulation so long, that we had not even awakened to the normal processes of thinking. We were Rip Van Winkles—awakening to a new world. Our desire was to touch, to feel, to make sure of what we saw.

That day, the doctors and nurses examined us briefly, and passed out much needed medicine. One of the doctors observed the condition of my only shirt and gave me one of his own. It was a much appreciated gift. My old one had been patched and mended to the point of exhaustion. In fact, the last time I had been working on it, one of the wits had asked:

"Colonel, what are you doing with that shirt—darning it, or just lacing it?"

The recovery party had everything organized for movement. Some of the conditions of surrender had been devoted to prisoners of war. The Japs had been told what to furnish, in the way of transportation, and they did. Trucks called for us early on the morning of September 9th and we moved out shortly thereafter. This time, everyone had plenty of room. The trucks took us to the assembly area, where trolley cars were scheduled for further movement to Fukui.

While waiting, Japanese served us hot tea!

Entering Fukui, we saw a city in ruins. It was far different than the city we had viewed on that evening in June, as we made our painful way to Rokuroshi. This had been a city of approximately 100,000 population.

We had known about the bombing of Fukui, which had occurred in the dead of night, sometime after our arrival at Rokuroshi. B-29's had circled near the camp with clock-like regularity that night. It seemed that they would never stop.

We had seen the huge glow in the sky to the west, knowing it could only be Fukui. New guards coming in had been overheard discussing it. But we were not prepared for the utter devastation which met our eyes.

The whole city had been flattened and burned. There were no structures, whatever, left standing. A few temporary buildings had been hastily erected, and it was to these, that we were taken to await the arrival of our train.

The Japanese Red Cross was in charge. They had installed tables and *chairs* for us, and served hot tea and Jap hardtack!

My old dysentery troubles had started again, and I felt like the "Wreck of the Hesperus." Being the senior officer of the particular contingent I was with, the head man of the Jap Red Cross, treated me with courtesy deluxe. He inquired if there was not something he could do for me. Not meaning to be serious, I asked him if there was a bed I could use while waiting for the train.

The Jap bowed and beamed—there was one ten minutes from there, and they would transport me. I told them it would be impossible; that I could not leave the contingent, and to forget about the request. He bowed again, and scurried away.

In about five minutes, the head man appeared again, this time really beaming. He was followed by three other Japs in solemn procession. Two were carrying a mattress, and the third had a pillow! I lay down and wallowed in this newfound luxury. The gang roared and cat-called. I thumbed my nose with great satisfaction!

Late that afternoon, our train arrived. It was a special and we had room to spare. No one slept a great deal that night. We were coming to life, and did not wish to miss anything enroute.

We arrived at Yokohama the next morning at 7:29 o'clock, to be exact! The train pulled into the station and stopped. We heard a band break out with, "California, Here I Come!" Nothing else was needed!

Literally, we tried to get through the door of our coach at the same time. Some gave up and went through the windows. Our eagerness knew no bounds.

General Eichelberger was on the station platform in person. He was shaking hands with any and all, slapping them on the back. G.I.'s were in position, guarding all approaches.

To us, they had the looks and the appearance of young gods. We were in American hands!

Clearing the station, we piled into trucks, and were taken to the port area. An immediate and most plentiful American breakfast was awaiting our arrival. Hot cakes! Syrup! Bacon! Coffee! All we wanted!

Then we were all run through a hot bath. At the other end, our few belongings were deloused and new clothing was issued. A line of doctors and nurses made hasty examinations to determine whether the individual was fit for travel. Without going into detail, many white lies were told that morning. We were all fit to travel—make no mistake about that!

A prisoner doctor friend of mine had stocked up on a fairly good supply of drugs. He knew my trouble, and gave me a good slug of sulphathyasol. It checked the dysentery within a matter of hours.

We were beginning to meet old friends, whom we had not seen since we had left Cabanatuan for Japan. Reunions were in order, and the process of getting oriented on 194th Tank Battalion personnel started. Many more had died on prison ships and in the various camps. It became apparent that only about twenty-five percent of the original outfit, had survived!

Our contingent was put aboard the U.S.S. Goodhue. It was an LST and had been named after the county of Goodhue in Minnesota. Early, on the morning of September 12th, we were on our way. Part of our fleet was at anchor and a good view was obtained. It was a sight!

A movie was held on deck that night. It was the first we had seen in nearly four years. Needless to say, it was thoroughly enjoyed.

Our first meal on board the ship was a revelation to the captain. He said that he had been warned to prepare for hungry people. But, he added, his imagination could never equal what he actually saw. Thereafter, he broke out everything there was on the ship, in the way of food!

In the wardroom mess, a waiter brought in a huge tray of white bread to our table. Before the tray could be set on the table—every slice was gone! The waiter stood there transfixed, as we gobbled it down! Then, he began to understand, and he took care of us properly.

Arriving at Manila, a convoy of trucks transported us

through the ruins and debris, and headed south. We noticed that everyone was driving on the right hand side of the road. The occupation forces had issued an order changing the old to the new. It seemed to be working out nicely.

Notification of promotion to full colonel had been handed to me shortly before leaving Manila. It was dated September 2nd.

At a point that looked very familiar in the dim twilight, we entered an area that proved to be Replacement Depots. Everything had been turned into Receiving Centers for prisoners of war, including allied prisoners as well. We were quartered in tents and then fed. The Red Cross issued needed articles, and clothing started to arrive. It was a busy evening.

The next morning, I discovered that my quarters were within 150 feet of the place where one of my old command posts had been located! We were at the old Muntinlupa position. It was a case of reminiscing.

It was here that I learned one of my sons had been killed on the Anzio beachhead in Italy.

My report to the Army was made here. It included not only my own affidavits, but also many other statements from the prisoners at Rokuroshi. My notes, buried at Zentsuji, contained two documents that the Army wanted very badly. An agreement was reached whereby the notes would be recovered without having to make a special trip myself. If I would furnish them with a map of the location, a party would be sent to Zentsuji. The Army would retain the two documents and would send me all of the other papers. This was done and I received my notes, intact, in February, 1946. There was very little deterioration. The two documents are in the confidential status. Receiving those notes was like the dead coming to life!

It was here, also, that I heard the gruesome report, on one of the most infamous, and vile incidents, of the entire war. The report was made to me personally, by one of the survivors, a member of the 194th Tank Battalion, from whom we had become separated in November, 1942. This man's testimony is unimpeachable. He was in the mess and survived. A number of our 194th were also in the mess, but did *not* survive. I relate only a part of that report, because a detailed account would serve no better purpose. I have set it down here, only to add more evidence to this manuscript, if that is necessary, for the sole reason of attempting to awaken the

American people from their lethargy. The report is as follows:

"About 1,639 Prisoners of War, from Cabanatuan, left Manila on December 12, 1944. On December 13th, the ship was bombed nine times by American planes, and finally beached. The Japs had put no markings, whatever, on the ship. Prisoners were made to stay on board all night. There was no water available. Some men went stark mad, and drank their own urine. Others, who had gone beserk, actually slashed the wrists of men, who were in a state of coma, to drink the blood. Some committed suicide. The sane prisoners, of necessity, had to kill some of the madmen, in order to stop the carnage.

"On the following morning, December 14th, the ship was bombed again before the prisoners were allowed to leave the boat. Many were trapped in the hold and suffocated. We had to swim to shore. The Japs shot at us as we were swimming, particularly if we drifted too far to one side of the ship or the other. The current was so strong, that some could not help being carried too far out. Quite a number were killed in this manner. Some were also shot on the ship.

"The Japs told us we had been left aboard overnight so we would be bombed again, in retaliation for the Japs killed on the previous day.

"We were sent by truck and train to San Fernando, La Union, and placed on another ship. Water was limited to about 6 to 8 spoonfuls per day. We reached Formosa, and again we were bombed. The dead were left in the hold of the ship for three days, along with the living. We were put on the third ship, and finally reached Japan on January 29, 1945.

"About 500 of the original 1,639 survived to reach Japan, but about 200 of these survivors died within thirty days afterwards."

That is the report in all its nakedness. *300 survivors out of 1,639! Almost two months of a super hell!*

And while I am setting down the facts of diabolical happenings in this war with the Japanese, it would not be amiss to mention another report told to me personally, which is also unimpeachable. The narrator was also a member of the 194th Tank Battalion—a corporal in Co. "A". I met him for the first time since Cabanatuan, after we had left Yokohama and were on our way to Manila.

The corporal was included in a group of 1,800 prisoners that left the Philippines in October, 1944. Other 194th personnel were also in this group. They were bound for Japan. As usual, the Japanese had no markings on the ship. Between the Philippines and Formosa, the ship was torpedoed. It received a vulnerable hit and was sinking. Many of the prisoners were shot by the Japs as they tried to escape from the hold.

Out of a total of 1,800—nine survived! The corporal was one of them.

Why did not the Japanese leave the prisoners in the Philippines, instead of trying to take them to Japan?

The answer is clear, and it is directly allied to the Japanese way of thinking. They wanted slave labor to begin with. When the war started to seriously go against them, they proceeded to do just what we knew they would do. The Jap honestly thought, that he could use his captives as a powerful collateral, with which to negotiate for peace. Therefore, he tried to take as many as possible to the homeland. He could not foresee the Emperor's final action. Had there been an invasion of Japan proper, every prisoner would have been executed summarily!

A glorious ending for most of the "expendables"—victims of the smug and idealistic thinking of Americans in the 20's and 30's—victims of the politics of Congress during those years—the poison of apathy with which the American people inoculated themselves!

And today?

The same cycle of thinking threatens to engulf us once again!

CHAPTER 38

The Japanese

MOST OF US, who became prisoners of war under the conditions described, are not embittered by those experiences. We do not wish to have the Japanese exterminated. Our only wish is that the parallel shall never happen again to America.

We wish to eliminate the unsound basis, on which Americans, all too often, evaluate other peoples. For the most part, in the prewar years, we dismissed the threat of Japan by a shrug of the shoulders, and the mouthing of uncomplimentary epithets—civilian and military alike. It nearly proved to be our Waterloo.

Oriental thinking is entirely different from that of the white man.

Japanese characteristics, for ages, have been motivated by instinct, and *not* design. When I use the word "instinct," I mean just what the dictionary says—"impelled inwardly; imbued." Granting this premise, we can proceed in analyzing the Jap.

Probably, they are more different than any other people on earth, because of certain inherent characteristics. We are most apt to look at the Jap from the Western point of view.

The Japanese are tricky and treacherous—not by design, but by *instinct*. They are cruel and sadistic. They shrug away the sufferings of those in their power. They are uncomplaining in their own sufferings. Their bravery stems from the ruthless and fanatical sense—not from moral courage. They are subject to extreme hysterical outbursts, and they are unpredictable (even to themselves). The Jap definitely has an inferiority complex. He practices deceit in every sense of the word, and recognizes only a master.

This sounds, perhaps, like a diapason of hate and prejudice.

Believe me, I do not hate, nor am I prejudiced. But, when we are examining characteristics, and evaluating other peoples, we must be practical and realistic. We must face the facts as they are, and not as we would like to believe they are.

Ambassador Grew, in the prewar period, specifically warned America of these characteristics. He *knew* the Japanese, and he warned of their capabilities. But Americans laughed it off, or agreed, and then went back to sleep!

Japanese characteristics are the direct result of Shintoism—ancestor worship—which is the basis for determining their way of life—even death itself. This education, indoctrination, and training has been poured down their mental gullets for centuries. *They think that way!* Therein lies the danger. That way of thinking cannot be changed by merely exploring the surface, nor can it be changed in a short time. The probing must be deep and thorough.

Shinto (Way of the Gods) means just that. These gods were invented centuries ago, and embody all the characteristics of the savage age—cruelty, trickery, obscenity, intent to murder, and downright dirtiness. Shintoism has no code of ethics as we understand them. There is no logical system of theology.

The Japanese have always known a natural world, but not a moral one. Our code of right and wrong, of good and bad as we know it, has not associated itself with the Japanese way of thinking. *He has never been taught moral and ethical codes. He has no concept of human dignity.* The Jap personal contact with the white man has been so little as to count for almost nothing, as far as moral and ethical influence is concerned.

There is no essential place in Japanese thinking for any sort of contract. A change of conditions, in personal business, voids a contract from the Jap viewpoint. If it is to his advantage, he will fulfill it to the letter. If it is not to his advantage, he will ignore it—calmly. Any moral necessity of abiding by a contract does not occur to his mind.

Here are some examples of Japanese logic:

A certain manufacturer of mineral water, complained to the court that a competitor had unlawfully imitated his registered label. Upon investigation, the charge was found to be true. However, the court ruled that the guilty party need not be restrained. It was winter time and not many people would be drinking the water. Therefore, the proprietor would not stand to lose a great deal!

A group of postmen protested, that they were getting no

promotions after long and faithful service. The claim was studied and found to be meritorious. Each man (all in the same grade) was promoted one rank. *But,* the salary of each grade was reduced to that of the next one below it. The men gained nothing but the title. No discontent was registered!

A successful hotel burned down in one of Japan's big cities. The proprietor immediately sought permission to re-build. The authorities ruled, that inasmuch as he had conducted a profitable business for a number of years, he must not re-build until one year had elapsed, so as to give his competitors a chance!

A report was published by a brewery company, showing an advertising item of 5,000 yen as an asset. They reasoned, that the increase to their business was an accomplished fact, when they advertised!

An insurance company was found with a deficit of 700,000 yen. An English expert, auditing the books at the request of the company, found the deficit. He advised that the company publish the facts and make it good from the reserve fund. However, the Japs pointed out that a government regulation obligated insurance companies to have a reserve of 500,000 yen. They then "doctored" the accounts. It was not thought to be dishonest, because they considered that obedience to official regulations was the first duty of every loyal subject!

During the war, an extra train was put on at Osaka. The announcement stated, that it would take care of the extra industrial workers due to the war effort. The train was actually put in operation. It did not take care of all the extra traffic. The fact that it did help the situation, was not recognized by the authorities. It was taken off, because it failed to complete-ly meet the desired objective!

The Japanese believe they are the master race, divinely created to conquer the world. It is disgraceful to surrender unless the Emperor wills it. Even then, it is not surrender as we would term it. The defeat suffered by the Jap in this war, is just one round. Underneath, he believes he will win the next one, and his way of thinking dictates there *will* be a next one.

The Jap does not really die, if he goes gloriously. He sim-ply leaves this earthly existence, and his spirit will return to guide the destinies of Japan. I quote an old Japanese Imperial Rescript, which will illustrate the foregoing:

"Duty is heavier than a mountain. Death is lighter than a feather. Go, Soldier, into battle where death awaits you."

This philosophy might be construed to be just the influence of militarists who have been in power. That is not true. The Jap mind believes, and underneath is loyal to that concept.

Professor Komaki of Kyoto Imperial University, defined the Japanese way of thinking when he said:

"Japan is the foundation and axis of the world. The world must be unified around Japan. Without unity there will be no peace. When the world is unified under one power, there will be eternal peace. Japan is the ruling nation of the world."

The notorious Tanaka Memorial was nothing more nor less than a re-hashing of age-old Japanese political philosophy. This philosophy was basically the plan of Hideyoshi, invader of Korea in 1592. Back as far as 660 B.C., Tenno advocated world rule by Japan in his Single Household Under Heaven principle.

The Japanese built the code of Bushido (Way of the Warrior) on this ideology. The concept was developed in the feudal age. It is the only ethical ideal the Japanese know. It does not contain honor, honesty, or morality unless coincidence makes it so. It embodies loyalty, complete and absolute, but only to the Emperor. Today, in the short space of five minutes, one can view both Nipponese modernism, and the feudalism of 500 years ago!

Spiritually and mentally, Japan is still in the Middle Ages. Her mental processes belong to a fantastic age. The patriotism of the Jap is completely beyond our conception. It is a religion. That is why they are always ready to do or die. If the Son of Heaven had commanded, "Fight on!" instead of calling on his people to lay down their arms, the Jap would have done just that. If he said today, "Rise up and cast the white man out!", I thoroughly believe the Jap would obey implicitly!

Even the Sons of Nippon have no answer for the tangents they suddenly pursue—the hysterical attack of the Jap, with no reason and even no preparation for what he is about to do. He is extremely suspicious—even of his own associates. When

he smiles and laughs, it is not always done in the same sense
as the Western world. He is curious to the nth degree. But
just because he asks a lot of questions does not mean that he
is so interested that he is going to accept, or intends to accept,
what you are telling him. He may nod his head and say,
"Hah" but that doesn't mean anything. He will accept your
mandates with alacrity (for the time being) *if you are the
master.*

The Japanese language is not adequate enough for proper
expression. In many ways, it may be misinterpreted. The
Constitution of Japan, in the prewar years, had to be drawn
up in English, so as to make it mean what it said!

Jap ideology teaches them to shed tears—"crocodile" tears.
They boast openly, in print, about shedding tears. I have seen
them give food and cigarettes to prisoners, and then for no
reason at all, bayonet, shoot or beat them. That ideology contains the belief, that if they feel sorry, it makes everything all
right, and justifies whatever they have done or are about to
do! *And they believe it!*

I have heard it said, and have read the statement, "In the
case of Japan, the Banzai shouting is over." Says who? And
why? Just because Banzai is not heard audibly over the land?

I do not say that the Jap is a son of the Devil and has no
good in him. I only say that the Jap is extremely dangerous—
and in a devilish way. He has mastered the machine age, but
is still a savage, mentally and morally—for the simple reason
that he was not required to develop his mind from the savage
to the civilized state.

He jumped that phase completely.

The theory has been advanced, that it will take only a
short time to change Japan into a democracy. These theorists
point to the Philippines as an example. Examining this claim
closely, and with an open mind, I can come to no such conclusion.

The Philippines had positive relations with the white man
for centuries. True, much of it was oppression and slavery,
but the fact remains that the white man's influence on cul-
ture, thinking, and doing things was pretty well established
when the United States took over at the beginning of this
century. It must also be remembered that the geographical
location of the Philippine Islands is in the tropics. Japan lies

in the temperate zone. Global wars do not start with tropical peoples. And even after centuries of indoctrination, the Filipino is still a long way from our way of thinking. Some of it is still counter-clockwise.

At the present time, Japan's acceptance of U.S. rule is on the surface only. The Jap is a past master in the art of passive resistance, and it is seasoned with a good dose of deceit.

It is very true that today, he is bowing and scraping and ingratiating himself with the occupation forces. *He did just that the day the war was over—to the same prisoners he was starving and beating to death the day before.* On the surface, he has apparently accepted democracy, *but he won't go in that direction very long—if we leave too soon!*

Therefore, because of the foregoing, I believe it will take a whale of a lot of democratic diet to wean the Jap from his way of thinking.

With the background of the Japanese, and their capabilities in a machine and atomic age, "The solution lies in education and mutual understanding" but not in the idealistic sense, nor for just a short period of time.

We have within our reach, the golden opportunity to strengthen our position in the Far East, and partially remedy the blunders we have made in China—if we have the wisdom and the will to do it.

We need Japan, desperately, as a buffer between ourselves and Russia. The two are deadly enemies—inherently so. Russian tentacles now reach into China. Russia is largely composed of Asiatics. Her tentacles will reach into Japan unless our policy is positive and definite. Japan is helpless to stop Russian aggression. We hold the key, to either lock or unlock the door.

Japan recognizes us as the master. She will work for and with us—*if we will assume the responsibility of guiding her destinies.*

CHAPTER 39

Who Should We Blame for Bataan?

WHERE CAN THE blame be placed for the tragedy of Bataan? To whom should we point the accusing finger? Should the military plead guilty?

My answer is given, in what I sincerely believe to be cold calculation. The findings, as I see them, are devoid of any prejudice whatever.

Most certainly, the military must accept the blame for not making use of those things, which they did have at their disposal. They must accept the blame for the system that allowed incompetent officers to retain their positions of command—and to be promoted. They must assume the guilt of inter-service jealousies, bickerings, duplication, hidebound policies, and red tape. Of a certainty, the military is guilty of maintaining a "spit and polish" establishment in those prewar days—a sunshine affair, when siestas were taken regularly, and the important business transacted at Officers' Call of the category as to who would tee off first at the golf club!

But—who was basically responsible for allowing any such condition to exist?

We had the Republican Party in control, and we had the Democratic Party in control between World Wars I and II. They were the chosen representatives of the American people. They were elected to do a job, and they did not! They were too busy playing at the game of politics—building up the votes for the next election—politically minded congresses. It all started after World War I, in the year 1920, when the National Defense Act became law. At last, we were to have an adequate defense. And then Congress, itself, voided the Act by not appropriating sufficient funds to carry it out. Niggardly appropriations became the rule, and the military stagnated while Congress fiddled.

Space will not permit going into detail on the "military policy" of Congress during the 20's and 30's. Suffice it to say, that it was a disgrace.

As was to be expected, Congress, after World War II, and hardly before the ink was dry on Japan's surrender document, demanded instant demobilization of the Armed Forces. Why? Because there was a chance of garnering a vote back home! To hell with our foreign policy and national commitments!

And then came the investigations, trying to place the blame, for the mistakes of the war and lack of preparation, on someone else.

I have often wondered why there have been no investigations of Congressional non-action in the prewar years?

Does Congress remember, that only a little more than three months before Pearl Harbor, a bill was presented in the halls of Congress, to allow the reserve components another year of active duty in the field, and that it finally passed by the stupendous majority of *one vote?*

We have had, and we do have, some mighty fine senators and representatives in Congress, who put Country above self, but as far as the security of America is concerned, the record indisputably shows they were far in the minority.

Should we stop with Congress in pinning down the blame? If we do, our classification as a people would, deservedly, be on the hypocritical side.

Congress will function as per the dictates of the American people—*if the people will make their wishes known!* About fifty percent of the eligible voters did not even cast a ballot in the last national election! The great, whopping majority of the people have never contacted their senators and congressman on *any* issue. Why place all the blame on Congress?

The majority of the American people are too busy with their own affairs, to seriously assume the obligations of citizenship. The greed for gain, the quest of the almighty dollar, the contest for creature comforts—these are the things too many of our people are pursuing with avid interest.

If the people had been truly interested in national defense in the 20's and 30's, our military establishment would have been adequate. We might not even have had a war. Apparently Congress did the right thing in its stagnation policy for the Armed Forces during that period. At least, there was no seriout protest from the people. Therefore, we must assume that it was acceptable.

Plenty was said and written relative to the state of our unpreparedness. But Congress and the people prerferred to emulate the proverbial ostrich, and bury their heads in the sands of idealism. We listened to that parroting statement made then (even as we hear it again today):

"There must never be another war!"

And so we became like the ostrich that will not see, or the mole that cannot see. *And we had the war!*

Failure to face realism brought on the war. We thought that by hastily appropriating billions of dollars overnight, we could purchase our security in the same period of time.

The shifting sands of pure idealism—the non-action of our vote-getting, fence-sitting, politically-minded Congress—an apathetic majority of the American people—*this vicious combination gave us the inevitable tragedy of Bataan.*

Therein lies the blame!

To those who would censure me for what I have said, and for the statement I am about to make, let me refer you to that familiar saying:

"If the shoe fits —————————."

To all Americans who helped keep America weak, directly or indirectly, *you are morally guilty of murder!*

CHAPTER 40

Unification of the Armed Forces

THE UNITED STATES has arrived at the crossroads of decision. The time is now, and the decision is yours. We must be vitally concerned about our present defense status, if we value the survival of America. Our concern cannot be confined to mere lip service as of the past. We must do better than that.

There are too many "arm strategists" in this country—people who know more about what is needed for defense, than do the experts. There are too many Americans, totally uninformed, who are reading "Buck Rogers" articles—based, for the most part, on conjecture—who are accepting those theories as actual fact. There are too many Americans who will allow themselves to travel a path that confirms only their own prejudices. Things they do not wish to hear—they will not allow themselves to hear. This, of course, is human nature and would not be so bad in itself, except that it has and can, influence legislation adversely.

Our first job is to inform ourselves, without prejudice, come down to earth, and to be practical and realistic.

It is obviously unfair to register unjustifiable and destructive criticism against the regular military establishment. Whatever criticism we have, should be based on informed knowledge of the facts. When that is the case, the charge should be made without any attempt to soften the blow.

Without a doubt, our professional military establishment needs a house cleaning. But, that does not mean that everyone in the service should be damned. Nor does it mean that everything is wrong. It is a recognized fact, in this world of ours, that we all need a "going over" periodically. There are many of our professional people in the military who would welcome a healthy interest, on the part of the American people, to accomplish that end. Some of the top Brass desire the clean-up. Some do not. Congress will do the job if you are interested enough to demand it and if you will confine your reasoning to an intelligent evaluation.

Generally speaking, our main trouble centers around the so-called unification of the Army, Navy, and Air Force. We have a law that is supposed to unify the three services. Although some things have been accomplished in that direction, we do not have unification. In the main, we have triplication.

The Secretary of Defense now asks Congress for more authority. Undoubtedly, he needs it. Congress should give him enough authority to actually consummate that unification. However, it has been charged, and I believe with some foundation, that the Secretary favors the Navy. If this is true, Mr. Forrestal should be promptly removed. Partiality can have no place in unification of our Armed Forces. The issue is too important.

The duty of Congress does not end with the enactment of legislation. It's duty is also to see to it, that the general intent of legislation is carried out. If Congress fails to perform this function, who will do it?

Prior to World War II, our wars were fought by separate operations on land and on sea. The advent of the airplane came in World War I, but was not sufficiently developed to play a major part, or to cause any serious argument. World War II gave birth to the third service—the Air Force—and third dimensional warfare. It brought forth the mandatory need for teamwork, between each of the services. It also brought into our realm of consciousness, something that had been brewing before World War II—inter-service jealousy. This should come as no surprise. Nor should the services be wholly condemned for that jealousy. There is much to be said on all three sides of that triangle.

Three thousand years of recorded history lies behind us to prove that the old, gives way only gradually to the new. At the advent of each new weapon, the enthusiasts have always made super-claims, without proper foundation to base them on. Always, they have found ready followers. At the advent of the machine gun, war was proved to be impossible (on paper) because of the impassable pattern in which machine guns could be laid. The submarine "knocked out" surface ships because of the "impossibility" to combat such a weapon. The invention of the tank made "infantry obsolete" because of its inability to cope with such a monster. In the 1930's, both the Army and the Navy was unnecessary because "the next war would be fought in the air." There were certain high ranking air enthusiasts that apparently believed this philosophy, because of the insistent demand that the Air Force bring about the capitulation of Hitler's minions, by air action!

All this, at the present time, sounds asinine. *But it did not at the time it was presented.* Why should we register surprise at inter-service jealousy? Certainly, *we the people,* are not immune to that sort of thing in our daily lives. We think we are right until we are proven wrong—and even then—some of us will not admit it.

Now, we have the atomic bomb. The same things are being said about it, that have been said with the advent of each new weapon. *All three services insist on carrying the bomb,* or something comparable. Each service tries to out-do the other as a vindication of their own pet beliefs.

And the American people, through Congress, still elect to sit on the sidelines—with indecision as their program!

The services must be told, in no uncertain terms, that unification is a *must,* and is the law of the land. They must know that it will become a physical reality—*or else!*

That, we have not done!

Traditions and prerogatives must be scrapped, if they interfere in any way with the plan for our national security. What is best for the nation, comes first.

Jealousy, bickerings, and unnecessary red tape are evils that will prevent the formation of a unified team. We don't give a hoot, who carries the ball. Our very survival demands immediate and wholehearted compliance with the rules of the game. There can be no reservations.

It must be realized that unification of the Armed Forces cannot be accomplished by merely rubbing Aladdin's lamp and wishing for it. There are many scattered pieces of the jigsaw puzzle to assemble and put together. Many wrinkles exist which must be ironed out. Procedures, of long-time standing, are on the list, to be torn apart and put together again in a composite whole. Thinking must be coordinated, and brought into line—both military and civilian. It is a tremendous job that can brook no interference from either "armchair strategists" or the Top Brass.

Time is the essence. At this late date, there is no time to waste!

The Secretary of Defense must act and function as the coach of the team. He must be given the authority to carry out the mandate. Leaning toward anyone of the three services will nullify that mandate. His job is to find the weak spots—take remedial action—perfect the team plays—remove the "grandstand players." In short, his job is to produce a team—with no alibis.

The under-secretaries must not only be responsible for the efficient building of their part of the team. They must also be held responsible that it can, *and does,* take its place as an integral part of that team.

This is an objective that calls for the unselfish devotion and unswerving loyalty of all three services. The time is long past due for that effort.

We have only to look at the operations of World War II to realize that realistic approach. Jealousy between the Army, Navy, and Air Force was most apparent in the Pacific Theater. This was, without doubt, due to the fact that we did not have a supreme commander in that part of the world. Much of the effort that should have been directed against the enemy, was expended in the inter-service war at Washington. The bare facts will record indisputable testimony, that time after time, leaders in all three services, failed to appreciate the capabilities and limitations of the other branch of service, with whom they were conducting (or supposed to be conducting) joint operations. Had there been a team, instead of lip service co-operation, casualties would have been far less, and the war prosecuted to completion in a much lesser period.

The lesson we should learn is crystal clear. Each branch of the service should be used for what it is trained to be. If the paramount issue happens to be ground operations, the Army should take over, with every other branch aiding it to carry the ball—and vice versa—all working as a closely coordinated team, and pointing toward a common objective, regardless of which uniform is designated to be the ball carrier.

This would be unification of the Armed Services. There can be no unification if the ground troops usurp prerogatives of the air, or of the Air Force becoming so high and mighty that it fails to recognize its proper place in the team. The same thing applies to the Navy. Every officer in the Armed Services, and especially those in the higher brackets, should receive positive indoctrination of the other branches, enough so, that he will be sufficiently conversant with the limitations and capabilities, so as to make an intelligent estimate of the situation when the need arises.

It is my belief that our present system of a Secretary of Defense, directly under the President, with three under-secretaries for the three services, is sound. Robert P. Patterson, former Secretary of the Army, is a vigorous opponent to that structure, basing his viewpoint, primarily, on the fact that the separate under-secretaries might become special emissaries for their own particular branch. For example—sometime ago, Air Force Secretary Symington went over the head of Defense Secretary Forrestal, and took his requests directly to Congress, totally disregarding the Army and the Navy. Naturally, this cannot be allowed if we are to have a team. However, I am not so sure that Mr. Forrestal's hands were clean. Nevertheless, if we are to have unification, proper legislation should be enacted, which would make a situation of this kind impossible to happen.

My basic argument for three under-secretaries (one at the head of each branch) is that we need a buffer between professional military thinking and civilian thinking. Our professionals are trained in military science. That is their career. It would be manifestly unjust, to expect them to be equally proficient in civilian channels and in the military profession—both at the same time. We demand a Dr. Jekyill and a Mr. Hyde in our military professionals. That demand is born of the inadequate system under which we have always operated. That system has created suspicion and lack of confidence. It has allowed military martinets to march forward, unimpeded, blanketing the whole military establishment under a mantle of distrust, besmirching the names of the good with the bad.

We, the people are responsible for that system.

A civilian under-secretary, at the head of each of our services, would owe no allegiance to that particular service, except to present the fair and impartial picture to the Defense Secretary. In turn, he would be held strictly accountable that decisions and mandates would be promulgated and prosecuted, in the service he represents. Proper selection of under-secretaries would guarantee a tempering of both civilian and military thinking. A happy medium is our objective. Mr. Patterson's proposal lacks personal, civilian contact with the services—and with no buffer.

CHAPTER 41

An Integrated Program for National Defense

OUR UNWILLINGNESS IN the past, to formulate an adequate military policy, has led to an unforgivable extravagance in deliberate waste of human lives, money, materials, and natural resources. Fortunately, we have had to reckon with little outside interference, in our growth as a nation, because of our isolation from the rest of the world, by two great oceans. Wars have not brought the Four Horsemen to our shores. As a consequence, we have been lulled into a smug and complacent security. As a people, we are living on borrowed time, and on a false premise.

Today, the two-ocean security no longer exists. We are sitting in a game of cold reality. The stake is survival of the fittest.

There have been fog, smoke screen, politics, and even subversive activities injected into the controversial issue of national defense. Positive hindrance to the consummation of an intelligent and integrated program, has been registered by uninformed, and/or prejudiced groups. The one salient thing we should fear in America, is an uninformed public that will take action without knowledge of the facts.

There can be no excuse for the American people, as a whole, to be ignorant of the basic needs for our national security. Many avenues are, and have been open, for those who seek to be properly informed.

Military preparedness in our country, which is dedicated to human rights and the ways of peace, is a far more difficult problem than in a nation under the domination of totalitarianism. The great bulk of our military strength must, of necessity, rest in the hands of the citizen reserve components. That is the guarantee against Absolutism.

An integrated program of national defense must meet this requirement, and be complete in the other elements in order that we have a balanced structure. We cannot sacrifice anyone of the elements for the other.

The American Legion is deserving of the highest commendation for its untiring and ceaseless efforts in the interests of an adequate defense. Ever since its inception, 30 years ago, the Legion has concerned itself with all phases of our security, working constantly on programs that allowed no dust to gather. Out of that wealth of experience and contact, The American Legion submits its program for our security, which meets with the unqualified approval of the President of the United States, the Armed Forces, the civilian reserve components, and the millions of Legionnaires and Auxiliary members who live in your own communities as Mr. and Mrs. John Q. Public. That program contains well tempered civilian and military thinking—the happy medium—so necessary in our deliberations. It is a nine point mandate, a small part of which, Congress has already enacted into law—but only by stop-gap and inadequate legislation.

The nine points are as follows:

1. Universal Military Training to be inaugurated without further delay.

2. That a unified command of our Armed Forces, with the Army, Navy, and Air Force on an equal level, is essential to adequate preparedness and economy of procurement.

3. The peacetime establishment of the Regular Armed Forces to be maintained at a minimum, consistent with necessity, to meet peacetime requirements, to be reinforced in time of emergency by organized units drawn from a citizen reserve, organized for this purpose in time of peace.

4. Scientific research in nuclear energy and in other scientific and technical fields, to be continued and expanded in order to contribute to the best interest of the nation, in peace as well as in war.

5. The merchant marine to be developed for commercial service in peace, and maintained for military service, as a vital arm of our national defense in war.

6. Stock piles of strategic material, difficult of procurement during emergencies, to be established and adequately maintained.

7. Our American department of World Intelligence Service to be expanded and maintained on a permanent basis.

8. A civilian defense program, to provide adequate protection for our civilian population, to be established as an integral part of the total defense policy of this nation.

9. Our nation to maintain necessary bases consistent with our policy of national defense.

It is not intended that any of the foregoing elements be given any priority over the others. Anyone of them has neither purpose nor effect except as a part of the balanced structure.

Universal Military Training is a controversial issue. Much has been said for and against it. Much that has been said eminates from misinformation of what the Legion program contains.

The only intelligent basis on which Universal Military Training should be accepted, is a demonstration that it is needed to insure our safety, in a world in which peace is not yet secure. An unprejudiced study of the facts, is that such a training program is a vital essential element in an integrated program of national security. The principal justifications for UMT are military security, peace for ourselves and for the rest of the world. It can be achieved under circumstances that will strengthen the spirit of democracy, and prove of lasting value from a physical, mental, and moral standpoint to our youths in training. However, these by-products should not be considered as an argument for UMT. The argument should be based on the need for military security for preservation of the American Way of Life.

It is apparent from the lessons of history and from the experience of the postwar period, that the only way in which we can lend authority and influence to our voice in international affairs, and inspire confidence in the ability of the United Nations to *enforce* peace, is to maintain our Armed Forces at a level of efficiency and comprehensiveness that will defy challenge by any would-be aggressor. Without strength to back up our moral positions, and discharge our national commitments, *we are impotent in a world where force is still, unfortunately, a determinant of the right. A weak nation can only beg, not command respect and reciprocity.*

If we value freedom, we must value a world in which freedom can endure. It will endure only with peace. And peace will be kept by those people who are willing to work for it, and to sacrifice, if necessary, their very lives in its defense.

Peace will be secured by leadership, by adherence to principle, and by maintenance of strength for enforcement. We may find security by compromise, but *not by appeasement.* We can no longer ignore the rest of the world and dwell in isolation.

It is extremely unfortunate that the mistaken idea has been planted in so many minds that the era of push-button warfare is now here. When it comes to transoceanic or transpolar ranges of intercontinental rockets equipped with atomic warheads, there is little or no possibility of such a weapon being produced and used effectively.

Our scientists and our military experts have testified, with the utmost conviction, that push-button warfare, in the sense that has gained such popular, widespread acceptance, is not a development of the forseeable future. The scientists and experts also testified, that the launching of guided missles from airplanes, submarines, and warships, at effective *shorter ranges,* was now a possibility. They also testified that some form of push-button warfare *might* become a possibility within twenty-five years. How far these developments may go, was indicated by the further testimony, that in less than ten years, there would be war planes capable of attaining supersonic speeds, and traveling at such altitudes, that interception by any variety of anti-aircraft fire would be highly improbable.

The foregoing is fact, and was derived from testimony before the President's Advisory Commission—all civilians of different religious and political beliefs. Their integrity has never been questioned, even by their severest critics.

The United Nations seeks to substitute the reign of law for the reign of force, in the world. During the formative period of the United Nations, it is all important that potentially aggressor nations be brought to clearly understand, *that they will not be permitted to use force, as an instrument, for gaining aggressive ends.*

We must have trained men, in every part of our country, ready and able, to meet sabotage, disorder, and invasion. Attacks may come so swiftly, and from so many directions, that it would be impossible for our regular establishment to accept, successfully, the dual role of an effective offensive and still take care of things here at home. Our chief reliance must be on a citizenry trained in advance.

Our iron ore docks at Superior and Duluth, have been classified as the third most vital and strategic point in North America, because about 80 percent, or more, of our iron ore passes through that area on its way to vital industries. Without iron, we cannot fight a war.

Invasion might be in the form of airborne attack by a comparatively small group of troops, charged with a specific mission of extreme strategic importance to the enemy, or it might be a large scale invasion by forces capable of sustained combat operations.

To meet such a universal attack, we need trained men everywhere. Thus, we come to Universal Military Training.

The UMT program of the Legion, was incorporated in a bill and introduced in Congress, early in 1948. It was the result of nearly thirty years of study and innumerable conferences with every type of group in America. It had the backing of all, who were interested in some form of UMT. Congress disposed of it, as was expected, by relegating it to the powerful Rules Committee. This is the committee, of which we heard a great deal about, in the first days of our 81st Congress, January, 1949.

The Rules Committee is the place where controversial bills are pigeonholed for the sake of convenience, and defense of the member of Congress, who must answer his constituents on the issue involved. The UMT bill was not allowed on the floor.

Why?

Because it was an election year, and votes were considered more important than was a debate on the security of America! My object, in setting forth these facts, is not to criticize Congress for not passing the UMT bill. *My object is to criticize, most emphatically, the malicious failure of the 80th Congress, to allow that controversial bill on the floor, in the democratic way, for a democratic debate, and to issue a yes or a no vote!*

I make the charge, with no fear of repudiation, that the 80th Congress, in this respect, *sat on the fence! And—for their own convenience.*

That program of UMT will again be presented to Congress, in its present session. It is expected that Congress will act—one way or the other.

That program proposes that UMT be administered by a

commission of three members—all civilians, appointed by the President and confirmed by the Senate. They would be responsible, directly, to the President of the United States. It would include full-time civilian inspectors, whose functions would be principally to keep the commission fully informed and advised, to provide an avenue through which any individual in training may submit complaints, and to locate any incompetent or irresponsible training personnel.

The young man would take his basic training *after* he has completed high school. While he is in training, it should be remembered that the young man is *not* in the service. He cannot be used as such. He would be subject to discipline, but *not* the Articles of war or military courts martial. Discipline administered would not be as conclusive as if he was in the service. *However, there would be discipline and proper penalties for non-compliance.*

The length of training would be one year, divided into two phases—basic and advanced training.

Basic training would be for a period of four or six months and would take place in the field. This period would include travel time to and from the camp, and processing. To the young man, who is planning for college after graduation from high school, he need have no fear that his education will be disrupted. Our educators have assured us that his basic training may be taken during the summer months, and the curriculum so adjusted that the individual will find his education uninterrupted.

The second phase of training takes place after the trainee has completed basic training. This would be in the form of options, selected by the trainee himself. The only proviso is, that in his second phase of training, he must take the equivalent of six months in the field. The trainee may select any of the following:

He may go to a college or university and enroll in the ROTC, or—

He may enlist in a National Guard Unit, or—

He may enlist in an organized unit of the Organized Reserve of the Army, Navy, Marines, Coast Guard, Merchant Marine, or—

He may pursue advanced technical training or basic scientific training in a college or university, industry, the Armed Forces, or—

He may continue in the National Training Corps for another six months, or—

He may enlist in the Unorganized Reserve, which calls for one month of field training each year for six years, or—

He may enlist in the Armed Forces in the beginning.

There are other options unnecessary to mention. Those in pursuit of clergical vocations, could so elect by taking the chaplain course, with no interruption of their normal studies.

No young man would be exempted from the training program, except those whose mental or physical condition made it absolutely impossible. For the lesser physically incapacitated, programs in keeping with their condition, have been designed.

The foregoing, in essence, is the program now proposed as an element in our national defense planning.

There have been many arguments registered against Universal Military Training. They range all the way from thoughtful, informed, and sincere to uninformed, emotional, and just downright prejudiced. *Some of the objections are most valid, and it becomes a matter of informed judgment to weigh the advantages against the disadvantages.*

We do not take unpleasant tasting medicine merely because we want to swallow it. We take it because we think it will cure some of our ills. The same thing is true of UMT. I honestly believe that it will cure some of our ills. I also honestly believe, that had we adopted UMT, when the Legion first asked for it in 1920, we might not have had World War II. Had we adopted it at the end of the war in 1945, as the Legion again asked for it, *we would not have Selective Service today!*

Some objections against UMT are of almost stereotyped frequency and will bear repeating here:

1. "Universal Military Training is conscription, un-American, un-democratic."

These three accusations, in my humble estimation, should never be used in any argument. They are epithets, merely name calling. These same three epithets were used against universal compulsory education in America, when it was first proposed and was being hotly opposed. Now, we have universal compulsory education, and we take a great deal of pride in the system.

Conscription can be used to define *anything*, that the individual citizen is called upon to do by this government—taxation, education, military training, service, or what-have-you.

Un-American simply means that it has not been done before in the United States. *But,* may I call your attention to the fact that it was done in the Thirteen Colonies, before we became a nation. If Americans want a certain thing, it suddenly becomes American. Many good Americans, down throughout our history, have consistently advocated Universal Military Training. *It started with George Washington!*

Un-democratic is a wholly improper characterization of UMT. If the program is adopted at all, it will be by the processes of our democratic government, exhibiting the majority will of the people. *How in the world can it be un-American and un-democratic?*

2. "If the United States adopts Universal Military Training, other nations of the world will be encouraged to do likewise."

The fact of the matter is, that the vast majority of all the nations of this earth, having any military organization whatever, *now have and did have Universal Military Training.* The most powerful (and some of the smaller) also have *Universal Military Service.* There is a vast difference between the two systems.

3. "Military preparedness leads to war."

There is no evidence to substantiate that statement. The indisputable evidence is, that the Axis Powers went to war because of the unpreparedness of France, England, and the United States. Captured documents, carefully assembled and analyzed, prove conclusively, that Hitler launched his wars of aggression when he did, because of the unpreparedness of the democratic countries. He initiated his campaign in 1939, instead of witing until 1943, *as originally planned!*

4. "Military training will make our people militaristic."

Once again, there is no evidence that will substantiate this statement. Is there any evidence, that the veterans of either World Wars I or II came back home and wanted more war or more military life? On the contrary, they were notably eager to get away from it all, once the necessary job was done. And also, in answer to the charge, it makes a great deal of difference, whether or not, UMT is conducted under a dictatorship, or under a democracy.

5. "We should make our regular services so attractive, and pay enlistees a lucrative bonus in such an amount, as to make UMT unnecessary."

I cannot believe that the American people want any such system. I can very readily believe, that *some* of our professional military people do want that system—a huge standing Army, Navy, and Air Force. However, this type of regular *does not* reflect the great majority opinion of the other regulars in our Armed Forces.

If the American people have deteriorated to such a low level that they wish to provide for their security, in total, by hiring it done, then in my opinion we are traveling the path of old Rome, and we will go out—just like a light!

The obligations of American citizenship should not be shouldered exclusively by those who volunteer to do so. Nor should they be shouldered by those whom we hire to do so. Those obligations must be shouldered by all, without favor or discrimination. *That is the essence of democracy.*

This, briefly, constitutes the general vein of arguments registered against UMT by those who would cloud the issue and confuse the public.

Never, in our nation's history, have our civilian components ever been allowed to progress beyond the basic training stage, during the times of peace. The reason? Simply because, in the meager time allotted, and having to depend entirely on voluntary enlistment, with its inherent ups and downs, it was strictly impossible to teach anything except a brand of below-par basic training. Advanced training, for the most part, had to be "learned" in the face of veteran enemy fire! My outfit was like that—and I wish to repeat—*about 75 percent did not come back!*

If UMT becomes a law, for the first time in our history, the National Guard and the Reserves—citizen soldiers—would engage in advanced training in their armory drill and field training curriculum—*because they would receive young men who had already graduated from a thorough basic training course.*

If that would be the only benefit, to be derived from UMT, the program would be more than worth while.

The United States has always awakened to find itself at war. Then, there has always followed a period of chaotic hysteria, political preferment. Factories and foundries are improvised. Graft and profiteering flourishes. Our untrained troops go forth upon the field of battle as cattle to slaughter.

We wave the flag.

Slowly, and by sheer weight of our inexhaustible resources, and by the loss and crippling of hundreds of thousands of lives—*human footballs*—we slowly wear the enemy out, and call it a glorious victory!

Then, we raise our hands in solemn vows—never to be caught in such a position of unpreparedness again! And a few of the faithful will attend the ceremonies honoring our war dead on Memorial Day.

It isn't very long after the war is over, before we cannot be bothered with the vows we have made—and the obligations of citizenship. Why bother ourselves with the efficiency or inefficiency of the Armed Forces—the fact that the establishment is tobogganing again into a "spit and polish" affair? To hell with it! Down with war! Up with brotherly love! The same old, time-worn, meaningless phrase—*"We must never have another war!"*

And so the cycle travels the same old rut—the pattern always the same—'round and 'round—just like a wheel.

Realism versus idealism is the issue.

We, the people cannot escape the decision.

CHAPTER 42

The Gray Board Report

THE DANGER OF PURE military thinking being allowed to run rampant, without going through the tempering process of analytical civilian thinking, is very well exemplified by a report issued on the Civilian Components. The average civilian, reading the report, or the excerpts appearing in news dispatches, probably would not realize the dangers to democracy contained therein, and might unwittingly, accept something entirely opposed to his best interests.

The Committee on Civilian Components of the Armed Services, commonly referred to as the Gray Board, recently made public their report to the Secretary of Defense. The Committee was composed of the following members:

Gordon Gray, Assistant, Secretary of the Army, Chairman.

John Nicholas Brown, Assistant Secretary of the Navy ;for the Air Force.

Cornelius V. Whitney, Assistant Secretary of the Air Force.

Raymond S. McLain, Lieutenant General, United States Army.

William M. Fechteler, Vice Admiral, United States Navy.

John P. McConnell, Brigadier General, United States Air Force.

The Committee's recommendation, relative to the National Guard, is:

"Establishing the reserve forces of the Army under the 'Army Clause' of the Constitution;

"Incorporating the National Guard and the Organized Reserve Corps into the Army reserve force under the name of the National Guard of the United States."

It is interesting to note that the civilian component of the Army most effected—the National Guard—was not represented on the Committee.

The report should serve as a potent lesson for the future, that our Secretaries and Assistant Secretaries, and other civilian personnel working in capacities that will recommend policies of the Armed Forces, be thoroughly informed, fully qualified for the job—men who will not lend themselves to one-sided thinking, and be swayed by the "honey" of some of the Top Brass.

The recommendation of the Gray Board, if adopted, would divorce the Guard from any and all State control. It would put the Guard—lock, stock and barrel—under control and jurisdiction of the Department of the Army.

In time of war, there can be no argument with federal control and jurisdiction of the Guard. During the time of peace, I believe there is much to be said against any such proposal.

The National Guard has a dual status of both militia and of Army Reserves. In time of peace, they are administered as militia but are trained and equipped under Army Training Directives and standards. This training is supervised by Regular Army personnel, detailed by the Department of the Army, as instructors and inspectors. When a national emergency is declared, the militia status becomes dormant and federal control becomes complete and absolute. There are pertinent reasons for this dual status which can best be covered in a brief commentary of the Gray Board Report and the answers thereto.

The principal reasons given by the Board, in defense of its recommendations, I do not believe will bear the sunlight of honest scrutiny:

1. "The National Guard has been assigned............a state mission and a federal mission, which might have to be executed simultaneously under the most dangerous circumstances............other units should be organized under state control to meet local demands of war."

The thinking here, to me, is inconsistent. No matter what state mission the Guard might be assigned to, the national emergency automatically puts it under federal control. It is entirely conceivable that federally controlled troops may participate in domestic situations during a national emergency. There must be federal planning and coordination, of both home defense forces and combat forces, in this atomic age and fifth column technique. This phase of defense at home is just as important for the major effort, as organization of the offensive against the enemy, and cannot be disposed of by simply tossing the responsibility over to the States. This part of the war effort is *not local in nature*. Certainly the States must help, but coordination and over-all planning must come from the Federal Government, which in war, is responsible for the defense of this country—both within and without. Those charged with planning have failed to give proper attention to the matter.

2. "The National Guard must be directly under Federal control. . . . It would eliminate two obstacles to quick mobilization—the legal anachronism which makes the National Guard unavailable for its Federal mission until Congress formally declares a national emergency, and the time-consuming re-transfer of property and equipment from the States to the Federal Government."

Strangely enough, the Gray Board fails to report, that the law dealing with the Organized Reserves (which is completely under federal control) also states that it shall not be mobilized "except in time of national emergency expressly declared by Congress" (Sec. 37 (a) National Defense Act). Why the omission? *Is it reasonable, that a national emergency can be declared for the Organized Reserve Corps, by Congress, any more rapidly than for the National Guard? This is a deliberate omission from the report to cloud and confuse the issue!* The Board has disregarded the fact that a bill now pending in Congress, sponsored by the Department of the Army, endorsed by the National Guard Association, the Reserve Officers Association, *and cleared by the Gray Board,* provides that the Guard and ORC can be ordered into the active federal service in an emergency declared *by either the President, or by the Congress.*

As to the "time-consuming re-transfer of property and equipment"—there is no evidence to substantiate that charge. There is no existing law, State or Federal, which has been cited that could cause any such difficulty. If such exists, it stems from unworkable Army Regulations and is due to the failure of proper Army planning. World War II clearly demonstrated the need for a renovation of both Army Regulations and Procedure. Anyone who was a member of the military establishment during the *prewar* mobilization of 1940 and 1941, knows that the "time-consuming" factor was not "re-transfer," but was the lack of proper planning, equipment, materiel, and supplies required to train the Army. The Gray

Board could well have directed their thinking which would have conceived a method whereby munitions of war could be moved and made available to troops as quickly as is planned to mobilize reserve components.

The Army was caught completely off balance in that prewar emergency, even though it was fully and forcibly warned at least two years before war actually came. The Army should have done its planning during the days of peace and before the emergency. *It did not! It did, however, attempt to cover up its own failures by using the civilian reserve components as a backstop!*

3. "It"—complete federalization—"would emphasize the Federal Government obligation in the organization, training and supply of the National Guard."

What emphasis? For the past two years, at least, the Reserve Officers Association and individual Reserve Officers have publicized and condemned the complete failure of the Army to make good the policies of October 13, 1945, affecting the Organized Reserve Corps. Ask your local reserve officer acquaintance what he does at so-called "drills." *And the Organized Reserve Corps is federally controlled, both in peace and war!*

The National Guard, is by law, a reserve component of the Army. What has been the obligation of the Federal Government up to now? Is there any reason to believe that the obligation would be recognized to a greater degree by divesting the Guard of the present militia status? If so, then the Army should be called to account for malicious disregard of the current law. As a matter of fact, the Army has demonstrated that as much attention has been paid the Guard, and probably more, as has been given the ORC. The reason, apparently, is because the Guard has had the organization necessary, to turn on the heat. It is rather difficult to understand just what the Gray Board had in mind, other than the avowed determination to give the nation a complete federally-controlled, citizen soldiery in time of peace.

4. "An officer commissioned in the National Guard must first have a state commission; he must then have a federal commission."

The Army should be concerned primarily with leadership, efficiency and physique. The Army promulgates the rules and regulations under which officers in the reserve components are selected, assigned, and promoted. *These rules and regulations are identical for both the National Guard and the Organized Reserve Corps.* The Army alone has the authority to either grant or withhold Federal Recognition. The States *cannot* force the State Guard officer on the Army. If the officer concerned does not possess the necessary qualifications, the Army has the authority to veto the candidate, whether for original commission, or for promotion. This means that the candidate does *not* get Federal Recognition.

What more does the Gray Board want?

Does the Board mean, that by eliminating the Guard's dual status and using some hocus-pocus method, it can then send federal agents in to the field and make super-appointments and assignments? Does the Board believe, that the advocates of strong central government, possess some superior capacity for picking the right men, in each of the towns and cities of our 51 States and Territories housing the Guard?

The Gray Board could have spent some of its time studying the reasons for the glaring failures of some of the officer personnel, of the regular services, brought into the spotlight by the recent war. But here, the shoe is on the other foot. *Here, the Federal Government selected, assigned, and promoted without any help (or interference) from the States!*

5. "If a unit does not comply with required training standards, they"—the Federal Government—"can withdraw federal recognition but they have no authority to correct a deficiency or to organize another unit in its place."

To the uninitiated, this perhaps seems to be a legitimate argument. To the initiated, however, it is just "baloney."

The training directive, program, and curricula of the Guard and the ORC is prescribed by the Department of the Army. *That training program is identical for both components.* Regular Army Instructors are assigned for the express purpose of supervision and inspection of officer personnel and units of the Guard—all to the end of determining whether they are up to standard, and federal recognition should be granted or continued. To my personal knowledge, many Regular Army Instructors have corrected deficiencies by the use of their veto—even to the extent of having certain officers replaced. If a unit is below standard, the fault certainly must lie with the officers. The veto is a very potent weapon. If some National Guard units and/or officers are below standard, the criticism should be levelled at the Instructors and Inspectors in their failure for not demanding proper standards.

6. "It is recognized that to bring the National Guard under the Army Clause of the Constitution..........may raise the question of encroachment on State's Rights. It is believed, however, that this issue can substantially be met since public concern over State's Rights applies more to the civilian functions of the government, than to the military force needed to protect it in case of war."

No greater misstatement of fact has ever been made. Any strong central government is backed up by federally controlled military forces. Otherwise, there would be no strong central government. The United States of America was founded on the premise of government coming from the people, and the government serving the people—not the other way around. That is the reason why the Constitution is written as it is.

The question of State's Rights is the very essence of the constitution, and holds just as much importance today as it did when adopted. The Fathers were not particularly afraid of "civilian functions." They were afraid of a strong central government backed up by a too-strong military. The Gray Board's assertion is, without doubt, the result of pure federal thinking, divorced from the channel of thought, that directed the framing of the Constitution!

7. "The use of the National Guard with its present powerful armament is not generally suitable for the execution of state missions in case of riot or other civil uprisings."

Under the Gray Board's recommendation, the Guard would be under federal control in peace as well as in war. Does the Gray Board mean that the Guard would have less "powerful armament" under complete federalization, when called to quell local disturbances? When civil law and order breaks down, it must either *be reestablished immediately or we have chaos.*

At the present time, reestablishing law and order in our local communities, is done by the National Guard in time of peace, *under State authority.* If the Gray Board's recommendation is adopted, civil law and order will be reestablished by the *federal soldier, with the federal gun and bayonet, and un-*

der federal order. *This would be totalitarianism—dictatorship!*

Under present arrangements, the Federal Government has no part in our local affairs unless federal rights are involved. Happily, we now have the Guard in a dual status, contributing both to peace and wartime service.

Why, in the name of common sense, should we divest the Guard of their dual status and then, in order to circumvent federal interference in our local affairs, form a separate State Guard at the expense of the State, for the express purpose of doing just what the Guard is now doing in time of peace? The advocates of strong central government, exemplified by the Gray Board, must be told in no uncertain terms, that *the National Guard will remain—as is!*

8. "Even the federal laws which have authorized taking militia troops for service outside the continental United States have never had final judicial determination and might still be questioned in the courts at a time critical to national security."

This is the last straw! That the Gray Board should so piously consider this angle of judicial procedure, is enough to bring tears to the eyes. In spite of this solicitude and worry of the Board, the Guard has already served all over the world in two wars. Why, at this late date, does the Board focus its attention on such asininity? Perhaps Guardsmen have a claim against the United States Government for sending them overseas illegally! It would seem to me that the Gray Board has reached to the bottom of the barrel, to drag out any and all things which might confuse the public. Perhaps it would be well to run the whole military establishment (including the Gray Board) through the wringer of judicial scrutiny!

The dual status of the Guard guarantees the sovereignty of the States, without which, the last vestige of the bastion in the fortress of State Rights would seriously be in danger of disappearing entirely. *This is no myth.*

There can be no argument that the individual state is far better equipped, than is the Federal Government with the knowledge of when and when not to use troops in local disturbances. *Time is the essence in these affairs.* It is entirely conceivable, that if the dual status of the Guard be destroyed, requests for troops might be used as a political cudgel on any state administration not of the same party color as the federal administration in power. This would be a sad state of affairs for the people, and would repudiate the local government that has been elected by the local populace.

The only question left—how well does the National Guard perform in time of war? In World War I, the Guard put into the field, 18 Infantry Divisions (combat), all of which went to France. Fourteen were engaged with the enemy. Practically all of the personnel of the other four, were sent to other divisions, where replacements were badly needed, and saw heavy combat service. Of the 8 divisions rated superior or excellent by the Imperial German General Staff, 6 were Guard Divisions! *The War Department never released this information officially! Why not?*

In World War II, the Guard again gave 18 Infantry Divisions, plus Army and Corp troops—about 300,000 men. It also furnished about 75,000 officers for the Army, and numerous cadres and instructors. The record of the Guard speaks for itself. Of the first eleven divisions to be engaged with the enemy, *nine were Guard Divisions.* The first armored unit to *ever* leave the continental limits of the United States was National Guard—the 194th Tank Battalion. Notable, in the ranks of the Guard, were the 32nd and 34th Divisions with from 500 to more than 600 days of combat!

The recommendation of the Gray Board is not new. In fact, the movement started in 1816. From time to time, the theory has been advanced without a great deal of variance. General Pershing said in a statement to the Senate Military Affairs Committee, shortly after the close of World War I:

"The National Guard never received the wholehearted support of the Regular Army during the World War. There was always more or less prejudice against them and our Regular Officers failed to perform their full duty as competent instructors and often criticized where they should have instructed."

The situation to which General Pershing alludes, was again prevalent in World War II. The main instigator was Lieutenant General Leslie McNair, aided by Lieutenant General Ben Lear. A goodly share of War Department Postwar Planning, *during World War II,* was devoted to plotting against the National Guard with the objective of removing its dual status, and bringing it completely under federal control in time of peace!

The Guard has never contended that it is without defects and faults. No organization can be that perfect. I can certainly testify that there are some things the Guard must and will correct. The same applies to the regular establishment. The Gray Board fails to list any defects of federally controlled troops. The reason is apparent. *It would boomerang right back in the Pentagon where the responsibility rests!*

In conclusion, we have the National Guard and the Organized Reserve Corps, functioning side by side, under exactly the same administrative procedures, with the same qualificational standards, and under the same training directive. But the ORC (completely federally controlled) is not organized yet into units ready to move. On the other hand, the Guard is an organization in being; a striking force, composed of over 4,500 units with a strength of 316,000—ready to move.

The Gray Board's recommendation is either prejudiced, or was conceived without knowledge of the basic factors involved. The dual status of the Guard *must not be taken away. The Army must be made to understand this. It must honestly help to eliminate the weak spots and defects—and the Guard must and will reciprocate.*

Elegy of a Prisoner of War

There's things about a prisoner's life—
To say the least—that I don't like.
The crowded place in which we rot—
The POW's hopeless lot.
The useless "tries" to think alone—
Thoughts mixed up with ceaseless drone.
The building up of spirits low
And smiling when you'd like to throw
A million things around and 'round!
And change the smile to a frown.
The peace of mind we often lack
And cannot have until we're back.
The loneliness for loved ones dear—
The wearing, anxious, gnawing fear.
The waking up from dreams of home
And hearing others groan and moan.
And seeing things you've seen for *years*—
In prison—*boy!* You're in arrears!
The childishness we often see
Of full grown men—I'd like to flee.
And everything I want or do—
A thousand others want it too!
The "crab" of some who whine and whine—
"He's got more rice and soup than mine!"
"My soup's all clear—no solids in it—
The way he's serving—I'm agin' it!"
The "Shylock's" trying to exact
The pound of flesh that others lack.
The hoarder's saving for a "rainy day"—
Hiding things that's hid to stay.
The mental quirks that go the rounds—
Some slow, some fast, by leaps and bounds.
The rumors coming by the score,
Some good, some bad—there's always more.
The pessimists with faces long—

No news is good. It's always wrong—
"We're here for years, we can't survive—
We're starving—sick—we all will die!"
The "heroes" of Corregidor,
Whose daring deeds grow more and more—
Who speak of Tunnel Rats as "They"
When "We" is what they ought to say.
And all the constant blow, blow, blow
Of "heroes" that we truly know!
The number tags on Nip bamboo
You wear all day to show who's you.
The water spigot's dribbling drops—
Stand in line to get a sop!
And stand in line for all your wants,
And stand and stand until you're gaunt.
The rags for clothes we have to wear—
"Sew" 'em up whene'er they tear.
The haircut once a month we get—
Clip 'em! Yank 'em! Yeah! Next!
The razor blade each month we get—
Just one, our tough old beard to whet.
The endless musters—bow just so—
Ichi—Ni—San—Shi—Go!
Inspections—heckling all the time—
Fold the blankets on a line.
And "Joto Ni"—the cry of guards
For doing things "not in the cards."
And smoking tea leaves—there's nothing more—
A butt's deluxe for a prisoner of war.
And sweep the floor with bamboo sticks—
Brooms in Nippon? Hells Bells! *Nix!*
A diet wholly without meat—
No chance for any body heat,
Waiting for the sun to shine—
The only heat in this damned clime!
The constant dripping from your nose
And shivers down to tips of toes.
The endless, cloudy, winter days—
No fuel or food, the cold to stay.
The crawling into bunks each night

And shivering 'till its broad daylight.
The endless walking up and down
To start the circulation 'round.
The chillblains—ears and hands and feet
That raise all hell with any sleep.
And washing clothes with fingers numb—
Water *cold*—chillblains bum.
Scrub and rub 'till fingers crack—
Tattletale gray? Why, no! It's *black!*
The lice that spread like blitzkrieg war
And feed upon your body sore.
The bedbugs, fleas, mosquitoes—*all,*
Scratching, scratching, *scratching raw!*
Your eyesight growing weak and dim
From just a lack of vitamin.
And scabs on hips, and aching backs—
From sleeping on a damned hard mat.
Coughs and hacks and swelling up—
Things that cause you to erupt.
Dysentery and cramps that gripe
And leave you flatter than a kite.
Beriberi—common place—
Some too weak to run the race.
Malaria too, and protein lack—
Cramps in feet and legs and back.
Athlete's foot and "dobe" itch,
Pellagra, scurvy, runs, and retch.
Legs that bend from lack of food—
Dengue fever—we're all imbued.
The men who die before our eyes—
"Who's next?" the inward, ceaseless cry!
And lying in your bunk at night
Hearing snores and groans—*some life!*
The Christmases, so bleak and drear—
The hardest time of all the year.
The hobbies that we all invent
To pass the time until its spent.
Propaganda of the Japs—
"Japaganda" on the map.
And ordered here and there by grunts

From little apish, bastard runts!
The gnawing hunger through the days—
The dreams of food at night—*it slays!*
The tastes we crave beyond our reach—
Oh Lord! Oh Lord! We do beseech!
The endless "soup" and endless rice
We know will not sustain our life.
The recipes from "out the hat"—
"Dip in egg, and fry in fat!"
Dividing up the so-called stew—
A spoon for me and one for you.
The tasteless rice that's always flat,
With worms and rocks and this and that.
The Red Cross boxes stored away,
Not issued 'till Bushido sways.
The slant-eyed Nips—worse than the Pox!
The food is spoiled. It's left to rot!
The beatings, if you fail to please
Sadistic minded Japanese.
The bravery they do not lack
Whene'er they find you can't fight back!
The yen we get in pay each month
To spend for worthless, useless junk—
Hoshi, Fish Pills, Vita Rays,
Pills and powder—aren't we gay?
All we get goes "down the hatch"—
Some comes up—rack and retch—
We put it down to fill the gap
Between our stomachs and our backs.
The constant wish of being home—
The promise to no longer roam.
Teeth decaying—bad to worse—
Grin and bear it—what a curse!

We've tasted brimstone long enough—
Our travel has been rough and tough.
Our rope is nearly at an end,
It's frayed and weak and hard to mend.
Oh Lord! We pray for Freedom's Song—
It can't be long. *It can't be long!*

▶ The following illustrations are repro-

ductions of originals made in Zentsuji

and Rokuroshi Prison Camps in the years

1943-44-45. These originals are in the

possession of the author.

Legion card carried by Colonel Miller throughout prison life.

Our contingent of prisoners arriving at Zentsuji—January 16, 1943.

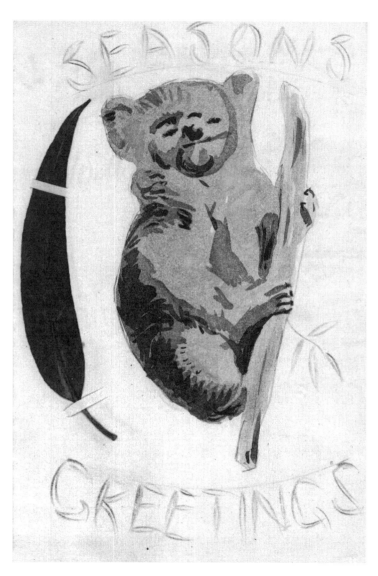

Australian greetings to U.S. Army, Zentsuji—Christmas, 1943.

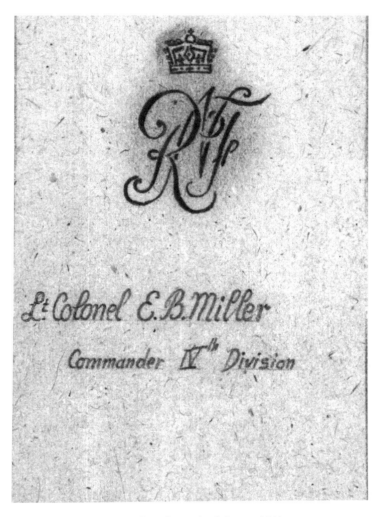

Greetings from the Dutch, Christmas, 1944.

May The Blue Bird
Of Happiness Sweeten
Your Yuletide Soup In '43
And
Wing You Home In '44

L. E. Johnson, s-3.

E.B.M.

A Merry Xmas

and

A Happy Victorious New Year

from

The Officers

of

The New Guinea Volunteer Rifles

Zentsuji.   1943

Christmas, 1944. Hopes of Dutch, American, British, and Australian prisoners to see Mt. Fuji for the last time—soon.

Greetings, New Year's Day, 1945. Depicting Australian, British, Dutch, and American prisoners homeward bound.

To:-
The _U.S._ Army.

The Season's Greetings.

From:-
The Officers of
The _British_ Army.

Zentsuji,
Xmas, 1943.

CHRISTMAS 1943

A.I.F.   CHRISTMAS
1943

A.M.F.

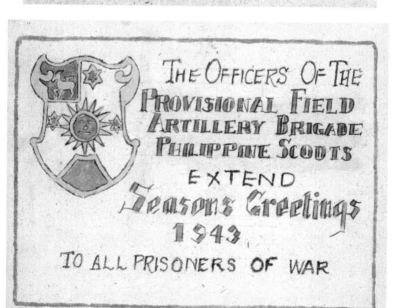

THE OFFICERS OF THE
PROVISIONAL FIELD
ARTILLERY BRIGADE
PHILIPPINE SCOUTS
EXTEND
Seasons Greetings
1943
TO ALL PRISONERS OF WAR

BIRTHDAY
GREETINGS

We, the officers of the United States Army, take this occasion to express our heartfelt thanks for your efforts and leadership in making our lives more tolerable in the face of the discomforts and the adversities attending a prisoner of war.

With the belief that the success of our armed forces will insure a better year in 1944 we sincerely wish you a very Merry Christmas and a Happy New Year.

Greeting card to Colonel Miller—Christmas, 1943.

Marine Corps greetings—Christmas, 1943.

Mindful of your efforts on their behalf
the officers of the Army of the United
States, in Zentsuji, take this opportunity to
express their thankfulness for your leadership and fellowship during the trying
past year — and to wish you a most

Merry Christmas
and
Happy New Year

Greeting card to Colonel Miller—Christmas, 1944.

The USS Perch was a submarine sunk in the Southwest Pacific.

HMS Encounter—sunk in Southwest Pacific.

One of the cardboard stars used for decorating—Christmas, 1944.

U.S. Army greetings.

Emblem of Zentsujians—organization formed secretly from Japs—for postwar
affliations. Colonel Miller served as National President until June, 1947.

"UNTO US A CHILD IS BORN"

CHRISTMAS SERVICES.

CATHOLIC
8·30, 8·53, 9·16, approx.   HOLY MASS

PROTESTANT.
7·0 HOLY COMMUNION   (C. OF E.)
10·0 MORNING SERVICE
11·0 HOLY COMMUNION (OTHER DENOMINATIONS)

R.C.R. Godfrey.
J.E. Davies
V. Turner H.
R.N. Harper Holdcroft
S. May A.I.F.

Chaplains program for Christmas, 1944.

Whenever one of the very few Red Cross boxes was issued, prisoners could be seen surrounded by empty tin cans and articles from the box, mixing up tastes of this and that.

Hurrying for Jap muster. Number tags had to be worn or face a beating.

Menu for Christmas—rice, bucket containing carrot and daikon soup, and the lowly sardine. Dippers used by the galley force for soup.

Minn. – N. Dak. – Mont.
Christmas Party
Zentsuji, Japan
December 26, 1944

Dinner Music
Thanksgiving
Pledge – Lt. Col. E.B. Miller
Supper

Sleight-of-Hand – Capt. Boggs
Imitations – Lt. Powell
Quasi Politico – Lt. Arnold
Song Medley
Toastmaster – Capt. Burke

Greetings to Colonel Miller—Christmas, 1944.

"Gus" was a naval officer prisoner. His home (when he was home)—Hawaii.

Serene It shines and gazes down
On battlefield and gutted town,
On vanquished and on victor brow
On broken spear and rusting plow,
On parapet and hasty grave
On twisted spar and sateless wave,
On smold'ring wood and gory streams
Its silvery light serenely beams.
Rises from the East again
To light a way for broken men . . . . . .
Could it be so — could it be true
It leads wise men to seek anew
The Peace He offered ages gone
Lead on, bright star, lead on !

Lt. F. W. Koenig

To "Boot Hill"—cemetery at the offspring of Hell—Camp O'Donnell.

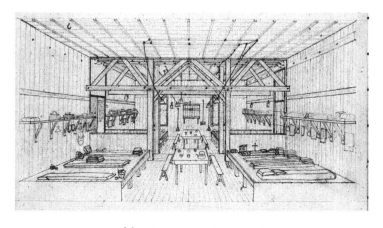

One of the prisoner rooms at Zentsuji, Japan.

One of the prisoner rooms at Rokuroshi.

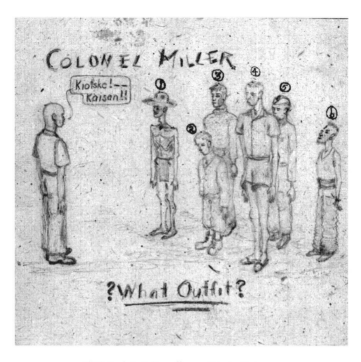

194th Tank Battalion officers at Zentsuji, Japan.

Left—Col. E. B. Miller

1—L. E. Johnson	4—J. S. Muir
2—R. L. Swearingen	5—J. J. Hummel
3—E. L. Burke	6—F. G. Spoor

SEASON'S GREETINGS

TO

Lt. Col. E. B. Miller

Inf. (A.F.) U.S. Army

HENRY   STANLEY   WILSON